THE FIRST ORDAINED WOMEN
IN THE CHURCH OF SWEDEN

LUND
UNIVERSITY
PRESS

LUND
UNIVERSITY

The first ordained women in the Church of Sweden

Narratives of vocation and recognition

FRIDA MANNERFELT AND
ALEXANDER MAURITS

Translated by Arabella Childs

Lund University Press

Lund University Press
The Joint Faculties of Humanities and Theology

**LUND
UNIVERSITY
PRESS**

P.O. Box 192
SE-221 00 LUND
Sweden
https://lunduniversitypress.lu.se

Lund University Press books are published in collaboration with Manchester University Press.

British Library Cataloguing-in-Publication Data
A catalogue record for this book is available from the British Library

ISBN 978-91-989941-3-1 hardback
ISBN 978-91-989941-4-8 open access

First published 2026

Lund University Press gratefully acknowledges publication assistance from the Thora Ohlsson Foundation (Thora Ohlssons stiftelse)

The publisher has no responsibility for the persistence or accuracy of URLs for any external or third-party internet websites referred to in this book, and does not guarantee that any content on such websites is, or will remain, accurate or appropriate.

EU authorised representative for GPSR:
Easy Access System Europe, Mustamäe tee 50, 10621 Tallinn, Estonia
gpsr.requests@easproject.com

Typeset
by Cheshire Typesetting Ltd, Cuddington, Cheshire

To Ella and Isak

Contents

Figures

Preface

'Could you help me with something?' The task that Lena Malmgren (1942–2020, ordained 1967) entrusted to us on that day in 2018 amounted to completing a collection of narratives which she had initiated fifteen years before, narratives about the path to ordination written by the first women to be ordained as priests in the Church of Sweden. Their narratives were to be kept in Lund University's Ecclesiastical History Archive (LUKA), where they would be accessible to future scholars.

Lena's question became the starting point of a research project which has been running for almost ten years. In early 2020, 34 stories were filed in the LUKA archive. One of them was Lena's own. In addition, there are large quantities of material about, and by, the 54 women who were ordained to serve as priests in the Church of Sweden from 1960 to 1970. We hope they will all be interesting and useful to researchers in the years to come.

It did not take us long to realise what a treasure trove these narratives were. With a few exceptions, they had never been heard before; consequently, they constituted a key piece in the jigsaw puzzle presented by the history of the 1958 reform of the priestly office in the Church of Sweden. In view of that realisation, it seemed self-evident to us that we would ourselves contribute to research in this area. Our book *Kallelse och erkännande: Berättelser från de första prästvigda kvinnorna i Svenska kyrkan* ['Vocation and recognition: narratives by the first ordained women in the Church of Sweden'] appeared in 2021, a hefty tome of some 500 pages written for a Swedish readership, full of details and incidents in the manner typical of Swedish church history and practical theology with a historical orientation.

The book has been followed by several scholarly articles in which, upon request, we have explored certain perspectives in greater depth. Our dual theological/theoretical approach has come in for a great deal of interest, as have the connections and parallels with other churches. Besides, we have had opportunities to discuss the book in a number of public contexts – podcasts, newspapers, blogs, TED talks, further-training courses, parish meetings and meetings of various organisations – in the course of which we have received a large number of expert queries and wise comments.

The present book is based on all this material. The Swedish book, reduced in size and adapted to an international readership, provided the foundation; but in some areas this volume goes into greater depth, incorporating perspectives that emerged as especially significant in academic and public discussion following the publication of the 2021 Swedish version. The comprehensive work of revision was made possible by generous financial assistance from the Einar Hansen Allhem Foundation, the Helge Ax:son Johnson Foundation, the Olle Engkvist Foundation, the Längmanska Kulturfonden Foundation and the Åke Wiberg Foundation.

We are also grateful to a number of people who have made essential intellectual contributions to this book. Special mention should be made of the Revd Christina Rees and the Revd Dr Isaac Munther, who agreed to be interviewed about their research, as well as about the processes through which the office of priest was opened up to women in the Church of England and the Evangelical Lutheran Church in Jordan and the Holy Land. Alexander's encounter with the Revd Dr Paula D. Nesbitt in Berkeley in the autumn of 2022, which gave him the opportunity to discuss her research in the field in the USA, provided crucial input, as did Frida's meetings with the Revd Marie Saltkjel, the Revd Dr Linn Sæbø Rystad and the Revd Hilde Marie Øgreid Movafagh, who contributed to the investigation of women in leading positions in the Church of Norway. Thank you all for taking the time to talk to us, thereby providing vital impulses for our work.

In the course of our research, we have had opportunities to present the project and parts of the text at seminars and conferences. Many thanks to helpful colleagues for essential input from the higher seminar for church history and practical theology at the Centre for Theology and Religious Studies at Lund University; to colleagues in the field of church history at the University of Glasgow; and to those fellow scholars who took part in a Norwegian whole-day meeting for practical-theology professionals in 2024.

We also wish to express our gratitude to the Right Revd Dr Teresia Derlén, the Revd Professor Anders Jarlert, the Revd Professor Fredrik Lindström, the Revd Daniel Strömner and the Revd Dr Andreas Wejderstam, who patiently drew on their specialist knowledge in order to help us with terminology and other matters, and to the two anonymous peer reviewers who scrutinised the manuscript for Lund University Press. The flaws that remain despite the assistance of our fellow scholars are entirely our own responsibility.

Two further people have been of decisive importance in the making of the book: our translator Arabella Childs, who transformed our Swedish script into an English text with meticulous care and constant attentiveness to our needs and wishes, and the Publishing Director of Lund University Press, Professor Marianne Thormählen, who encouraged us and led us 'onward!' through the whole process with unparalleled kindness and wisdom. From the bottom of our hearts: thank you.

In addition, we owe a tremendous debt to Lena and the other 33 women priests who have given us an insight into what it was like to be called to serve as a priest during a turbulent period in the history of the Church of Sweden. Warmest thanks to all those who took the time to write down their narratives, or who allowed themselves to be interviewed. Treasuring the memories of all conversations and correspondence with you, we thank you for your piercing comments, your warm sense of humour and your insightful expertise.

A final observation: in the course of our work on this book, it has become obvious to us that the issue of women in church leadership positions is a topic of great and constant interest. All around the world, processes are in motion with a view to opening up the priesthood to women. Likewise, jubilees commemorating the initial ordination of women are taking place all over the world, forming events where churches come together in order to understand their own history and what it might mean for the way ahead. Every church has its own history and its own process. At the same time, there are many common features in the course of events that ensued when women who received a vocation from God went on to pursue their church's recognition of that vocation. Parallels to the narratives we have attempted to give a voice to recur in dissimilar contexts and periods, and so do elements in the historical processes described in this book. By foregrounding the narratives of vocation and recognition told by the first women to be ordained as priests in the Church of Sweden, we hope to be able to contribute to a deeper understanding of historical and contemporary processes of change in other churches and societies.

Frida Mannerfelt and Alexander Maurits
Lund, spring 2025

Note on terminology

Priest(s). The Swedish word *präst* is a tricky concept, and it can be translated in a variety of ways depending on the context. Despite its Roman Catholic/High Church connotations, we have chosen to use 'priest' for four reasons. First, the word indicates that in the Swedish Lutheran context, the theology of the ordained ministry emphasises the Episcopalian structure and tends to embody a more exalted view of the office than other Lutheran churches. For example, Holy Communion can only be administered by an ordained person. By opting for 'priest' rather than 'pastor', we hope to guide the reader's associations in a direction that facilitates the understanding of, for instance, why the so-called New Ecclesiology and the idea of apostolic succession gained such a strong position in the theology of the Church of Sweden during the twentieth century. That realisation makes it easier to comprehend why the idea of a woman performing the altar service was felt by many to be downright offensive. Second, while 'minister' is a useful concept, we find it too broad; it is apt to obscure the fact that the women on whose experiences this book is based experienced a call not just to any ministry, but to a very particular one. Third, the use of 'priest' helps to remind the reader that there are important theological and organisational differences between *präst* (in the Church of Sweden) and 'pastor' (in the so-called Free Churches). Finally, 'priest' is the term preferred by the first ordained women themselves in international contexts. For instance, in her chapter 'The Ordination and Consecration of Women in the Church of Sweden' in the volume titled *Women and Ordination in the Christian Churches: International Perspectives*, edited by Ian Jones, Kirsty Thorpe and Janet Wootton (London: T&T Clark, 2008), Bishop Christina Odenberg employs the concepts of 'priest' and 'priesthood'.

The first ordained women. Throughout this book, we use the term
'the first ordained women in the Church of Sweden' in a narrow
and particular sense to designate women who were ordained as
priests to the office of preaching. However, some of the women
priests speak about having been ordained before, as deaconesses,
and one might wonder how these two kinds of ordination relate to
each other. In the Swedish context, the deaconesses were members
of a movement that was independent of the Church of Sweden. A
movement which emerged in the mid-nineteenth century, inspired
by similar movements in Germany, it was organised as orders with
a mother house that sent out deaconesses for service, for example
to the Church of Sweden. Throughout the twentieth century the
connections between these organisations and the Church of Sweden
gradually grew stronger, not least as a result of liturgical developments. For example, the 1942 liturgical handbook of the Church of
Sweden contained a ritual for the ordination of deaconesses, male
deacons and missionaries. However, in the Lutheran context of the
Church of Sweden, 'the office' [*ämbetet*] was primarily understood
as 'the office of preaching' [*predikoämbetet*]; and it was only with
the 1999 Church Order that deacons were fully integrated into the
Church of Sweden as an official part of 'the ordained ministry'.

Core episode. While Dan P. McAdams uses the concept of 'nuclear
episodes' to designate those narrative components that stand out
because of their dramatic qualities and/or psychological significance (such as turning points, climaxes and difficulties), we have
chosen to employ the concept of 'core episodes' throughout this
book.

Parish. The Swedish word *församling* can be translated as 'congregation', 'community' or 'parish'. We have chosen 'parish' in order
to stress that in the context of the Church of Sweden, in its capacity
of state church for the whole nation (as it was in the twentieth
century) and as governed by a territorial parish principle, *församling* connotes people who are members of the Church (almost the
entire population at the time) in a particular geographical area.

Lena Malmgren, ordained for the diocese of Karlstad in 1967, the initiator of the collection of vocation narratives submitted by the first ordained women in the Church of Sweden. That collection forms the core of the present book. (Image: copyright Bilder i Syd. Reproduced by permission.)

Chapter 1

Writing the history of a reform: narratives of vocation and recognition

Jo: Well, it's just about our little life.
Amy: So?
Jo: Well, who will be interested in a story of domestic struggles and joys? It doesn't have any real importance, does it?
Amy: Maybe it doesn't seem important because people don't write about them.
Jo: No, writing doesn't confer importance, it reflects it.
Amy: I don't think so. Writing them will make them more important.[1]

People understand themselves and the world through storytelling. They create meaning by assembling various events and phenomena into coherent narratives. As a result, their own story will always exist in relation to other, shared stories. Groups, cultures, communities and denominations also create narratives that influence and are influenced by the individual story.[2] This phenomenon sometimes occurs by reinforcing and confirming, sometimes by challenging and questioning. Consequently, that mutual influence links narratives to power.[3] As Amy March wisely replies to her sister Jo in the

---

1   Quotations from Greta Gerwig's 2019 film adaptation of *Little Women*, Louisa May Alcott's classic 1868 novel.
2   Anna Johansson, *Narrativ teori och metod: Med livsberättelsen i fokus* (Lund: Studentlitteratur, 2004), pp. 15–17, 86; Ari Antikainen, 'In Search of Life History', in Ivor Goodson (ed.), *The Routledge International Handbook on Narrative and Life History* (Abingdon: Routledge, 2017), pp. 131–139; Dan P. McAdams, 'How Stories Found a Home in Human Personality', in Goodson (ed.), *The Routledge International Handbook*, pp. 34–37.
3   Ken Plummer, 'Narrative Power, Sexual Stories and the Politics of Storytelling', in Goodson (ed.), *The Routledge International Handbook*, p. 281; Ivor Goodson, 'Introduction: Life Histories and Narratives', in Goodson (ed.), *The Routledge International Handbook*, p. 4.

quotation above from *Little Women*, when Jo asks who would be interested in a story about four young women: stories influence what is considered important, and bringing new stories to the fore can change the shared narrative. That is what this book is about.

On Palm Sunday 1960 three women were ordained as priests in Sweden's state Lutheran Church. Elisabeth Djurle Olander (1930–2014), Ingrid Persson (1912–2000) and Margit Sahlin (1914–2003) were the first women to be ordained in the Church of Sweden after its highest decision-making body, the General Synod, voted on 28 September 1958 to open up the ranks of its priesthood to women. Over the next decade a total of 54 women would be ordained.

In 2004, more than forty years after the first ordinations, work began on collecting these women's stories about their path to ordination. Thanks to this initiative by the priest Lena Malmgren (1942–2020, ordained 1967), Lund University's Ecclesiastical History Archive (LUKA) now holds 22 such stories, in which the first ordained women describe their memories in their own words. Twelve other women priests chose not to write anything new, citing other occasions when they had described or written about their life as clergywomen. This book is, to put it in simple terms, a collective story – a historical narrative – put together on the basis of these 34 stories. Individually, these stories are of interest as expressions of how the Church of Sweden received its first ordained women; but they are also of interest because they problematise shared historical narratives about this reception, narratives that have been relevant in various contexts.

The first aim of this book is therefore to make available a source which has hitherto been relatively unknown and overlooked: the first ordained women's stories about their path to ordination and their first years serving in a parish. Using these individual narratives as a starting point, we aim to highlight and discuss some frequently recurring key themes and relate them to their historical context in church and society, as well as to relevant theoretical perspectives.

This approach also achieves the book's *second purpose*: to supplement, deepen and also problematise the historical narratives about the opening up of the priesthood to women in the Church of Sweden during the twentieth century. In the Swedish context these historical narratives vary a great deal, but they have one thing in common: they all stress that this event should primarily be understood as something national and intra-church. That attitude contributes to obscuring the fact that the processes of opening up the clergy to women in one church influence, and are influenced by, what happens in other churches. *The third purpose* is therefore to explore connections and parallels between the process of change in the Church of Sweden and that which took place in other denominations at this time.

Various historical narratives and their consequences

The Swedish historical narrative about the opening up of the priesthood to women in the Church of Sweden is a variegated one. In another context, we have argued that this narrative may be categorised according to three different approaches: the 'thesis' historical narrative, the 'antithesis' historical narrative and the 'synthesis' historical narrative.[4]

The 'thesis' historical narrative can be said to be the dominant one of the three. In brief, its proponents assert that the Church of Sweden's decision to open up the priesthood to women was the result of political pressure. They describe it as a struggle between two main actors: on the one hand the state, representing a not very church-going public, and keen to implement the reform on the basis of secular ideals of equality between men and women plus a politically driven theology about the 'folk church'; and on the other hand the church, represented by its clergy and active members, who opposed the reform for theological reasons.[5] This idea of a political power struggle occupies a prominent position in most of the textbooks used in theological training programmes in Sweden.[6]

---

4 We develop the issue of a variety of historical narratives in Frida Mannerfelt and Alexander Maurits, *Kallelse och erkännande: Berättelser från de första prästvigda kvinnorna i Svenska kyrkan* (Stockholm: Makadam, 2021), pp. 28–42.
5 See, for example, Carl Arvid Hessler, *Statskyrkodebatten* (Stockholm: Almqvist & Wiksell, 1964); Dag Sandahl, *Kyrklig splittring: Studier kring debatten om kvinnliga präster i Svenska kyrkan samt bibliografi 1905–juli 1990* (Stockholm: Verbum, 1993); Dag Sandahl, *En annan Kyrka: Svenska kyrkan speglad genom Kyrklig samling och Kyrklig samling speglad genom Svenska kyrkan* (Helsingborg: Gaudete, 2018); Dag Sandahl, *Förnyarna: Mer än en historia om arbetsgemenskapen Kyrklig förnyelse* (Skellefteå: Artos, 2010); Erik Petrén, *Kyrkan och synoden* (Lund: Signum, 1984).
6 Oloph Bexell, 'Kyrkligheter i Svenska kyrkan', in Stephan Borgehammar (ed.), *Kyrkans liv: Introduktion till kyrkovetenskapen* (Stockholm: Verbum, 1993), pp. 134–135; Lars Österlin, *Churches of Northern Europe in Profile: A Thousand Years of Anglo-Nordic Relations* (Norwich: Canterbury Press, 1995), pp. 267–275; Ingmar Brohed, *Sveriges kyrkohistoria, 8: Religionsfrihetens och ekumenikens tid* (Stockholm: Verbum, 2005).

The thesis of the politically controlled church has also grown strong in parts of the Church of Sweden that have challenged this reform. One such context, to which we will return, is the collaborative forum known as the Church Coalition for the Bible and Confession [Kyrklig samling kring Bibeln och bekännelsen]. This historical paradigm also holds a strong position in the conservative Lutheran association called the Mission Province [Missionsprovinsen] (founded in 2003), which has its roots in the Church of Sweden. The Mission Province encompasses a distinctive account of twentieth-century Swedish church history, an account which is centred upon the reform of the priesthood caused by 'the political control of the church'.[7] According to the narrative cultivated within this circle, the true church is suffering under the yoke of democratisation and politicisation.

The 'antithesis' historical narrative has largely been formulated in contrast to the 'thesis' historical narrative. Proponents of this approach have emphasised the connection between church and society, arguing that the parishes mobilised to push through the reform and that the decision was grounded in Lutheran theology.[8] Perhaps the clearest example of this position can be found in theologian Maria Södling's contribution to an anthology published in 2008 on the occasion of the fiftieth anniversary of the General Synod's decision to open up the priesthood to women. In her essay, Södling stresses that the ecclesiastical historical narrative has been shaped by the opponents' strategy of systematically invalidating and making invisible the ordained women's vocation and will, as well as the theology supporting their vocation. As an example, she refers to the latest overview of Swedish church history. This overview was published in collaboration with the Church of Sweden Unit of Research, and the volume on the twentieth century

---

7 Carola Nordbäck, '"Att återvända till början": Historia och identitet inom Missionsprovinsen', in Urban Claesson and Sinikka Neuhaus (eds), *Minne och möjlighet: Kyrka och historiebruk från nationsbygge till pluralism*, Forskning för kyrkan, 22 (Stockholm: Makadam, 2014), pp. 140–147 (p. 141).

8 Eva Brunne et al., *Myten om madonnan: En bok om kvinna och man under förtryck och befrielse* (Stockholm: Verbum, 1978); Boel Hössjer Sundman (ed.), *Äntligen stod hon i predikstolen! Historiskt vägval 1958* (Stockholm: Verbum, 2008); Christina Odenberg, 'The Ordination and Consecration of Women in the Church of Sweden', in Ian Jones, Kirsty Thorpe and Janet Wootton (eds), *Women and Ordination in the Christian Churches: International Perspectives* (London: T&T Clark, 2008), pp. 113–122.

was written by the former head of the Church of Sweden's research department, Professor Ingmar Brohed. Södling argues that the resulting overall impression is that the historical view and the interpretations presented in this volume are sanctioned by the Church of Sweden. Södling asserts that Brohed pits theology and politics, church and society against each other. In addition, she maintains that Brohed promotes the idea that ordaining women was an issue of gender equality and not a theological issue, driven by the feminist movement rather than by church opinion. As one example, she cites Brohed's description of the expiry of the 'conscience clause' [*samvetsklausulen*] in 1982 as indicating that 'society's demands for gender equality had fully taken hold here'.[9] Södling regards this as a serious oversimplification of the historical course of events, one that she believes is particularly egregious given that the book in question was compulsory course literature in Swedish academic programmes for future priests at the time of her essay's publication.

Brohed responded to Södling's criticism in a review, defending the emphasis he chose to place on the influence of state and society. He describes Södling's essay as 'a rather shameless attempt to impose on me as a church historian the label of representative of the history of the "losers" and of researching on their terms'.[10] This dispute is one example of the intense debate that exists among Swedish scholars, a debate in which differing interpretations of historical events are pitted against each other.

The 'synthesis' historical narrative has emerged in recent years. This approach draws inspiration from both of the other historical narratives, stressing the complexity of the issues and the importance of allowing for several explanatory models. Two contributions to the 'synthesis' narrative published in recent years are by theologians: Johanna Andersson's dissertation *Den nödvändiga manligheten: Om maskulinitet som soteriologisk signifikant i den svenska debatten om prästämbete och kön* ['The necessary manhood: on masculinity as a soteriologically significant phenomenon in the Swedish debate about the priesthood and gender'] (2019) and Maria Eckerdal's book *Slaget om kyrkan: Yngve Brilioths ecklesiologiska och kyrkopolitiska strävanden*

9 Maria Södling, 'Ingen kvinna synes än: En historia om kvinnliga präster', in Hössjer Sundman (ed.), *Äntligen stod hon i predikstolen!*, pp. 150–161.
10 Ingmar Brohed, 'Review of *Äntligen stod hon i predikstolen! Historiskt vägval 1958*', *Kyrkohistorisk årsskrift*, 109 (2009), 267–273 (271–272).

1931–1958 ['The battle for the church: Yngve Brilioth's ecclesiological and church-political endeavours 1931–1958'] (2018).[11] Andersson applies a gender-theoretical and power-critical analysis to show how masculinities were constructed in the debate on the priesthood in a series of General Synods that preceded the decision to admit women to the priesthood. Eckerdal uses a biographical method and contributes new perspectives on a decisive period in the modern history of the Church of Sweden, not least the 1958 reform of the priesthood, through her examination of the then Archbishop Yngve Brilioth's extensive writings. Andersson and Eckerdal may thus be said to pose new questions to already known source material.

Our contribution to the historical narratives of the reform of the Church of Sweden priesthood might also be labelled as belonging to the 'synthesis' approach, but our depiction is based on a previously ignored source: the vocation stories of the first women to be ordained. This gives a voice to a group that has not been able to express itself to any significant extent in previous research. We bring out the practical consequences of the main arguments when the decision on the reform became embodied in the women who felt called to become priests. Their stories help to complement, nuance and complicate other narratives about the issue of women's admittance to the Church of Sweden clergy.

Clearly, then, there are a variety of different approaches to the historical narrative about this reform of the priesthood. Although these three ways of understanding this historical event differ, the reform has often been regarded as an isolated phenomenon in Sweden and/or the Church of Sweden. Connections and parallels with other churches and denominations, nationally as well as internationally, have rarely been considered. In the few cases where such considerations have been presented, it has mainly been a matter of drawing attention to what came to be known as the 'ecumenical argument' in the 1950s, that is, the belief that implementing

---

11 c.f. Martin Berntson, Bertil Nilsson and Cecilia Wejryd, *Kyrka i Sverige: Introduktion till svensk kyrkohistoria* (Skellefteå: Artos, 2012), pp. 317–320; Johanna Andersson, *Den nödvändiga manligheten: Om maskulinitet som soteriologisk signifikant i den svenska debatten om prästämbete och kön* (Gothenburg: Institutionen för litteratur, idéhistoria och religion, University of Gothenburg, 2019); Maria Eckerdal, *Slaget om kyrkan: Yngve Brilioths ecklesiologiska och kyrkopolitiska strävanden 1931–1958* (Skellefteå: Artos, 2018).

this reform would damage the Church of Sweden's ecumenical cooperation with the Church of England.

Upon closer inspection, however, clear connections and parallels emerge with developments in other churches, both in and outside Sweden, and not only Lutheran ones. One common denominator of these connections and parallels is found in the driving forces – the motives – for change. This book focuses on two driving forces which we believe were key to developments in the Church of Sweden and also in several other denominations: vocation and recognition. Consequently, these are the two central concepts in our investigation.

In the following analysis, we have chosen to place the 34 stories side by side and consider them as narratives. The next chapter sets out our theoretical starting points in greater detail, but to put it briefly, narrative analysis is based on the idea that a story always has a central theme that runs through it and structures it.[12] This theme is usually referred to as a 'plot', which is made up of components called 'episodes'. Core – or, as Dan McAdams calls them, 'nuclear' – episodes are particularly important as turning points, climaxes or difficult events that drive the story forward.[13] Storytelling may be compared to stringing beads on a thread to make a necklace. Depending on what the narrator believes the necklace will be used for, he or she selects which beads will be included and in what order they will appear.

When the stories of the first ordained women are assembled and analysed as narratives they shed light on one another, creating additional dimensions and causing significant patterns to emerge. Particular types of episodes and a similar way of structuring them recur in many narratives. A basic plot emerges in which the thread that carries the beads of the story is the theme of *vocation* – a concept that is deeply connected to the concept of *recognition*, as we will show. Analysing the narratives in the light of the concepts of vocation and recognition lends greater depth to the interpretation of the episodes. The whole thus sheds light on the parts and on

---

12 Ivor Goodson, 'The Rise of the Life Narrative', in Goodson (ed.), *The Routledge International Handbook*, p. 4; Marianne Horsdal, 'The Narrative Interview', in Goodson (ed.), *The Routledge International Handbook*, p. 266.

13 McAdams, 'How Stories Found a Home in Human Personality', pp. 38–39; Johansson, *Narrativ teori och metod*, p. 95.

how the various parts relate to one another, and may also be related to other collective narratives of vocation and recognition.

As will become apparent, the themes of vocation and recognition are also found in other churches and other denominations. We therefore believe that the narratives about and descriptions of the historical course of events in Sweden can contribute to a new understanding of stories about corresponding reforms of the clergy in other churches and denominations. In other words, and to reiterate: by presenting new stories, we can change the shared narrative.

Contributing to three scholarly debates

In publishing this study we contribute to an international scholarly discussion, particularly in three fields: first, the writing and the use of history in relation to women's leadership in the Christian church; second, research on women in church leadership roles on the basis of their own narratives, such as interviews; third, research on the process of opening up the priesthood to women in various churches, with a particular focus on links and parallels between different Protestant denominations.[14] In the remainder of this chapter, we supply examples of research published in the last few decades. These examples are selected representatives of a research field that is so wide-ranging that it cannot be covered in one chapter. Consequently, we have chosen to present and discuss the Scandinavian contributions separately in Chapter 9. Finally, we define our own contribution to the scholarly debate.

Writing and using history

Since the turn of the century, a number of ecclesiastical historical works have been published about women's leadership and their execution of church offices during various historical periods in the Christian church. The aim has been to supplement the generally accepted historical narrative in this field with the aid of previously unrecognised source materials or new theoretical perspectives. One example is the anthology *Patterns of Women's Leadership in Early Christianity* (2021), which assembles a number of texts

---

14 Consequently, we do not discuss the extensive and long-lasting debates about opening up the priesthood to women in the Roman Catholic Church and in Orthodox Churches.

on the theme of women's leadership in churches during the first
millennium. In the introduction, the editors of the anthology –
the historian of religion Joan E. Taylor and the theologian Ilaria
L. E. Ramelli – discuss how the various authors, by using previously ignored sources or by approaching previously used source
materials from different perspectives, contribute to deepening and
complementing the historical narrative. The contributors mainly
focus on the practices – the activities – that the women carried
out in their religious communities, demonstrating that in actual
practice, the women undertook various leadership roles. A number
of the contributions also highlight evidence that women's perfor-
mance of church offices was officially recognised and sanctioned by
the church through liturgical practices, as there are orders of service
from the early Middle Ages that were used to distinguish women
who carried out church offices, such as 'widow' or 'prophet'.[15]

This argument is also put forward by the theologian Gary Macy
in his book *The Hidden History of Women's Ordination: Female
Clergy in the Medieval West* (2008). Drawing on source material
consisting of liturgical orders, references in papal and canonical
documents, and theological texts from the early Middle Ages,
Macy argues that women were indeed ordained as holders of
clerical office, even though many scholars claim that this did not
happen. He asserts that the various source materials are not the sole
influence on the historical narrative; the theoretical and theological starting points used to analyse the sources have also influenced
the research results. Macy points out that many scholars have
approached the sources with a modern definition of what a church
office is. In fact, he says, the early church had a different understanding of what 'ordination' is, namely, a process and ceremony
by which an individual is set apart from others for office within the
church community. On the basis of this definition, he argues that it
is possible to claim that women were indeed ordained.[16]

Other types of sources and perspectives on women's ordination
to church offices may thus help to complement and add complexity to the historical narrative. However, as the historian Kathryn
Kerby-Fulton, co-editor of the volume *Women Intellectuals and*

---

15 Joan E. Taylor and Ilaria L. E. Ramelli, 'Introduction', in Joan E. Taylor
and Ilaria L. E. Ramelli (eds), *Patterns of Women's Leadership in Early
Christianity* (Oxford: Oxford University Press, 2021), pp. 1–10.

16 Gary Macy, *The Hidden History of Women's Ordination: Female Clergy in
the Medieval West* (Oxford: Oxford University Press, 2008).

Leaders in the Middle Ages (2020), points out, such an approach comes with a number of frequently occurring pitfalls. First, it is common for women to be portrayed as exceptions and victims. Second, there is a tendency to overemphasise such source material as vernacular texts and material culture, for instance works of art, textiles, jewellery, church windows and the like. This emphasis may lead scholars to overlook sources which show that women were intellectuals who read and wrote Latin, Greek and/or Hebrew. Third, Kerby-Fulton perceives a tendency to focus too much on the occasions when women went beyond the doctrinal framework, made new discoveries or questioned established doctrines.[17] Even so, according to her, it is possible to add nuance to the historical narrative if we avoid these pitfalls.

Kerby-Fulton also observes that varying ways of using history will exercise different influences on the historical narrative about women's service and leadership in the church. People today, she argues, employ narratives in order to justify differing attitudes towards women's leadership, and she suggests that 'whoever controls the historical narrative wields the power'.[18] As historians, we must hence be alert to the ways in which our writing of history affects the debates in our own time. The same challenge is mentioned by Taylor and Ramelli, who argue that 'Christianity can look to biblical and ancient precedents to justify current practices'.[19]

One of the disadvantages of using historical analyses in today's debates is identified by the historian of religion Catherine A. Brekus. In the introduction to her book on women revivalist preachers in the United States from 1740 to 1845, she points out that a major contributing factor to the paucity of research about these women is that they were 'biblical feminists'. They believed that God had called them to preach as 'labourers for the harvest', and therefore they did not insist on being ordained. Because the women's rights movement did not consider these preachers to be radical enough, feminists have not wished to draw attention to them; and because they were not conservative enough, they have been of no interest

---

17 Kathryn Kerby-Fulton, 'Introduction: Taking Early Women Intellectuals and Leaders Seriously', in Kathryn Kerby-Fulton and J. Van Engen (eds), *Women Intellectuals and Leaders in the Middle Ages* (Martlesham, Suffolk: Boydell & Brewer, 2020), pp. 1–18.

18 Ibid., p. 17.

19 Taylor and Ramelli, 'Introduction', p. 4.

to opponents of women's ordination.[20] In other words, as these preachers did not serve the purposes of today's debates, they have been ignored.

One scholar who has discussed issues related to the writing and use of history specifically in relation to the ordination of women is the theologian Frances Young. In a review of arguments for and against women's ordination, she assesses how history is used in the current debate. Young points out that both proponents and opponents tend to refer to the past to support their position. Depending on their respective stances, the narrative is written in dissimilar ways and often makes use of different sources. Young points out that using historical arguments is therefore problematic for several reasons. These include issues of interpretation and the risk of terminological anachronism. In brief, she believes that using history as an example is fraught with difficulty irrespective of whether one is arguing for or against the ordination of women. Instead, she says, the argument should be based on hermeneutics and biblical interpretation.[21]

Clearly, then, the scholarly conversation about women in church leadership roles in the history of the Christian church appears to raise questions about how history is written. What sources are used, and what perspectives are applied? In this situation, using other types of sources and analytical perspectives may help to supplement and add complexity to established historical narratives, even calling some of them into question. In addition, this type of research appears to raise questions about how history is being used to shed light on, and even steer, the orders and practices in churches today. With our own study, we wish to contribute to this dialogue in two ways. First, we want to apply the above-mentioned research approach that draws on other sources and perspectives to complement and nuance the historical narrative. Second, we aim to contribute an in-depth, theoretically grounded discussion of the relationship between writing and using history in relation to the issue of women in church leadership.

---

20 Catherine A. Brekus, *Strangers & Pilgrims: Female Preaching in America, 1740–1845* (Chapel Hill, NC: University of North Carolina Press, 1998), pp. 3–17.

21 Frances Young, 'Hermeneutical Questions: The Ordination of Women in the Light of Biblical and Patristic Typology', in Jones, Thorpe and Wootton (eds), *Women and Ordination*, pp. 21–39 (p. 26).

Studies of narratives

The second scholarly debate we would like to join is that of studies of women in church office and leadership roles on the basis of their own narratives. The turn of the twenty-first century saw a number of such investigations, particularly ones based on interviews.

One such study is Paula D. Nesbitt's 1997 longitudinal study of two American churches. At issue is whether the entry of women into the clergy has actually led to a change in – or a feminisation of – the church and the office of the clergy. Nesbitt analysed a large number of occupational biographies of both female and male clergy from 1920 to 1993 (399 female and 974 male priests from the Episcopal Church and 77 female and 119 male ministers from the Unitarian Universalist Association). Has the entry of women into the clergy resulted in structural changes of the kind that are frequently associated with feminisation, such as the loss of prestige and power; or has a difference arisen between women and men in terms of their tasks, entailing segregation? Nesbitt argues that changes which predated the opening up of the priesthood to women had a great impact on clergymen's careers, and that the feminisation of the office is occurring concurrently with the feminisation of other, secular professions. Her findings thus reflect not only a change within various denominations but also a change in society at large.[22]

Helen Thorne's study *Journey to Priesthood: An In-depth Study of the First Women Priests in the Church of England* (2000) proceeds from an extensive survey (1,247 responses) plus interviews with 29 ordained women priests. It focuses on the experiences of those women who have been ordained since the 1992 reform of the priesthood in the Church of England. The study 'records the history of the women ordinands by examining women's backgrounds, their journey into priesthood and their post-ordination experiences'; but Thorne also sheds light on 'women's approach and attitude to ministry'.[23]

---

22 Paula D. Nesbitt, *Feminization of the Clergy in America: Occupational and Organizational Perspectives* (Oxford: Oxford University Press, 1997), pp. 1–32.

23 Helen Thorne, *Journey to Priesthood: An In-depth Study of the First Women Priests in the Church of England* [CCSRG Monograph Series 5] (Bristol: Department of Theology and Religious Studies, University of Bristol, 2000), pp. 1–7 (p. 4).

Another interview-based study is Kornelia Sammet's *Frauen im Pfarramt: berufliche Praxis und Geschlechterkonstruktion* ['Women in parish ministry: professional practice and gender construction'] (2005). Sammet's primary material consists of 14 interviews with ordained women in the Evangelical Church in Germany [Evangelische Kirche Deutschland, EKD], most of them belonging to the first generation to be ordained after the church permitted women to become members of the clergy. Sammet applies a distinctly sociological perspective and does not analyse theological arguments; instead, she concentrates on the question of how gender in the office of the clergy is constructed: on the one hand historically and on the other in the narratives of the ordained women.

Sammet's interview study reveals that established patterns and gender roles persist even among the ordained clergy as a group. The group displays a clear gendered division of labour, whereby male clergy are more often in charge of worship services and – because they are believed to be more caring – female clergy are assigned pastoral duties. The women clergy have various strategies for dealing with this situation. Some choose to adapt to established patterns while others question these patterns, placing an emphasis on personal qualities and suitability. Ordained women who are daughters of clergymen would appear to be more likely to fall into, or live by, the church's more traditional gender constructions/patterns. However, Sammet notes that the churches do contain an inherent potential for change: through theological re-evaluation and reinterpretation, gender can be understood in new ways.[24]

The tension between different ways of understanding the office of the clergy is also the starting point of Eliana Coelho da Silva's thesis 'Chamadas por Deus' (2014), for which she interviewed 11 ordained women from various Protestant churches in Brazil. She identifies a tension between a biblical ideal which prescribes that women should be submissive and what happens in practice when women pastors do not adhere to this ideal.[25] Like us, Coelho da Silva is interested in the ordained women's stories and their path to ordination. She also wants to shed light on what it means to be

24 Kornelia Sammet, *Frauen in Pfarramt: Berufliche Praxis und Geschlechter-konstruktion* (Würzburg: ERGON, 2005), pp. 162–163, 448–464.
25 Eliana Coelho da Silva, 'Chamadas por Deus: características do pastorado feminino na cidade de Fortaleza', PhD dissertation, Universidade Federal do Ceará (UFC), 2014.

a woman and a pastor, describing two theological ideal types: the egalitarians and the differentialists. Egalitarians stress that God created man and woman as equals, and even though the Fall led to inequality, Christ has cancelled that punishment because in Christ 'there is no longer male and female' (Gal. 3:28). Differentialists cite the order of creation and justify women joining the clergy on the grounds that women have special qualities which complement those of men.

Regardless of whether an egalitarian or differentialist inter-pretation is chosen, the emphasis is on vocation (hence the title of her thesis: *Chamadas por Deus* means 'called by God'). A recurring theme in the interviews and the women's stories is the idea that when God calls, we have a responsibility to obey the call and carry out the task. Not to do so would be to go against God's will. Out of their love for God, the ordained women follow their calling even if it leads to persecution and harassment. The task is difficult, but ordination gives legitimacy to their vocation. Additional support can be obtained through others who already have a position within the church (such as a husband or father who is also a pastor, a theology professor, or the congregation).[26]

A similar conclusion is drawn by Frederick W. Schmidt in his study of women set apart for service as pastors in American Baptist churches in the USA (2019). On the basis of a survey in which 81 women pastors responded to questions about their experiences, Schmidt found that '[t]he advocacy of others was often central to their experiences'. Both bureaucratic and formal regulations, plus a permissive ecclesiastical culture, are required for women to feel suf-ficiently supported in their role as pastors. However, Schmidt points out that legal provisions are not enough. Their legitimacy must also be rooted in biblical texts and theological categories.[27]

Yet another interview study is presented in Mindy Makant's *Holy Mischief: In Honor and Celebration of Women in Ministry* (2019). This study was carried out in connection with the fiftieth anniversary of the date when the two American Lutheran churches which later formed the Evangelical Lutheran Church in America (ELCA) first permitted the ordination of women in August 1970. The study is based on a total of 85 interviews with ordained

---

26 Ibid., pp. 142–148.
27 Frederick W. Schmidt, '"How Long, O Lord?": Women, Ordination and the American Baptist Churches, USA', *American Baptist Quarterly*, XXXVIII (2019), 369–386 (p. 374).

women, including nine bishops, and focuses on their experiences: their vocation or call stories, experiences from their training and being a candidate for the clergy, and the challenges and joys of their role.[28] Makant analyses the stories with reference to recurring themes. She finds multiple examples of experiences of opposition and harassment. These were rarely expressed in congregations or in ecumenical contexts; instead, they usually came from strangers as comments or hate mail in public contexts. The interviews also mention direct violence, threats and sexual harassment. The narratives also describe experiences of explicit support from bishops and male colleagues, which the ordained women felt was important. Bishops in particular are central figures, both in cases where they welcomed women's vocation and in cases where they were sceptical or dismissive.[29]

A further interview study from the American context is *She Preached the Word: Women's Ordination in Modern America* (2018) by political scientists Benjamin Knoll and Cammie Jo Bolin. They explore why there are still far fewer women than men in leadership roles in religious denominations in the United States, and what consequences this state of things may have in the long term. The low proportion of women among religious leaders is often explained by theological convictions, the association of women leaders with liberal values, the absence of hands-on support from denominations that are in favour of women leaders in principle, and the lack of role models. The uniqueness of Knoll and Bolin's study is that they examine multiple denominations, and not only from the perspective of leaders, but also from the perspective of parishioners/congregants. They use both quantitative methods in the form of surveys and qualitative methods in the form of interviews.[30]

Knoll and Bolin's study shows that whether people are for or against women in church leadership, they justify their position by referring to theology and the Bible, personal experiences of ordained women, or gender stereotypes. It is noteworthy that the most important factor when it comes to whether someone is for or against women clergy is not theological conviction but rather the institutional

28 Mindy Makant, *Holy Mischief: In Honor and Celebration of Women in Ministry* (Eugene, OR: Cascade Books, 2019).
29 Ibid., pp. 60–102.
30 Benjamin Knoll and Cammie Jo Bolin, *She Preached the Word: Women's Ordination in Modern America* (Oxford: Oxford University Press, 2018), pp. 14–16.

context (denominational or parish/congregational policy), and the question of whether or not the individual has had personal experience of female religious leaders. Unsurprisingly, people who have already interacted with a female religious leader are more favourably disposed than those who have not. The study also suggests that when a woman leads a parish/congregation, the impact is greater on women than on men. Whereas men are basically not influenced at all, the study shows that girls and young women in adolescence who encounter female religious leaders display greater self-confidence and self-reliance, have higher levels of education and better-paid jobs, and have more children than their counterparts in parishes/congregations with only male religious leaders.[31]

How denominational and parish contexts and the experiences of ordained women influence attitudes towards women in religious leadership roles is also a central part of Alex David James Fry's thesis, for which he interviewed 41 male priests from Anglo-Catholic and Evangelical devotional traditions within the Church of England. On the basis of narrative analysis, and drawing on various sociological and psychological theories, Fry found that the male priests' perceptions of gender are shaped by their religious traditions. He argues that their resistance is due to the ordained women's being perceived to threaten the male priests' identity and thereby their self-confidence.[32]

Narratives about the opening up of the Church of England priesthood in 1992 also form the starting point of Clare Walsh's study *Gender and Discourse: Language and Power in Politics, the Church, and Organizations* (2001). In addition to interviewing ordained women, Walsh analyses the narratives that appeared in the media debate leading up to the decision to open up the priesthood to women in 1992. Using a theoretical framework that combines critical discourse analysis with feminist perspectives, Walsh finds that the women's negotiation with institutional obstacles during and after the debate contributed to a 'counter-tendency' which, in turn, created a discursive restructuring.[33]

---

31 Ibid., pp. 63–146.
32 Alex David James Fry, 'Gender Attitudes amongst Anglo-Catholic and Evangelical Clergy in the Church of England: An Examination of How Male Priests Respond to Women's Ordination as Priests and their Consecration as Bishops', PhD dissertation, Durham University, 2019.
33 Clare Walsh, *Gender and Discourse: Language and Power in Politics, the Church and Organizations* (Harlow: Longman, 2001), pp. 1–3.

Narratives about ordained women in the media are also at the centre of Else Marie Wiberg Pedersen's study of how female priests and theologians were represented in Danish newspapers between 1885 and 2022. Wiberg Pedersen found a number of recurring themes: St Paul and women (women should not become priests); priestesses (sex is an identity marker based on the idea that women are different from men); female dominance (having a greater number of ordained women is described as a problem); the church's gender shift (more women means that the church changes, i.e. is feminised); and the caring church (the church becomes more focused on care than on theology and preaching). She notes that interviews with ordained women nuance the banal and stereotypical descriptions, indicating the complexity and the wide range that ordained women represent.[34]

In Sweden there is little or no research on women in church leadership that is based on their own narratives or statements. Internationally, however, the picture is different. To summarise the above review: first, many of these research efforts were made in conjunction with anniversaries of decisions or the first ordinations of women, when the issues were once again topical.[35] It is also clear that the narratives tend to be analysed *either* from theological perspectives *or* from theoretical ones (the latter encompassing sociology, political science, discourse analysis, gender studies). By contrast, we believe it is important to analyse the narratives from both these points of view. Consequently, this study attempts to achieve a dynamic tension between theological and theoretical perspectives, through the theologically grounded concept of *vocation* and the social-science concept of *recognition*.

Research on connections and parallels between various churches

The third scholarly conversation we wish to connect with is historical research which discusses connections and parallels between the respective processes of opening up the clergy to women that took place within various churches. Just as for the Church of Sweden,

---

34 Else Marie Wiberg Pedersen, 'Kirkens kønsskifte? Nedslag i medieomtalen af kvindelige praester', in Else Marie Wiberg Pedersen (ed.), *Guds Ord i kvindemund: Om køn og kirke* (Aarhus: Nord Academic, 2023), pp. 281–315.

35 Ibid., pp. 281–315; 'Om bogen', in Wiberg Pedersen (ed.), *Guds ord i kvindemund*, pp. 8–11.

for virtually every church that has permitted women to become ordained there is a specific national and/or intra-church research field about the process.[36] However, the question of connections and parallels between various denominations has not attracted as much interest. Knoll and Bolin's above-mentioned study of women in religious leadership roles in various American denominations is one of a small number of exceptions.

The comparative perspective has been treated sparingly. Such discussions are nevertheless sometimes found in introductory chapters of various anthologies. One example is the introduction to the anthology *Religious Institutions and Women's Leadership: New Roles Inside the Mainstream* (1996), which brings together discussions of women's leadership in various Christian and Jewish denominations in the United States. The book's editor, Catherine Wessinger, argues that three factors unite the denominations that display openness to women's leadership: these denominations have 1) an image of God that is not exclusively masculine, 2) a view of humanity that does not blame women for the Fall, and 3) a conviction that women can have roles other than those of wife and mother. Wessinger says that when combined with favourable social and economic conditions, these three factors can contribute to change.[37]

It is also clear that increasing women's ability to take up leadership positions in religious denominations is a slow process. Moreover, the events and dates that often appear significant – for example, Palm Sunday 1960 for the Church of Sweden – are in reality merely symbolic. Wessinger writes that '[t]he date that women are first ordained in a patriarchal denomination does not

---

36 See, for example, Miki Mei, 'A Church with Newly-opened Doors: The Ordination of Women Priests in the Anglican-Episcopal Church of Japan', *Japanese Journal of Religious Studies*, 44 (2017), 37–54; Jane Steen, 'Women's Ordination in the Church of England: Conscience, Change and Law', *Ecclesiastical Law Journal*, 21 (2019), 289–311; Stephen Asol Kapinde and Eleanor Tiplady Higgs, 'Global Anglican Discourse and Women's Ordination in Kenya: The Controversy in Kirinyaga, 1979–1992, and its Legacy', *Journal of Anglican Studies*, 20 (2022), 22–29; Lesley Orr, 'To Build the New Jerusalem: The Ministry and Citizenship of Protestant Women in Twentieth Century Scotland', *Religions*, 13 (2022), 1–17.

37 Catherine Wessinger, 'Women's Religious Leadership in the United States', in Catherine Wessinger (ed.), *Religious Institutions and Women's Leadership: New Roles Inside the Mainstream* (Columbia, SC: University of South Carolina Press, 1996), pp. 6–7.

mark the full inclusion of women in that organisation's leadership. Rather, these dates are beginning points for additional struggle by women to be represented fully in their religious tradition.'[38] What is common to different denominations, then, is that decisions to – for instance – ordain women as priests are rarely the end point, but perhaps rather the starting point for a new struggle to put structures in place so that these women can exercise their leadership on equal terms. Theological arguments alone are usually not enough; they need to be supported by a social expectation of equality.

Whereas Wessinger and Knoll and Bolin focus on connections and parallels in a national context, the anthology *Women and Ordination in the Christian Churches: International Perspectives* offers – as the title indicates – an international angle.[39] The anthology addresses the issue of women becoming ordained clergy from theological, historical and sociological perspectives. As the editors observe, there are a number of 'intriguing parallels' between both the theological reflection and the experiences of women pioneers in various churches and denominations. Despite the contextual differences, it would hence appear that both debates and experiences '"translate" from one culture to another'.[40] Recurring themes across churches and denominations include an equality perspective, questions about the nature of women and men (are there any uniquely female characteristics?) and the importance of the norms of the surrounding social culture. As was the case in the American context, another recurring theme was that the struggle often did not end with the decision to open up the clergy to women, as those women who were ordained soon hit 'the stained-glass ceiling' or encountered other types of resistance.[41] In the anthology's afterword, Ian Jones stresses the need for further research into women's experiences of being ordained clergy, not least in terms of inter-church connections.[42]

In his book *The Bible in History* (2023), David W. Kling emphasises how Galatians 3:28 has been a central interpretative key and one of the cornerstones of those biblical arguments that have been

---

38 Ibid., p. 31.
39 Ian Jones, Kirsty Thorpe and Janet Wootton, 'Introduction', in Jones, Thorpe and Wootton (eds), *Women and Ordination*, p. 4.
40 Ibid., p. 7.
41 Ibid., pp. 12–16.
42 Ian Jones, 'Afterword', in Jones, Thorpe and Wootton (eds), *Women and Ordination*, pp. 225–228.

cited in a number of different churches and denominations to justify the ordination of women. In his analysis of how this passage has been interpreted, Kling shows how this statement, which for most of the church's history has been considered to be about *coram Deo* (humans' relationship with God), is instead assumed to be about *coram hominibus* (interpersonal relationships) and came to be the *locus classicus* for defending women's right to be ordained. Kling writes:

> As in the nineteenth-century debate, contemporary proponents of women's ordination uplift Galatians 3:28 as *the* crucial text. The text is, it seems, as ubiquitous as the John 3:16 banners displayed at professional sporting events. Its appeal cuts across denominational boundaries and a wide spectrum of theological positions [...] In his programmatic essay *The Bible and the Role of Women* (1958; English translation, 1966), Krister Stendahl, the Swedish Lutheran New Testament scholar and professor at Harvard Divinity School, referred to Galatians 3:28 as Paul's 'break-through.' Other proponents of women's ordination call it the 'Magna Carta of Humanity,' 'the women's text,' and 'a cardinal statement in the Scriptures FOR the emancipation of men and women.' Opponents retort that Galatians 3:28 has been 'grossly misused,' 'does not concern ministries,' and is 'wholly irrelevant' to the questions of women holding office.[43]

In other words, Kling sees clear parallels between different denominations and revivalist movements which have opened up the clergy to women both in the past and in the present, given that they cite the same biblical text. Also noteworthy is his mention of Krister Stendahl, who contributed to the debate that led to the Church of Sweden's decision that same year to permit the ordination of women.

Kling's discussion of the relationship between hermeneutics and culture is interesting as well. Although this biblical text has been cited in support of women's ordination since the mid-nineteenth century, it was not until the 1970s that women began to join the ranks of the clergy to any great extent. Does this mean that this text had no real influence on decisions to permit women's ordination, and instead it was the women's rights movement that enabled this change? Kling asserts that there was an interaction

---

43 David W. Kling, *The Bible in History: How the Texts Have Shaped the Times* (Oxford: Oxford University Press, 2023), p. 270.

between culture and hermeneutics: changes in society made people return to Galatians 3:28 and interpret the text in a new light, which in turn led to the discovery of interpretative possibilities in the text that had been there all along.[44]

Applying a comparative perspective to women's path to church leadership and the processes geared to opening up the clergy to women is thus not very common. With this study, we hope to remedy this shortcoming; but we also wish to deepen the analysis, primarily by identifying connections and parallels between the Church of Sweden and other churches and denominations. It is interesting to note that the comparisons that have already been made and that we have touched on above emphasise both theological and other types of perspectives, and that issues related to the interaction between theology and social changes occupy a central place. These are self-evident starting points for us.

∞∞∞∞

In conclusion, our aim with this book is to contribute to various scholarly discussions in several ways. To start with, we wish to show what the process of opening up the clergy to women might look like in a church that did so at a relatively early stage for Lutheran churches. The Church of Sweden has also attracted international attention for the rapid growth in the number of its women priests.[45] Although there are many scholarly studies of this event in Swedish, there is none aimed at an international readership. This circumstance is bound up with the first aim of the book: to make the vocation stories of the first ordained women – their narratives – accessible. This source material has previously been virtually ignored in the writing of Swedish ecclesiastical history.

Together with other material, including the Sigtuna Foundation's large collection of articles from Sweden's biggest daily newspapers categorised under the heading 'the woman holding office', we seek to complement and nuance the Swedish historical narrative. We thereby hope to contribute to the international discussion about the writing and use of history, analysing an example from a period

---

44 Ibid., pp. 280–281, 294–296, 305.
45 Rakel Lennartsson and Kristoffer Morén, '1533 kvinnor och 1527 män blev världsnyhet', *Kyrkans Tidning*, 31/32 (2020). See, for instance, the *Daily Telegraph*, 'Smash! Another glass ceiling destroyed', 22 July 2020, and the *Guardian*, 'Church of Sweden's female priests outnumber men', 23 July 2020.

that is not very often discussed. We also wish to deepen the theoretical discussion about the relationship between writing and using history. In addition, we want to contribute to the research based on ordained women's own narratives by applying both a theological and a theoretical perspective to our analysis. As was shown above in the overview of previous research, usually one *or* the other of these perspectives is employed. In this study, we try to apply a dual perspective by showing how the concepts of vocation (theological) and recognition (theoretical) can be used to understand the change that occurs over time.

Finally, we wish to contribute to the debate about connections and parallels between various churches and denominations, but with a somewhat different approach from the ones that have been applied before. Instead of juxtaposing several separate studies of churches or denominations and examining their similarities and differences, we want to use the process in the Church of Sweden as an example of what such connections and parallels might look like in practice.

The nine ensuing chapters are structured as follows: in Chapter 2, we present the methodological and theoretical starting points in more detail. We describe the connections between narrative analysis and historical narratives, as well as the two key concepts in the analyses: vocation and recognition. Chapters 3 to 7 present the themes and core episodes that we have found to be particularly prominent in the narratives. Chapter 3, 'The path to vocation', focuses on childhood and adolescence and, where relevant, previous occupational life. This chapter also places the vocation stories in their historical social context, an era characterised in many ways by the struggle of different groups for recognition. Chapter 4, 'The theology of vocation', discusses the first ordained women's theological understanding of their vocation and the theological atmosphere exuded by their narratives. The following chapters discuss, in chronological order, some of the core episodes in the vocation stories. Chapter 5, 'The path to recognition', looks more closely at the period of training and what is often highlighted as the vocation stories' high point: ordination as the church's formal recognition of vocation. Two subsequent chapters examine the period after ordination. Chapter 6, 'Recognition of the vocation', explores how this recognition was expressed in practice in relation to parishes, fellow priests and ordaining bishops. A complex picture emerges of a heartfelt and warm recognition on the one hand, and an ambivalent, even withheld, recognition of the ordained women's vocation on the other. Chapter 7, 'The struggle for recognition', shows how the first ordained women dealt with the fact that the church which had recognised their vocation by ordaining them also had a provision – the 'conscience clause' (*samvetsklausulen*, briefly mentioned above and explained in a subsequent chapter) – which permitted a refusal to recognise that same vocation. The chapter also presents the retrospective perspectives and meta-reflections that meet in the narratives as the women look back on the past.

Chapters 8 and 9 examine connections and parallels with other denominations, both inside and outside Sweden. In addition, we show how these connections specifically relate to vocation and recognition, which emerge as the combined driving force behind the processes of change. In Chapter 8, 'Ecumenical entanglements', we look more closely at connections and parallels to other denominations in Sweden, while Chapter 9, 'Links and parallels', examines the international connections, especially to the neighbouring Nordic countries of Denmark and Norway. The book ends with a summarising chapter.

In a feature article about Ingrid Persson, published on 5 July 1997, the newspaper *Västernorrlands Allehanda* wrote of the photograph taken by press photographer Kjell Jonsson: 'Kjell crept into the church with only a few photos left in his camera, borrowed a roll of film from a colleague and captured the image of Ingrid Persson [...] The photo became a classic, and the following day [the major tabloid] *Expressen* led with the image splashed across its front page.' Persson's own account of the day of her ordination in 1960 forms part of her article 'Min väg till prästämbetet' ['My path to the office of priest'] (1994) and includes the observation by a worshipper that just as she came in through the back door of the cathedral, the congregation was singing 'Come, come, oh Shulamite, thou bride of Christ –'. (Image: reproduced by courtesy of Profilbild i Härnösand AB/Kjell Jonsson.)

Chapter 2
Narratives of vocation and recognition: theory and method

> When you are in the middle of a story it isn't a story at all, but only a confusion; a dark roaring, a blindness, a wreckage of shattered glass and splintered wood; like a house in a whirlwind, or else a boat crushed by the icebergs or swept over the rapids, and all aboard powerless to stop it. It's only afterwards that it becomes anything like a story at all. When you are telling it, to yourself or to someone else.[1]

Vocation narratives

This study is based on the vocation narratives of the first women to be ordained in the Church of Sweden. By using the term 'vocation narrative', we wish to emphasise that we regard the source material as narrative and to indicate how we have gone about analysing it.

Narrative is fundamental to the human ability to understand, acquire knowledge and create meaning. As we hear in the above quotation from a novel by Margaret Atwood, creating a narrative involves assembling various fragments into a whole. At the outset, the different fragments may seem disparate and incoherent. A similar situation exists in the work of historians, who create understanding of and meaning in the past by constructing historical narratives. The historian's scholarly work, however, also involves being aware of the components of the narratives: how they were created, selected, interpreted and, not least, structured.

Narratives are often structured according to particular patterns and themes. In the case of the narratives we are examining here, we believe that the common thread on which the beads of the narratives are strung comprises two intertwined concepts: *vocation* and *recognition*, 'vocation' being the narrators' fundamental concept.

---

1 Margaret Atwood, *Alias Grace* (London: Bloomsbury, 1996), p. 298.

We therefore understand the source material we have worked with as vocation narratives, and we analyse them as such.

This chapter presents research-methodological considerations and approaches. We describe what we mean by narrative and how narratives and the construction of history writing relate to issues of meaning making, identity and power. We also introduce the two concepts we regard as fundamental to the narratives of the first ordained women: on the one hand, the theological concept of vocation, and on the other, the sociological concept of recognition as developed by the philosopher Axel Honneth. In addition, we examine the ways in which these two concepts may be said to relate to each other.

Narrative and the writing of history

Narrative research methodology has its roots in two ideological currents of the twentieth century. The first is post-war humanism, which was strongly critical of scientific positivism and instead focused on individuals, drawing on case studies, biographies and life stories to explore how people describe and understand themselves. The other is structuralism and poststructuralism, which are concerned with the structure and content of narratives as well as with their performative function. Most researchers working with narrative today apply both of these approaches, usually combined into the idea of narrative as a means of resisting power structures.[2] That is also what we do in this study. There are, however, many different ways of proceeding on a practical level, and the choices we have made are presented in some detail in the following pages.

Narratives create meaning

How can we humans actually gain knowledge of and understand something about the reality in which we live? One way to describe this is to talk about narrative. A thinker who has played a major role in the development of this approach is the philosopher

---

2 For an extensive overview of the roots of narrative analysis, see, for example, Ivor Goodson, 'The Story of Life History', in Goodson (ed.), *The Routledge International Handbook*, pp. 23–33; Molly Andrews, Corinne Squire and Maria Tamboukou (eds), *Doing Narrative Research* (London: Sage, 2008), pp. 1–18.

Paul Ricoeur (1913–2005). In *Temps et récit*, he discusses the hermeneutics of narrative and the relationship between narrative, time and the construction of historical narratives. Ricoeur describes how narrative or plot (*intrigue* in French) creates a meaningful whole. He distinguishes between *transformation*, which occurs when individual events are assembled into a coherent narrative, and *configuration*, which occurs when a series of completely different phenomena are combined into a single unit.

When humans assemble narratives, it becomes possible to talk about time in the paradoxical way we human beings do. On the one hand, time is seen as a chronological sequence of hours, minutes and seconds, a constant flow within which we exist. On the other, time is seen as something non-chronological, a view tied to a human existential experience of time, something that can be retold as a narrative with a beginning and an end. In turn, time makes it possible to refigure narratives – in short, to change them. Ricoeur argues that narratives are constantly in flux. They are transformed when new events are inserted into the plot and when new factors are configured by being combined into a single unit.[3]

For Ricoeur, this situation has implications for our understanding of what history is. He asserts that historical knowledge derives from our narrative understanding of experiences and comes into being when we configure praxis by assembling various temporal factors. Historical knowledge is thus rooted in our practical skill, which helps us to process actions that occur *in* time. In addition, this view implies that the purpose of historical knowledge is to refigure praxis and thereby our understanding of what it is to exist in this world. Ricoeur emphasises this indirect link between history and narrative. On the one hand, he opposes scholars who claim that there is no connection between narrative and the writing of history and that it is possible to write history objectively. On the other, he also goes against those who assert that there is a direct relationship between history and narrative, with full continuity between the present day and historical time.[4]

Ricoeur's understanding of historical knowledge is one of the starting points for the doyen of historiography as a field of research, the historian Jörn Rüsen (1938–). Rüsen also believes that all

---

3 Paul Ricoeur, *Time and Narrative* (Chicago: University of Chicago Press, 1984), I, pp. 52–89.
4 Ibid., pp. 91–92.

history is to be regarded as narrative, but according to him, not all narratives are history. For something to be considered a historical narrative, two things are required: first, that the individual historical events linked together in the narrative are considered to have actually taken place; and second, that the narrative helps to establish a connection between the past, present and future which can be described and in which our experience of the past is interpreted in a way that contributes to our understanding of the present and our expectations of the future.[5]

These lines of reasoning by Rüsen and Ricoeur form the foundation of our approach to writing this book. We interpret and construct a historical narrative, in which a number of events are transformed by being put into chronological order and various factors are configured by being brought together. The history we write is based on (but is not the same as) the narratives of the first women ordained in Sweden, stories which, in turn, constitute their ways of understanding events and experiences that once occurred. Our text adds something to the historical narratives that already exist about these women and about the Church of Sweden and thereby changes them. In that respect, this text is no different from other historical narratives. As its reader, you also contribute to it. Our book is open to a multitude of readings, whereby you read the text in relation to your own narratives and interpret it on the basis of your own specific situation.[6]

Narratives create identity

Narratives make human experience meaningful, helping to create, sustain and change how we understand ourselves and the world around us. Consequently, narrative is crucial to the formation and transmission of both identity and culture, for individuals as well as groups.[7] Psychologist Dan P. McAdams argues that identity is fundamentally narrative, defining it as the ongoing story that an individual constructs in order to explain how they became the person they are becoming. The capacity for autobiographical

---

5 Jörn Rüsen, *History: Narration – Interpretation – Orientation* (Oxford: Berghahn Books, 2005), pp. 1–74; Jakob Dahlbacka, *Framåt med stöd av det förflutna: Religiöst historiebruk hos Anders Svedberg* (Åbo: Åbo Akademi, 2015), p. 35.
6 Johansson, *Narrativ teori och metod*, p. 31.
7 Ibid., pp. 15–17, 86; Antikainen, 'In Search of Life History', pp. 131–139.

reasoning develops during adolescence, and throughout life the narrative framework organises all the various and contradictory parts of the past, present and future, providing that sense of inner wholeness and social continuity which we call 'identity'. Human beings may hence be said to be living their story as they write it.[8] However, the narrative identities of individuals do not stand in isolation from one another; they are strongly influenced by the collective narratives of groups, cultures and societies.[9]

Historical depictions are also narratives in that they create, sustain and change identity. Various historical disciplines play a central role in contributing to the narratives that are necessary for people to understand themselves and orientate their actions towards the future in a sensible way.[10] According to this view, history is a deeply meaning-making discipline, and the narratives that are produced in research have existential implications.

This is particularly true of churches. Church historian Carola Nordbäck argues that the writing of history has been used to shape a collective Christian identity for virtually the entire history of the Church. As early as the work of Eusebius of Caesarea (263–339, the man usually called the father of church history), it is possible to discern a model of historical narrative that aims to define the right faith versus heresies and apostasy. With Eusebius, according to Nordbäck, there is a historical pattern of interpretation and a Christian self-understanding – an identity – which recurs up to the present day and whose continuity is strong. Nordbäck even speaks of a specific Christian historical consciousness that has the aim of creating context and meaning, both for individuals and groups and over time and space.[11]

Theologian Rowan Williams has also discussed the relationship between historical narrative and (Christian) identity. Like

---

8 McAdams, 'How Stories Found a Home in Human Personality', pp. 34–37.
9 Johansson, *Narrativ teori och metod*, p. 90; Philip Manning, *Erving Goffman and Modern Sociology* (Cambridge: Polity, 1992), pp. 72–117.
10 Martin Wiklund, 'Inledning', in Jörn Rüsen, *Berättande och förnuft: Historieteoretiska texter*, trans. Joachim Retzlaff (Gothenburg: Daidalos, 2004), p. 13. See also Sinikka Neuhaus, 'Vad är det vi gör när vi berättar historia?', in Claesson and Neuhaus (eds), *Minne och möjlighet*, pp. 44–52; Sinikka Neuhaus, *Reformation och erkännande: Skilsmässoärenden under den tidiga reformationsprocessen i Malmö 1527–1542* (Lund: Lund University, 2009).
11 Carola Nordbäck, 'Kyrkohistorisk historiebruksforskning', in Claesson and Neuhaus (eds), *Minne och möjlighet*, pp. 16–21.

Ricoeur, he maintains that a good and nuanced historical narrative is indirect, recognising that there are both differences and similarities between the present and the past. For Williams, however, it is above all the dissimilarity – the fact that the past is radically different – that is important for identity. By engaging with what is different and therefore often hard to understand, Williams believes that an understanding of who we are is created.[12] History writing thus not only creates identity; it also demonstrates that this identity is constantly changing.

Narratives and power

Because narratives help to create meaning and identity, they have a performative function, and narratives are therefore also related to power. For better or worse, narratives have the capacity to influence and control the voices of both the narrator and others, thereby creating and maintaining power structures.[13]

The performative function of narratives, however, can also be used to reveal and resist power structures. By constructing other narratives, known as 'counter-narratives', and giving them space to be heard, the balance of power can be changed.[14] This realisation is important in societies and cultures in which women's voices and histories are ignored or undocumented.[15] One example of this phenomenon, taken from a Swedish context, is found in the way in which the prevailing theological narrative of woman's vocation as wife, mother and housewife came to be challenged, in the latter half of the nineteenth century, by a counter-narrative based on theological grounds. The new view of the Bible and history that spread at this time favoured the theological counter-narrative, gave it

---

12 Rowan Williams, *Why Study the Past: The Quest for the Historical Church* (London: Darton, Longman & Todd, 2005), pp. 23–24.

13 Ken Plummer, 'Narrative Power, Sexual Stories and the Politics of Storytelling', in Goodson (ed.), *The Routledge International Handbook*, p. 281; Goodson, 'Introduction: Life History and Narratives', p. 4.

14 Ricoeur, *Time and Narrative*, I, p. 75.

15 Sanela Bajramovic Jusufbegovic, 'Muntliga berättelser om kvinnoaktivism i Bosnien-Hercegovina: Med källkritik och analys i fokus', in Greger Andersson, Christina Carlsson Wetterberg, Carina Lidström and Sten Wistrand (eds), *Berättande, liv, mening* (Örebro: Örebro University, 2014), p. 108. See also Maria Tamboukou, 'A Foucauldian Approach to Narratives', in Andrews, Squire and Tamboukou (eds), *Doing Narrative Research*, pp. 102–120.

priority and interpretative primacy, and came to drive the Swedish emancipation process.[16] Historiographical research also recognises the performative aspect of historical narratives and the link to power. For example, Jörn Rüsen argues that history has a clearly normative and performative side.[17] In particular, the issue of the 'use of history' – that is, how historical narratives are employed for particular purposes – has been much discussed since the turn of the millennium. The historian Peter Aronsson sums up 'the basic concepts of the use of history' as historical culture, use of history and historical consciousness. By 'historical culture', Aronsson means the artefacts, rituals, customs and assertions with reference to the past that offer tangible opportunities to bind together the relationship between past, present and future.[18] As Nordbäck has pointed out, communicative contexts that produce historical narratives and statements may also be regarded as historical cultures.[19] In our opinion, it is hence reasonable to consider the Church of Sweden as a historical culture.

When a historical culture is activated for a specific purpose, the procedure is referred to as 'use of history'. Use of history might engender enhanced or modified historical consciousness. 'Historical consciousness' creates connections between past, present and future, and it helps with orientation in time and space.[20] To put it another way: in order to create a specific historical consciousness and nudge public opinion in a particular direction, use of history enables the application of historical consciousness.[21]

In the discussion on history writing and power, the concept 'misuse of history' has also become established. Nordbäck stresses that it is important for historians to identify various forms of

16 Inger Hammar, *Emancipation och religion: Den svenska kvinnorörelsens pionjärer i debatt om kvinnans kallelse ca 1860–1900* (Stockholm: Carlsson, 1999), pp. 11–19, 246–247.
17 Jörn Rüsen, *Zeit und Sinn: Strategien historischen Denkens* [Neuausgabe] (Frankfurt am Main: Humanities Online, 2012), pp. 77–105. See also Dahlbacka, *Framåt med stöd av det förflutna*, p. 16.
18 Peter Aronsson, *Historiebruk: Att använda det förflutna* (Lund: Studentlitteratur, 2004), p. 17.
19 Nordbäck, 'Kyrkohistorisk historiebruksforskning', pp. 16–21.
20 Aronsson, *Historiebruk*, pp. 17–18.
21 Urban Claesson, 'Introduktion', in Claesson and Neuhaus (eds), *Minne och möjlighet*, p. 8.

history misuse, especially representations of history that stigmatise or discriminate against groups in various ways, thereby fuelling conflicts. We share the conviction that the more active research on, and discussion of, history is in a society, the more the risk of such misuse going unchallenged decreases.[22] It is partly in the light of this conviction that we have written this book: our ambition is to bring out voices that have been largely ignored in the past. By presenting these narratives, we hope to complicate and supplement received truths. To some extent, we also hope to help give voice to people who have been silenced and marginalised by the dominant narratives.[23]

At this point, it should be observed that the term 'marginalised' might not really be an adequate description of people who have after all held leading positions in the Church of Sweden, published books, frequently been interviewed by newspapers, obtained doctorates, and so on. Even so, we believe that there are grounds for maintaining that the first ordained women were definitely marginalised in the 1960s, the period covered by this study. Regardless of one's position on that issue, however, it is certain that we are presenting stories that have not been heard before, in the hope that they will shed light on the historical narrative about the 1958 reform in the Church of Sweden and help to complement and nuance it.

Narratives in the source material

When a researcher gains access to a narrative, it is important to bear in mind that this narrative is not the same thing as the internalised, gradually emerging and ever-changing story that the individual carries within himself or herself. At best, the researcher can only access fragments of that story.[24] Scholars must also be aware that the accessed narratives occur in the present. They form a kind of snapshot of what the inner narratives looked like at the time when they were written down.[25] Research on narratives thus focuses on the story as it is told by the narrator himself/herself at a

---

22 Nordbäck, 'Kyrkohistorisk historiebruksforskning', p. 27.

23 Johansson, *Narrativ teori och metod*, pp. 23–24; see also pp. 218–219, in which the emancipatory potential of the narrative method is discussed.

24 McAdams, 'How Stories Found a Home in Human Personality', p. 40.

25 Jaber F. Gubrium and James A. Holstein, 'Analysing Novelty and Pattern in Institutional Life Narratives', in Goodson (ed.), *The Routledge International Handbook*, p. 156.

specific moment.[26] Consequently, it is essential to be familiar with the conditions of this specific moment in order to gain a satisfactory understanding of the source material. This is particularly true of a source such as the one we are working with, material which was created at different times, in different contexts and by different people.

Most of the narratives on which this study is based were written in the early 2000s on the initiative of Lena Malmgren, herself one of the first women to be ordained in the Church of Sweden (1967). In late 2004 she wrote to all the women who had been ordained in the Church of Sweden from 1960 to 1970, asking them to write about their path to ordination. These stories were to be placed in Lund University's Ecclesiastical History Archive (LUKA) and made available to future researchers. After about a year, 17 such narratives had been collected. They varied in length and narrative style, ranging from a single page to about 40 pages. Among those who did not submit texts, two instead referred to a book to which they had contributed, *Kvinnlig präst idag: Tio kvinnliga präster berättar* ['A woman priest today: ten women priests tell their stories'] from 1967, in which ten ordained women talk about their lives in active ministry. These ten stories are therefore also included in our primary source material.

Several of those who did not submit a text explained that they were in active service and unfortunately did not have time to write, but that they would be happy to do so after they had retired. In 2018 we were asked to take over the project and finalise the collection. After the research-ethics review had been performed,[27] in May 2019 we sent letters to the 16 priests who were still alive and who had not submitted a narrative, whereupon eight new narratives were added to the collection. Some of the priests preferred to be interviewed rather than writing down their story themselves. We conducted four such interviews, using the same questions: 'What was your path to ordination like?' and 'What were your first years in ministry like?'

Eight did not respond or chose to decline. Three referred to other publications in which they had already told their story. These three were Ulla Nisser (1941–, ordained 1968), who had published an autobiography in 2016; Margareta Brandby-Cöster

---

26 Goodson, 'The Story of Life History', pp. 23–33.
27 Case number 2018/853, approved 7 November 2018.

(1947–, ordained 1970), who had recently celebrated the fiftieth anniversary of her ordination and in connection with this put her memories on paper, producing a book on the subject; and Birgitta Nyman (1945–, ordained 1970), who referred to an interview she gave in 2008 in conjunction with the fiftieth anniversary of the General Synod's decision to open up the priesthood to women.[28] The publication to which Nyman referred also contains interviews with two more of the first ordained women. These three interviews are also included in the source material for this study.

In the period since the first narratives were written down in 2004, a book had also been published that contains a selection of Margit Sahlin's diary entries, selected and annotated by Elisabeth Nordlander.[29] This book is also included in our source material.[30] In total this study is thus based on 34 of the first ordained women's narratives about their path to the priesthood, of whom 12 had not previously published anything on this topic. We also have information about a further 11 ordained women via diocesan annals, personal archives and obituaries, as well as from relatives and close friends. Another important supplementary source material is the newspaper articles in the Sigtuna Foundation's clippings archive (more on this below).

In May 2019 we also contacted the five women priests who had already submitted their stories and who were still alive, informing them that a research project had been initiated. Four of them then wished to review their stories once more, but no changes were made.

All source materials from the LUKA archive, both interviews and stories written by the priests themselves, are subject to research-ethics rules governing confidentiality. This is required both to

---

28 Ulla Nisser, *Hopp från trampolin: Mitt liv som flicka, kvinna och präst* (Mjölby: Atremi, 2016); Margareta Brandby-Cöster, *Hur gick det till? Hur blev jag präst? Erinringar 50 år efteråt* (Stockholm: BoD – Books on Demand, 2020); Boel Hössjer Sundman and Lina Sjöberg, *Du ska bli präst: Livsberättelser 50 år efter kyrkomötets beslut* (Stockholm: Verbum, 2008).

29 Elisabeth Nordlander, *Margit Sahlin: På väg mot verklighet* (Skellefteå: Artos, 2010).

30 Since Sahlin's life and work are relatively well researched, we have chosen to focus primarily on the source materials from the LUKA archive and the Sigtuna Foundation's clippings archive, and used Nordlander's excellent sample from Sahlin's voluminous archive. Sahlin's archive is currently in the possession of the director of the Margit Sahlin Academy, Madeleine Åhlstedt.

protect personal data such as religious affiliation and because these narratives might contain sensitive information. We will therefore subsequently refer to the source material and the vocational narratives from the LUKA archive by number. In a number of cases, the names of people and places have been removed and replaced with [name] and [place]. However, when we refer to individuals who were acting in their public capacity as bishops, professors, teachers and the like, we have generally allowed the name to remain.

Still, this ethical requirement for confidentiality had to be weighed against the desire of some of the priests to own their personal story, a desire rooted in concern about the risk of being misinterpreted and having opinions imposed on them that they might not have held. The fear of being misinterpreted was sometimes combined with a wish not to be lumped together in a group, as if all ordained women were cast in the same mould. The correspondence from both 2004 and 2019 makes it clear that the experience of an earlier study from 1982 was particularly discouraging.[31] That study was based on questionnaires distributed to all women who were ordained from 1960 to 1977, and the results were used by opponents of the reform to argue that it should never have been implemented. When the study was published in 1982, some of the first ordained women reacted strongly. For example, Else Orstadius (1926–, ordained 1967) wrote in *Svenska Dagbladet* that she felt obliged to 'clearly mark my repudiation of her [Ulla Carin Holm's] way of depicting us women priests'.[32] Margit Sahlin's statement about the future publication of her diary entries summarises her concerns and those of some of her fellow priests:

> A significant element in this context is the behaviour of women priests, behaviour that is detrimental to their own cause and, above all, to the church. This is the case with Ulla Carin Holm and her thesis 'Her works shall praise her', in which she maintains, among other things, that women priests do not read the Bible and cannot accept traditional Christianity, which they find masculine. As was to be expected, [the well-known opponent of the reform] Gustaf Adolf Danell later wrote that this is what happens when you 'ordain ladies'.[33]

---

31 Ulla Carin Holm, *Hennes verk skall prisa henne: Studier av personlighet och attityder hos kvinnliga präster i Svenska kyrkan* (Båstad: Plus Ultra, 1982).

32 Else Orstadius, 'Jag tar avstånd', *Svenska Dagbladet*, 27 December 1982.

33 Nordlander, *Margit Sahlin*, p. 289.

Some of the priests concerned also directly questioned the issue of confidentiality, arguing that names should be disclosed. One priest who did so was Margareta Brandby-Cöster, in the introduction to her above-mentioned book:

> On two occasions I have received an invitation from the Ecclestiastical History Archive in Lund, which went out to us women who were ordained in 1960–1970. We were invited to write about our path to ordination and perhaps something about our early days as priests. It is a commendable initiative. The first time, however, I declined. I have always found it difficult and boring to write about myself, and I still do. Consequently, I have never kept a diary. The second time I said 'yes', but I changed my mind after a while. Everything I've written and said as a priest I've done publicly, so why should I now write directly for an archive? Because it is nevertheless important to document eras and events, and despite my inner resistance, I decided to try to say something about my path to the priesthood and make it available to any interested reader. If the Ecclesiastical History Archive would like to add this story to their records, that's fine.[34]

In this book, despite the confidentiality imposed by the Swedish Ethical Review Authority [Etikprövningsmyndigheten], we have therefore endeavoured to supply names as far as possible (as was mentioned above, it could not be done when referring to the source material in the LUKA archive for reasons of research ethics). The ordained women have published books, they have given interviews and written opinion pieces, and some even have personal archives. With the help of this material, we hope to show the breadth and diversity that exists in the different vocational narratives. It has also been important for us not to contribute more than is required by research ethics to silencing and concealing women's voices. Our hope is that this approach has resulted in an acceptable balance between our informants' right to protection and their right to be heard as individual theologians and priests.

Analysing narratives

Whenever a narrative is to be analysed, a thematic content analysis is usually undertaken, and this is done here, too. What themes and patterns emerge and recur? To understand what is being told, however, it is essential to pay attention to when, by whom and for

---

34 Brandby-Cöster, *Hur gick det till?*, p. 6.

whom it is being told, and through what medium. Two more things are also important to the analysis, namely, finding the plot of the narrative and establishing its anchorage.

One aspect to consider during analysis is the question of *when*. The analysis needs to take into account how close in time the recording of the retold events is to the events themselves. In this study, the time distance between event and recording is generally wide. That might be seen as a disadvantage, as it affects – for example – the informants' ability to remember exact dates and the names of people and places. One exception is the vocation narratives published in the book *Kvinnlig präst idag* from 1967, which was written close in time to the events recounted.[35] An advantage of having material from both 1967 and the 2000s is that it is possible to highlight changes in the informants' reflections on what happened, for instance how things changed over time and what they would have liked to have done differently. We will return to such so-called meta-reflections in Chapter 7.

Then comes the question of *who*. To begin with, the informant herself is in focus. Does she have what is known as narrative competence, demonstrated by her skill in telling stories and making observations using a large vocabulary; or is this an informant who has difficulty expressing herself? How does the informant talk about herself? As an active participant in the story or as someone who was being victimised? Are the events portrayed neutrally or emotionally?[36]

The question of *who* applies to researchers, too. This question is particularly prominent in the interview situation when the narrative is being created; but it is also crucial in the analysis of those texts that the researcher has not taken part in creating. In the case of this source material, for example, there is a certain difference between being asked to write down one's narrative by a friend and fellow priest, with the argument that 'one day someone might want to do research on this', and being asked by two researchers whom one does not know and who intend to carry out a research project in the near future. In the narratives collected on the latter occasion, a greater degree of caution can be discerned in how the priests chose to express themselves. The collected texts also show

---

35 *Kvinnlig präst idag: Tio kvinnliga präster berättar* (Stockholm: Natur och Kultur, 1967).

36 Ibid., pp. 265–267.

that the ordained women have thought in quite dissimilar ways. Some have worked extensively with literary form with the aim of having posterity read the narrative as a whole; others have written in bullet-point form with precise dates; and still others include long explanatory digressions that suggest that the future recipient is not expected to have prior knowledge of theology or history.

Another aspect of the analysis is the *medium* through which the narrative is conveyed. For this study we received most of the narratives in text form. This creates some challenges in the interpretation. Usually, narratives are created through an interview, in which the researcher hears voice inflections and pauses, and sees gestures and facial expressions, laughter and tears, glances and other kinds of body language, all of which may contribute to the analysis.[37] In this case, with the exception of four interviews, we received the narratives in one-dimensional text form, which might be said to make analysis more difficult.

An analysis of narratives also needs to pay attention to *genre*. The way narratives are told is shaped by how narratives of the same type are usually formulated.[38] It is essential to be aware of this for several reasons. First, because some things are not said, as they do not fit into the way this particular type of narrative is structured. For example, if interviewees are asked to describe the time before, during and after their ordination, they are unlikely to include their passion for football or their family life in their story. It is therefore important to be careful about assuming causal relationships that the interviewees themselves do not explicitly state. There may be no connection at all, or there may be something unspoken that is the real cause.[39]

Second, paying attention to genre enables researchers to examine the structure of the narrative. Such an examination supplies an idea of how the narrator makes sense of her life; and if several stories of the same type are put side by side, it becomes possible to distinguish interesting patterns and recurring themes. That is how we have worked with the narratives on which this book is based. Although they are different from one another, there is a recurring structure of themes that return in the vast majority of narratives.[40]

---

37 See, for example, Andrews, Squire and Tamboukou (eds), *Doing Narrative Research*.
38 Goodson, 'The Rise of the Life Narrative', p. 4.
39 See Andrews, Squire and Tamboukou (eds), *Doing Narrative Research*.
40 Horsdal, 'The Narrative Interview', p. 266.

Most narratives of some length consist of structuring components. The aforementioned Dan P. McAdams, who has studied
the role of narrative in identity, has identified four such frequently
occurring components. The first is *nuclear episodes* (which we
prefer to call 'core episodes'), scenes that stand out because of
their dramatic qualities or psychological significance. These can
be turning points, climaxes or moments of greatest difficulty. The
second is the *imago*, personified representations of the self, a kind
of semi-autonomous protagonist in the narrative. Examples are
the good son, the rebel and the future priest. A third common
component is *ideological setting*, that is, the beliefs and values that
place the narrative within a particular epistemological, ethical,
social and religious context. The fourth component is *generativity
script*, which is about the desire to leave a favourable legacy that
might guide and inspire people in the future.

According to McAdams, all these components relate to content,
and the most common approach consists in adhering to some
kind of broad thematic line.[41] This thematic line, or foundational
element, in the narrative is sometimes referred to as the *plot*.[42] The
ideological circumstances that leave their mark on the narratives we
analyse are to be found in the Swedish church context. The central
structuring component – the main plot, which recurs in almost all
core episodes – is vocation.

Vocation

Vocation is a central theological concept in the Lutheran tradition
to which the Church of Sweden belongs. Traditionally, we speak of
inner and outer calling. In both cases, it is God who calls, but the
call is experienced in either of two ways. In one way, the individual
personally experiences that God is calling them to service, and in
the other, church representatives see that the person is suitable and
express a desire for them to take on a role. Sometimes people talk
about 'God's call' and 'the call of the church/parish'; but the idea is,
of course, that it is God who calls, also via his church/parish. Both
aspects of vocation are components of *rite vocatus* – being 'properly
called' – according to Article 14 of the Augsburg Confession, the
shared confession of faith of the Lutheran churches.

---

41 McAdams, 'How Stories Found a Home in Human Personality', pp. 38–39.
42 Johansson, *Narrativ teori och metod*, p. 95.

The ordained women describe their inner and outer vocation in many different ways. For example, Ingrid Persson says that her answer to Archbishop Gunnar Hultgren (1902–1991), when asked if she could see herself being one of the first women to be ordained, was 'it is to your, the Church's and God's call that I answer yes'.[43] Inner and outer calling are thus linked. At the same time, it is possible to distinguish between the different aspects; for example, Birgitta Nyman does so when she says in an interview that it was rarely the case that 'the inner call from God was supported by an outer call from the church leadership'.[44]

In the narratives of the first ordained women, the core episodes are repeatedly linked to their vocation: the decisive moments have to do with their experience of being called. Difficult moments, such as death and serious illness, tend to be interpreted in relation to the call from God. High points and moments of joy are also linked to vocation, in particular the ordination ceremony, which is represented as the external confirmation that they have been called. A number of the narratives begin and/or end with accounts of or reflections on vocation. One telling example is found in the introduction to the longest story, Ulla Nisser's autobiography *Hopp från trampolin* ['Jumping from a trampoline'] (2016):

> Some years later, I am leafing through a memoir written by some of the first ordained women. At first I am struck by how many of them can point to a concrete event that triggered their sense of vocation. One speaks of a bicycle ride at the age of eleven, another of her vocation as a bolt of lightning in her life [...] As for me, though, I have nothing tangible to present with regard to my vocation. No supernatural intervention. Just something that emerged without clear contours. But that's enough for me, and perhaps that is what's most important after all.[45]

When Nisser compares her own story with those of other ordained women, it is hence the vocation that she notices and describes, even though the experience itself differs.

The source material thus provides evidence that the underlying theme is one of vocation. Another reason for regarding these

43 Yvonne Landström, 'En stilla stund 40 år efter prästvigningen', *Västernorrlands Allehanda*, 5 July 1997.
44 Lina Sjöberg, 'Kyrkan måste vara ömsint och stå på människors sida: Birgitta Nyman, prästvigd 1970', in Hössjer Sundman and Sjöberg, *Du ska bli präst*, p. 59.
45 Nisser, *Hopp från trampolin*, p. 6.

stories as vocation narratives is that such narratives constitute a kind of unofficial genre within the ecclesiastical context, implied but very much in use, especially when recruiting to various types of training programmes. In the application for the Salvation Army's officer-training programme, a mandatory part of the application was the so-called conversion story. In this section, the applicant would describe how she felt called to take up the battle under the sign of the Cross and how she longed to become a female warrior in the army of God. The stories depicted childhood, sin and hardship, and they described the experience of happiness when the individual realised their vocation.[46] Similarly, applicants to deaconess-training programmes were expected to describe how and in what way they had been called to serve.[47]

Vocation was also the central theme for the women revivalist preachers in the United States between 1740 and 1845, as studied by the historian of religion Catherine A. Brekus. This focus on vocation is based on the fact that the purpose of the narratives was, among other things, to defend the right to preach. Having begun in childhood, the narratives describe a conversion and a subsequent call to preach. The call is often represented as being so powerful that it is impossible to opt out, because God refuses to let the women deny their calling.[48]

As we mentioned in the research overview, the idea that rejecting the call amounts to going against God's will is also a major theme in the narratives of the Brazilian pastors examined by Eliana Coelho da Silva.[49] This theme also appears in a number of the narratives on which this study is based: the idea that there is something compelling, something unavoidable, in God's call, and that the call to the priesthood which the narrators have experienced is profoundly connected to their identities, that is, to their innermost selves.

Priests in the Church of Sweden did not have to declare their vocation in writing, but there appear to have been discussions on this topic in conjunction with the bishops' decisions to ordain priests.[50] There is also evidence in the source material to the effect

---

46 Johan A. Lundin, *Predikande kvinnor och gråtande män: Frälsningsarmén i Sverige 1882–1921* (Malmö: Kira, 2014), pp. 83–91.

47 See, for example, letters kept in the archives of Marie Cederschiöld University in Stockholm.

48 Brekus, *Strangers & Pilgrims*, pp. 160–183.

49 Coelho da Silva, 'Chamadas por Deus', pp. 142–148.

50 Vocation narrative No. 7. The narratives are hereafter referred to by number.

that this was something that the first ordained women had to explain more than once. It is striking that in the cases where we have access to several narrative versions of the path to priestly ordination, core episodes relating to the call are recounted in similar ways. We have about ten pieces of evidence for this, cases where it is possible to compare the source material in the archive with statements expressed in *Kvinnlig präst idag* from 1967, *Du ska bli präst* ['You shall become a priest'] from 2008, and various interviews in newspapers and the like.

Many of the vocation narratives that we analyse emphasise that a call from God is something that must be heeded. The call 'beckons and pulls' in an irresistible manner.[51] Giving up on the call makes a person so unhappy that she can hardly bear to live. One of the priests describes how she tired of the resistance from the male priesthood candidates during her training, decided to ignore it all and tried to become a secondary school teacher instead. However, this led to great anguish: 'What had I done? How could I let God down, how could I let myself and my future down? I could neither eat nor sleep. I could not concentrate on my studies. My will to live was failing. Everything was chaos.'[52] Finally, her fiancé made her realise that 'if I didn't follow my calling, become a priest, I would no longer be the person he loved'.[53]

In the interviews we ourselves conducted, this experience was expressed with great clarity. When the interviewer (AM) began to say 'so then you had decided to become a priest', the informant (I) interrupted firmly and somewhat irritably:

> I: Or if God had decided it! Yes, I just had to.
> AM: There was a call?
> I: Yes![54]

The idea of the vocation as something compelling is sometimes linked to the idea that it is deeply connected to the priest as a

---

51 No. 29.
52 No. 42.
53 Ibid.
54 Most of the first women to be ordained share similar thoughts; for example, Kerstin Lindqvist-Bolling (1939–2015, ordained 1964), 'Förstadspräst', in *Kvinnlig präst idag*, pp. 43–44; Inger Svensson (1945–1996, ordained 1969), in Oloph Bexell, Kjell Hagberg and Viveka Posse, *Kvinnliga präster i Växjö stift?! Handlingarna i en kyrklig stridsfråga* (Uppsala: Pro Veritate, 1969), p. 15; Britta Olén-van Zijl, 'Att få vara präst', in *Kvinnlig präst idag*, p. 104.

person.[55] An example is provided by Lena Malmgren in an opinion piece entitled 'Omöjligt skilja på sak och person i prästämbetet' ['Impossible to distinguish between the issue and the individual in the priestly office']:

> The reason I am a priest is because I believe I am called by God to be one, and by a parish to exercise my ministry there. I build my life, my work, my courage, my entire existence on the fact that I am a priest, called by God and willing to obey that call to the best of my ability in parish and church. Anyone who does not respect my faith in God and his calling of me as a priest does not respect anything that is important to me, not the innermost part of my person; he violates my very person.[56]

Malmgren believes that a division between 'priest' and 'human being' is not possible, especially since it is God's compelling call that one cannot avoid obeying. In Malmgren's view, this vocation is so closely tied to one's identity that its being questioned by others amounts to a kind of violation.

The argument that questioning an individual's vocation is perceived as a violation of her personhood and identity is put forward by a number of the women priests.[57] In an article in *Norrköpings Tidningar* in June 1977, Barbro Westlund (1936–2016, ordained 1967) stresses that she considers it to be a rejection of her entire life and her life's work when someone says that her priestly actions are not valid because she is a woman: 'I have devoted my life to serving as a priest. To reject me as a priest is to reject the entirety of who I am.'[58]

With this background in mind, we maintain that vocation is the key plotline around which the narrative unfolds, and therefore

---

55 This is mentioned, for example, in Olén-van Zijl, 'Att få vara präst', p. 104; Ylwa Gustafsson (1937–2010, ordained 1967), in Anna Lena Wik-Thorsell, 'Kvinnlig präst söker aldrig konflikterna', *Svenska Dagbladet*, 3 September 1967.

56 Lena Malmgren, 'Omöjligt skilja på sak och person i prästämbetet', *Göteborgs–Posten*, 31 October 1978.

57 'Margit Sahlin till kvinnoprästmotståndarna: Hur ska framtiden se ut inom kyrkan?', *Sydsvenska Dagbladet*, 17 September 1977; Barbro Westlund (1936–2016, ordained 1967), in Eva Jansson and Christer Dandels, 'Stiftets första kvinnliga präst: – Vi har kommit för att stanna!', *Norrköpings Tidningar*, 10 June 1977; Caroline Krook, *Prästens identitet och kyrkans trovärdighet* (Stockholm: Verbum, 1996), p. 31.

58 Jansson and Dandels, 'Stiftets första kvinnliga präst'.

it becomes the central component of our analysis. It is, however, important to be aware of what the practical theologian Sune Fahlgren calls 'the language issue'. Different church traditions have dissimilar ways of theologically understanding such things as vocation and leadership and how they should be organised; consequently, they employ very dissimilar terminologies. The terms themselves vary; sometimes the same phenomenon may be described using different terms; and sometimes one term means different things depending on the context.[59]

The language issue takes on an additional dimension when a scholarly study is translated from Swedish into English. The Swedish concept of *kallelse* contains elements of both the concepts in use in English, that is, 'calling' and 'vocation': it is both about something existential and about being active in a profession. In this book, we have chosen to use the term 'vocation', but the reader should be aware of this dual connotation. Similar challenges apply to the Swedish word *präst*. Depending on the ecclesiastical context that one is addressing, or that one comes from, different terms such as 'pastor', 'priest' and 'minister' are employed. In this study we have chosen to use the term 'priest' to denote the first ordained women, perceiving it as being the most common one in an Anglican context in order to denote how the office is understood in the Church of Sweden. As for the concept of *vigning* (ordination), the act is formally carried out during a church service that includes prayers and the laying on of hands by a bishop. The title of priest is thus linked to the individual rather than to the office in a parish (one is hence a priest even if one is not currently called and employed by a parish); but the right to exercise the office of priest can be revoked by the Church if a priest does not adhere to the promises made in connection with the ordination.

Anchoring narratives

In addition to the plot, there is another important component of narrative analysis, namely the anchoring of the narrative. One downside of the performative function of narratives is that they sometimes risk losing their connection to real events. As the linguist

---

59 Sune Fahlgren, 'Ämbete, kallelse och tjänst', in *Präst och Pastor: Ämbete, kallelse, tjänst*, Nordic Ecumenical Series, 28 (Uppsala: Nordic Ecumenical Council, 1996), pp. 17–18.

Christian Salmon has observed, the boundary between fiction and reality can sometimes be suspended, so that ultimately it is only a question of which narrative is perceived as most credible, not which narrative best describes real experiences. Salmon views credibility as a problematic criterion because it tends to be based on fitting into and confirming the worldview that the audience already has, or on fulfilling an expectation of what the audience would like it to be. Credibility risks becoming a matter of what 'feels right'. According to Salmon, one way of counteracting such tendencies when analysing narratives is to ensure that contradictions, complexities and nuances are clearly stated.[60]

Another leading thinker in the field of narrative theory, Ivor Goodson, highlights two further ways of anchoring narratives: they need to be analysed both in relation to theoretical perspectives and in relation to their context, since individual narratives are always closely tied to their surrounding culture, circumstances or life situation.[61] In the following analytical chapters we have integrated the statements of the source material with historical context and theoretical reasoning, so that the analyses do not float away and lose their grounding in real events and phenomena.

As far as the historical context is concerned, of course we draw on previous research and other relevant sources from this period, but also on voices from the debate in newspapers of the day. It is not only the voices of the ordained women that have not been given much space in the research to date. Contemporary newspaper debates have also been overshadowed by source materials such as church council minutes and the presentations and reports of bishops and prominent theologians. We believe that the interaction between the media and the church is a very important piece of the puzzle when it comes to understanding the era in question. Mediatisation processes are a key to understanding Christian practice and theology, not only in the present but throughout church history. Moreover, from the 1950s onwards the importance of the media increases.[62]

---

60 Christian Salmon, *Storytelling: Bewitching the Modern Mind* (London: Verso, 2010).

61 Goodson, 'Life Histories and Narratives', pp. 4, 18–19.

62 See, for example, Peter Horsefield, *From Jesus to the Internet: A History of Christianity and Media* (Chichester: Wiley Blackwell, 2015); Mia Lövheim and Stig Hjarvard, 'The Mediatized Conditions of Contemporary Religion: Critical Status and Future Directions', *Journal of Religion, Media & Digital Culture*, 8 (2019), 38–39.

In this book we have mainly drawn on the clippings archive of the Sigtuna Foundation, which has a solid collection of newspaper articles on the theme of 'women in the service of the church' from the entire twentieth century. The selection of articles has been governed by the primary source material, that is, the ordained women's narratives; and it has been made with regard to which pieces are able to shed light on the themes that emerge. In some chapters we draw on this press material to engage in greater depth with one or more specific events, individuals or phenomena. By adopting this approach, we wish to convey a sense of what contemporary debates and conversations might have sounded like, and to situate the vocation narratives safely and clearly in their context.

One particularly important aspect of the historical context is how the vocation narratives relate to contemporaneous ideological circumstances, that is, to the overarching theological narratives of vocation and ministry that prevailed at the time. These overarching theological narratives are the very air that the vocation narratives breathe, and they become incomprehensible if they are disconnected from this context. We therefore devote a good deal of space to analysing the theology expressed by the women priests in their vocation narratives, and to situating their theology in the context of some of the key theologians and theological movements of the time.

In terms of theoretical perspectives, we allow the narratives to be illuminated by a number of relevant theories that not only anchor the source material but also contribute critically and constructively to the understanding of the narratives. Central to this endeavour is the theory of *recognition*.

The theory of recognition

In parallel with vocation, philosopher Axel Honneth's moral and socio-philosophical theory of recognition is an important interpretative key to understanding the narratives. To a large extent, the narratives – but also their counter-narratives – deal with issues of intersubjective recognition.[63]

With his 1992 book *Kampf um Anerkennung: Zur moralischen Grammatik sozialer Konflikte* (published in English as *The*

---

63 The following section is based on Frida Mannerfelt and Alexander Maurits, 'Kallelse och erkännande: Perspektiv på de första prästvigda kvinnorna i Svenska kyrkan', *St Sunniva*, 2 (2021), 6–24.

Struggle for Recognition: The Moral Grammar of Social Conflicts, 1995), Honneth laid the foundations of his theory of recognition. Since then, he has developed this theory further in a large number of books and articles. A central starting point for Honneth, who stands in the tradition of the Frankfurt School, is that social change is driven by various struggles for recognition. Besides, he believes that all human development depends on well-established ethical relationships between people and various groups of individuals. A cornerstone of Honneth's way of perceiving the world is human intersubjectivity. With an oversimplification, this means that a human being comes into being – and thus also risks being destroyed – in relation to other people. In becoming a human being, three aspects are fundamental: self-confidence, self-respect and self-esteem. These three aspects are created and maintained through mutual recognition. This recognition occurs in the context of three different types or levels of relationships: close relationships; legal and institutional relationships; and social networks with shared values.

An individual's development of a healthy self-identity requires close relationships to be characterised by love and self-confidence, that is, by the ability to express their needs without running the risk of being abandoned. This is a matter of rights and self-respect, meaning that a person possesses universal human dignity and is seen as morally responsible and capable of participating in collective negotiations about the shape of society (it should be noted that a person can have self-respect without legal recognition, but self-respect can only be fully realised if they do have it). It is also a matter of solidarity and self-esteem, meaning that their contribution to the various social networks of which they are a part is perceived as a valuable contribution to the community.[64] In simple terms, Honneth believes that becoming a human being requires the development of a healthy self-image and identity through being recognised on these three levels. It is vital that this recognition should come from those whom the individual himself/herself recognises.

However, the reverse is also true: denial of recognition has a negative impact on identity, and the experience of not being respected or recognised can cause extensive damage and, in the

---

64 Axel Honneth, *The Struggle for Recognition: The Moral Grammar of Social Conflicts* (Cambridge: Polity, 1995), pp. x–xxi, 91–130.

worst case, lead to a collapse of the human identity.[65] According to Honneth, withheld or denied recognition is expressed in three forms of contempt. The first case has to do with a violation of physical integrity, where someone usurps control over another person's body against her will. This experience of powerlessness leads to a loss of self-confidence. In the second case, denied recognition means that the person feels structurally excluded from the rights held by others in society. When, as a subject, a person is not deemed capable of making moral judgements, a loss of self-respect ensues. The third case involves a denial of recognition of a person's ability to contribute to their culture and community, a denial which makes it impossible for them to fully realise their own potential.[66]

This is where one of the strengths of the theory emerges in relation to our source material. As we have shown above, it is clear that vocation is deeply connected to the women priests' identity, and that it is highly offensive to have one's vocation – and thus one's person – questioned. Honneth's concept lends visibility to the connections between recognition at different levels and an individual's identity, demonstrating the fatal consequences of denied recognition. These connections would not have been as clear if we had chosen a more general concept, such as 'affirmation' or 'confirmation', to denote this phenomenon.

Honneth further argues that every historical and social process of change can be interpreted as a *struggle for recognition*. This means that if we examine conflicts in society, a clear pattern emerges: they are all collective reactions to denied recognition. With or without violence, these reactions are an expression of struggle. Honneth calls this pattern *moral grammar*. It is moral because the struggle is not about an egocentric quest for better material conditions but rather about morality, about what is right and just. By labelling this as grammar, Honneth shows that the actors are not always aware of the pattern.[67] Since Honneth's theory contains this moral aspect, he is able to diagnose social pathologies, that is to say, evaluate the current time period and determine which struggles should be recognised.[68]

---

65 Axel Honneth, *The Fragmented World of the Social: Essays in Social and Political Philosophy* (Albany, NY: State University of New York Press, 1995), p. 249.

66 Honneth, *The Struggle for Recognition*, pp. 131–140; Honneth, *The Fragmented World of the Social*, pp. 252–256.

67 Honneth, *The Struggle for Recognition*, pp. 160–170.

68 Christopher F. Zurn, *Axel Honneth* (Cambridge: Polity, 2015), pp. 8–10.

This is where another of the theory's strengths becomes clear. The theory places the Church of Sweden's reform of the office in relation to a longer historical process and, as we will show, helps to shed light on the processes of change. Indeed, some of the first ordained women do perceive such links between their own and other groups' struggles for recognition, such as the struggle against apartheid in South Africa (see Chapter 4), the struggle of homosexuals for the right to marry[69] and the #MeToo movement.[70]

Recognition theory has proved useful in a variety of contexts and has met with appreciation. However, like all wide-ranging theories, it has also been criticised. Among the objections raised by critics are that Honneth accords freedom a special position among other values; that the theory is adapted to the post-Enlightenment age; and that it risks having an overly optimistic view of the development of history and might therefore result in an anachronistic and almost moralising attitude to the past, an attitude in which the ideals and values of the present become normative for the assessment of the past. Furthermore, Honneth has been accused of simplifying and not taking account of the diversity that characterises a globalised world in which it is difficult to talk about shared fundamental values. The theory has also been criticised for being too idealistic in its view of power, structures and systems. There is a risk that a struggle for recognition becomes symbolic and does not really affect how groups actually express themselves or behave.[71]

---

69 It is well known that parallels exist between views on homosexuality and views on women's access to the priesthood. This was expressed not least in the debate leading up to the Church of Sweden General Synod's decision to open its doors to same-sex marriage in the late 1990s and early 2000s. Some of the first women to be ordained, such as Margareta Brandby-Cöster, drew this parallel themselves. In the text she wrote on the occasion of the fiftieth anniversary of the General Synod's decision in 1958, she says, 'Instead of celebrating or commemorating the 1958 decision, we should learn from this particular decision, so as not to make seemingly tolerant and enabling decisions again, for example regarding gay marriage, where the burden and the struggle may be placed on individual homosexuals or on priests who affirm same-sex marriage.' Margareta Brandby-Cöster, 'Dubbla budskap – vilket ska firas?', in Hössjer Sundman (ed.), *Äntligen stod hon i predikstolen!*, p. 164.

70 Tuulikki Koivonen Bylund, 'Ett ytterligare #metoo? Berättelsernas egenvärde', *Svensk kyrkotidning*, 11 (2018), 328–330.

71 Zurn, *Axel Honneth*, pp. 192–202.

Several of these problems are discussed by the church historian Sinikka Neuhaus. In addition to those listed above, she points to a further tension in the theory: even if one group's struggle for recognition can be described as moral, in practice it often leads to the denial of recognition to another group. She notes that '[r]egarded as a struggle, the morally motivated struggle is thus morally ambivalent'.[72] In other words, Honneth's theory of recognition raises questions about how to proceed when two groups can be said to be engaged in a struggle for recognition where they are in opposition to each other. Who or what should be recognised, and who recognises what?[73] Honneth himself has pursued a continuous discussion about this. As was mentioned above, the moral aspect of change processes is crucial in his thinking. Already in *The Struggle for Recognition*, he wrote that there must be a normative element in order to assess how the struggle develops. He is not looking for a measuring stick that is valid for all times, but rather a hypothetical approximate goal to aim for. He bases this goal on anthropology: a desirable development is that an individual, through the recognition of others, will have an increasingly favourable relationship with himself/herself as a person with positive qualities who is able to contribute to the common good.[74]

Ten years later, when he discussed justice and recognition with the philosopher Nancy Fraser in their book *Redistribution or Recognition? A Political-Philosophical Exchange* (2003), Honneth explained why he believes that there is value in having a normative concept of what is a desirable direction for development. He emphasises the reciprocity of recognition. The 'good' – in the form of justice – is only possible if everyone involved has the best possible relation-to-self, which entails individual autonomy, freedom. Here, reciprocity is the key.[75] Honneth argues that the definition of the good/justice changes over time because the idea of social equality has a 'semantic excess', that is, the notion is able to expand and

---

72 Sinikka Neuhaus, *Reformation och erkännande: Skilsmässoärenden under den tidiga reformationsprocessen i Malmö 1527–1542* (Lund: Lund University, 2009), pp. 54, 83–84 (p. 83).

73 Cecilia Wejryd, 'Kallelse och erkännande', *Kyrkohistorisk årsskrift*, 122 (2022), 196–198; Andreas Wejderstam, 'Recension av Kallelse och erkännande', *Svensk pastoraltidskrift*, 11 (2023), 27–28.

74 Honneth, *The Struggle for Recognition*, 168–175.

75 Nancy Fraser and Axel Honneth, *Redistribution or Recognition? A Political–Philosophical Exchange* (London: Verso, 2003), p. 258.

create new interpretations. Each time the sphere of recognition expands or deepens, it becomes possible to imagine a broader and deeper recognition of more people. In this way, says Honneth, we may argue that a moral evolution occurs.[76]

Christopher Zurn, an expert on Honneth, has devoted detailed discussions to this aspect of his theory and to the ways in which he works to diagnose social pathologies. Among other things, Zurn singles out Honneth's distinction between ideological recognition and justified recognition, whereby ideological recognition is the kind that virtually amounts to a confirmation of oppressive social structures. It is characteristic of such unjustified ideological recognition that whatever the institution or group recognises will not eventually achieve full recognition. One of the examples Honneth uses is the novel *Uncle Tom's Cabin*, where Uncle Tom is recognised by the institution of slavery for his submissive manner, but where it is clear that through this institution he will never achieve self-esteem, self-regard and self-respect. Zurn also notes that while Honneth's theory is a powerful tool for identifying and explaining the cause of social pathologies, it is not as well formulated with regard to how the problems might be solved in practice.[77]

Honneth's book *Freedom's Rights* (2014) is a step towards clarification. In it, he expands on the idea of freedom as a social phenomenon created and maintained by mutually beneficial give-and-take. In order for freedom to exist at all, a social environment is needed in which actions can be given meaning and become part of a common social context. This environment is based on mutual recognition. In *Freedom's Rights*, too, Honneth develops a theory of democracy – that is, how social freedom should function in practice. Here he emphasises the processes of democracy in the form of discussion, debate and negotiation. In relation to this issue, he discusses nationalism as an example of a struggle for recognition that is morally questionable, the reason being that nationalism tends to demand recognition but is then apt to use this recognition and the freedom it has gained in order to restrict the right of others to recognition and democratic processes.[78]

Clearly, then, if this aspect of Honneth's theory of recognition raises questions about the limits of recognition, it also offers

76 Ibid., pp. 260–263.
77 Zurn, *Axel Honneth*, pp. 96–98, 113–126.
78 Ibid., pp. 155–165, 182–189.

possible answers. Recognition is characterised by reciprocity in the giving of freedom; its aim is to keep expanding the concept of recognition to include more people; and the goal of the struggle for recognition should be equality, solidarity and symmetrical relations. When a struggle for recognition does not lead to this outcome, that is a warning sign. If the freedom and recognition that people seek is to be used to restrict the freedom of others and deny others recognition, then there is every reason to question whether such recognition should be granted. However, as Honneth also points out, the limits of recognition are a matter of negotiation in an ongoing process. On their journey towards the goal of total recognition, people must negotiate, discuss and find compromises. In this democratic – and in the ecclesiastical context also theological – dialogue about recognition, justice and freedom, everyone has the right to participate.

In our opinion, Honneth's theory is well suited to the issues of meaning making, power and identity addressed in this study.

The links between vocation and recognition

In analysing the vocation narratives, we thus regard two concepts as crucial.[79] As we will show, in the twentieth-century debate one or the other of these was often cited as the motive for the reform: either vocation (reasons of theology) or recognition (reasons of equality and justice). This duality is to some extent reflected in the Swedish historical narrative, in which proponents of the *thesis narrative* emphasise the equality reasons, while proponents of the *antithesis narrative* stress the theological ones. As we discussed in our research overview, international research commonly emphasises either of the perspectives. Conversely, we believe that vocation and recognition should be regarded as two inextricably intertwined driving forces for the reform of the Church of Sweden ministry.

It is, however, reasonable to ask whether an explicitly non-metaphysical sociological concept can really be linked to a key theological concept such as vocation. We believe that it can, and we would like to present two approaches to this question.

The first example of how Honneth can be used in a theological reflection is provided by Sinikka Neuhaus, who relates Honneth's

---

79 The following section draws on Mannerfelt and Maurits, 'Kallelse och erkännande', pp. 6–24.

theory to theology by depicting the processes of the Reformation and the emergence of Evangelical Lutheran theology as indeed being struggles for recognition. Neuhaus argues that such a perspective is particularly fruitful because the Reformation was not primarily a conflict over material goods. She also points out that Honneth discusses this aspect in relation to the philosopher and sociologist G. H. Mead (1863–1931), who held up Jesus as an example of an individual who energised social struggles for recognition. Neuhaus herself observes that this theme recurs in both the Old and the New Testament. In the Old Testament, humanity's ability to discern righteousness is invoked in relation to the Lord's covenant with Israel, and in the New Testament the same ability is seen through Paul, who in Galatians 3:28 establishes equality in terms of duties and rights in baptism.[80]

In Neuhaus's study, it becomes clear that the theological re-evaluations that occurred in Reformation-era Malmö were a response to the experience of the denied recognition of the laity's ability to lead a righteous life. The Evangelical Lutheran theology of the priesthood of all believers and the calling to service pertaining to practically everybody, in all social classes and official positions, was a response to these experiences and helped to support the laity's struggle for religious recognition.[81] Although women's ordination was not a matter of discussion in sixteenth-century Malmö, this issue does situate this process of change within a longer historical and not least theological perspective. The struggle of the first ordained women for their vocation to be recognised may thus be said to have its roots in the Reformation-era struggle for recognition of the vocation of every human being through baptism.

Even so, Neuhaus points out that Evangelical Lutheran theology could also result in oppression, of which there are countless historical examples in the form of enforced social constructions, social disciplining, repression and war.[82] She cites the Lutheran concept of the three orders/estates as an example.[83]

---

80 Neuhaus, *Reformation och erkännande*, pp. 101–140.
81 Ibid., pp. 134–136.
82 Ibid., p. 136.
83 This is the idea that society is organised into three orders/estates (the church, the government and the household), every individual having a definite hierarchical position and set of obligations within each. See John Witte, Jr, *Law and Protestantism: The Legal Teachings of the Lutheran Reformation* (Cambridge: Cambridge University Press, 2002), pp. 5–9, 89–94, 199–202.

In a theological commentary on the major survey performed among the Church of Sweden membership in 2010, the ethicist Johanna Gustafsson Lundberg builds on Neuhaus's examination of the connection between recognition and vocation. It is interesting to note that Gustafsson Lundberg perceives a number of parallels between Honneth's reasoning and the theologian whom a number of the first ordained women cite as central to their view of vocation, Gustaf Wingren (1910–2000); she lays particular stress on Wingren's thought on human life as *recapitulatio*, restoration of the truly human.[84] Gustafsson Lundberg also links this aspect to the 1958 reform of the Church of Sweden, asserting that this reform can be understood theologically as both an updating of the priesthood of all believers and a result of what we might describe, employing Honneth's terms, as a struggle for recognition.[85]

∞∞∞∞

This study is based on what we have chosen to call vocation narratives, that is, those narratives that were formulated in various contexts by the women who were ordained to the priesthood in the Church of Sweden during the period 1960 to 1970. Our primary source material is the 34 narratives found in Lund University's Ecclesiastical History Archive (LUKA).

In the present study, we analyse these stories by means of a narrative methodology according to which we identify tropes, key elements of the plot, core episodes, and so on. We also consider the ideological circumstances (the theology) that influence the narratives. Our analysis of the narratives is anchored partly in the historical context through supplementary source materials – in particular extensive newspaper materials – and partly in various theoretical arguments.

The theological concept of vocation emerges as fundamental and structures the women priests' narratives. It appears abundantly in the source material, particularly in relation to crucial events, so-called core episodes. The concept is so essential to the priests that in cases when they did not experience a single decisive event, they choose to say that their vocation came to them in another way. The vocation can be something an individual is absolutely sure of or

---

84 Johanna Gustafsson Lundberg, *Medlem 2010: En teologisk kommentar* (Uppsala: Church of Sweden Research Unit, 2010), pp. 17–21, 29–31.
85 Ibid., p. 30.

a question they are struggling with; either way, it is something to which they relate. In other words, vocation appears as the overall plot in the narrative analysis.

The second important starting point for our analysis is Axel Honneth's theory of recognition. He argues that it is crucial to a person's identity and self-esteem that she should be recognised. Withheld or denied recognition has serious consequences for the individual's identity and well-being. Analysing the vocation narratives of the first ordained women in the following chapters, we will encounter many examples of the consequences of lacking, denied or ambivalent recognition; but there will also be numerous examples of extensive and warm-hearted recognition.

Our analysis is based on the assumption that there is a close relationship between narrative and the construction of a historical school of thought. In both cases, these are parallel and partly intertwined processes that create meaning and are closely linked to issues of identity and power.

Chapter 3
The path to vocation: the historical context

> It is a truth universally acknowledged, that a single man in possession
> of a good fortune, must be in want of a wife.[1]

Jane Austen's introduction to her novel *Pride and Prejudice* (1813),
quoted above, is one of the most famous opening sentences in
literary history. It sets the (ironic) tone of this iconic story about
the conditions for women in a society where their lives and futures
are largely dependent on men, establishing the direction of the
narrative. The opening of the story is thus of key importance to its
continuation. Unlike the novel's assertion, however, the starting
point of the vocation narratives examined in this book is a
question: 'What was your path to ordination?' It is a question that
has a chronological perspective. It is therefore not surprising that
almost all the collected vocation narratives are structured along a
time axis.

In this chapter, we analyse the first core episodes that are threaded
on to the narrative plotline. In most of the vocation narratives the
ordained women mention their childhood, their confirmation and
their church involvement in youth. Other common core episodes
that occur early on chronologically are, on the one hand, professional life and, on the other, belonging to a family of priests. Our
analysis is anchored in the historical context of Sweden and the
Church of Sweden during the first half of the twentieth century.
This context also partially links back to the opening quotation, in
that the ideal of womanhood implied in Austen's sentence was also
very strong during the period investigated in the present study. It
is an ideal that was used as an argument against opening up the
priesthood to women.

---

1 Jane Austen, *Pride and Prejudice* (New York: W.W. Norton, 2001), p. 3.

Childhood

Narratives about being called to the priesthood often begin in childhood. A number of the ordained women testify that early in their lives, sometimes even before confirmation, they experienced a longing to become a priest.[2] One of them even experienced a direct call from God at the age of 11:

> 'You are going to be a priest.'
> 'But that's not possible. I'm a girl.'
> I can still see the image of the 11-year-old girl on the church steps, 'hear' the voice and relive the strange event. It was a summer Sunday. My parents and my sister, who is four years older than me, and I had gone on a cycling trip to the [locality] church in the north of [province]. It was my grandmother's home church. It was afternoon, and we had been inside looking at the church. I remember standing alone on the church steps and feeling that God was speaking to me. But the whole thing was so irrational that I did not tell anyone about it. The memory of what I later considered to be my first calling was forgotten, and it was not until [year], after I had been a priest for ten years, that the memory came back, very strongly during a period of illness.[3]

A number of the vocation narratives contain extensive accounts of childhood, especially in cases featuring a strong presence in the church. Out of a total of 34 narratives, about half supply a comparatively detailed picture of the narrator's childhood years. In most cases, the childhood home is portrayed as having had a favourable effect on the future priest's spiritual life; that is to say, a Christian life was experienced as being natural and part of the family's customs and traditions. Another recurring theme is that the attitude of parents and grandparents had a major impact on the priest's Christian faith.

In a handful of the narratives, the future priest grew up in a non-Christian home and came to her Christian faith later in life. In relation to the issue of vocation, these episodes might seem unimportant. Far from it! One core episode in a narrative is often related to others, and they serve to explain one another. Moreover, these particular core episodes show the range that characterises the first women to be ordained; they are far from being cast in the same mould.

---

2 No. 17; No. 24, No. 28; No. 35.
3 No. 28.

But let us begin with those priests who report that their vocation was rooted in their birth family's Christian faith. A prominent theme in their narratives is the significance of the staunch faith of their parents or other close relatives.[4] One priest describes a childhood home where Sunday worship and evening prayer were considered essential. She also says that both her mother and grandmother read the Bible: 'At my grandmother's house, next to her bed, I saw her worn Bible sitting there – just as my mother had her Bible within reach at home.'[5]

Britta Olén-van Zijl also describes how her vocation gradually emerged in her early years:

> The desire to become a priest has been with me since my childhood. My parents' example meant a lot to me. I grew up in a Low Church rectory, where a deep spiritual life was lived. Both my mother and my father preached and testified about God in their own straightforward way. A steady stream of seekers passed through the rectory doors. Many of them experienced spiritual renewal and salvation. My mother in particular meant a lot. She was an invaluable help to me. It was she who helped me to make a full and complete commitment to God. She was a spiritual guide like few others. And her prayers sort of encompassed my life. We became more and more one in spirit. We fought together for the Kingdom of God.[6]

Olén-van Zijl's narrative not only shows how important a Christian upbringing can be for the vocation to become a priest; it also highlights something that recurs in a number of other narratives, namely, that a Christian background could be influenced by or even come from denominations other than the Church of Sweden. This is implied in her comment that her mother preached, which was not permitted in the Church of Sweden at that time and so must have occurred in other denominational contexts. We will return to this later in the chapter.

One example of Christian education occurring within the framework of a denomination other than the Church of Sweden is found in the case of the priest whose parents were Salvation Army soldiers. She says that this had consequences for the place of religion in her childhood home: 'It was prayer and Bible reading in the home,

---

4 No. 21; No. 24; Birgitta Nyman in Sjöberg, 'Kyrkan måste vara ömsint', p. 60.
5 No. 20.
6 Olén-van Zijl, 'Att få vara präst', p. 105.

Sunday school in the morning at the Salvation Army and for a time also with the Methodists in the afternoon. Early on I was given a children's bible with colourful illustrations.'[7]

The importance of regularly attending church services while growing up is noted in a number of vocation narratives.[8] One priest describes how she gradually came to attend church more and more: 'I became a regular church-goer long before I had to attend services in preparation for my confirmation.'[9] Another priest also describes how she attended several services every Sunday, not only because her father was a clergyman but also because as a child she had always wanted to 'attend both Sunday services'.[10]

It is also interesting to note that some of the priests describe religion as 'a private matter'. They include the priest who described herself above as 'a frequent worshipper'. She describes a childhood in which saying evening prayers and grace at meals was taken for granted, while at the same time the family's religious life was not discussed or problematised to any great extent. Her parents, or at least her mother, went to church on the major holy days and maybe once or twice in between. It could be said that she broke with her parents' habits in that she gradually came to attend church regularly.[11] Another priest says that although religion was quite a powerful presence in her childhood, the family regarded it as a private matter. Everyone said their evening prayers privately, because 'displaying religious expressions was hypocritical'.[12]

One priest says that her family's attitude to religion was characteristic of 'a typical Swedish family'. She describes it as rather lukewarm, and that it was a matter of allowing the children to take part in the church rites (baptism and confirmation) and then going to church for the Christian holy days.[13] This 'typically Swedish' attitude is also described by four other priests.[14] They include a priest who says that her parents were Social Democrats, and that this had consequences for her view of religion and the church:

7 No. 28.
8 No. 35; Margit Sahlin in Nordlander, *Margit Sahlin*, pp. 18, 21; Siv Bejerfors, 'Lärare och präst', in *Kvinnlig präst idag*, pp. 116–117; No. 44.
9 No. 8.
10 No. 17.
11 No. 8.
12 No. 44.
13 No. 30.
14 No. 45; No. 42; No. 44.

My parents were old-school Social Democrats, back when it was still about socialism. They believed in everyone's equal value and right to education. Those who held such beliefs did not trust people in authority. The mill owner, the doctor, the teachers and the church all belonged to the same pack. Faith became a class issue. We did not belong to that class. Of course all the big holy days were to be celebrated in church, as were weddings and funerals, but in everyday life God was at leisure, as it were.[15]

Accordingly, and perhaps not surprisingly, a Christian upbringing seems to have been a common factor. In a few cases, however, a different picture emerges. One priest describes how she 'grew up in a non-Christian home. You could almost say *anti*-Christian.'[16] Another priest stresses that she grew up 'in a religiously rather indifferent home'.[17]

However the priests describe their childhood, it is interesting to observe how often they choose to stress whether they came from a Christian, non-Christian or 'typically Swedish' family. In many ways, these statements are an expression of the social context into which the women ordained in 1960 to 1970 were born.

Sweden in the twentieth century

The first half of the twentieth century in Sweden was characterised by major social changes.[18] It was an economically expansive period in which the Swedish welfare state was established. From the 1940s onwards the nation was gradually transformed from a country of full- and part-time small farmers into an industrial nation. *Industrialisation* also led to *urbanisation*. The movement of people into towns and cities was a trend that was particularly strong in the 1960s, when urban industrial production increased. The result was an extensive transformation of Swedish society.

The period from 1900 to 1950 was also characterised by *democratisation*. In line with Axel Honneth's theories presented in the previous

---

15 No. 42.

16 No. 34.

17 No. 29.

18 The general historical overview that follows is mainly based on the following: Yvonne Hirdman, Urban Lundberg and Jenny Björkman (eds), *Sveriges historia 1920–1965* (Stockholm: Norstedts, 2012) and Kjell Östberg and Jenny Andersson (eds), *Sveriges historia 1965–2012* (Stockholm: Norstedts, 2013).

chapter, this was a period when more and more social groups gained recognition both legally and socially. For example, royal authority finally gave way to a parliamentary system of government. In the first half of the twentieth century a number of different political parties were formed and consolidated, many of which still exist today.

From a gender perspective, however, this was a time when an older social order – based on the Lutheran doctrine of the three estates[19] – largely remained intact, but the relationship between the sexes gradually came to be manifested in different terms. As before, it was basically only men who could move around in the public space and participate in paid employment. For women the good housewife was the ideal, and the focus was therefore on domestic labour. In this way, the prevailing gender order was largely (merely) a recodification of the Lutheran view that had dominated Swedish society for several hundred years.

The first decades of the twentieth century, however, saw some *emancipatory reforms*, and women came to be legally recognised as a group. These reforms included the introduction of universal and equal suffrage in 1921; the 1920 marriage legislation, which no longer viewed married women as legal minors; and the 1925 *behörighetslagen* ['the authorisation law'], which gave women the right to hold various official posts – but not in the priesthood or in positions that might involve the use of physical force, such as the police and the military.

Despite these reforms, however, the household remained the primary arena for women. One example of this is the fact that until 1939, women who became pregnant could be dismissed from their paid employment. Throughout this period, few women were elected as members of Sweden's legislative assembly, the Riksdag. In 1937 nine out of a total of 233 members of the second chamber of the Riksdag were women, that is, 4 per cent. In 1970 the corresponding figure was 15.5 per cent. Women's participation in the political sphere was thus severely limited for much of the twentieth century. It is hence not surprising that the spontaneous reaction of the 11-year-old girl called by God to become a priest on the church steps was 'But that's not possible. I'm a girl!'

---

19 This will be discussed in the next chapter but, in brief, the Lutheran doctrine of the three estates held that everyone had a vocation that called them to live in one of three estates: church, state and household, the last-mentioned being the foundation on which the others rested. See Witte, *Law and Protestantism*.

Compared with most other European countries, Sweden was unusual in having remained outside both world wars. The Swedish manufacturing apparatus was therefore intact at the end of the war in 1945, which meant that Swedish companies were able to supply the great demand for goods and services that came to characterise the post-war period. The period from the end of the Second World War to the beginning of the 1970s was thus characterised by vigorous economic growth and a doubling of the standard of living in Sweden. This growth was a prerequisite for the emergence of the welfare state. The Social Democratic Party – which held a hegemonic position in Swedish politics in the post-war period – implemented a series of welfare reforms. These reforms were centred on education and healthcare and were only made possible by means of a substantial enlargement of the public sector, financed by increased taxation.

One result of the expanding welfare sector was a need for more female labour. In view of the established gender order, this need required a change in the view of gender roles, a change that often ran counter to the theory of distinctive natures that had dominated the relationship between women and men until then. The movement of women into arenas previously reserved for men was not without controversy, and it led to various forms of conflict. Naturally, the risk of women taking jobs from men was thought to be a danger; but the right to be able to work for pay and have a family was also much discussed. Over time, the issue of equal pay became central as well.

The policy reforms implemented in post-war Sweden included improved pensions, reformed health insurance, social services, child benefits, extended holiday entitlement, free school meals, new working-time legislation and new housing policies. One consequence of this highly expansive and reform-orientated Social Democratic policy was that it prompted leading representatives of the Church of Sweden to act. Among other things, the Church regarded the new tax reforms as being a threat to the family (which, according to Lutheran thinking, was the key component of society). Apparently, the fact that both men and women could take paid work was perceived by the Church as a threat to certain core values.

The late 1960s and early 1970s saw the introduction of individualised social security and the abolition of family taxation. The welfare reforms of the time also required an expansion of the public sector, and it was mainly women who found work in the expanding health and caring services. In a short time, Sweden became one of the countries in the world with the highest number of gainfully employed women. In simplified terms, they were hired by the state to perform for pay the work they had previously done at home. Consequently, the first women to be ordained were children during a tumultuous time of great social change when women were increasingly gaining legal recognition in society, a development which also gave them the opportunity to support themselves. This was a time of profound change for the Church of Sweden, too – not only because the Church had to operate within this society, but also because it was the nation's state church.

The Church of Sweden in the twentieth century

With the Reformation in the sixteenth century, Sweden became an Evangelical Lutheran nation with a state church. The Reformation principle of *cuius regio, eius religio*, that is, the religion of the ruling prince governs that of the people, exercised an indirect influence in Sweden right up until 1951, when – after a long struggle, not least on the part of the so-called Free Churches (see below) – freedom of religion was introduced. In several different contexts, including the 1734 legislation, it was emphasised that Swedish subjects should be faithful to the Evangelical Lutheran confession.

Scholars of ecclesiastical history point out that a gradual loosening of the Lutheran unity of society began to make itself felt in the course of the nineteenth century. One important reason for the changes was increased religious diversity, in particular various revivalist movements, whose social and ecclesiastical-historical significance must not be underestimated.[20] Over the course of the century, a number of movements and denominations emerged that (re)vitalised religious life in Sweden. Some revivalist movements stayed within the Church of Sweden, such as the Swedish Evangelical Mission [Evangeliska Fosterlands-Stiftelsen, EFS] (founded in 1856), while others broke away, such as Svenska Missionsförbundet [Swedish Mission Covenant, later the Mission Covenant Church of Sweden (Svenska Missionskyrkan)] (founded in 1878). Revivalist movements with foreign roots were also important. These included the Baptist Union of Sweden [Svenska

---

20 Anders Jarlert, 'Reform in Sweden: From Confessional Provincialism towards World Ecumenism', in Anders Jarlert (ed.), *Piety and Modernity: The Dynamics of Religious Reform in Northern Europe 1780–1920* (Leuven: Leuven University Press, 2012), III, pp. 286–306.

Baptistsamfundet] (founded in 1857), the United Methodist Church in Sweden [Metodistkyrkan i Sverige] (founded in 1868), the Salvation Army [Frälsningsarmén] (in Sweden from 1882) and the Swedish Pentecostal movement [Pingströrelsen] (in Sweden from 1907). At the beginning of the 1930s these movements and denominations, often referred to as Free Churches, encompassed around 600,000 Swedes, that is, around 10 per cent of the population. The largest was the Mission Covenant Church of Sweden with almost 114,000 members, followed by the Baptist Union of Sweden with just over 64,000 members. These denominations came to have a major impact on society, not least because several of them were characterised by their political activism, which involved a social commitment pertaining to all of society.[21] It is in this context that the church that had previously been 'the (only) church in Sweden' was given the name 'Church of Sweden' to emphasise its position as the state church.

The encounter between the Church of Sweden and these movements and denominations was anything but frictionless. The Swedish state and the Church of Sweden regarded them as a threat to unity and Lutheran doctrine, and initially both institutions engaged in various forms of repression. For their part, the movements and denominations harshly criticised a church they perceived as 'lukewarm in the faith' and steered by the state. The memory of these conflicts was very much alive in the mid-twentieth century; and in various ways, as we will show, they served as a joint sounding-board in the debates about women's access to the priesthood.

The state responded to the increased religious diversity by introducing 'dissenter laws' in 1860 and 1873, laws which granted limited religious freedom. However, Swedes who wished to leave the Church of Sweden had to join a state-approved Christian denomination instead. In other words, limited religious freedom did exist, but always within a Protestant framework.[22] One result

---

21 Erik Sidenvall, 'Frikyrkligheten i Sverige 1920–1965', in Hirdman, Lundberg and Björkman (eds), *Sveriges historia 1920–1965*, pp. 83–88. See also Oloph Bexell, *Sveriges kyrkohistoria, 7: Folkväckelsens och kyrkoförnyelsens tid* (Stockholm: Verbum, 2003), pp. 198–245, and Berntson, Nilsson and Wejryd, *Kyrka i Sverige*, pp. 269–300.

22 To our knowledge, there is only one overview of Swedish Church history in English: Lars Österlin, *Churches of Northern Europe in Profile: A Thousand Years of Anglo-Nordic Relations* (Norwich: Canterbury Press,

of this was that the Roman Catholic Church and Catholics came to be regarded as a threat, and other expressions of religious faith were considered to be exotic exceptions. Socially and culturally, the Lutheran mindset thus continued to have great social significance well into modern times, even though the Lutheran faith gradually ceased to be an explicit part of the ideology underpinning Swedish society.

Another consequence is that when complete freedom of religion was introduced in 1951, and citizens were permitted to leave the Church of Sweden and join any religious denomination they wished (or even renounce membership of a denomination), this development had very little to do with diversity. In 1974, 95 per cent of citizens still belonged to the Church of Sweden; and until 1996, any child who had at least one parent belonging to the Church of Sweden automatically (that is, not through baptism) became a member of the Church.[23]

During the period at the centre of this book, that is, the 1950s, 1960s and 1970s, the Church of Sweden was hence a majority church. In the mid-1960s virtually the entire population of Sweden were members of some religious denomination. As many as 96 per cent belonged to the Church of Sweden, and of the remaining 4 per cent, the majority belonged to a Free Church.[24] Although almost everyone was formally a member of the Church of Sweden, worship attendance was low. In addition to being a majority church, the Church of Sweden was also a governmental church and responsible for various ecclesiastical functions (that is, baptism, confirmation, marriage and burial), civil registration and parish activities. In other words, this is the 'typical Swedish' situation that some of the first ordained women describe in their childhood narratives. In view of this context, it becomes understandable why those who came from Christian homes where faith was actively practised emphasise this fact in their narratives. It was quite simply not the norm.

1995). The issue of the reform of the priesthood in the Church of Sweden and the reaction in the Church of England is discussed on pp. 267–275.

23 Martin Nykvist, 'A Superfluous Legislation? Historical and Contemporary Perspectives on Religious Freedom in Sweden', *Religion – Staat – Gesellschaft: Zeitschrift für Glaubensformen und Weltanschauungen*, 18.1–2 (2017), 95–108.

24 David Thurfjell, *Det gudlösa folket: De postkristna svenskarna och religionen* (Stockholm: Molin & Sorgenfrei, 2015), pp. 17–37; David Thurfjell, 'Världens mest sekulariserade land?', in Östberg and Andersson (eds), *Sveriges historia 1965–2012*, pp. 156–160.

If the increased religious pluralism of the nineteenth century meant that different denominations and churches profiled themselves against one another, the twentieth century brought an increased desire for ecumenical cooperation. In Sweden, this ecumenical endeavour led to the Free Churches entering into various collaborative ventures with one another, but rarely with the Church of Sweden. When this did occur, it was mainly locally and regionally, at the parish level. At the national level, the Church of Sweden primarily turned to churches in other countries, initially German Lutheran ones but gradually more and more to the Anglican Church. Among other things, cooperation between the Church of Sweden and the Church of England resulted in an agreement on communion in 1922.[25] A central figure in this ecumenical work was Archbishop Nathan Söderblom (1866–1931), who initiated the so-called Stockholm meeting in 1925 between representatives of the Orthodox and Protestant churches. This meeting has been recognised as the starting point of that international ecumenical effort which became the basis for the World Council of Churches, established in 1948.[26] The Church of Sweden had a strong ecumenical self-image, and the general feeling was that it was very open to other churches (albeit not to Swedish Free Churches). It felt able to act as an influential bridge between denominations.[27]

At the time, the great changes that were taking place in society were often interpreted in terms of secularisation. The churches worked actively to meet and counter this secularisation, not least by trying to appear relevant to society. That, however, was a real challenge at the time when the first women to become ordained were still in their childhood and youth.

In the late 1940s Ingemar Hedenius (1908–1982), Professor of Philosophy at the University of Uppsala, initiated a fierce cultural debate on faith and knowledge. Hedenius and others who thought along similar lines attacked theology and the Christian faith, especially its claims to truth. The cultural debate that arose and the resulting criticism of the Church of Sweden and its leading theologians had a number of unfavourable consequences. For the Church, the 1950s has been described as being 'a miserable decade of increasing secularisation and repeated scandals surrounding

25 See, among others, Carl Henrik Lyttkens, *The Growth of Swedish–Anglican Intercommunion between 1811 and 1932* (Lund: Gleerup, 1970).
26 Berntson, Nilsson and Wejryd, *Kyrka i Sverige*, pp. 323–325.
27 Brohed, *Sveriges kyrkohistoria*, p. 160.

dubious appointments, crowned by the great controversy over women priests, the effects of which it still lives with in many ways'.[28]

The relationship between faith and knowledge was, of course, discussed in other countries, too; but the Swedish debate initiated by Hedenius occurred earlier than elsewhere. In other countries, such a frontal attack from agnostics and atheists did not occur until the 1960s and 1970s. Sweden, which had not been involved in the devastating world war, was clearly not affected by 'the post-war mood of moral traditionalism' in the same way as other countries.[29] These thought currents form an underlying context for the first ordained women when they speak of the need for priests in a secularised age, and for those women priests who speak of having had a distinctly 'non-Christian' childhood.

Even though there is good cause to speak of a period of crisis and a Christianity in retreat, a way of living and a sense of commitment that were strongly Christian persisted both in Sweden and in the Church of Sweden. In the early twenty-first century, scholars have stressed the dynamic Christian semi-public sphere with its thriving Christian publishers, newspapers and magazines promoting encounters between culture, science and Christianity.

The Church of Sweden of the 1950s and 1960s has been aptly described as a multifaceted institution, encompassing a range of theological and political positions. More conservative factions were pitted against more liberal ones. A number of issues divided these factions, including views on the Bible, family and morality; but opposition to women priests became an issue that reinforced such differences of opinion and intensified opposing views on Christianity.

The issue of opening up the Church of Sweden's priesthood to women spanned virtually the entire twentieth century. It is also in all likelihood the topic which – alongside the relationship between the Church of Sweden and the state – was accorded the most attention in that era's Swedish religious debate. The issue was discussed as early as the turn of the century in relation to women's legal adulthood, right to education and right to hold public office. In 1925 it was ruled that women could hold civilian public office

---

28 Hirdman, Lundberg and Björkman (eds), *Sveriges historia 1920–1965*, p. 400. See also Berntson, Nilsson and Wejryd, *Kyrka i Sverige*, pp. 301–344.

29 Hugh McLeod, *The Religious Crisis of the 1960s* (Oxford: Oxford University Press, 2007), pp. 31–59 (p. 55).

with the exception of the priesthood. When this issue was examined further, the theological faculties of Uppsala and Lund universities, among others, concluded that there were no theological obstacles to ordaining women as priests, but all the cathedral chapters and Svenska Prästföreningen [the Association of Swedish Priests] opposed the idea.

When, in 1938, the Church of Norway decided to open up its priesthood to women, the issue arose again in Sweden. One proposal was to establish a special position for women, but this idea was not put into practice. In 1946 a new government commission of inquiry was appointed. Presented in 1950, its report proposed that the priesthood should, with some reservations, be opened to women. A number of consultative bodies rejected this proposal.

In 1957 the government took the initiative, proposing that the priesthood be opened up to women in a letter to the General Synod. The Synod voted against the proposal. However, after the Riksdag had supported a bill to open up the priesthood to women and upon the initiative of the Minister for Education, the Synod reconsidered the proposal a year later and voted in favour. As part of the decision, the so-called 'conscience clause' [samvetsklausulen] was included, which guaranteed opponents to the reform that they would not have to serve alongside ordained women priests. Furthermore, ordinands who were opponents would be able to take their vows without having to affirm the new arrangement, and no bishops would have to ordain women priests against their will. Following intense debate, the conscience clause was repealed in 1983.[30]

In the 1960s and 1970s various political movements existed both in the Swedish Christian community in general and in the Church of Sweden. The post-1968 left-wing movement, which came to characterise the Church of Sweden to some degree, has often been singled out; but it should be borne in mind that both a conservative and a clearly liberal trend existed as well.[31]

Despite these nuances, church life in Sweden was characterised by relative homogeneity for a long time. Apart from various forms

---

30 Berntson, Nilsson and Wejryd, *Kyrka i Sverige*, pp. 317–320; Andersson, *Den nödvändiga manligheten*, pp. 4–8, 31–42.

31 Johan Östling, Anton Jansson and Ragni Svensson Stringberg, *Humanister i offentligheten: Kunskapens aktörer och arenor under efterkrigstiden* (Stockholm: Makadam, 2022), pp. 165–209 (p. 200).

of Protestant Christianity, other denominations and religions were virtually invisible. The period after the 1950s featured a decline in the traditional belief in God and in organised church membership, but not in religiosity in general. Church ceremonies in particular, such as baptisms, marriages and funerals, continued to hold a strong position.[32] This was true not least of confirmation. While confirmation was not compulsory, most Swedes were confirmed because an acceptable knowledge of the Christian faith was a requirement for being allowed to receive Communion. Since confirmation took place in the lower teenage years, it was often regarded as a rite marking the transition to adulthood. However, this was not the only reason why the confirmation period is a core episode in many of the vocation narratives of the first ordained women.

The confirmation period

An important core episode in a number of the vocation narratives is confirmation and the confirmation period. For some narrators it was the day of confirmation itself, especially the 'holiness' of the service, that was significant.[33] One priest even recounts how she experienced God speaking to her directly in connection with the confirmation service.[34]

Most of the women, however, highlight their confirmation classes as being essential to their vocation.[35] For example, Mailice Wifstrand (1923–2017, ordained 1968) describes how this training led to the realisation that she wanted to become a priest. 'Then it was clear to me that I wanted to become a priest. I suppose I was not sufficiently aware to call it a vocation – that was just the way it was.' Wifstrand says that she told her confirmation priest of this experience.[36]

Another way in which the women's vocation and their confirmation period were connected is that their confirmation priest came to have an impact on their future career choice. One vocation

---

32 Thurfjell, *Det gudlösa folket*, pp. 54–66; Thurfjell, 'Världens mest sekulariserade land?'

33 Margit Sahlin in Nordlander, *Margit Sahlin*, pp. 29–39 (pp. 29–30); No. 8; No. 42.

34 No. 37.

35 No. 8; No. 20; No. 29; No. 42.

36 Mailice Wifstrand, 'Dröm, plan och verklighet', *Svensk Kyrkotidning*, 10 (2004), 138.

narrative underlines that the confirmation priest 'was a brilliant teacher with a great sense of humour and warmth. He made us youngsters curious about what the church and the Bible could say to us in our lives and, at least for me, sparked an interest in thinking further.'[37] This same woman priest says that for a couple of years after her own confirmation, she was a leader for other confirmands with the priest in question. Besides, her confirmation priest and his family remained close to her after she was ordained.[38]

Another priest emphasises the close ties she developed with her confirmation priest – who in this case had a more liberal stance on theological issues than the one prevailing in the diocese where he served. This confirmation priest also became involved in the public debate and spoke against some of the most prominent opponents of the reform of the priesthood. The relationship between the woman priest and her confirmation priest was so close that he assisted at her ordination.[39]

Another vocation narrative also stresses the great importance of the confirmation priest, but in this case the narrator's future career choice eventually became a problem for their relationship, because the confirmation priest opposed the reform of the priesthood. Even so, it is clear to this narrator that her path to ordination began with her confirmation period. It was prior to her first Communion and the confirmation priest's teaching of the meaning of Communion that she experienced a strong Christian conviction and began to attend Mass every Sunday.[40] Caroline Krook also recounts an event during her confirmation period that she connected with her vocation: 'My confirmation priest said that maybe one of you will become a priest. That was the first time I thought: Maybe it's me.'[41]

Involvement in Church youth and student organisations

Among the core episodes significant for the vocation to the priesthood, the ordained women's narratives also mention involvement in various Church youth organisations, which emerge as important seedbeds of growth. Sveriges kristliga gymnasistförbund [the Swedish Christian Secondary School Association, KGF], a national

---

37 No. 30.
38 Ibid.
39 No. 34.
40 No. 45.
41 Kerstin Weigl, 'Jag lekte med bilar och slogs', *Aftonbladet*, 3 April 2004.

organisation for Christian young people in their upper teens with local associations around the country, is mentioned in at least ten of the vocation narratives. A number of the priests discuss KGF and emphasise how crucial it and its various local organisations were to their spiritual development and interest in service in the Church. One priest writes as follows in her vocation narrative:

> During my school years I became involved in KGF, and especially the winter camps at the Sigtuna Foundation came to mean a lot to me: the spirituality, the friendship with other Christian young people, the Masses, the discussions came to deepen my faith. Through my believing friends I could feel affirmed as a young Christian.[42]

Similar descriptions of KGF recur in several of the vocation narratives.[43] One priest describes that 'that was the way I stayed in the church' (after confirmation), and that when she later graduated from secondary school, 'there was only one path somehow, and that was to start studying theology'.[44]

Another priest describes her involvement in KGF during her secondary school years, including evangelisation weeks, known as *kårfärder* ['corps trips'], during a couple of summers in the early 1950s, which she believes were important for her spiritual development. When the invitation to such a trip came, she could sense a calling: 'It became a turning point in my career focus: a calling to work in the service of the church and pass on Christ's message.'[45]

KGF thus seems to have been a context in which the calling to become a priest was felt by a number of the first ordained women. In addition, though, it was a context in which some of the women were able to express their Christian faith publicly, for example by giving lectures, leading morning prayers or preaching.[46]

---

42 No. 37. The Sigtuna Foundation was founded in 1915 and aimed to be a centre for what was known as *ungkyrkorörelsen* ['the young church movement']; see below.
43 No. 29; No. 34; Mailice Wifstrand in Wifstrand, 'Dröm, plan och verklighet', p. 138; Britta Olén-van Zijl in Olén-van Zijl, 'Att få vara präst', p. 105; Birgitta Nyman in Sjöberg, 'Kyrkan måste vara ömsint', p. 60. Notably, in his obituary for Eva Lindqvist Olofsson (1941–1991, ordained 1967), Nils Parkman points out her engagement in KGF. See 'Minnesteckning över Eva Lindqvist Olofsson', in *Härnösands stifts prästmöteshandlingar* (1994).
44 No. 45.
45 No. 20.
46 No. 18; No. 45.

Still, KGF was not the only 'plant nursery' for future priests. Though that movement is mentioned most often, there are examples of other contexts that played a similar role. One such environment was Kristliga föreningen av unga kvinnor [the Young Women's Christian Association, KFUK]. Caroline Krook, for example, says: 'Looking back, I can see how early I practised leadership. At the age of 17 I took a gap year from school and became a KFUK volunteer. That's where my vocation to become a priest grew.'[47]

For Margit Sahlin, it was the student movement that had a similar impact. In her diary she recalls 'highly inspiring student meetings' from the summer of 1936.[48] She was also involved in the *ungkyrkorörelsen* ['the young church movement'], which was a nationally orientated revival movement within the Church of Sweden during the first part of the twentieth century. In her diary, she describes how she felt put to use and given the opportunity to serve through her missionary work.[49]

Even though it is outside the bounds of what might be defined as church youth and student work, a political party might also serve as a context for spiritual growth and maturity. Marianne Westrin (1920–2015, ordained 1965) stresses how important her political involvement in the Centre Party was for the maturation of her 'Christian faith from childhood and youth'.[50]

Childhood, confirmation and adolescence thus stand out as core episodes of importance to vocation that recur in most of the narratives of the first ordained women. Alongside these, there are two other frequently occurring core episodes. One focuses on career choice.

Career choice – 'something like a priest'

In her contribution to the anthology *Kvinnlig präst idag* (1967), entitled 'Lärare och präst' ['Teacher and priest'], Siv Bejerfors writes:

When it came to making serious plans for the future after graduating from secondary school, I knew that I wanted to study theology

---

47 Petter Karlsson, 'Caroline Krook: Jag kan nog till och med säga att jag föddes religiös', *Dagen*, 27 May 2011.
48 Nordlander, *Margit Sahlin*, pp. 45–47.
49 Ibid., pp. 51–53 (p. 53).
50 Marianne Westrin, 'I elfte timmen', in *Kvinnlig präst idag*, pp. 80–81.

above all else, but this did not mean that I could focus on becoming a priest. After all, women were not eligible for the priesthood. One of my fellow students described my situation very well when we were discussing career choices. She said: 'It is not difficult for you to choose. You're going to be something like a priest.' She clearly knew me quite well. I had to focus on becoming something 'like a priest', something in the priestly direction, and it was almost the same as deciding to become a schoolteacher of Christianity. That path was practically the only one available to the few female theology students of the time. I thought about it a lot. I didn't really want to be a teacher. But the desire to become something 'like a priest' was too strong.[51]

Many of the first ordained women were in the situation Siv Bejerfors describes: they felt a calling to serve within the church, they wanted to study theology; but the priesthood was not open to women. What remained was to become 'something like a priest', to aim for another profession where they could utilise their longings and talents. Working as 'something like a priest' is a recurring core episode in their narratives. All in all, the issue of having an alternative career is raised in at least 21 of the vocation narratives. Thoughts or experiences of working as a missionary, deaconess, parish secretary and secondary school teacher of religion, with an emphasis on Christianity, recur regularly.

One possible path for a female theology student was to become a missionary. The fact that the missionary movement was borne up by women, both in Sweden and out in the field, and that the role of missionary created greater room for manoeuvre for women has been noted by a number of researchers.[52] One woman priest, whose vocation narrative was formulated by a close relative, is described as having had far-reaching plans to become a missionary. She had a solid theological education, but when she married a clergyman she thought she would have to shelve her own missionary plans. However, the fact that her husband was stationed abroad for a while in a country occupied by Nazi Germany gave her a partial chance to realise her dream. During her time abroad, she helped

51 Bejerfors, 'Lärare och präst', p. 138.
52 Karin Sarja, 'Ännu en syster till Afrika': Trettiosex kvinnliga missionärer i Natal och Zululand 1876–1902 (Uppsala: Svenska institutet för missionsforskning, 2002), pp. 309–315; Jonas Jonson, Missionärerna: En biografisk berättelse om Svenska kyrkans mission 1874–1974 (Stockholm: Verbum, 2019), pp. 259–267.

Jews and others escape from the Nazis, and on one occasion she herself was mistaken for a Jew and beaten.[53]

Another priest describes how she, with a Bachelor of Theology degree, worked for ten years as a missionary in an African country, where she taught at a Bible school and simultaneously translated the New Testament into one of the local languages. She describes doing top-quality, meticulous translation work, often in dialogue with prominent biblical scholars, especially in the UK. While she obviously possessed the academic knowledge necessary for doing advanced Bible translation work, she did not have the right to use her knowledge as a preacher, a circumstance that made her unhappy. She summarises her plight as follows:

> Translating the Bible is of course very much in the service of the Word. I was careful not to wake sleeping bears [the Swedish equivalent of 'let sleeping dogs lie'], and I gratefully accepted the excellent further training that daily study of the Greek text with thick commentary books gave me. But it felt hard to be almost transported by all the Bible material and never be allowed to express it to a worshipping congregation, just because I was a woman. Filipo, my co-worker, was often allowed to preach, even though he was not a theologian. But he was a man![54]

Several of the women priests studied here say that they longed to work as missionaries but that this did not materialise. However, their missionary dream made them venture to study theology.[55] Out in the mission field, they were assigned tasks that matched their previous vocational training. For one woman it was her profession as a teacher of Christianity that made her particularly suited to missionary work, and she was sent to India.[56]

Another alternative career choice for those who could not become ordained priests before the 1958 reform was to become a deaconess. Ingrid Persson was one woman who tried this route. She describes how, after having been director of studies at Diakonistiftelsen Samariterhemmet [now Samariterhemmet Diakoni, 'The House of the Good Samaritan'], she considered becoming a deaconess for some time. She writes: 'I had also realised that the ordination of a deaconess was the only ordination that the church

---

53 No. 2.
54 No. 17.
55 No. 24; No. 25.
56 No. 19.

had to offer women. And I felt the lack of an ordination. So it was decided that I would be ordained as a deaconess.' Persson was ordained a deaconess in September 1949.[57] It is noteworthy that she emphasises that her choice to become a deaconess was partly because it was the only opportunity for ordination available to her. This is also a first example of a recurring theme in the vocation narratives: the importance of the inner calling being recognised through an outer calling in the form of formal ordination.[58]

Another of the priests studied here also says she chose deaconess training because it was the only option available. In the mid-1940s Samariterhemmet offered an experimental programme that afforded trainee deaconesses the opportunity to study theology. She writes: 'So I still got to do exactly what I wanted to do, but as if I was flying blind, without knowing whether my theology degree could be used for anything.' After completing her Bachelor of Theology degree, she was sent by the director of Samariterhemmet to St Etienne in the French Massif Central as a fieldworker for the World Council of Churches, 'and suddenly found myself in a harsh coal-mining environment, sent to serve in a small, poor Reformed congregation in a dense Catholic setting'.[59]

For a woman who wanted to be 'something like a priest', there could also be other types of posts in the Church of Sweden. Ingrid Persson tried this as well, in the form of a youth secretary position which focused on teaching the Christian faith to children and young people in the diocese of Härnösand. She writes that she was hired thanks to Bishop Torsten Bohlin (1889–1950), who 'had a vision of women's service in the Church of Sweden'. Persson describes how, as a youth secretary, she was expected to preach.[60] Another priest relates that she worked both as a secretary in the Swedish civil service and as a parish assistant, that is, the leader of children's activities in a parish, a few years before she was ordained.[61]

---

57 Ingrid Persson, 'Min väg till prästämbetet', in Urban Råghall (ed.), *Härnösands Stiftshistoriska sällskap: Studier och uppsatser IV* (Härnösand: Härnösands stiftshistoriska sällskap, 1994), pp. 41–42 (p. 41).
58 The diaconate as an alternative to the ordination of women as priests is discussed by Elisabeth Christiansson in *Kyrklig och social reform: Motiveringar till diakoni 1845–1965* (Skellefteå: Artos & Norma, 2006), pp. 145, 166.
59 No. 17.
60 Persson, 'Min väg till prästämbetet', pp. 33–35 (p. 33).
61 No. 5.

Several of the priests recall that for some time before their ordination they had been employed as parish secretaries, a position similar to that of youth secretary but with a focus on teaching for all ages. One priest describes how she worked as a parish secretary in a large urban parish and had almost every task imaginable: 'I was also allowed to deliver sermons in the various services, but the altar service had to be performed by the clergymen.'[62] The priesthood being closed to women, she had studied theology before she held this post with a view to obtaining a bachelor's degree, because she knew she wanted to work through helping people.[63] Another priest writes that she and a number of her fellow female theology students regarded becoming a parish secretary as a future career choice.[64]

The fact that church leaders viewed the position of parish secretary as a preferred option for female theology students who wanted to serve in the Church of Sweden is evident from two vocation narratives.[65] Barbro Westlund describes a meeting with the bishop of her home diocese; they were going to talk about priestly ordination, but he then raised the possibility of her becoming a parish secretary instead. This was because there was opposition within the diocese to women's ordination, but also because of the vulnerability that he believed ordination as a priest would entail for her. Only when he was satisfied that this was not an option did he agree to ordain her:

I sat there for many hours. Finally he says: 'Now I'm going to ask you the very last question: could you still not consider becoming a parish secretary instead, Miss Westlund?' 'No', I said. 'I have been called to be a priest, and if I can't be one then that's the end of it.' 'Then so be it', said the bishop. 'I will ordain you on the seventeenth of December.'[66]

The most common alternative career path, however, as Siv Bejerfors pointed out above, was to become a teacher – especially a teacher of

62 No. 21.
63 Ibid.
64 No. 37.
65 One of the two was Inger Svensson, whose story is told in Tom Alandh's TV documentary *Förlåt oss våra skulder*, broadcast by Swedish Television on 13 February 2014; see also Bexell, Hagberg and Posse, *Kvinnliga präster i Växjö stift?*, pp. 9–12.
66 Lina Sjöberg, 'Jag är så tacksam över att leva i en tid då det är möjligt: Barbro Westlund, prästvigd 1967', in Hössjer Sundman and Sjöberg, *Du ska bli präst*, pp. 51–52.

religion, with an emphasis on Christianity – in an upper secondary school. A number of the priests repeatedly state that they studied theology with a focus on becoming teachers because that was an alternative to being a priest.[67] For these women, though, becoming a teacher necessitated a period of study that was longer than the one for men who wanted to become priests. Studying at university meant first taking a three-year Bachelor of Arts degree, then another year for a four-year Bachelor of Theology degree, and finally a fifth year resulting in a Master of Arts degree. 'Since we female theology students were not permitted to become priests, we had to study more subjects than the male theology students, so that we could become secondary school teachers.'[68] In one case, one of the ordained women, born in the early 1930s, had attended a training college for primary school teachers, whereupon she had studied subjects such as political science, history, Nordic languages, literary history and pedagogy at university before working for a number of years as a teacher at a Christian folk high school.[69]

Several of the priests, including Christina Odenberg, Ulla Nisser and Birgitta Nyman, say they had originally planned to train as teachers.[70] However, two of the priests in the archive material point out that they chose a teaching career owing to the resistance to the reform of the priesthood. One mentions that she opted to become a teacher because she did not think she could 'cope with the resistance'.[71] Another says: 'Not many of us dared to say out loud why we were studying theology [...] Fear was everywhere. I decided that I would finish my theology studies, and then I would study the history of literature and become a secondary school teacher.'[72]

A handful of priests testify that they worked in ways that were not as close to being 'like a priest' as the majority. One of the priests in our material was married to a farmer, which meant that she had to work on the farm as well. In addition, she states that while conducting long-distance theology studies, she also worked as an unauthorised

67 For example, Mailice Wifstrand in Wifstrand, 'Dröm, plan och verklighet', pp. 138–139; Siv Bejerfors in Bejerfors, 'Lärare och präst', p. 131.
68 No. 18.
69 No. 19.
70 Lina Sjöberg, 'Kristus som livshypotes: Christina Odenberg, prästvigd 1967', in Hössjer Sundman and Sjöberg, *Du ska bli präst*, p. 42; Nisser, *Hopp från trampolin*, p. 65; Sjöberg, 'Kyrkan måste vara ömsint', p. 60.
71 No. 28.
72 No. 42.

secondary school teacher in Swedish and English.[73] Another priest, Birgitta Fogelklou, describes working as an advertising consultant before going on to work for the Church of Sweden Mission [Svenska kyrkans mission, SKM] and finally as general secretary of KFUK in the 1960s.[74] Three of the ordained women say that they received training from or worked closely with S:t Lukasstiftelsen [the St Luke Foundation], an ideas-based organisation with psychotherapy clinics and organised groups throughout Sweden. One of these priests stresses that she trained as a psychotherapist in order to equip herself for a possible future role as a priest.[75]

Margit Sahlin is a well-known example in Sweden of how long and winding the road to priestly ordination could be. After obtaining a Bachelor of Theology degree, she worked as a spiritual counsellor at the City Mission [Stadsmissionen] in Stockholm from 1943 to 1945 on a salary that was less than half that of a primary school teacher. Her job was provisional, too. She writes in her diary that she was grateful for her tasks but that she also longed to be ordained as a priest.[76]

> Above all, I longed for an ecclesiastical ordination [...] To be obliged in this way to forge my own path, borne only by a personal faith in my vocation, without any external ecclesiastical authority to fall back on, constituted an unreasonable pressure. My belief in myself had long been undermined by an inferiority complex, fuelled by the questioning and criticism to which I was always exposed as a pioneer.[77]

In this passage, Sahlin speaks about the importance of the inner vocation being supported by an outer one, and she is not afraid to point out the lack of recognition that was reflected in her often temporary posts. She returns to this topic when describing one of her other jobs as parish secretary for the Church of Sweden's National Board for Parish Life. The board offered inspiration and practical services to parishes for those of their activities that were not regulated by law, that is to say, voluntary parish work:

> To work in the service of the church without any kind of ordination is unacceptably stressful; [one is] constantly exposed to criticism

---

73 No. 7.
74 Georg Franzén, *In memoriam: Minnesteckningar av präster i Lunds Stift 1987–93* (Lund: Arcus, 1994).
75 No. 17; No. 19; No. 37.
76 Nordlander, *Margit Sahlin*, pp. 73, 80.
77 Ibid., p. 80.

and dependent on the shifting judgements of others and on one's own self-criticism. You hang in the air and have nothing objective to fall back on, with a vocation that is always being questioned and without any task assigned directly by the church.[78]

Like Ingrid Persson above, Sahlin also believes that the church's legal recognition of inner vocation through some form of ordination is crucial. To act as 'something like a priest' in the service of the church without this recognition is 'unacceptably stressful'.

Two other priests also discuss this issue at length:

[W]e were simply at a disadvantage, much like immigrant academics in Sweden today, whose education is not utilised but who are reduced to working as cleaners, pizza bakers and taxi drivers. Well, we could become secondary school teachers. We could get *venia concionandi* [special authorisation for a layperson to preach and conduct the church service]. Becoming a parish secretary was a possibility, of course. And it is true, as Charles de Foucauld said, that those who have Jesus within them cannot help but convey him to others, but we so dearly wished to be able to do this with the support provided by a priestly ordination.[79]

Birgitta Fogelklou expresses similar views in a letter to Stig Hellsten (1913–1999, a bishop in the diocese of Luleå), probably written in 1957:

Because I believe that ordination helps us to become identified not with ourselves and the burden that can involve – but with the office. The position of being a servant is expressed more clearly – and I believe that the example is important, too – we demonstrate that we want to commit something to God – the idea of vocation becomes emphasised.[80]

These quotations highlight the importance of receiving recognition at all those three levels that Honneth outlined. It is not enough to receive recognition from close relatives only, and within a larger social context; in addition to this there is a need for legal recognition that formally legitimises one's identity as being called to serve as a priest in the Church of Sweden. Recognition of vocation is also a central theme in the core episode we have labelled 'from a clerical family'.

---

78 Ibid., p. 89.
79 No. 18.
80 Letter from Birgitta Fogelklou to Stig Hellsten, undated but probably 1957, Stig Hellsten archive, Umeå University Library.

From a clerical family

In seven of the narratives, the priests emphasise that they have other priests in their family, for example that they come from a clerical family or that they have a father and/or brother who is a clergyman.[81] Being from a clerical family appears to have had both positive and negative aspects.

One woman describes how the 'priest gene' in her family dates back to the seventeenth century, and observes that it affected her own vocation, but that at the same time it created an awareness of limitation because she was a woman: 'As early as my teens, I experienced a real sorrow that I could not become a priest because I happened to have been born a girl. So what did God want with my life?'[82] Another priest describes the support she received from her father and her husband, who were both clergymen. At the same time, she describes how one of her brothers, also a clergyman, refused to attend her ordination 'because of his High Church beliefs at that time', even though both the bishop and their mother had asked him to be present.[83]

For two of the first women to be ordained, it appears that their fathers, who were also priests, came to have a strong influence on their daughters' vocation and struggle to be ordained. One of these is Inger Svensson. Her father, Einar Svensson (1903–1984), was a dean, a member of the General Assembly in 1957 and a high-profile advocate for reforming the priesthood. In debate he very often encountered G. A. Danell (1908–2000), an opponent of the reform and cathedral dean of the same diocese, that of Växjö.[84] The relationship between Einar Svensson and his daughter was portrayed in detail in a documentary broadcast on Swedish television in 2014. In addition to the father's battle for his daughter's ordination, the

---

81 See No. 7; No. 18; No. 35; No. 37.
82 No. 17.
83 No. 18.
84 Oloph Bexell, *Präster i S:t Sigfrids stift: Minnesteckningar till prästmötet i Växjö 1990* (Växjö: Växjö stiftshistoriska sällskap, 1990), pp. 240–247; Tom Alandh's TV documentary *Förlåt oss våra skulder*. See also 'Eko efter kyrkomötet: KVINNO-präster NEJ/JO', *Kyrka och hem: Kyrkligt månadsblad för Växjö Stift*, 11 (1957), 230–233; Göte Fridner, 'Prästbråket bara växer: Skrämselaktion mot ung kvinnlig teolog?', *Expressen*, 11 May 1969; Per-Eric Simonsson, 'I tre år har G A Danell tjatat på henne: Snälla ni – bli inte präst', *Arbetet*, 14 May 1969; Bexell, Hagberg and Posse, *Kvinnliga präster i Växjö stift?*, pp. 12–14.

documentary paints a clear picture of the devastating personal consequences that the opposition had for Inger Svensson.[85] The other daughter of a priest is Britta Olén-van Zijl, daughter of the vicar Gunnar Olén (1890–1990). The present chapter concludes with a comparatively detailed account of her path to ordination, in order to reveal something of the complexity that emerges from studying how decisions of principle are realised in practice. One aspect that appears particularly clearly is that women might need the support of a man in order to be recognised in a homosocial – that is, same-sex (usually male) – context.

The Gunnar Olén Collection in the University Library in Lund and the archive of Archbishop Gunnar Hultgren at the Central Church Office in Uppsala contain material relating to Britta Olén-van Zijl's path to ordination.[86] Olén-van Zijl, who worked as a secondary school teacher and had an extensive theological education, including the final elements of pastoral training, wished to be ordained as a priest, preferably as soon as possible after the General Synod's decision to open up the priesthood to women. An article from September 1957 in connection with the General Synod of that same year makes it clear that Olén-van Zijl hoped to be the first woman to be ordained as a priest in the Church of Sweden. The article begins by pointing out that her choice of profession was encouraged by her father, a senior parish priest who has 'accepted the idea of a woman in the pulpit'.[87] In the article, Olén-van Zijl describes her current work as a secondary school teacher as 'a surrogate'.

As a priest, Gunnar Olén represented an unambiguously Low Church and revivalist line.[88] He was heavily involved in various associations and organisations, including the EFS and the Swedish Association of Christian Social Democrats [Sveriges kristna socialdemokraters förbund]. Olén adopted a strongly ecumenical approach with a focus on the Free Churches, and he was deeply involved in the issue of opening up the priesthood to women.[89]

85 Alandh, *Förlåt oss våra skulder*.
86 Gunnar Olén Collection, Lund University Library (LUL).
87 'Malmölärarinna första kvinnoprästen', *Morgonbladet*, 2 September 1957.
88 Gunnar Carlquist (ed.), *Lunds Stifts herdaminne: Från reformationen till nyaste tid. Ser. II Biografier 13A Östra och Medelstads kontrakt* (Lund: Bokhandeln Arken, 2006), p. 194.
89 Ibid., pp. 194–196.

Olén appears to have shared his commitment to various issues, not least the matter of women's access to the priesthood, with his wife, Nelly. Being distinctly Low Church, they had a correspondingly high regard for the Lutheran doctrine of the priesthood of all believers. They did not regard the priesthood as a divine institution but more as a point of order.[90]

In the memorial sketch he wrote about his wife, Gunnar Olén stresses that it was she who provided the strongest support to their daughter, Britta. As we saw, Britta herself held the same view. Nelly Olén believed that women were legal adults in terms of their religion. She also felt that the key element in the Lutheran Church is the Word and not the preacher. She strongly opposed the idea that, according to the order of creation, man is the head of woman, instead maintaining that the position of women was different now from what it had been in New Testament times.[91] She argued that those who opposed the reform of the priesthood had introduced a Catholic-type view of the office that was not compatible with a Lutheran standpoint.[92] Gunnar Olén supplies the following account of his wife's battle for her daughter's ordination:

> Nelly's fight for women priests took a very personal, almost dramatic turn towards the end of her life. It concerned the ordination of our daughter Britta. She fought for this cause with great fervour and deep empathy. She courted the bishops, she wrote letters and newspaper articles. And, first and last, she assailed the God of heaven with fervent prayers.[93]

Gunnar Olén himself had been strongly influenced by women preachers early in his life. His first encounter with the Baptist preacher Ida Andersson (1889–1974) in 1922 had made a permanent impression on him.[94] Olén brought this experience into the discussion about opening up the priesthood to women, writing in his book *Möte på vägen* ['An encounter on the road'] (1967):

> Ida Andersson on the plain of Skara [a municipality in western Sweden] is a powerful refutation of their [the opponents of the

---

90 Gunnar Olén, *Kavajprästens hustru* (Jönköping: Hall, 1965), pp. 97–98. See also Gunnar Olén, *Kavajprästen berättar: Del II. Mannaåldern och livsinsatsen* (Stockholm: Gummessons, 1962).

91 Olén, *Kavajprästens hustru*, p. 99.

92 Ibid., p. 102.

93 Ibid., p. 104.

94 Gunnar Olén, *Möte på vägen* (Jönköping: SAM-förlaget, 1967), p. 92.

reform] theories, that Jesus does not like women priests. God has blessed her work in an extraordinary way. She has been more than a priest for the members and evangelists of the various congregations. She may well be compared to a bishop, for she has been given the gift of governance to a high degree.[95]

It is thus evident that Gunnar Olén encouraged his daughter to follow her vocation. In addition, Britta both preached and worked as a personal assistant and holiday substitute for her father in Karlskrona parish, where Olén was vicar and hence the senior parish priest.[96]

Britta married the missionary Jan van Zijl, a minister of the Dutch Reformed Church, and they lived for a time in Cofimvaba, South Africa. However, the marriage became an obstacle to Olén-van Zijl's plans to become a priest. The bishop of the diocese of Lund, Nils Bolander (1902–1959), was dismissive. He made several statements to the newspapers about the issue, including the following:

> She explained that it was her great dream to be ordained and that she wanted to please her elderly parents. I ordain neither men nor women on such grounds. I do not ordain a candidate for her personal pleasure, but to have priests in the diocese [...] The theology graduate Britta Olén will not be a Swedish missionary but will work as a wife alongside her husband, who belongs to the Boer church, which is very foreign to us.[97]

The article makes it clear that Olén-van Zijl had also appealed to Archbishop Gunnar Hultgren but that he shared Bolander's opinion, feeling that those ordained to the priesthood 'must have the intention of fulfilling a task in the church to which they are ordained'. The archbishop repeated this message directly to Olén-van Zijl in correspondence between them.[98]

95 Göran Janzon, 'Driftig församlings- och kapellbyggare', in Göran Janzon and Berit Åqvist (eds), *I kallelsens grepp: Om sex baptistkvinnors liv och tjänst* (Karlstad: Votum & Guller, 2016), p. 51. See also Olén, *Möte på vägen*, p. 93.
96 See the report from Gunnar Olén on 1 January 1959 regarding the *venia concionandi* issued by Bishop Nils Bolander on 15 December 1958, and the letter from Gunnar Olén to the Lund Cathedral Chapter on 7 March 1960, both in the Gunnar Olén Collection in LUL.
97 Stig Alkhagen and Gudmund Sandblad, 'Råddes att vänta och se: Fyller ej lagliga krav', *Expressen*, 13 January 1959. See also 'Uppskov i två år med kvinnopräst: Biskoparna avgör', *Svenska Dagbladet*, 24 December 1958.
98 Alkhagen and Sandblad, 'Råddes att vänta och se'. In a notice in *Svenska Dagbladet* with the headline 'Britta Olén fick venia för ett helt år', the

For his part, Gunnar Olén wrote letters to both the Lund Cathedral Chapter and the Lutheran bishops in South Africa, asking them to help make his daughter's ordination possible. His plea met with little interest.[99] He also contacted Archbishop Hultgren. A letter dated 12 March 1960 states that Olén had 'repeatedly been in telephone contact with the Archbishop' [i.e. 'you', 'the Archbishop' being an address in the third person, as was customary in Swedish until the late twentieth century] on this matter. He said that while the future was uncertain, he did believe that his daughter would eventually be able to work as a priest either in Sweden or in some Lutheran context in South Africa. This was not least because in his opinion she was a more skilful preacher than her already ordained brother:

> Although I am a party to this case, I can assure you that she is a good preacher, perhaps slightly ahead of her younger brother Benkt, who has already been ordained and is currently on leave of absence to study towards a licentiate's degree in church history. A third son is studying in Lund for a Bachelor of Theology degree and has about a year left.[100]

---

following is emphasised towards the end with regard to Olén-van Zijl not being ordained: 'For formal reasons the archbishop has previously not permitted her to be ordained because she would be travelling outside her home country.' See letter from Britta Olén-van Zijl to Gunnar Hultgren, dated Lommaren, 15 January 1959, in the Gunnar Hultgren archive in the Central Church Office, Uppsala; letter from Britta Olén-van Zijl to Gunnar Hultgren, dated Cofimvaba, 18 April 1959, in the Gunnar Hultgren archive in the Central Church Office, Uppsala; letter from Gunnar Hultgren to Britta Olén-van Zijl, dated Uppsala, 24 June 1959, in the Gunnar Hultgren archive in the Central Church Office, Uppsala.

99 Letter from Gunnar Olén to Helge Fosséus, dated 7 January 1960, Gunnar Olén Collection, LUL; letter from Gunnar Olén to G. A. Pakendorf, 25 January 1960, Gunnar Olén Collection, LUL. 'My daughter has a great desire to serve God as a preacher. She is willing to serve as an assistant preacher without salary in your parish. Perhaps she could hold services for Scandinavians in your church. I believe that a call as an assistant preacher to your parish will be of great importance. No bishop in Sweden will ordain her as a preacher if she has no work in a Lutheran parish. It is therefore very important that she receives such a call. I will be very grateful if you will lend your support.' Letter from Gunnar Olén to Helge Fosséus, 27 January 1960, Gunnar Olén Collection, LUL.

100 Letter from Gunnar Olén to Gunnar Hultgren, 12 March 1960, Gunnar Olén Collection, LUL. The letter is also in the Gunnar Hultgren archive in the Central Church Office, Uppsala.

Olén then stressed the good travel links between South Africa and Sweden – a person could travel between the two places in a day and a half – which would enable his daughter to work 'both here at home and in Africa'.[101] In his letter to the archbishop Olén also emphasised his wife's work as a preacher, perhaps as a way of demonstrating the openness that existed in Karlskrona for women to perform church leadership functions and maybe also, in the longer term, for women priests:

> It should be added that my wife has for many years served as a teacher in the City of Karlskrona's elementary schools alongside extensive voluntary parish work and much preaching activity both in the parish and elsewhere. Not least because of her efforts, the city parish is largely in favour of women priests.[102]

These various efforts did not bear fruit immediately, though, and it was almost another three years before Britta Olén-van Zijl was ordained as a priest in Lund Cathedral on 16 March 1963 by Bishop Martin Lindström (1904–2000). Although the Lund Cathedral Chapter had decided as early as March 1960 to call Olén-van Zijl to serve as a priest in the diocese, there was no bishop who could ordain her. After Bolander's death in December 1959, the bishopric was vacant and the cathedral dean, Yngve Ahlberg (1903–1983), failed to persuade any other bishop to perform the ordination. Five bishops, including the archbishop, declined 'on the grounds that they only want to ordain priests who will belong to their own dioceses', and when Martin Lindström took over as bishop at the end of 1960, it took a few more years before the ordination could take place.[103]

The cases of Inger Svensson and Britta Olén-van Zijl reveal some interesting things that complicate and deepen the historical narrative about the reform of the priesthood in the Church of Sweden. The struggle here is not between a secular society and a theologically motivated church. Nor is it between parishes and priests. Instead, it is priests with strong positions in the Church of

101 Ibid.
102 Ibid.
103 'Brita Olén får inte bli präst förrän Lund får egen biskop', *Dagens Nyheter*, 19 March 1960. See also 'Två biskopar avböjer prästviga Brita Olén', *Sydsvenska Dagbladet*, 18 March 1960, and 'Missionärshustru ny kvinnlig präst. Domkapitel röstade för. Fem mot ett', *Dagens Nyheter*, 17 March 1960.

Sweden who are working for women to be ordained as priests, and they are doing so for theological reasons. Nor are these just any women, but their own daughters.

∞∞∞∞

In this chapter we have seen how the first Swedish women to be ordained to the priesthood describe their childhood and adolescence in their vocation narratives, and how they relate their experiences from these core episodes to their vocation to serve as priests in the Church of Sweden. An important observation is that these women had different experiences of childhood and adolescence and that their background is quite varied. It becomes apparent that the first ordained women were a very diverse group who came from different segments of Swedish society. In other words, there is no such thing as a typical woman priest, supposing anyone ever had that idea.

Even so, some common aspects do emerge in the parts of the vocation narratives that concern childhood and adolescence. It appears, for example, that despite the 'typically Swedish' religious adherence in society in general, it was fairly common to have had a Christian background and to have been socialised into a Christian context by parents or grandparents. These processes took place within the framework of Church of Sweden traditions as well as the traditions of other denominations. In addition, we have noted that a number of the first ordained women emphasise their confirmation period and their involvement in Church youth organisations as being central to their Christian identity, and not infrequently also to their growing awareness of their vocation to become a priest.

Furthermore, this chapter has shown that the women priests who describe their previous occupational experiences in their vocation narratives often had jobs where they could act as 'something like a priest'. A number of them worked as missionaries, deaconesses, parish secretaries and/or teachers. However, it is clear from the vocation narratives that for some of them, being 'something like a priest' was not enough. They 'yearned to be able to do this with the support provided by ordination as a priest'. In other words: a legal recognition of their vocation.

Moreover, a not inconsiderable number of the first women to be ordained came from clerical families. Two of them had fathers who were themselves priests in leadership positions in their respective dioceses and who were also in favour of the reform of the priesthood. The support that Britta Olén-van Zijl and Inger Svensson received from their fathers testifies to the complexity of this reform and its consequences.

These vocation narratives thus complement and complicate the historical narratives about the reform of the Church of Sweden priesthood that we have presented in previous chapters. In contrast to the assertion frequently made by proponents of the historical narrative according to which the change with regard to women priests was impelled by secular motives, this change was actually driven by theological reasons. Nor was there a clear conflict between supposedly secular-lenient parishes and conservative priests, as representatives of the antithetical historical narrative have sometimes claimed.

Britta Olén-van Zijl was ordained in Lund Cathedral in 1963. Cathedral Verger Oscar Jönsson assisted her in putting on the liturgical vestments before her ordination. The cathedral was full to bursting point. A couple of years after her ordination, in the book *Kvinnlig präst idag: Tio kvinnliga präster berättar* (1967, p. 104), Olén-van Zijl wrote: 'One is grateful for every moment when one's allowed to be a priest, to convey the Word of God, God's gifts to mankind [...] To be a human being, to be a Christian, to be a priest – it all comes together. For me, the office of priest is not a profession or a lifelong obligation among others. Nor, of course, is it a kind of post-apostolic monopoly for men only. It is a divine vocation – for women as well as for men.' (Image: copyright Bilder i Syd. Reproduced by permission.)

Chapter 4
The theology of vocation: the theological context

It is important to stress that what drove the three female theologians to take on, in such a difficult situation, the burden of being the first Swedish women to request ordination to the priesthood was not a zeal to assert general equality between women and men nor a personal need for self-realisation. Above all, it was an expression of fidelity to the living Word of God and co-responsibility for the church's vocation in keeping with the times, knowing that if the church did not take this step, she would fail in her mandate to proclaim the Gospel to today's evolving society – to bear witness through action to the applicability and creative power of God's Word in our own time.[1]

This chapter focuses on the theology of vocation – what Chapter 2 referred to as the ideological setting of the vocation narratives. The narratives of the first women priests regarding their paths to ordination are, of course, told in relation to the various collective narratives of the Christian church, in which theology is a crucial component. As Margit Sahlin, one of the three women ordained in 1960, pointed out when she looked back twenty years later, there were several prevailing theological narratives about the priesthood and vocation. Therefore, the question at the centre of this chapter is: How do the first ordained women express vocation in their narratives in theological terms, and how can this mode of expression be understood in relation to the contemporaneous theological context?

As we turn to the source material to answer these questions, it is important to remember that it is not easy to describe one's vocation. As Caroline Krook put it in an interview about the

---

1 Margit Sahlin, *Dags för omprövning: Kring Bibel, kyrka och kvinnliga präster* (Stockholm: Proprius, 1980), pp. 32–33.

process of receiving a call to the priesthood: 'You can't describe it – and you shouldn't. Some things break up when you put them into words. For example, a great experience of love can only be expressed in poetry. We don't have the words.'[2] It is also worth keeping in mind the priests' experience of opposition to the reform. Those who spoke of their vocation risked having it analysed and dismissed.[3] When the priests wrote about their vocation, it was thus as something that is difficult to capture in words, and it sometimes made them vulnerable to criticism. In view of these obstacles, the multifaceted accounts and abundant details that are after all found in the source material are remarkable.

It is also essential to recall the nature of the source material. The vocation narratives are personal accounts in a relatively short format; they are hence not theological treatises that delve deeply into definitions of specific concepts. In addition, the priests who were writing their accounts assume that their readers have some prior understanding; consequently, they do not always take the time to explain and elaborate on what they mean. For that reason, this chapter devotes a relatively large amount of space to describing the theological context to which the statements in the vocation narratives relate.

Within this theological context, there was an intense debate about vocation in the Church of Sweden. Although the question of women's ordination became a major focal point of the discussion, it was far from being the only issue that prompted a resurgence of theological reflections about the significance of vocation and how it should best be organised and legitimised. Several of the developments described in the previous chapter contributed to this renewed focus. Vocation and the priesthood were key topics in the encounter with the ecumenical movements and other denominations. Criticism of religion and the presumption of the secularisation of society also provoked debate about what type of priests were needed in such times.

In this chapter we will present key theological concepts, currents of thought and ways of theologically understanding vocation and the priestly office in the late nineteenth and early twentieth centuries. The starting point is the first ordained women's statements about their theological understanding of vocation through

---

2 Kerstin Weigl, 'Jag lekte med bilar och slogs', *Aftonbladet*, 3 April 2004.
3 No. 18.

three frequently occurring themes that emerge when these narratives are juxtaposed: the vocation to point to Christ, the vocation to be a servant of the divine Word, and various theological narratives about the link between vocation and gender.

Pointing to Christ

When the first women priests describe the priest's central mandate, it is common for them to express it as 'pointing to Christ'.[4] This is often linked to the Lutheran concept of the priesthood of all believers, as in the case of Margit Kolfeldt when she writes about being a 'signpost' to the 'Cross of Christ', a mandate that she says applies to everyone who is baptised. 'Yes, this applies to all of us who profess to be disciples of Christ, whether we are priests or not. The mandate to be a letter from Christ among our fellow human beings applies to all professing Christians.'[5]

It is significant that this 'universal' vocation appears in the hymns that four of the first ordained women mention, independently of one another, as a key to interpreting their work as priests. All four hymns were written by theologians in the so-called folk church tradition: J. A. Eklund (1863–1945), Einar Billing (1871–1939) and C. R. Sundell (1857–1947) (see further below). The hymns emphasise the vocation that God gives to every human being to assume responsibility for the gifts laid down in him or her.[6]

The same theological motif as in the hymns is found in a Bible passage that one of the priests says she received from her

---

4 See Olén-van Zijl, 'Att få vara präst', p. 104.
5 Margit Kolfeldt, 'Långt mellan byarna', in *Kvinnlig präst idag*, pp. 97–98, 102. See also, for example, Barbro Nordholm-Ståhl, 'Nära livet', in *Kvinnlig präst idag*, p. 29; Christina Odenberg in Göran Skytte, *Biskop Christina: Ett samtal med Göran Skytte* (Lund: Arcus, 1998), pp. 18–21, 45.
6 Britta Olén-van Zijl speaks of Hymn 257 and quotes: 'He gave me of his wealth / My home, my calling with the times' (Olén-van Zijl, 'Att få vara präst', p. 113); Margareta Brandby-Cöster 'leans on' Hymn 380 in the 1937 hymnal (Brandby-Cöster, *Hur gick det till?*, p. 71); a priest in the LUKA archive states that Hymn 596 has been 'hers' throughout her ministry, especially verse three: 'So teach me too, Lord, to your delight / to administer the talent [in the sense of 'money'] that was given to me'(No. 20); Lena Malmgren chose 'her' hymn 'God gave in the words of Creation', Hymn 580, for her funeral because for her it signalled her vocation both as a person and as a priest.

confirmation priest. He had chosen 'So then you are no longer strangers and aliens, but you are fellow citizens with the saints and also members of the household of God, built upon the foundation of the apostles and prophets, with Christ Jesus himself as the cornerstone' (Eph. 2:19–20). She interpreted this verse as a description of the vocation of the priesthood of all believers.[7]

Siv Bejerfors (1924–2017, ordained 1965) also uses the expression 'pointing to Christ' and stresses that the priest must not stand in Christ's way:

> [W]hat I am referring to now is the greatest thing that a priest – he or she – can experience, namely that the priest as a person gives way completely to the Lord of the church, who himself meets his congregation and is received by it [...] It is my prayer that I may become a priest who lets Christ work unhindered. For a person to be able to meet the incarnate God, another person must not put themself in the way and thereby, even if only partially, obscure him. The right position for the person who might be able to help is the side position. To be at the side of the one who seeks contact with Christ, to be at the side of Christ and from there, without drawing any attention to my own person and remembering the obscured side position, to point to Christ and say: 'Ecce homo – Behold the man!', that must be my deepest mission as a priest.[8]

Here the side position is emphasised, and the idea that a person could stand in the place of Christ is rejected. This is probably a veiled jab at a theology of the priesthood that emphasises representation, that is, that the priest in the service represents Christ himself through the so-called apostolic succession.

Vocatio and consecratio

The notion that the priest represents Christ through the apostolic succession was well established among representatives of the 'New Ecclesiology' (den nya kyrkosynen). This view began to emerge in the Church of Sweden in the first half of the 1940s. Along with the ecumenical movement, and as a reaction against liberal theology and the concept of the folk church, came a new emphasis on the church. According to this view, the church had not arisen in the form of various congregations that eventually joined together.

---

7 No. 20.
8 Siv Bejerfors, 'Lärare och präst', in *Kvinnlig präst idag*, pp. 125–126.

Instead, according to the New Testament, Christ had founded the church with the first Easter and Pentecost. Christ's intention had been that God's work of salvation would continue through the church, the body of Christ in the world. The church could thus be said to represent Christ, and the church's ministry was understood to be a representation of Christ. This view of the church also emphasised the collective aspect – the church as community in opposition to individualism. Another notion was that salvation only existed within the church. In the era studied here, this new view of the church was well established among both university theologians and bishops in the Church of Sweden.[9]

While this new view's understanding of the priesthood was dominant, it was not the only one. For example, Professor of Practical Theology Sven Kjöllerström (1901–1981) was of a different opinion. In his 1974 overview of the ecclesiastical history of the episcopate, he argues that two ways of thinking about the office and the vocation have existed in parallel throughout the history of the Church of Sweden. At different times one or the other has been emphasised, but they always exist side by side. One he calls the *vocatio* (vocation) of the Reformation and the other the *consecratio* (consecration) of the Middle Ages.[10]

Consecratio emphasises *essence*: that the priest is a representation of Christ guaranteed by an unbroken chain, whereby the mandate is passed on through the laying on of hands and prayer from bishop to bishop in what is known as the apostolic succession. The ordination ceremony is thus regarded as a decisive moment when this succession is formally passed on to a new generation of priests by the bishop laying his or her hands on the ordinands and praying for them.

Vocatio emphasises *function*: what the priest (or bishop) should do. He or she exists for the sake of order: to ensure that the Word is

---

9 Brohed, *Sveriges kyrkohistoria*, pp. 148–150; Berntson, Nilsson and Wejryd, *Kyrka i Sverige*, pp. 320–322; Andreas Wejderstam, *Personlig och kyrklig förnyelse: Svenska kyrkan och Vadstenamötena 1943–1985* [Acta Universitatis Upsaliensis: Studia Historico-Ecclesiastica Upsaliensia 51] (Uppsala: Uppsala University, 2020), pp. 53–54. Representatives of the new view of the church included Anders Nygren (1890–1978), Gustaf Aulén (1879–1977), Bo Giertz (1905–1998), Ragnar Bring (1895–1988), Anton Fridrichsen (1888–1953), Olof Linton (1898–1980), Hjalmar Lindroth (1893–1979) and Ruben Josefson (1907–1972).

10 Sven Kjöllerström, *Sätt till att ordinera en vald biskop 1561–1942* (Lund: Gleerup, 1974), p. 31.

purely proclaimed and that the sacraments are rightly administered. In principle, anyone who has been baptised and therefore belongs to the universal priesthood can become a priest; but he or she must have a *rite vocatus* – that is, be regularly called – in order to do so. A person who is regularly called is one who feels an inner call to become a priest and who is considered suitable by the church and thus given an outer vocation. The church may be understood as being the church leadership, but so may the parish.

In discussing views of the priesthood during the twentieth century, Kjöllerström says that the *consecratio* model came to dominate, largely because of strong influence from High Church Anglicanism. This influence arose out of a desire for more cooperation and intercommunion. He asserts that the emergence of the Church of England as such a crucial ecumenical dialogue partner for the Church of Sweden from the beginning of the twentieth century was somewhat surprising to many people at the time, as Sweden was in those days fully integrated into the German cultural sphere. However, it was largely a result of informal, personal contacts between an inner circle of influential theologians. The Swedish theologians included Nathan Söderblom (1866–1931), Erling Eidem (1880–1972) and Yngve Brilioth (1891–1959), all of whom eventually became archbishops of the Church of Sweden.[11]

The pursuit of intercommunion with the Anglican Church raised the issue of apostolic succession. A number of researchers, including the aforementioned Yngve Brilioth, investigated the issue in the 1920s and 1930s and argued that there was historical evidence that the apostolic succession had remained unbroken in the Church of Sweden despite the Reformation. Kjöllerström's doubts both about the existence of the apostolic succession in the Church of Sweden and about the *consecratio* view in general are unmistakable, not least through the recurring expression 'the Anglican sourdough'.[12] As we will see in the following chapters, Kjöllerström also seems to have been clear about this in his professorial work and in his role as a teacher of ordinands. One of the

---

11 For a thorough investigation of the relations between the Church of Sweden and the Church of England, see Mikael Hermansson *'En allians av något slag': Förändrade relationer mellan Svenska kyrkan och Church of England, 1909–1954* (Malmö: Universus Academic Press, 2018), and Lyttkens, *The Growth of Swedish-Anglican Intercommunion.*

12 Kjöllerström, *Sätt till att ordinera en vald biskop*, pp. 33–45, 153–188.

first women to be ordained refers to his history of the episcopate in appreciative terms.[13]

Kjöllerström's two theological models may be regarded as an overly schematic way of describing developments in the twentieth century. At the same time, they reveal the preconceptions that underlie the various possible positions in a way that is easily understood: is being a priest something you essentially *are* or something you primarily *do*? As we shall see, the theological reasoning of the first women priests very much emphasises the priesthood as a *function*. As Siv Bejerfors put it in an interview in 1977:

> I think that many priests – consciously or not – have built their opinion on the idea of representation, the idea that a priest represents Christ and that it is therefore a strength if he is a man. I cannot share that view. After all, one of the central ideas of Christianity is that Christ is present everywhere; and if he is, he does not need to be represented. When the king travels somewhere, he hardly sends a representative to the same place. He only does so if he is himself unable to go. For me, the priest's duties are more of a practical nature: a parish requires a leader or chairperson. If you regard the priest's office in that way, it is not such a solemn business. Nor does it matter so much who is exercising it – a woman or a man.[14]

In this quotation, Bejerfors describes the priesthood as primarily a practical function; and she rejects the idea of representation, which she regards as being linked to the idea that the priest must be a man. However, the division between function and representation is not entirely clear-cut. As we discussed in Chapter 2, several of the first ordained women stress that their vocation is interwoven with their person and deepest identity. In this sense, 'priest' is something they are and not merely something they do.

Ministers of the Word

The most common way for the priests in this study to describe the task they feel called to perform is in terms of preaching.[15] Bodil Fredfeldt (1942–, ordained 1965) puts it this way:

13 No. 34.
14 Anders Franck, 'Sluta tala om kvinnopräster', *Göteborgs-Posten*, 18 September 1977.
15 For example, No. 18; No. 17; Inger Svensson in Bexell, Hagberg and Posse, *Kvinnliga präster i Växjö stift?*, p. 15; Britta Olén-van Zijl in Olén-van Zijl,

To be a priest is to be a minister of the Word of God, that is to say, to adhere to the Bible and to emphasise in preaching what he shows us in terms of both Law and Gospel. But we also recall the equating of the Word and Christ in the Gospel of John. In every action, then, a priest must always be first and foremost a servant of Christ.[16]

Some of the women stress that the priest is an instrument through which the Word of God reaches people.[17] On one preaching occasion, Kerstin Lindqvist-Bolling reflects on some worshippers who had begun to worship frequently in the church where she serves:

Why are they sitting here? I have to ask myself this question again and again. It is of great importance to my raison d'être. Many of my fellow priests have God's word for it that I should not be standing here. Last week, the two [in the congregation] who follow the service seriously and fervently testified, independently of each other, how they found life and meaning in Christianity after they happened to visit the church when I was preaching. I wanted to tell them that it was not me, it was Christ – it was his message that was getting through. Would it not therefore be Christ they had met, because it was not his instrument that had spoken of him.[18]

Here again we see the tension between the priestly office as something you do and something you are. As a priest, Lindqvist-Bolling is functioning as a minister of the Word, an instrument by which Christ reaches out. At the same time, her choice of expression – 'raison d'être' – also suggests that the mandate of being a priest is linked to who she is, her identity.

There is probably a link between the idea that the priest is the minister of the Word and the abundance of episodes in the narratives that are related to preaching. Reading the source material through the lens of the narrative-analysis method, it is striking that many of the core episodes concern occasions when the women, as future priests, had the opportunity to preach.

A number of the vocation narratives contain episodes when the ordinand's first opportunity to preach became something of

'Att få vara präst', p. 111; Barbro Westlund in Sjöberg, 'Jag är så tacksam över att leva i en tid då det är möjligt', p. 53.

16 Bodil Fredfeldt, 'Vid Öresund', in *Kvinnlig präst idag*, p. 60.

17 See Barbro Nordholm-Ståhl, 'Nära livet', in *Kvinnlig präst idag*; Bejerfors, 'Lärare och präst', pp. 129–139; Olén-van Zijl, 'Att få vara präst' .

18 Lindqvist-Bolling, 'Förstadspräst', p. 41.

a spiritual breakthrough. For example, in her narrative Ingrid Persson often refers to occasions when she preached and relates them to her vocation as a priest. She describes writing her first sermon on the theme of sin and forgiveness as a confirmand, how she stood in the pulpit for the first time in Härnösand Cathedral in 1939, and that she held the bishop's *venia*.[19] She also talks about when she preached in connection with the practical element of priestly training, saying that her male fellow students thought that she 'preaches like a real man'.[20]

The source material is filled to the brim with similar stories about preaching activities that were vital to the writer's vocation. One example is being allowed to preach as a child or teenager.[21] Elisabeth Djurle Olander mentions the evangelisation weeks in the diocese of Växjö, when the young members of KGF were asked if any of them could say a few words during an open-air service:

> Then I felt I had something to say and I went up to the leader and said: 'If you trust me, I can say something.' He affirmed it, and it was a crucial experience for me, which led me to change my life path. The call made my choice a natural one.[22]

There are many episodes describing occasions when the women, as future priests, were allowed to preach during their training, often in combination with serving at the altar.[23] One of the priests describes her experience of the 'practice service' that formed part of the practical element of her training as holding great meaning for her; it included altar service as well as preaching:

> I can never forget the liberating feeling of deep joy and peace that filled me! I was like a fish in water, in my own natural element. And serving at the altar, in all the years since, has always given me a special joy.[24]

---

19 The bishop's written authorisation to preach in the diocese. *Venia* could be issued for a single occasion or as *venia concionandi*, the bishop's permission to preach at any time.
20 Persson, 'Min väg till prästämbetet', pp. 28–51.
21 No. 18; No. 45.
22 Lina Sjöberg, 'Närhet och glädje: Elisabeth Djurle Olander, prästvigd 1960', in Hössjer Sundman and Sjöberg, *Du ska bli präst*, p. 26.
23 No. 8; No. 28; Birgitta Nyman in Lina Sjöberg, 'Kyrkan måste vara ömsint och stå på människors sida: Birgitta Nyman, prästvigd 1970', in Hössjer Sundman and Sjöberg, *Du ska bli präst*, p. 60; Margareta Brandby-Cöster in Brandby-Cöster, *Hur gick det till?*, p. 39.
24 No. 17.

The women priests stressed the continued importance to them of preaching and administering the sacraments after their ordination. For example, Siv Bejerfors writes that it is a profound joy and 'feels natural' to preach and serve at the altar, which has 'helped make my awareness of my vocation even firmer and stronger'.[25]

One decisive piece of the puzzle in terms of understanding the first ordained women's emphasis on the priest as a minister of the Word, and the calling embodied in the priesthood of all believers to 'point to' Christ while not representing him, is Gustaf Wingren's theology. His theological model is the one mentioned most often in the vocation narratives of the first women priests.[26] Margareta Brandby-Cöster, for example, mentions that 'Wingren's theology had a great influence on me',[27] and Margit Sahlin says that 'Wingren's shadow' lies over her entire theology.[28]

Gustaf Wingren and the concept of the 'folk church'

Gustaf Wingren (1910–2000) was a priest in the Church of Sweden and Professor of Systematic Theology at Lund University from 1951 to 1977. In his biography of Wingren, the theologian Bengt Kristensson Uggla maintains that he waged a constant battle for the legitimacy of the reform of the priesthood. He also claims that the question of women priests was a cardinal issue in Wingren's theological thinking and thus formed an undercurrent in many of the conflicts he was involved in. In addition, Kristensson Uggla points out, this reform is a recurring topic in almost all of Wingren's books;[29] indeed, what Wingren wrote about vocation and the priesthood could fill an entire book. In addition to the public debate in which he participated, however, two publications are crucial for understanding his theological position on this issue: *Luthers*

25 Bejerfors, 'Lärare och präst' p. 124.
26 No. 26; No. 34; Margareta Brandby-Cöster, 'Wingrensk homiletik', *Svensk teologisk kvartalsskrift*, 1 (2011), 87–90; Margareta Brandby-Cöster, 'Vad skall kyrkan förkunna i klimat-orons tid?', in *Sagt och gjort: Texter och tal från mitt prästliv* (Stockholm: BoD, 2015), p. 234; Nordlander, *Margit Sahlin*, p. 210; Nisser, *Hopp från trampolin*, pp. 71–72.
27 Brandby-Cöster, *Hur gick det till?*, p. 33.
28 Nordlander, *Margit Sahlin*, p. 210.
29 Bengt Kristensson Uggla, *Becoming Human Again: The Theological Life of Gustaf Wingren* (Eugene, OR: Cascade Books, 2016), pp. 14, 236, 315.

lära om kallelsen (1942) [translated as *Luther on Vocation*] and *Kyrkans ämbete* ['The church's ministry'] (1958). In Wingren's interpretation of Luther, everyone has a vocation. This vocation is in relation to fellow human beings, not to the church, and involves following Christ in caring for everyone, regardless of their faith. The central aspect of this vocation is the proclamation of the Gospel. Humans are called through the Word, and they grow by means of it. Preaching is thus a mission to which one is called by God; and like all other vocations, it is performed for the sake of other people.[30] Even so, Wingren is careful to point out that the works that humans are called to do are not necessary in relation to God, only in relation to their fellow humans.[31] He also carefully distinguishes between following and imitating: 'Christ is not to be imitated by us, but rather to be accepted in faith, because Christ also had his special office for the salvation of man, an office which no one else has.'[32]

The 1958 pamphlet *Kyrkans ämbete* is a partisan contribution that summarises Wingren's views on the priesthood in general, not only in relation to the issue of admitting women. In many ways the pamphlet sums up the debate that he was deeply involved in throughout the 1950s.[33] In the debate, Wingren criticised the idea that what he called a High Church view of the priesthood – above all the concept of apostolic succession – was Lutheran. He said that while Sweden did indeed have a church that happened to have apostolic succession, the Book of Concord, that is, the Lutheran Confession of 1580, prevented the church from assigning any fundamental importance to it. Wingren adds that no evidence exists for the doctrine of apostolic succession, either in the three Creeds or in the Bible.[34]

---

30 Gustaf Wingren, *Luther on Vocation* (Eugene, OR; Wipf & Stock, 2004), pp. 1–50.
31 Ibid., pp. 162–171.
32 Ibid., p. 172.
33 This debate, which took place in *Svensk Kyrkotidning* from 1953 to 1956, has been analysed by Dag Sandahl and Tomas Fransson, both practical theologians: Sandahl, *Kyrklig splittring*, pp. 44–67; Tomas Fransson, '*Kristi ämbete*': *Gunnar Rosendal och diskussionen om biskopsämbetet i Svenska kyrkan* (Skellefteå: Artos, 2006), pp. 187–224.
34 Gustaf Wingren, 'Bekännelseskrifterna och högkyrkligheten', *Svensk Kyrkotidning*, 10 (1954), 149, 155.

Like the debate, then, the pamphlet *Kyrkans ämbete* is not primarily focused on the reform of the priesthood. The central question for Wingren is what view of the priesthood may be said to be supported by the Bible and the Book of Concord. According to Wingren's interpretation of the latter, the priest's mandate is to preach the Gospel and administer the sacraments in accordance with Christ's command to the church. However, Christ has not issued any instructions as to how the individuals who are to carry out this mandate are to be appointed; it is up to the church in each age to decide how this is to be organised. 'Everything to which the church is *obliged* is anchored with extraordinary certainty in *the Gospel*. And in all other things there is *freedom*, but freedom under the highest responsibility, freedom in the choice of ways to bring this Gospel *to the people of every age and nation*.'[35]

Wingren argues that the understanding of his contemporaries – the exponents of the 'new ecclesiology' – regarding what a priest is does not exist in the Bible. The word 'priest' is used in the New Testament of Christ and also of everyone who in faith receives Christ and shares in his priesthood: the priesthood of all believers.[36]

Only in the very last pages of the pamphlet does Wingren relate his ideas to the issue of opening up the priesthood to women. Since the office is there to fulfil a function, there should be no obstacles to ordaining women. As long as the Word is purely preached and the sacraments rightly administered, it is not important how this is organised and who holds the office. Wingren also points out that women were already involved in the mandate of spreading the Gospel as missionaries. However, the fact that they are permitted to preach but not to administer the sacraments is wrong from a biblical and Lutheran perspective, because it amounts to dividing Word and sacrament. According to Wingren, there is no support for this division in Scripture or the Book of Concord.[37]

As was pointed out above, a number of the first ordained women emphasise Wingren's importance for their own view of vocation and ministry as a priest. In this context, it is easy to imagine that the first women priests appreciated Wingren for coming to their defence. It is clear, though, that his main purpose was not to explain

---

35 Gustaf Wingren, *Kyrkans ämbete* (Lund: Gleerup, 1958), pp. 16–17. Italicisation in original.

36 Ibid., p. 10.

37 Ibid., pp. 34–35.

why women had the right to become priests, but rather to promote what he believed to be a genuine Lutheran view of the priesthood that was in accordance with the Church of Sweden's Confessions and the Bible.

The similarities between the first ordained women and Wingren's theological understanding of vocation also arise from the fact that they are rooted in a current of theological thought that was widespread within the Church of Sweden. It emphasised the Word as being constitutive of the church, the church as the place where the Word is proclaimed and the sacraments administered, and the priest as an instrument for conveying these means of grace. This current of thought is very much related to the Church of Sweden's status as a state church in Sweden, and it is usually referred to as the 'folk church' concept.

The folk church concept offers a number of variations, but it comprises some central trains of thought. Leading first-generation folk church theologians were Einar Billing, J. A. Eklund and Manfred Björkquist (1884–1985), who were also the authors of some of the hymns that the priests in the present study refer to as essential to their understanding of their call to the priesthood. Despite these theologians' differences, they shared a number of features. First, they criticised the Free Churches' understanding of what a parish is. Second, the divine Word (or the Gospel) was regarded as being constitutive of the church. Since the proclamation of the Word is necessary for the faith of the individual, the church comes into being when the Word is proclaimed and the sacraments administered. This Lutheran view was stressed by a number of the theologians (Wingren included) who wrote after Billing and formulated variants of folk church theology.

Third, the folk church concept contains elements of a historical understanding of the idea of revelation, that is, that God reveals himself in and through human history. This idea could take various forms. In Billing's concept of the folk church, it is manifested through the church as an institution that mediates grace. Everything focuses on how the Word of God's grace will reach the individual. Eklund and Björkquist anchor their view of the Church more tangibly in a conception of the creation and argue that the people are also an expression of how revelation appears in and via history. God simply creates different groups of people who have particular characteristics that indicate different aspects of life with Christ. There is an eschatological dimension here, too. God's intention is that each group of people should be brought into its own as a result of the increasing permeation of culture and social life by the Christian faith, and it is the mission of the church to contribute to this development.

This relates to a fourth idea shared by several of the folk church theologians: the notion that the church is involved in a continually ongoing process. The idea of process and creation-orientated revelation may also be expressed in the idea that popular movements outside the church can be expressions of God's revelation, for example in the form of ethical ideals.[38]

There was also a huge variety in folk church theologians' understanding of what constituted a 'people' [folk in Swedish]. This concept could be understood on a national and ethnic basis, but also as referring to people who lived in a specific territorial area. It could be linked to ideas such as 'God's chosen people', which in turn could relate both to the laypeople in the local parish and to the early twentieth-century development whereby the territorial nation-state became increasingly important in shaping people's identity. In addition, the idea of a 'people' might be linked to the idea of the church's responsibility for holding this 'people' together by acting as a unifier and bridging divides for the good of society. Finally, it might be understood in relation to democracy – the influence of the people or of the laity.[39]

Folk church theology thus has many variations and emphases, but they share a common core. It is on the foundation of this theology that both Wingren and many of the first women priests built their understanding of vocation.

Vocation and gender

It is well documented in Swedish research that the theology underlying the view of the priesthood is closely linked to ideas about gender.[40] This also applies to the theology of the first women priests. When they express their theological views on vocation and

38 Jonas Ideström, *Folkkyrkotanken – innehåll och utmaningar: En översikt av studier under 2000-talet* (Uppsala: Svenska kyrkans forskningsenhet, 2012), pp. 53–57.

39 Ibid., pp. 55–56.

40 Ninna Edgardh, *Diakonins kyrka: Teologi, kön och omsorgens utmattning* (Stockholm: Verbum, 2019); Johanna Gustafsson, *Kyrka och kön: Om könskonstruktioner i Svenska kyrkan 1945–1985* (Eslöv: B. Östlings bokförlag Symposion, 2001); Alexander Gustavsson, 'Manlig bekännelsetrohet i

the priesthood, their reasoning often connects with issues of gender, gender differences, male and female characteristics and tasks, women's and men's rights and obligations, and so on. Some of the women anchor their view of the priesthood and vocation partly in a complementary view of humanity – that is, one of the arguments in favour of ordaining women is that they contribute something that men do not. This is justified in terms of creation theology. For example, one priest writes that she is convinced women are needed as priests 'because, according to the first Creation story, God "created humans in his image [...] male and female he created them"'.[41] Christina Odenberg expresses herself in a similar way:

> For me, it is inherent in the very foundation of the Creation that man and woman interrelate with each other. God created humans, he created them male and female, i.e. man and woman in polarity constitute the human. If there is anywhere in society where it is important that men and women are always present, side by side, it is in all human caring professions [...] Man and woman together in church, before the altar.[42]

Odenberg testifies that her theological reasoning in this regard was strongly influenced by Margit Sahlin.[43]

Some of the first women priests hold a somewhat different view, however, maintaining that while there might well be differences between women and men, the priestly office itself is gender-neutral. Siv Bejerfors, for example, returns several times in her vocation narrative to the idea that we should spend more time thinking in terms of human roles than in terms of gender roles.

---

motvind: En mikrohistorisk studie av prästen Bo Giertz', in Anders Jarlert (ed.), *Bo Giertz – präst, biskop, författare* (Gothenburg: Församlingsförlaget, 2005); Martin Nykvist, *Alla mäns prästadöme: Homosocialitet, maskulinitet och religion hos Kyrkobröderna, Svenska kyrkans lekmannaförbund 1918–1978* (Lund: Nordic Academic Press, 2019); Maria Södling, *Oreda i skapelsen: Kvinnligt och manligt i Svenska kyrkan under 1920- och 30-talen* [Acta Universitatis Upsaliensis: Uppsala Studies in Faiths and Ideologies 26] (Uppsala: Uppsala University, 2010); Andersson, *Den nödvändiga manligheten*.

41 No. 7.
42 Skytte, *Biskop Christina*, p. 73.
43 Lina Sjöberg, 'Kristus som livshypotes: Christina Odenberg, prästvigd 1967', in Hössjer Sundman and Sjöberg, *Du ska bli präst*, p. 43.

This is not, of course, a denial of the female sex but rather an attempt to go into greater depth, which may be justified precisely in the context of the priesthood. There we should be able to be free to consider only the bringing together of God–human and of human–human without any further categorisation of humans. God calls a human being to be a priest. He invites that human being to serve his or her fellow human being as a priest.[44]

This example comes from the portion of the source material that dates from 1967 and the book *Kvinnlig präst idag* ['Women priests today']. The book contains other statements of a similar nature. For example, Margit Kolfeldt (1915–2007, ordained 1964) writes: 'To be a woman priest is – in the same way as for a male priest – to be inserted into a large context where it is not about oneself, where it is not about one's own will or wishes, but where it is about God's will: It is about serving God in and among one's fellow human beings.'[45]

The prominence of this theme in these texts is very probably due to the focus of the book itself – that the priests who are speaking are women. The introduction to the book states that it was written partly in response to the book *Att vara präst: Tjugo präster berättar om sitt kall* ['Being a priest: twenty priests talk about their vocation'] from 1965, in which none of the 20 participating priests was a woman. *Kvinnlig präst idag* is mentioned in an article from 1967, in which Elisabeth Djurle Olander, Ingrid Persson and Ylwa Gustafsson are interviewed, and it is clear that they are tired of journalists' questions about what it is like to be a woman priest. The three colleagues are quick to reply: 'It's presumably just like being a male priest. There's nothing special about us.'[46]

It is interesting to note that this wide range of opinions appears to be reflected in other times and contexts as well. As we pointed out in our account of the scholarly discussion about research into ordained women's own narratives, Eliana Coelho da Silva also discovered dissimilar viewpoints in her analysis of what it means to be a woman and to be called to church leadership in various Protestant churches in Brazil in the 2010s. On the one hand there

---

44 Bejerfors, 'Lärare och präst', pp. 124–125.
45 Margit Kolfeldt, 'Långt mellan byarna', in *Kvinnlig präst idag*, pp. 97–98. See also in *Kvinnlig präst idag*: Olén-van Zijl, 'Att få vara präst', p. 104; Bejerfors, 'Lärare och präst', pp. 124–125; Lindqvist-Bolling, 'Förstadspräst', pp. 42–43.
46 Wik-Thorsell, 'Kvinnlig präst söker aldrig konflikterna'.

are differentialists who refer to the order of creation, justifying women's access to the priesthood on the grounds that women have special qualities that complement those of men. On the other hand, there are egalitarians who cite Galatians 3:28 and stress that in Christ there is no difference between man and woman.[47]

It is also common in the source material for the first women priests to express ambivalence regarding the gender-equality discussions that were going on in their time. For example, another priest says:

> In the fifties, the issue of women holding the office was often discussed at political gatherings. I was divided in my opinion. I was convinced that women were needed as priests because, according to the first creation story, God 'created humans in his image [...] male and female he created them' [...] I didn't like the undertones of feminist struggle that were sometimes heard.[48]

Similarly, it was very common in newspaper interviews for the first ordained women to point out that women's access to the priesthood was a theological issue, not a question of gender equality or fairness.[49] For example, Barbro Westlund stated that:

> It is unfortunate that the debate on women priests too often becomes a sex-role debate. Many people who say 'yes' to women priests regard it as a women's issue. But the idea that it is only a women's issue is alien to me. People become priests because they feel they are called to it. Regardless of whether you are a man or a woman.[50]

The emphasis on the theological reasons for the reform and the marking of a boundary from the social debate on the status of women is also very often an important theme in slightly longer texts in which the first women priests present their views on the office. In *Man och kvinna i Kristi kyrka* ['Man and woman in Christ's church'] (1950), Margit Sahlin emphasises that this is not

---

47 Coelho da Silva, 'Chamadas por Deus'.
48 No. 7. See also Margit Sahlin in Nordlander, *Margit Sahlin*, p. 92.
49 For example, Britta Olén-van Zijl in 'Radiopredikande Brita Olén övertygad om sin kallelse', *Sydsvenska Dagbladet*, 17 November 1957; Elisabeth Djurle Olander, Ylwa Gustafsson and Ingrid Persson in Wik-Thorsell, 'Kvinnlig präst söker aldrig konflikterna'; Siv Bejerfors in Eva Jansson and Christer Dandels, 'Stiftets första kvinnliga präst: – Vi har kommit för att stanna!', *Norrköpings Tidningar*, 10 June 1977.
50 Jansson and Dandels, 'Stiftets första kvinnliga präst'.

a women's rights issue; instead, her favourable attitude to women's access to the priesthood is based on theological considerations.[51] In the introduction to *Ordets tjänst i en förändrad värld* ['The ministry of the Word in a changing world'] (1959), she says that while the issue might have begun as a question of equality, this then raised theological questions about views of humanity and the relationship between man and woman, which in turn clarified the solid theological foundations of the idea of women priests.[52] Another example is Caroline Krook, who in her book *Prästens identitet och kyrkans trovärdighet* ['The priest's identity and the credibility of the church'] (1996) puts it this way: 'For me personally, women in the priesthood means something more than that it is a practical and good order in our modern society. For me it is a consequence of the Gospel, a profound matter of faith.'[53]

What lay behind this distancing from the women's rights movement and this strong emphasis on the contention that opening up the priesthood to women is a theological issue? In all likelihood it was because opponents of the reform often stressed the theological foundation of their arguments by referring to themselves in the debate as 'faithful to the Bible and the Confessions'. Explicitly or implicitly, they argued that supporters of women's ordination lacked theological motives and were imposing a secular ideal on the church.

In her 2020 account of her path to ordination, Margareta Brandby-Cöster says that this was precisely what she, Birgitta Nyman and their colleague Anne Strid (1948–, ordained 1974) wanted to address when they published the text *Kvinna – kyrka* ['Woman – Church'] in 1978. Feeling that women priests were constantly being accused of not having acceptable and Christian arguments, she quotes from the joint publication from the 1970s:

> We have arguments in favour of women priests. We represent a tradition that is faithful to both the Bible and the Confessions, and this is important. To be in favour of women priests is not to be any less scrupulous than those who adamantly work to oppose the reform.

---

51 Margit Sahlin, *Man och kvinna i Kristi kyrka* (Stockholm: Diakonistyrelsen, 1950), p. 208.
52 Margit Sahlin, *Ordets tjänst i en förändrad värld: Några linjer till ett kyrkligt program* (Stockholm: Diakonistyrelsen, 1959), pp. 7, 18–19.
53 Krook, *Prästens identitet*, p. 34.

Quite the contrary. To be in favour of women priests is to be rooted in the Word of God. A rootedness that must have consequences in other areas where faith operates, that is, in all areas of life.[54]

However, contrasting theology and the church to the equality of secular society was not only something done by the opposing side. As can be seen from Barbro Westlund's quotation above, equality between women and men was a common argument, for example for the women's movement, and not least in the cultural debate in the press. As we will show below, it was not unusual for statements by opponents of the reform to be harshly criticised by means of pitting modern, enlightened equality thinking against naive, outmoded, patriarchal beliefs. It is not surprising that some of the first ordained women sought to distance themselves from such a negative view of theology – and church leaders who represented such a view.

Underlying the statements of the first women priests, as well as criticism of the church by the women's rights movement and in the Swedish cultural debate, was the Lutheran doctrine of the three estates.

The dominant theological narrative on vocation and gender: the Lutheran doctrine of the three estates

In the first half of the twentieth century, the theological understanding of gender and vocation was based on the Lutheran doctrine of the three estates. The doctrine was founded on the idea that God has established three orders – three ways of organising human life. The purpose of this order was to lead to salvation and a good life for humanity as a whole. It was often said that these three estates ensured the survival of society and were part of God's plan of salvation.

The three estates consisted of the spiritual (the church), the temporal (the state) and the domestic (the household). Everyone participated in all these estates and had specific vocations within each of them. The temporal or secular estate concerned the organisation of society and the vocation to, for instance, a profession or a task. The spiritual estate concerned everything to do with a

---

54 Brandby-Cöster, *Hur gick det till?*, p. 65; Margareta Brandby-Cöster, Birgitta Nyman and Anne Strid, *Kvinna – kyrka* (Stockholm: Verbum, 1977), pp. 3–4.

person's spiritual life, and vocation was understood in the categories of priest/teacher and listener. The domestic or household estate included the family, the male head of the household being ultimately responsible for and thus superior to the housewife, children and servants.[55]

All three estates were linked to one another. In particular, the spiritual and household estates were closely connected. Within the family, the head of the household had a priest-like function. He was responsible for the spiritual welfare of the family in the same way that the priest was responsible for the spiritual welfare of the parish. In reverse, there was an idea that the order of the spiritual estate should reflect the order of the household, the priest acting like a household head of the parish. What they had in common, however, was that in each of them the highest position was held by a man. This superiority was thought to be modelled on Christ, who, although he held all power, sacrificed himself out of love for the sake of the world. Likewise, the priest and the head of the household were called on to sacrifice themselves for their subordinates. Because this vocation emanated from God, the male priest or head of household was also ultimately responsible to God himself.[56] In the Swedish context, this concept found concrete expression in the theological programmes of leading representatives of the church.[57]

The fact that the Lutheran doctrine of the three estates, with its theological arguments about creation, was articulated in various contexts within which the first women priests operated is reflected in one of the vocation narratives. One of the priests describes an occasion when she gave a talk in the summer of 1959. When she saw a priest in the audience, a man whom she liked, she took the

55 Alexander Maurits, *Den vackra och erkända patriarchalismen: Prästmannaideal och manlighet i den tidiga lundensiska högkyrkligheten, ca 1850–1900* (Malmö: Universus Academic Press, 2013), pp. 76–82. See also Witte, *Law and Protestantism*.

56 Maurits, *Den vackra och erkända*, pp. 76–82. A number of scholars argue that the doctrine of the three estates is very important for understanding the theology of the Church of Sweden. See, for example, Gustafsson, *Kyrka och kön*, pp. 145–151; Gustavsson, 'Manlig bekännelsetrohet'; Södling, *Oreda i skapelsen*, p. 300; Urban Claesson, 'Lutherska begrepp och nordisk samhällsteologi', in Jenny Ehnberg and Cecilia Nahnfeldt (eds), *Samhällsteologi: Forskning i skärningspunkten mellan akademi, samhälle och kyrka* (Stockholm: Verbum, 2019); Andersson, *Den nödvändiga manligheten*, pp. 325–331.

57 Södling, *Oreda i skapelsen*, p. 300.

opportunity to ask him for his views on the debate about the reform of the priesthood.

> He replied with a long exposition on the order of creation, on Christ as the head of man and man as the head of woman, etc. I had heard this before but still became very upset. The following night I had a dream: People are dragging me by both arms towards a guillotine some distance away. I tear myself free and stamp on the ground, saying: 'I refuse, on behalf of myself and half of humanity, I refuse to allow myself to be beheaded by you.' I wake up with a pounding heart and immediately see the connection: If people want to deny me and other women the self-evident right to a direct relationship with Christ, because we are women, I experience that as an attempt at decapitation! I do not accept a man as an authority over me. (I'd barely heard the word 'feminism' back then!!)[58]

In other words, the fact that she had heard the argument of a God-given order of creation many times before did not make it any easier to swallow. This quotation points to another important aspect: she was almost unfamiliar with the concept of feminism. That period in time was instead characterised by the relationship between the sexes that was described in Chapter 3, where men and women were perceived as complementary and women were subordinate within the framework of the housewife ideal. This viewpoint was almost a matter of course at a time when the gender-equality debate of our time had not yet had any major impact in Sweden.

Although the Lutheran doctrine of the three estates was the dominant theological narrative on vocation and gender at this time, a theological counter-narrative had begun to emerge that also claimed to be genuinely Lutheran.

A theological counter-narrative: equality in Christ

The ambivalent nature of Luther's views on the role of women in society is well known. As theologian Sasja Emelie Mathiasen Stopa's overview of the scholarly debate on Luther's views on women shows, opinions differ a great deal. Some academics claim that Luther cemented patriarchal structures; others maintain that his theology emphasised freedom and equality, which gradually laid the foundation for women's emancipation. On the basis of her analysis of Luther's lectures on the Book of Genesis, Stopa argues that the conflicting interpretations of his view on women are not so strange because that view is itself based on a patent paradox. On the one hand, Luther believes that woman is equal to man in relation to God and that she has also been given the power to rule over creation, primarily by being the leader of the household. On the other hand, Luther expresses a traditional view of women as being weaker and subordinate. Stopa argues that this paradox is rooted in the duality of Luther's theological anthropology, where humankind is seen as simultaneously sinful and righteous.[59]

It is equally well known that this ambivalence in Luther's view of women was also reflected in the attitude of Lutheran churches towards women's church leadership. For example, in his study of the role and ministry of women in early Lutheranism (seventeenth century), the professor of Reformation history Kenneth G. Appold shows that Luther's ambivalent attitude both enabled and prevented women's church leadership. As a result of the patriarchal structures of pre-modern society, however, the view that favoured the subordination of women came to dominate over the view that women were part of the priesthood of all believers with the ability and vocation to preach the Gospel. As socially determined barriers to women were gradually removed, for example when women gained access to higher education, a theological reassessment also occurred which enabled the alternative view to flourish.[60] Drawing on Honneth's theory, we believe that this development might be described as an expanded recognition that enabled a different understanding of priestly vocation.

In the Swedish church context of the mid-twentieth century, this view of vocation was theologically rooted in Galatians 3:28.[61] As was mentioned in the introduction to this book, this situation

59 Sasja Emelie Mathiasen Stopa, 'Women as Wives and Rulers in Martin Luther's Theology', *Dialog* (April 2023), 1–14.
60 Kenneth G. Appold, 'Frauen im frühneuzeitlichen Luthertum: Kirchliche Ämter und die Frage der Ordination', *Zeitschrift für Theologie und Kirche*, 103 (2006), 253–279.
61 Another debater in the Swedish context who used Galatians 3:28 as a key to interpretation and a justification for opening up the priesthood to women was Lydia Wahlström (1869–1954), who had a doctorate in history and was a well-known cultural figure who campaigned for women's political suffrage. However, when it came to the reform of the priesthood, she emphasised that 'it was not a feminist issue when it came to work for the Kingdom of God: here, according to Paul, it is "neither slave nor free, neither Jew nor Greek, neither man nor woman".' 'Kvinnan och prästämbetet', *Dagens Nyheter*, 27 April 1914.

was by no means unique to the Church of Sweden. According to biblical scholar David W. Kling, this biblical text is known as the 'Magna Carta of Humanity', 'the women's text', and 'a cardinal statement in the Scriptures FOR the emancipation of men and women'.[62]

One example of a theologian who contributed to such a reinterpretation – a theological counter-narrative of a Lutheran view of vocation that some of the first ordained women say they listened to and were inspired by – was Margit Sahlin.

Margit Sahlin on vocation

In the vocation narratives, Margit Sahlin (1914–2003) is mentioned on several occasions by the other women priests, both as an inspiring mentor and as someone they respected but could not regard as a role model.[63] Whether or not they shared Sahlin's views, her fellow ordained women knew of her thoughts on vocation and the priesthood.

Margit Sahlin was undoubtedly one of the best-known advocates, and in due course representatives, of women priests. After obtaining a doctorate in Romance languages in 1940, she studied theology and took a Bachelor of Theology degree in 1943. Between 1945 and 1970 she was secretary of the Church of Sweden National Board for Parish Life [Svenska kyrkans diakonistyrelse], and as such she had the task of assisting the Church of Sweden's parishes with inspiration in the form of lectures, courses, books, materials and the like. She founded diocesan women's councils throughout Sweden to promote women's opportunities for regular employment in the Church of Sweden, and also the Women's Church Council [Kvinnliga kyrkorådet] which organised the diocesan councils. She founded and was director of the St Catherine Foundation [St:a Katharinastiftelsen] from 1950 to 1970. In 1960 she was one of the first three women to be ordained as a priest, and in 1970 she became Sweden's first vicar [kyrkoherde]. Uppsala University awarded her an honorary doctorate in theology in 1978. She also wrote a number of books, including three on the theme of ministry and vocation. Two of

---

62 Kling, *The Bible in History*, p. 270.
63 No. 30; Caroline Krook in Karlsson, 'Caroline Krook'; No. 17; Mailice Wifstrand in Wifstrand, 'Dröm, plan och verklighet', p. 138; No. 24; No. 18.

them were published in the 1950s, the aforementioned *Man och kvinna i Kristi kyrka* (1950) and *Ordets tjänst i en förändrad värld* (1959).

In both books, but especially in *Man och kvinna i Kristi kyrka*, Sahlin anchors her thoughts on the priesthood in the story of the creation. She argues that the creation story is an expression of the fact that man and woman in union comprise the image of God.[64] This order of creation slipped into the background, but in Christ this relationship that God desired for his creation was restored. That message was passed on by St Paul in his letters, where he made no distinction between men and women. Sahlin cites a number of examples from the Pauline letters, but first of all Galatians 3:26–29, which is crucial to her argument.

However, owing to the prevailing patriarchal social context, Jesus only chose men to be apostles (in the Jewish context, women would not have been able to fulfil the mandate of an apostle); and it is the patriarchal social order that makes Paul utter the much-referred-to dictum according to which women should be silent in church.[65] This contrast between the 'genuinely Christian' and the 'pagan, Jewish, conservatively bourgeois, or whatever garb it adopts'[66] becomes the underlying theme in Sahlin's historical narrative.[67] This dark view of Judaism is problematic, particularly the tendencies towards supersessionism and replacement theology, which assumes that a superior Christianity will replace an inferior Judaism and emphasises the contrasts rather than the continuity between the two religions. This way of describing Christianity was, however, common in Sweden at the time.[68]

Sahlin's depiction of women's situation and position in ecclesiastical history stresses that the Church Fathers were influenced by the surrounding Roman society, which further reinforced ideas about

---

64 Sahlin, *Man och kvinna*, p. 13.

65 Ibid., pp. 18–37.

66 Ibid., p. 86.

67 As an example of that era's replacement theological tendencies, see, for example, Anton Fridrichsen's popular collection of sermons *Fyrahanda sädesåker: En kommentar till Evangeliebokens högmässotexter* (Stockholm: Svenska kyrkans diakonistyrelses bokförlag, 1958).

68 See Marianne Moyaert, *Christian Imaginations of the Religious Other: A History of Religionization* (Chichester: Wiley Blakwell, 2024). This has been the very foundation of Christian identity formation since the early days of the Christian church.

the subordination of women in the early church. According to Sahlin, these ideas are still present in the Roman Catholic Church in the idea that ordination does not 'take' on a woman. In her view Luther restores the authentic Christian concept of the creation and breaks away from the devaluation of women, the concept of different holy estates and the false view of the priestly office.[69] Sahlin describes how Luther's rediscovery faded from view over time, something that was 'reinforced by the strong Old Testament influence in the seventeenth century' – in other words, the Lutheran doctrine of the three estates – and the woman's role was limited to domestic life and housework.[70] What is truly Lutheran, though, is the view of humanity described in Galatians 3:28.

It is interesting to see how this egalitarian view to some extent goes against the final section of the book, which discusses the implications of this view for the contemporary church and its practices. Here, the discussion is characterised by a complementary approach. Sahlin emphasises that this creation-given, Christian equality does not mean uniformity. Man and woman are created 'to embody the image of God in their living unity, with its polarity between two elements that belong together yet are different'.[71] The church, however, has failed to capitalise on women's distinct nature, talent and power. It is not enough to have sewing groups; there need to be stable positions with adequate salaries, sanctioned and confirmed by the church through ordination.[72] Sahlin writes:

---

69 Sahlin, *Man och kvinna*, p. 84.
70 Ibid., p. 86.
71 Ibid., pp. 41–45.
72 Ibid., pp. 91–104. Sewing groups were an expression of the 'associational activity' that was characteristic of church life in Sweden from the mid-nineteenth to the late twentieth century. Exclusively for women, they convened on a regular basis in order to practise sewing and other handicrafts. A sewing group would frequently be attached to a Christian denomination. The sewing groups of the Church of Sweden were normally independent associations, but it was common for a priest, deacon or deaconess to join the group's meetings and provide a spiritual element. It was not unusual for a sewing group to arrange auctions where they would sell their handiwork, or arrange collections for charity. The purposes ranged from needs in the parish via missionary and local welfare work to refugee aid. In Sweden, the financial contribution from sewing groups to, for instance, mission work has been very considerable over the years. See Cecilia Wejryd, *Svenska kyrkans syföreningar 1844–2003* (Stockholm: Verbum, 2005).

It can feel oppressive for them [women] to have no real authority to fall back on when doing such responsible work, where they are in a sense the representatives of the church; to enter into the work merely based on a personally sensed inner call, a *'vocatio interna'*, or a short-term private mandate, and not to be able to rely on any external, 'objective' call, a *'vocatio externa'*, given by the parish or the church itself.

Just having an inner vocation is thus not enough; recognition is required as well. In Sahlin's view, however, this did not necessarily have to be the priestly office itself. Other types of ministry that could make use of women's special gifts were also a possibility.

Sahlin was not the only debater to advocate such a solution on the basis of a complementary view of the sexes. The then Archbishop of the Church of Sweden, Yngve Brilioth, also argued that the best solution was to arrange for some type of office specifically for women. Although he perceived no biblical arguments against the reform entailing the admission of women to the priesthood, he considered that this might threaten ecumenical relations, especially with the Church of England (more on this in Chapter 9). In addition, it would run counter to what he believed 'active church people' wanted: the Lutheran doctrine of the three estates. 'A Swedish church parish wants to view its priest as it does the father of the household in the parsonage. I believe this view is led by a correct instinct.'[73]

Brilioth does not wish to deny that there are advocates of reform who act 'on the basis of religious reasons', but he argues that the primary motive behind the calls for reform is secular equality, and that those who are pushing the demand are people who are not otherwise interested in the work of the church.[74] Newspapers report that in a talk on the theme 'Why not women priests?', he answered the question as follows:

The weakness in the campaign for women priests is that it has been propelled not as a wish from inside the church but as part of the demand for basic equality between the sexes [...] As far as the ordination of women priests is concerned, I believe that a serious split in the church would result if this issue were to be raised in our country. Such a thing would cause more harm than the benefit that could be gained by a woman's contribution in such a position. The fact is [...] that the somewhat politically orientated demand for

---

73 Yngve Brilioth, *Herdabrev till Uppsala ärkestift* (Stockholm: Diakoni-styrelsen, 1950), pp. 159–173 (p. 172).
74 Ibid., pp. 159–173 (p. 171).

the priestly ordination of women is currently the greatest obstacle to finding a suitable path for women's involvement.[75]

The archbishop also warned that Galatians 3:26–29 had been misused. According to Brilioth, the passage did not mean that no difference exists between the sexes, but that 'everyone should fulfil the task assigned to them according to their gifts and talents without envy or the desire to dominate'.[76]

Brilioth's reasoning is thus a clear example of the dominant theological narrative based on the Lutheran doctrine of the three estates, and on the associated belief that the desire for reform was driven by gender-equality motives and not theological ones – an idea that (as mentioned earlier) the first ordained women strongly opposed. The ways in which the archbishop's pronouncements on the reform were received in the public debate are intriguing, too. One comment in the newspapers was that Brilioth showed that an enlightened modern view of humanity stood in opposition to the conservative church.[77]

Both Brilioth and Sahlin were also criticised for proposing special job categories for women in the church.[78] It is therefore interesting to examine the wording of Sahlin's book that was published once the reform had been implemented: *Ordets tjänst i en förändrad värld* ['Serving the Word in a changed world']. In it she returns to her idea of a creation order in which man and woman complement each other and together form the image of God. She nuances her earlier reasoning somewhat, but still argues that while it may not be possible 'to identify certain constitutively female qualities', it is 'reasonable to think that such traits as maternal care, intuition and tender understanding of the deeply personal should generally be characteristic of women'. Although the priesthood is now formally open to women, it may therefore still be appropriate for women to be given specialised positions, such as those focused on pastoral care or missionary work, for which women with their distinctive nature would be well suited. However, Sahlin is careful to point out that it is important that these be priesthood posts, both so that their holders would have the support and security of ordination and

75 'Prästvigning av kvinna ett politiskt önskemål', *Dagens Nyheter*, 5 April 1954.
76 Ibid.
77 'Är kvinnans "Orenhet" bommen för predikstolen?', *Göteborgs Handels- och Sjöfarts-Tidning*, 23 September 1950.
78 Birgit Rodhe, 'Man och kvinna', *Sundsvalls Tidning*, 7 April 1951.

so that they can fulfil their role in practice by offering confession and Communion.[79] Once again, she stresses the importance of legal recognition to the ability to answer God's call.

Even so, the main purpose of *Ordets tjänst* was to provide principles for interpreting the Bible and arriving at an adequate view of the church. Regarding the former, the same ideas already appeared in *Man och kvinna i Kristi kyrka*, but they were not developed in depth until the new book was published in 1959.[80] It contains many references to Gustaf Wingren, and Sahlin was clearly inspired by his thinking when she formulated her ideas. She advocates that biblical texts should be interpreted in relation to their context and a functional understanding of the priestly office.[81] The idea that the essential message is incarnated in every time and culture also means that at a time when Christ's radical view of humankind has finally permeated Western thought, human beings may need to reassess how – and by whom – the Word can be communicated.[82]

This brings Sahlin to the issue of how to view the church. She stresses the importance of the priesthood of all believers and that the church is comprised of people who are living stones in a spiritual building, and that the only limit is at baptism.[83] Asserting that the entire church has a role to play in Christ's mandate to the world, she concludes:

> All the limbs of the Body of Christ, all the Christians of the church, are co-responsible in the life of the church, co-bearers of her debt, co-participants in her mission, co-trustees of her message and her action. The priest, therefore, cannot very well be Christ's representative in the specific sense that he personally embodies Christ's role and, for example, 'represents' Christ in the celebration of the Eucharist; instead, Christ is present in the Eucharist in that 'in, with and under' the form of bread and wine he gives himself to us, in the very communion of the meal, in which all share equally and in which the priest has the special mission of servant.[84]

As is apparent from this paragraph, Sahlin vigorously rejects the concept of representation and instead emphasises the importance of the priesthood of all believers and the idea of the folk church.

---

79 Sahlin, *Ordets tjänst i en förändrad värld*, pp. 52–57 (p. 51).
80 Sahlin, *Man och kvinna*, pp. 99–111.
81 Sahlin, *Ordets tjänst i en förändrad värld*, pp. 23–34.
82 Ibid., pp. 28–40.
83 Ibid., pp. 46–48.
84 Ibid., p. 49.

Ordets tjänst i en förändrad värld thus argues primarily from perspectives on the Bible and the church. The historical aspects are largely absent. Whether this is the reason why the negative view of Judaism corrupting egalitarian Christianity has essentially disappeared is something we must leave unexplored. Instead, another thought comes to mind: that a parallel exists between the question of women's access to the priesthood and racial issues. This idea may be expressed the way Sahlin does when she speaks of a

corresponding conflict between literal fidelity to certain words of the Bible and personal obedience to Christ [...] in the South African controversy over race. Those who assert a rigid concept of segregation and in its name permit what in Swedish eyes are unchristian atrocities claim to have the Word of God on their side.[85]

Sahlin is far from being the only person to draw these parallels; this is a recurring theme in the debate. The source materials compare the way in which the first women priests were treated to apartheid in South Africa as well as to discrimination against black people in the United States, often with reference to Galatians 3:28. For example, this is how one priest expressed himself in connection with the General Synod's refusal to ordain women in 1957:

I believe there is no difference in the relationship between the 2,091 priests who [in a survey] opposed women priests and the people of the African Union and the American South who refuse to allow Negroes [*sic*] to attend their services. They are all affected by the words of St Paul: 'There is no longer Jew or Greek, slave or free, male and female, for all of us are one in Christ Jesus.' How can an opponent of women priests react against the abuse of blacks by whites when they are guilty of the same abuse against their own family members who are women, or against fellow students and parishioners[?][86]

Because he was writing in the 1950s, the priest used a word that is unacceptable today because of its derogatory connotations. The same word appears on two other occasions in the source material, too,[87] and also in the 1970s, when the ordained women were denied recognition by their fellow priests and bishops.[88]

---

85 Ibid., pp. 30–31.
86 'Präst lämnar kyrkan: Skäms över beslutet', *Dagens Nyheter*, 3 October 1957.
87 No. 19.
88 Ann Lindgren, 'Söder får ingen kvinnlig präst', *Aftonbladet*, 12 June 1968; Brandby-Cöster, Nyman and Strid, *Kvinna – kyrka*, p. 20.

Similar parallels could be drawn to the Holocaust, as in the work of Sten Rodhe (1915–2014), who compares opponents of the reform to Nazis who want to 'explain away' what is written in Galatians 3:28 by saying that this equality only applies 'in Christ', that is, before God and not in society. Rodhe says that the Nazis interpreted this biblical passage in the same way in relation to the Jews. He continues: 'There have always been such Christians who, against the proposals to free slaves, to make Negroes [sic] equal to whites, to make women equal to men, have argued that the words "There is no longer Jew or Greek…" apply only "in Christ".'[89] Such an analogy might be viewed as problematic – both the comparison itself between two such different contexts and likening one's thought-opponents to racists or, as in Rodhe's case, implying that the opponent thinks like a Nazi. At the same time, this simile reminds us of two things that are important for understanding the theology that was being formulated at that time: first, it was not only the opponents of the reform who could be described as using harsh language; and, second, the expressions of opposition to the reform were perceived to be deeply offensive and unjust – and indeed they were in many respects. As Honneth has pointed out, denial of recognition usually leads to a reaction in the form of strife or conflict. It is also common for a group that has been denied recognition to compare its situation to that of other groups from whom what they regard as rightful recognition has been withheld. In the light of Honneth's theories, we might add that even though the comparison might be described as problematic, it is obvious why it is used.

To summarise, then, this debate featured two opposing theological narratives about vocation and gender. This tension between different understandings of vocation – between the ideal of the priesthood and the ideal of womanhood – recurs in the vocation narratives of the first women priests, particularly when they talk about family and having children.

Incompatible vocations?

Some of the first women to be ordained say that because of their calling to become a priest, they chose not to have a family.

---

89 Sten Rodhe, 'Manligt – kvinnligt – bibliskt', *Sydsvenska Dagbladet*, 10 March 1958.

For example, Birgitta Nyman mentions that 'not many women priests of my generation started a family, there wasn't the energy or time for it'. The reason, according to her, is that the first women priests were few in number and also in high demand to conduct various types of ceremony. She stresses that she and her female colleagues often felt that they 'were forced to prove our legitimacy and competence' by working almost all the time, saying 'yes' in all situations and ensuring that they were present in all contexts where they ought to be.[90] Many of the first women priests clearly believed that they had to overachieve in order to gain recognition for their vocation. For some of the priests in our material, this recognition obviously came at a high price, as other things had to be sacrificed.

Caroline Krook spoke in a similar vein in an interview with the newspaper *Aftonbladet* in 2004. When asked why she does not have any children, she replies that it stems from an older Catholic ideal of the priest by which 'the parish becomes your family' and you therefore do not have 'time or energy for anything else'. She states that she certainly does not share this priestly ideal, but that she would never have had the energy to have a family as well. In the article Krook implies that many of the first women priests might have refrained from starting a family because they 'entered a male profession on men's terms', which, according to her, was necessary but at the same time required sacrifices.[91]

The ordained women who did marry and had children not infrequently delineate a conflict between the demands of their vocation as priests and the various obligations they were under as wives and mothers. Britta Olén-van Zijl describes the challenges she faced as a priest but also relates these experiences to the situation of other working women at the time. She argues that it can be difficult in general for married women with children to combine paid work with the demands and expectations of family life. Judging from her story, it appears that she was expected to perform not only the tasks of the priest and the housewife, but also the role of the priest's wife.[92]

Olén-van Zijl and other ordained women had to live up to both the prevailing ideal of the housewife and the ideal of the

90 Sjöberg, 'Kyrkan måste vara ömsint', pp. 59–60.
91 Kerstin Weigl, 'Jag lekte med bilar och slogs', *Aftonbladet*, 3 April 2004.
92 Olén-van Zijl, 'Att få vara präst', pp. 109–110.

priest's wife. As the ecclesiastical historian Ulrika Lagerlöf Nilsson and the ethnologist Birgitta Meurling have noted, the work of a parish priest required a close partner who assisted with such tasks as providing support services in the home, supplying refreshments for meetings, teaching in and running Sunday schools, and leading sewing groups. In most cases, the priest's wife filled this role; otherwise a sister or some other female relative might step in. Under the Lutheran doctrine of the three estates, the priest was regarded as the head of the parish, and his wife was its mother and spiritual role model.[93] As the church historian Alexander Maurits has shown in his study of the role of the priest's wife from 1920 to 1987, that role underwent major changes during this period, in relation both to the social changes described in Chapter 3 and to the increasing professionalisation of church life, with employees increasingly taking over the tasks that the priest's wife had performed on a voluntary basis.[94] During the period studied here, though, the idea that a priest should have a wife was still very much alive. Olén-van Zijl was thus expected to plan and lead a Bible study group and also to take on the role of a priest's wife in providing food and drink for the participants.[95] This was obviously a challenge; but she notes that 'combining the duties of the priest with those of the housewife works quite well', because the priest has the freedom to organise her work as she wishes and can do a lot of household chores while others are working.[96]

Similar thoughts are expressed by Elisabeth Djurle Olander, who talks about the challenges of combining her profession as a priest 'with being a wife and mother'. She emphasises that coping with what contemporary Swedes call 'the jigsaw puzzle of life' would not have been possible if she had not had her husband's support in looking after the children and the household. In so doing he, too, went against the prevailing norms regarding responsibility for the

93 Ulrika Lagerlöf Nilsson and Birgitta Meurling, 'Vid hans sida – en introduktion', in Ulrika Lagerlöf Nilsson and Birgitta Meurling (eds), *Vid hans sida: Svenska prästfruar under 250 år – ideal och verklighet* (Skellefteå: Artos & Norma, 2015), pp. 7–12.

94 Alexander Maurits, 'Prästfrurollen under förändring: Prästfruar verksamma i Växjö stift omkring 1920–1987 berättar', in Lagerlöf Nilsson and Meurling (eds), *Vid hans sida*, pp. 75–100.

95 For a discussion of the demands on a priest's wife in the middle of the twentieth century, see ibid.

96 Olén-van Zijl, 'Att få vara präst', p. 110.

home and family.[97] The preconceptions about women's role and function that the first women priests wrestled with also appear in an obituary of Gunilla Öman (1942–2015, ordained 1967). Her husband, Hilding, was also a priest; and evidently Gunilla was expected to accept that her primary task was to perform the role of a priest's wife and help her husband.[98]

The expectations placed on priests are also addressed in a newspaper interview from 1967. It discusses the practical problems that might arise from being a woman priest, noting that 'you are your own priest's wife, and you have to be your own hostess'. Besides, it emphasises that '[n]obody really expects home-baked cookies in the parsonage or the parsonage apartment, but people do expect more than they would from an unmarried male priest'.[99] Consequently, the first ordained women would seem to have had a lot to live up to.

One of the priests in the material describes how these expectations about organising domestic arrangements might be expressed. She recalls the dinner that her future vicar and supervisor held the day before she was to be ordained. At the dinner, the priest stressed that it was important that those priests who served the large parish of up to 42,000 parishioners 'had their support services organised' and that '[t]here should be a housewife'. The woman priest notes that this was not possible for her and that she felt 'rather squashed'.[100]

Being a woman and a priest was hence not always easy owing to the prevailing norms and expectations in society at the time. Some of the priests in our material found it impossible to combine family life with the role of priest. The difficulties of having a full-time job as a woman in the 1960s were not unique to the first women priests, however; they were a general problem in society. The priests in our material who did start a family succeeded thanks to help from other people. This dependence on others and the support that the priests sometimes received is memorably illustrated in one of the vocation narratives. There, the priest describes how the women in the parish sewing group gave her home-made food one Christmas, because they realised that she did not have

---

97 Lina Sjöberg, 'Närhet och glädje: Elisabeth Djurle Olander, prästvigd 1960', in Hössjer Sundman and Sjöberg, *Du ska bli präst*, pp. 27–28.
98 'Minnesord Gunilla Öman', *Sundsvalls Tidning*, 10 January 2015.
99 Wik-Thorsell, 'Kvinnlig präst söker aldrig konflikterna'.
100 No. 42.

time to both discharge her duties as a priest and prepare all the food for the Christmas table.[101]

∞∞∞∞

This chapter has examined the ideological settings of the vocation narratives. We have presented some central themes in the first women priests' theological understanding of their vocation and discussed how these relate to theological schools of thought and to the contemporary theological context.

Both the first ordained women and Gustaf Wingren, the theologian whom a number of them cite as an inspiration, emphasise that the priestly office is a function – that the priest is at the service of the Word and the mission is to point to Christ. It is understandable that Wingren's strong criticism of apostolic succession and his view of the office-holder as being a servant of the Word became an important source of inspiration. Both the women priests and Wingren can be understood in relation to the theological school of thought that is so important for Sweden: the concept of the folk church. This is a theology that emphasises the priesthood of all believers – that everyone has a vocation and a mandate to communicate the Gospel.

In addition, we have discussed how the first women priests felt about ideas concerning gender and vocation. Again, there is a wide range of views, and far from all the writers comment on this topic in their vocation narratives. Among those who do, though, there are some interesting themes. We found that a number of the women strongly emphasised that they welcomed the reform of the priesthood for theological reasons, not for reasons of equality. This fits in well with the emphasis that they place on their being priests, purely and simply, not women priests. At the same time some of the ordained women had a complementary view of gender, a view according to which men and women are assumed to complement each other. This view might be cited as one reason for ordaining women to the priesthood, as women could be said to add something different since they possess qualities that men lack.

Their statements were placed in the context of the two collective theological narratives about gender and vocation that were prevalent at the time. In this case, the dominant narrative's Lutheran doctrine of the three estates was challenged by the words

---

101 No. 34.

of Galatians that in Christ, human beings are 'no longer male and female'. What is genuinely Lutheran is hence not a doctrine of the three estates in which woman is subordinate; rather, it is a view of humanity in which the categories of man and woman are cancelled in Christ through baptism. This theological counter-narrative, together with the functional *vocatio* understanding of the priest as servant of the Word, justified the women priests' struggle for the recognition of their vocation.

How this manifested itself in practice when different theological understandings of vocation faced off against one another is the focus of the next chapter.

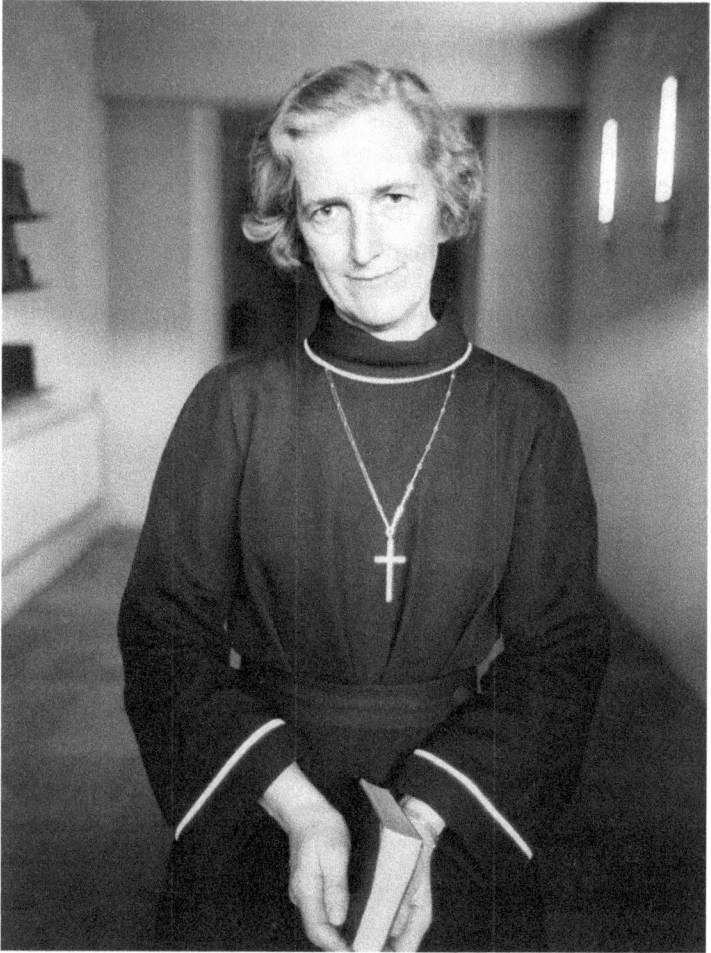

Margit Sahlin was not merely one of the first three women to be ordained; she also made essential contributions to theological reflection about vocation and ministry for a large part of the twentieth century. In her book *Dags för omprövning: Kring Bibel, kyrka och kvinnliga präster* (1980, pp. 32–33), she emphasises the theological reasons for the decision to introduce the reform, as well as for its implementation in practice: 'The crux of the matter was a desire to express fidelity to God's living Word, as well as joint responsibility for the vocation of the church in our own time. It was borne by a conviction that if the church were not to take this step, she would fail in her duty to preach the Gospel to today's changing society – to perform an act of testimony-in-action to the validity of the Word of God and his creative power in our own time.' (Image: copyright TT Nyhetsbyrån. Reproduced by permission.)

Chapter 5
The path to recognition: training and ordination

Memories have life. They don't resemble a herbarium with dry petals.
No, sometimes they flare up and hurt. The path to holy service was
difficult, a Way of the Cross. It is not possible to describe it in detail,
as the events are too close to us in time.[1]

If the question 'What was your path to ordination?' forms the
starting point of a narrative, its natural end point is, of course,
ordination itself. A number of vocation narratives do adhere to this
pattern: childhood, confirmation, adolescence, theological studies,
the pastoral training period and finally ordination. This chapter
shows how the first women priests describe the period leading up
to the climax of their narratives: ordination, the formal recognition
of their vocation.

In the Swedish context this path is sparsely researched, largely
because of a lack of source material. Britta Olén-van Zijl's comment
quoted above is one of the few occasions when the student years are
mentioned in published material; and when she did speak of this
period, she did so in order to emphasise that it was too painful and
sensitive to talk about. To what extent this is an experience shared
by more ordained women is impossible to say – perhaps accounts
of it were just not regarded as relevant – but it is clear that the first
women who were ordained to the priesthood very rarely speak
about their student years in interviews and in their own published
texts.

This is reflected in the present chapter, in which depictions of
student years are almost entirely based on the vocation narratives
from the LUKA archives. Unlike other material about the first
women priests, these narratives offer a relatively large amount of
information about the priests' education. The core episodes in the

1 Olén-van Zijl, 'Att få vara präst', p. 106.

narratives relating to the student years are often particularly long and detailed. Together they paint a picture of what it might have been like for a woman to train to be a theologian and priest in Sweden in the 1950s and 1960s. The narratives are not unanimous, though: not one shared experience applied to everyone. It is nevertheless possible to perceive recurring themes and patterns in these narratives, not least in relation to the environments in the two educational settings, Lund and Uppsala, and to the ecclesiastical context that was closely linked to the academic one.

Although the women's impressions and experiences during their student years have been veiled in obscurity until now, their ordinations were all the more public. They were covered by the media, and some were even broadcast live by Swedish television.

As a reader today, it is important to remember that what follows is an account of the situation in the 1950s and 1960s. The standpoints people assumed back then regarding the reform of the priesthood were not necessarily the same as those they held later on. It may also be worth pointing out how the term 'High Church' is used in the source material. The concept can mean a number of different things. In the Swedish ecclesiastical context, High Church might be used to describe everything from a liturgically based revitalisation movement within the Church of Sweden to an upward revaluation of the priestly office.[2] In other words, the epithet High Church does not necessarily mean that an individual opposes the reform of the priesthood. Similarly, opponents to the reform were present in other ecclesiastical groupings, such as revivalist-inspired piety movements.

In the vocation narratives, High Church is widely used as a synonym for opposition to the reform and in relation to two groups. The first is the Church Coalition for the Bible and Confession [Kyrklig samling kring bibeln och bekännelsen], a collaborative organisation for those in the Church of Sweden who wish to work together to ensure that the Bible and the Book of Concord should be the sole guiding principle within the church, and which was formed in 1958 in opposition to the decision to open the priesthood to women. The second is the Church Renewal Movement [Arbetsgemenskapen Kyrklig Förnyelse], a High Church

---

2 Carl Sjösvärd Birger, 'Den katolicerande riktningen i vår kyrka': Högkyrklig rörelse och identitet i Svenska kyrkan 1909–1946 [Acta Universitatis Upsaliensis: Studia Historico-Ecclesiastica Upsaliensia 52] dissertation (Uppsala: Uppsala University, 2022), pp. 14–19.

organisation that regards itself as a defender of the universal – Catholic – Christian heritage within the Church of Sweden. Some priests, Margit Sahlin among them, mourned the fact that because of this association between the High Church movement and opposition to the reform in the public debate, she was forced to renounce some features of the movement that she considered good and valuable, such as its liturgical and ecumenical endeavours.[3]

The educational period

Anyone who wanted to study theology in the 1950s and 1960s in order to become a priest in the Church of Sweden had a set path to follow. According to the curriculum, which had been in force with a few minor revisions since 1903, a four-year bachelor's degree in theology and a final term devoted to pastoral training were required.[4] The recommended approach was to complete the theoretical studies first, starting with exegesis and ecclesiastical history and moving on to ethics and dogmatics, and finally crown one's efforts with practical-theological studies, which were viewed as the transition to the actual practical training.[5] Judging from the vocation narratives of the first women priests, however, this outline was rarely followed in practice. The order of the subjects varied, and a few of the priests report that they had not completed all the theoretical courses when they started their practical-theology training.

A book list was supplied for each course, and there were oral examinations for each subject. According to the revised curriculum from 1936, no more than three students were permitted to attend each exam.[6] However, the most common thing was to do the exam alone. The student contacted the teacher to arrange a time and place, usually at the examiner's home but sometimes on university premises. The student was then expected to answer the questions posed by the teacher. The examiner's decision was recorded in a so-called grade book, which was then used as the basis for the degree awarded on completion of studies.

---

3 Nordlander, *Margit Sahlin*, p. 210.
4 Frida Mannerfelt, 'Kontrast och kontinuitet: Predikoideal i Svenska kyrkans prästutbildning 1903–2017', in Stephan Borgehammar (ed.), *Predikan i tid och otid* (Skellefteå: Artos, 2018), pp. 123–162.
5 *Studieplaner Lund* (1936), p. 4.
6 Ibid., p. 4.

The university was responsible for the pastoral training term as well. Although knowledgeable priests taught the course, the director would usually be the professor of practical theology.[7] The training was intended for candidates for ordination (that is, men); but where appropriate, women who aimed to become missionaries and teachers could also choose to take it. These women were expected to perform such tasks as leading morning prayers in schools and preaching in the mission field. Ordination normally followed completion of the pastoral training term. As one of the first women priests notes, until 1960 the last line of the curriculum read: 'Under Swedish law women cannot be ordained.'[8]

For people who wanted to be ordained, there was no set admission procedure. An individual usually contacted a bishop, often by telephone, and after a possible meeting with the bishop was told 'yes' or 'no'. Applicants were usually not completely unknown to the bishops. The pastoral training term included a two-month internship, which was normally arranged so that during the summer months, the student served as a pastoral assistant [*tjänstebiträde*] in a parish in the diocese for which they wished to be ordained. However, it was possible to work in some kind of social welfare function, such as health and social care, instead. Some of the first women to be ordained chose this option.

The bishop also gained information about the candidates for the priesthood when they applied for a scholarship to help finance their studies. The diocese administered money donated for this purpose, money that was distributed by the cathedral chapter, which included the bishop and the cathedral dean. The theology student groups in which the candidates were expected to participate could also function as meeting places. These groups were for candidates who would be working in a particular diocese, such as the theology student group of the diocese of Gothenburg. The purpose of the groups was to offer in-depth study and create good relations between future fellow priests who would be working in the same diocese.

A future theologian and priest had two places of study to choose from: Uppsala or Lund. From 1958 onwards, there was also an organisation in Stockholm called Stockholms teologiska institut [the Stockholm Theological Institute]. This not-for-profit organisation

---

7 *Studieplaner Lund* (1904), p. 5; *Studieplaner Uppsala* (1904), p. 5.
8 No. 25.

worked to promote the training of priests and teachers, to support theological training at Ersta-Sköndal (a college that trained future deacons) and to alleviate the severe shortage of priests in the diocese of Stockholm. Various courses were given in the afternoons and evenings, usually by teachers from the University of Uppsala.[9]

The university years

Theology students at Lund at this time were mainly taught what was known as 'Lundensian theology'.[10] In her autobiography, Ulla Nisser vividly describes what it was like:

> In a packed lecture theatre I listened to a lecture by Torgny Bohlin, who was an associate professor of dogmatics. He spoke about Eros and Agape, human and divine love [...] The book he drew on was written by Professor Anders Nygren – a groundbreaking book with the same title as the lecture we were listening to [...] The lecture on Eros and Agape, but also the study of Martin Luther and his book *On the Freedom of the Christian*, became essential [...] The theology teacher who came to mean an especially great deal to many of us who studied in Lund was Professor Gustaf Wingren. For me, who had been used since childhood to the Free Church's sharp division of spiritual and worldly, his way of holding the heavenly and the earthly together was something new. He said that our hope of eternity and our attachment to life here on earth are closely linked.[11]

Other priests also mention the great importance of Lundensian theology and Gustaf Wingren. However, Lundensian theology was not always appreciated by Lund professors. Another priest describes an occasion when she had to take an exam in dogmatics. At first the examiner did not want to permit her to take an exam on

---

9 ITH was dissolved as an association in May 2009, and its assets were used to create Stiftelsen för teologisk utbildning och forskning i Stockholms stift ('The foundation for theological education and research in the diocese of Stockholm').

10 Lundensian theology emerged in the 1920s as a reaction against liberal theology. Its leading figures, Anders Nygren (1890–1978), Gustaf Aulén (1879–1977) and Ragnar Bring (1895–1988), pursued a scientifically sound basis for theological work and distanced themselves from metaphysical speculation. Gustaf Wingren's theology was developed partly in relation to and partly in reaction against Lundensian theology, not least via a marked upward revaluation of the significance of human agency in the Christian faith.

11 Nisser, *Hopp från trampolin*, pp. 71–72.

the syllabus for the entire term because, she says, he thought it was 'too difficult for girls'. She stood her ground.

> I: So I took the exam in April and he began by asking, 'What's wrong with Lundensian theology?' and I was furious, so I said, 'There's nothing wrong with Lundensian theology.' It was not a good start. But the Lundensian theologians Nygren, Billing, Gustaf Wingren have meant so much to me, to the whole of Lund, so that theology in Sweden is orientated towards Denmark, Kierkegaard, Grundtvig and Germany, and not, as in Uppsala, towards English philosophy [...] then he questioned me for an hour and a quarter, and then he failed me. Then he said to me: 'Are you going to become a priest?' 'Yes', I said, because by then it was known, and I was almost ready to graduate [sighs]. And then he said: 'Do you have a talented brother?' 'Yes,' I said, 'I have two of them.' 'Then you should know that what you believe is your calling from God is just penis envy.'
>
> AM: And he said that during this exam
> I: Yes.
> AM: – when it was just you and
> I: Him.
> AM: – your teacher.
> I: Yes. But I left there in tears [... and went] straight to Benkt-Erik Benktson, whom you are welcome to mention. He was an associate professor of dogmatics and I also knew him privately through a mutual friend. His wife came to the door and saw me crying and said: 'Benkt-Erik is in the library. I'll put on some coffee.' And I told him all about it and he said, 'You could consider a public exam, but I think you've stuck your nose out enough. But I can give you credit for half.' He had permission to credit parts of this exam, and so he did. And then I calmed down.[12]

Benkt-Erik Benktson (1918–1988) appears to have used this method of helping students with their exams on several occasions. Another priest describes meeting Benktson in 1967 at the Sigtuna Foundation, at which time he encouraged her to become a priest. When she told him that she balked at having to supplement her degree by taking an oral exam with a well-known opponent of the reform of the priesthood, he offered to let her take the exam with him.[13]

The incident with the examiner is an example of how standpoints held in the ecclesiastical context might inappropriately and calculatedly influence language and behaviour in the academic

12 No. 34.
13 No. 19.

context. This case is also an example of a situation in which a woman needed a man's help to be recognised on her merits.

Another Lund teacher who is warmly mentioned is Associate Professor Per Erik Persson (1923–2019), in relation to his book *Kyrkans ämbete som Kristus-representation: En kritisk analys av nyare ämbetsteologi* ['The ministry of the church as a representation of Christ: a critical analysis of recent theology of ministry'] (1961), which, according to Margareta Brandby-Cöster, 'provided important insights into the issue of the ministry'.[14] The historical overview *Sveriges kyrkohistoria* ['The church history of Sweden'] mentions it as a book that led to an intense debate.[15]

In his book Persson discusses the New Ecclesiology, which he believed had led to a new view of the ministry. According to Persson, the prime example of this reorientation is the anthology *En bok om kyrkans ämbete* ['A book on the church's ministry'] from 1951, edited by Hjalmar Lindroth (1893–1979), which brought together many of the representatives of this new view of the church. Persson bluntly argues that it is scientifically dishonest for people not to openly state that they base their view of the ministry on the post-biblical theological tradition, instead trying to claim that they are expressing Reformation theology rooted in the Confessions and the Bible.[16] This standpoint was probably a major reason why he was appreciated by the first women priests.

It is interesting to note that none of the priests mentions anything about tuition in relation to the Lund theologian and university teacher Gustaf Wingren, who they say was so important for their view of the theology of vocation. The two occasions when Wingren is mentioned other than as a theological inspiration centre on the fact that his clear theological standpoint was not always expressed in action. Two of the priests mention that although Wingren strongly supported women's right to be ordained, he was less self-evidently supportive of women's career opportunities in the academy. He often encouraged male students to continue doing research but never female ones, and the female doctoral students he did have never received any doctoral scholarships.[17] Wingren could thus be an example of how taking a principled stand on the issue

---

14 Brandby-Cöster, *Hur gick det till?*, p. 33.
15 Brohed, *Sveriges kyrkohistoria*, p. 215.
16 Per Erik Persson, *Kyrkans ämbete som Kristus-representation: En kritisk analys av nyare ämbetsteologi* (Lund: Gleerup, 1961), p. 352.
17 Brandby-Cöster, *Hur gick det till?*, p. 34; No. 34.

of women's ordination did not necessarily mean that an individual also stood outside the patriarchal structures of the day.

The Lund Faculty of Theology was thus home both to theologians who strongly favoured the reform and had a view of the ministry that would support it, and those who expressed a contrary view. Some of the latter taught Biblical Studies. In 1951, together with colleagues at Uppsala, they formulated a consultation response known as the exegetes' declaration [Exegetdeklarationen], which played a major role in the debate over the opening-up of the priesthood to women.

Biblical Studies was a core subject in the training programme, and several of the priests mention how difficult the Biblical Studies courses were in their vocation narratives. Despite the curriculum recommendation that these courses be taken early on, several priests say they put off exegesis as long as they could. It is not surprising that both women and men were apprehensive about the study of ancient languages. However, women had additional reasons to be anxious about certain courses, particularly Biblical Studies. In the exegetes' declaration of 1951, virtually all the Biblical Studies teachers at both Lund and Uppsala had rejected the proposal to admit women to the priesthood.

The background to the exegetes' declaration lay in the context of the church. Five years earlier the General Synod had commissioned 14 experts, led by the Bishop of Härnösand Torsten Bohlin (1889–1950), to investigate the question of women's eligibility for the priesthood. The results of this commission of inquiry were presented in early February 1951. The experts were not unanimous, but the majority, including Bohlin, concluded that there were no obstacles to ordaining women. The majority view was that the idea that women should be silent in church was an expression of the ancient world's view of women and could not be considered binding on the church in all times. Besides, the commission recognised that women were already active in parish work, including preaching. Most of the experts argued that whether or not someone could become a priest depended on personal suitability and not on biological sex. However, five of them dissented from the commission's report. One said she felt the proposal did not go far enough; the other four were of the opinion that the priesthood should not be opened up to women at all.[18]

---

18 Kvinnas behörighet till kyrkliga ämbeten och tjänster: Betänkande av inom ecklesiastikdepartementet tillkallade sakkunniga, SOU [Swedish Government Official Reports], 1950:48.

The proposal was submitted for consultation to a number of bodies, and the exegetes' response was one of those that attracted particular attention. The response document was signed by those individuals who were teaching New Testament studies at Lund and Uppsala at that time, namely the professors Anton Fridrichsen (1888–1953) and Hugo Odeberg (1898–1973) and the associate professors Bo Reicke (1914–1987), Harald Riesenfeld (1913–2008), Ernst Percy (1901–1968), Henrik Ljungman (1917–1998) and Evald Lövestam (1921–2009). In November 1951 they issued a joint statement in which they argued that the introduction of women priests in the Church was incompatible with New Testament perspectives. The statement was quoted by the newspapers:

> We, the undersigned, professors and associate professors of New Testament exegesis at the nation's two universities, hereby declare as our firm opinion, based on careful research, that the introduction of so-called women priests into the Church would be incompatible with New Testament beliefs and would constitute a departure from fidelity to Holy Scripture. Both Jesus' selection of apostles and St Paul's words on the position of women in the congregation are a matter of principle and independent of temporal circumstances and opinions. The current proposal that women should be admitted to the priesthood in the Church of Sweden must therefore be said to encounter serious exegetical obstacles.[19]

The exegetes' declaration may be regarded as an expression of the New Ecclesiology, which many of the exegetes embraced.[20] However, the reception of the biblical scholars' declaration in the public debate was lukewarm to say the least. The exegetes were considered to have 'undoubtedly exceeded their remit as exegetes' by speaking as 'Church Christians and Church politicians', and 'have thereby revealed their strange way of conducting research and written their own declaration of incompetence'.[21] The various consultation responses were so widely publicised in the debate that it was easy to overlook the fact that only a few people stood behind expressions such as 'the exegetes' declaration' or 'the theologians' groups'.

---

19 'Exegeterna emot kvinnliga präster', *Dagens Nyheter*, 9 November 1951.

20 Brohed, *Sveriges kyrkohistoria*, pp. 148–150; Berntson, Nilsson and Wejryd, *Kyrka i Sverige*, pp. 320–322; Wejderstam, *Personlig och kyrklig förnyelse*, pp. 53–54.

21 'Exegeterna har överskridit sina befogenheter', *Svenska Morgonbladet*, 19 November 1951.

It is, of course, impossible to know how much influence the biblical scholars' declaration actually had on the first women priests' experience of their student years; but since their future as priests depended on passing Biblical Studies, this statement by influential teachers must have had some impact. Although a teacher's attitude to the reform was not always known, the exegetes' declaration suggests that the individual responsible for teaching the course was very likely to have had a negative attitude to the women's aim with their studies. As in the example of the exam that ended with the future priest being accused of penis envy, it was not rare for examiners to ask about a student's plans for the future, and the vocation narratives contain examples of how this could in some cases lead to being failed or not being credited for the course. It is therefore not surprising that succeeding in an exam was considered to be an unusual and important event and thus functioned as a nuclear, or core, episode in the narrative of the path to becoming a priest.

Per Erik Persson writes that there was a difference in attitude to the reform between Uppsala and Lund.[22] This view is supported by the vocation narratives. Although there are examples from Lund of Biblical Studies causing concern, it is especially the priests who studied at Uppsala who dwell on this aspect. One priest who studied at both places says that she took all her Biblical Studies exams with well-known opponents of the reform, Bertil Gärtner (1924–2009) and Hugo Odeberg, and describes the nervousness she felt. However, it went 'perfectly well' in both cases.[23] Another priest tells of her relief after passing the exam in New Testament studies with Odeberg, which she passed 'because I carefully read up on the professor's so-called hobbyhorses'.[24]

Some of those who studied Biblical Studies at the faculty in Uppsala describe similar agonies when facing Professor Harald Riesenfeld. One priest, who is otherwise tight-lipped about her teachers, writes: 'On 21 November 1969 I took my last exam, and it was in NT exegesis for Prof. Riesenfeld. A good feeling filled me when I saw that I had received a top grade.'[25] One priest says that

---

22 Per Erik Persson, 'Glädjebudet – det allt avgörande', in Hössjer Sundman (ed.), *Äntligen stod hon i predikstolen!*, pp. 43–60.
23 No. 26.
24 No. 24.
25 No. 19.

she was really nervous, but also that she was pleasantly surprised by her meeting with the professor.

> The Novum exam – the study of the New Testament – I put off until the last minute. I was well aware of my insecurity in Greek, the language in which the New Testament is written and which I had to read and translate. I also had some fear of my examiner, Professor Riesenfeld. He was considered to be extremely strict and meticulous at his job. In short, I feared that he would be my Waterloo! [...] Pale and worn out, having read myself half to death, I entered Professor Riesenfeld's office nervous and on trembling legs. With a friendly smile he asked me to sit down comfortably in the chair he indicated so that we could talk! [...] I don't know how long this exam took. Time just flew by. But we got a lot done, so it must have lasted about an hour [...] This learned man opened wide for me the door to the New Testament world with Christianity's emergence and origin in Jesus Christ in a way I would call a revelation! He took me up the Mount of Transfiguration.[26]

In the above examples, we can see that despite the justified concerns expressed by several priests about taking an exam on a subject known to be difficult with an examiner who had publicly opposed the reform, several of the women end by saying that they were favourably surprised by their friendly reception. Consequently, it appears that a stand taken on principle was not necessarily reflected in inappropriate language or bad manners; indeed, the opposite might be true.

Even so, the reception by the exegetes does not always seem to have been so amicable. One priest who studied at Uppsala says that for her exam, she was given the task of translating the Beatitudes. She passed the exam, but the professor refused to enter any grade in her grade book and only noted that she had sat for it.[27]

Like Per Erik Persson, several of the first women priests testify to the general feeling that there was stronger resistance to the reform at Uppsala than at Lund. One reason for this might be that the New Ecclesiology was particularly well represented at Uppsala. Not only the biblical scholars but also several teachers of systematic theology sympathised with this view of the Church, whose idea of the priesthood frequently resulted in an unfavourable attitude to the reform. However, the vocation narratives reflect both the rule and the exception. One of the priests who studied for her Bachelor

---

26 No. 8.
27 No. 5.

of Theology degree at Uppsala at the end of the 1950s reports as follows:

> As far as I can remember, none of my female colleagues dared to say a word about any possible plans to become a priest. The opposition among the teachers was sometimes very obvious, but even more frequently unspoken. It was assumed that this was so. I cannot recall a single one declaring a favourable attitude.[28]

Another teacher from Uppsala mentioned in the narratives was the Professor of History of Religions, Geo Widengren (1907-1996). He features in a core episode of one priest's vocation narrative. She says: '[t]here were many tall tales about the dangerous Professor Widengren in History of Religions. He walked around Uppsala attired in riding breeches, boots and a riding crop.' She further describes how difficult it was to book a date for the exam with him and that he became annoyed when she persisted in securing an appointment. Before the exam itself she was very nervous, not least because he had been grouchy when she was making the appointment. She writes:

> My legs felt like boiled spaghetti when I finally managed to get there. The professor didn't look up after shouting 'come in'. He just sat there glowering at his papers. I did not know what to do. Suddenly he said in a loud voice: 'ONE thing I thank God for every night in my evening prayer is that I was not born a woman.' Even a mouse can get angry at a cat. I snapped back, 'Unfortunately, I cannot of course thank and praise God for that reason.' He looked up in surprise, asked me to sit down and began the oral exam [...] Suddenly there was a conversation, a real conversation, in which I dared to ask questions, but did not receive any pat replies. It was a journey of discovery, and I no longer felt stupid. We exchanged ideas. That exam took several hours, but I got my pass with distinction plus a friendly exhortation to continue studying the history of religions. At first I was extremely flattered, but later I began to wonder whether it was a smart move to avoid seeing me be ordained.[29]

In the light of this description, it is understandable why another priest, who is more reticent about her student years, still chooses to mention that she was particularly proud of being been passed in history of religions by Widengren, whom she describes as 'a feared

---

28 No. 28.
29 No. 42.

examiner'.[30] However, judging from the first priest's narrative, the experience could also be a good one.

The fact that Widengren stood out as an intimidating examiner, and that he sometimes wore riding garb when lecturing or examining students, is well known. In his biography of Widengren, the history of religions scholar Göran Larsson touches on the misogynistic attitude that both teachers and students at the Uppsala faculty could hold towards women who were studying theology in order to become priests. According to Larsson, it is difficult to categorise Widengren as belonging to this group, and he cites a couple of examples when Widengren actually supported female students. The biography also makes it clear that Widengren often mentioned what he regarded as students' lack of knowledge in general and knowledge of history of religions in particular.[31] If this attitude was widely known among the students, it might have contributed to the impression of Widengren as a dreaded examiner.

Nevertheless, there are occasional stories from women priests who studied at Uppsala about faculty members who explicitly supported the reform and encouraged the women students of theology to become priests. Astrid Andersson Wretmark (1939–, ordained 1966) describes how the Professor of Practical Theology, Åke Andrén (1917–2007), encouraged her to be ordained for the priesthood: 'Miss Andersson, you will take holy orders.' These words had a decisive impact on her, because before this conversation she had not been certain that she would indeed become a priest.[32]

Another reason why the women theology students at Uppsala experienced their study environment as more difficult than did their counterparts at Lund probably has to do with their fellow students and social environment. Considerably more narrative episodes from Uppsala describe an unfavourable attitude on the part of fellow students. One priest began her studies at the Stockholm Theological Institute but moved to Uppsala in 1963 to complete the programme:

30 No. 25.
31 Göran Larsson, *Geo Widengren: Stridbar professor i en föränderlig tid* (Stockholm: Bokförlaget Langenskiöld, 2023), pp. 90–93, 116–120.
32 Lina Sjöberg, 'Jag har aldrig blivit bibringad föreställningen att livet skulle vara enkelt: Astrid Andersson Wretmark, prästvigd 1966', in Hössjer Sundman and Sjöberg, *Du ska bli präst*, p. 31.

[I] experienced an isolation there, even among my fellow theology students in Uppsala, that I had not experienced before. I found it difficult to be myself. I had difficulty talking about my thoughts about becoming a priest, which were increasingly beginning to take shape in me. It felt forbidden, even when nothing was said about it.[33]

Another priest who studied at Uppsala from 1957 to 1961 says that the atmosphere in the student residence where she lived was tense on the day when the first ordinations of women priests were announced, and that someone even played Chopin's funeral march on the piano.[34] Narratives from the latter part of the 1960s also describe hostile reactions from other students. Ulla Nisser, who by then had moved from Lund to Uppsala, supplies a detailed account of how, in breaks between lectures, the female students might be interrogated by male fellow students about their future plans, and how an affirmative answer often led to vigorous questioning.[35] Another priest who was studying at Uppsala at the same time says that some women students were badly affected, but that she herself was fortunate because she was well informed about the arguments for and against the reform. But she says that those among her colleagues who were not so informed 'suffered a lot from spiteful but also childish attacks by students who were opposed'.[36] Some of the priests studied here, however, did not experience any opposition or resistance on the basis of beliefs about the priesthood. One of the priests we interviewed states that '[t]here were never any unpleasant incidents or bad behaviour from anyone'.[37]

While reports of negative treatment by fellow students who opposed the reform are far more common from the women priests who studied at Uppsala, they are not completely absent in the narratives from Lund. For example, one priest who came to Lund in 1958 says, '[m]any of my fellow students in the theological survey course were fanatically opposed to the decision and the waves of discussion ran high, not always in a warm comradely spirit'.[38]

As was mentioned earlier, some of the first women to be ordained studied at the Stockholm Theological Institute. Compared

33 No. 37.
34 No. 25.
35 Nisser, *Hopp från trampolin*, pp. 74–76.
36 No. 30.
37 No. 33.
38 No. 29.

to the Faculty of Theology at Uppsala, the Institute had a more Low Church profile.[39] The director of the Institute, Gösta Hök (1903–1978), was a well-known name among the proponents of the reform and often participated in the public debate.[40] When the vocation narratives mention Hök, they stress his support for the female ordinands.[41] One of the women comments on what an important support Hök was in his role as an academic teacher, and says that he took her 'vocation profoundly seriously'.[42] However, the vocation narratives reveal that opposition could exist among the students at the Stockholm Theological Institute as well. Here, too, female candidates might find themselves compelled to defend their vocation and their future career choice. Some of the narratives describe how the women students tried to support one another. One of the priests who studied at the Institute writes about her friend and future fellow priest:

> She was small and dark, delicate, but my goodness when she raised her voice ... Oh yes, the 'male theology students' would tremble. [She] was never mean, but she was stubborn and she knew what she wanted. Straightforward and genuine. She became my strength, my crutch for many years.[43]

Theology student groups

Candidates for ordination were expected to participate in a group of theology students in their place of study. The groups were organised on a diocesan basis, so that the students could get to know their future priestly colleagues. Usually, the bishop would visit 'his' candidates in the group on a fairly regular basis. The groups normally met in the evenings and invited various guest speakers to dispense additional theological and pastoral insights.

The few mentions of the theology student groups in the vocation narratives portray episodes when the female candidates were treated badly. Two priests, both from the diocese of Gothenburg, say that they had a frosty reception when they joined their theology student group. The diocese of Gothenburg – and apparently also

39 No. 42.
40 'Stockholmspräster protesterar mot kyrkomötet i kvinnofrågan', Stockholms-Tidningen, 1 October 1957.
41 No. 44.
42 No. 42.
43 No. 42.

its theology student group at Lund – was home to high-profile opponents of the reform. Any woman who visited this theology student group would be expected to 'bond with the male theologians', and she would aim to become a priest's wife, not a priest.[44]

Another example of how the first women priests might experience a theology student group was Inger Svensson's relationship with the diocese of Växjö's group at Lund. The primary-source collection *Kvinnliga präster i Växjö stift?!* ['Women priests in the diocese of Växjö?!'] contains a number of extracts from minutes and letters from the theology student groups and the diocesan youth council. The collection reveals that the Växjö diocesan theology student group intervened in ways that were unconventional for the times to try to persuade Bishop David Lindquist (1905–1973) not to ordain Svensson.[45] Prior to her impending ordination, Svensson spoke in an interview about the resistance she had encountered from other theology students from her home diocese: 'A group of my own fellow students paid me a personal visit and said that I must not destroy Växjö diocese and cause division within the Church of Sweden. Since then the group has contacted me at regular intervals.'[46]

No more statements about theology student groups appear in the vocation narratives of the first women priests. However, some priests report participating in a different type of gathering: ones exclusively for women candidates for ordination. For example, two priests say that they were invited to the home of Bishop Martin Lindström (1904–2000) in Lund together with other future female theologians.[47]

Other meetings might be organised by the students themselves. Margareta Brandby-Cöster describes two such occasions at Lund:

> The meetings, as I recall, were held quite late at night, and as I walked there in the dark, I saw other women fellow students walking in the same direction and thought: Oh, I can't believe she is one! Once Margit Sahlin (1914–2003) was invited to talk about what it was like for a woman to be a priest. I remember that we sat in a semicircle around her and listened. The second time, Britta van Zijl (1927–2017) was invited. She was ordained in 1963 and had

44 Brandby-Cöster, *Hur gick det till?*, pp. 30–31. See also No. 34.
45 Bexell, Hagberg and Posse, *Kvinnliga präster i Växjö stift?*, pp. 58–62, 82–85.
46 Simonsson, 'I tre år har G A Danell tjatat på henne'.
47 No. 34; No. 45.

experience of South Africa. It's mostly the atmosphere of those meetings that I remember vividly. We sat there in the dark, as if we were alone in the world and as if this was something very important. That's how it felt.[48]

Birgitta Nyman attended the same event. She says that she and her fellow students had looked at Margit Sahlin with uncomprehending eyes and laughed when Sahlin said it was vital to stick together, create networks and support one another. They had believed it was self-evident that the Church of Sweden would receive and accept them. Looking back, she says that Sahlin's advice was important, and that she and other women priests 'needed to have stuck together'.[49]

A third priest who studied at Lund also attended the meeting. She says she spent a lot of her time at the St Lawrence Foundation [Laurentiistiftelsen] student residence, where many theology students lived. She regularly took part in devotional life and had been promised a place high up on the waiting list for a room at the residence, but after attending this meeting with Margit Sahlin she had slipped far down the list. She does, however, end by saying that this was the first occasion when she had encountered such expressions of opposition to the reform and that she had found it strange.[50]

Trainee periods

Candidates for ordination also had to serve at least two months as a trainee. The core episodes depicting memories of this period are usually more light-hearted in character. As we showed in Chapter 4, experiences of preaching and leading services at the altar as a trainee often had a great impact on the sense of vocation.

---

48 Brandby-Cöster, *Hur gick det till?*, p. 36.
49 Sjöberg, 'Kyrkan måste vara ömsint', p. 59.
50 No. 45. The St Lawrence Foundation is an independent residential organisation with accommodation for students; it has its own church, which belongs within the Church of Sweden. Services have a High Church profile, and its clergymen superintendents have traditionally belonged to this tendency within the Church of Sweden. There is a similar foundation with a High Church orientation in Uppsala, the St Ansgar Foundation. See Sven-Oscar Berglund, *Laurentiistiftelsen i brytningstid: Minnen från ett studenthems tillkomst och uppbyggnad* (Lund: Lunds universitets kyrkohistoriska arkiv, 2000).

Two of the priests devote a particularly large amount of space in their vocation narratives to this trainee period.

One of these two priests initially had a bad experience. She had applied to be an assistant priest in the diocese of Luleå, but was told by the diocese that this would be too controversial. However, she would be welcome as a 'guest'. According to her, the summer as a guest was a short one, and one contributing factor was that the parish priest's wife was very sceptical about the reform.[51] The guest therefore broke off her traineeship and went home. But when she returned to the same diocese a year later, things had changed. The meeting with the dean and his wife was an entirely different story:

> I was warmly welcomed by the dean and his wife [...] Wearing a grey silk jacket, the dean came hurrying out of the office door. His water-combed grey-white hair shone beautifully against his friendly, sun-tanned face. His eyes assessed me with scrutinising benevolence and a good measure of curiosity. And then I got a big hug!! So this was the dean! And then came his wife – mother [name]. Bright, warm, cheerful eyes, well-groomed wavy hair à la 1920s, hands that spoke of much housework interspersed with parish work as the parish's unpaid assistant. She pressed me tenderly to her heart. Even then I realised that I had found friends and so-called 'mentors' for life.[52]

The other priest who gave an unusual amount of space to trainee periods says that she first worked with Ingrid Persson in the diocese of Härnösand. In this case, too, the supervisor became a mentor. 'Ingrid Persson became a friend and, above all, a supporter, a role model and an intercessor. "I pray for my girls", she used to say, referring to me and all the others who came after me as assistants or trainees.'[53] How much it could mean to have a woman priest as a supervisor during one's traineeship is also testified to by another priest, for whom Elisabeth Djurle Olander became a role model.[54] After her time with Ingrid Persson, the future priest also got a taste of what it was like to serve in the diocese of Lund. She describes her senior parish priest as 'original'. A man with a distinctly Low Church profile, he thought it self-evident that women could be priests.[55]

---

51 No. 24.
52 Ibid.
53 No. 28.
54 No. 33.
55 No. 28.

A number of interesting themes emerge from these narratives. First, the importance of being welcomed – to use Honneth's term: of receiving social recognition – by future fellow priests, but also how discouraging it was when this recognition was denied. Second, the importance of mentors and role models. Not infrequently, these appear to have had a distinctly Low Church profile and a view of the priestly office that emphasised function rather than representation and gender. Nevertheless, it should be pointed out that just like High Church priests, Low Church ones could also react to the reform in different ways: even the latter might have an unfavourable opinion of it.

The pastoral training term

The last part of a priest's training before the final examination before the cathedral chapter was the pastoral training period. A number of the women priests describe this term as definitely the hardest part of their training. It could be demanding for several reasons. One priest who went through this training at Uppsala in the autumn of 1969 notes that it was a tough term with regard to studying, because she had three other courses with final exams at the same time.[56] The reason given most often, however, is the behaviour of some of the opponents of the reform. For example, one priest says: 'During the training term I encountered the toughest and most compact resistance to women priests that I have ever experienced.'[57] Another observes that the pastoral training term 'was a real trial. For the first time the resistance was open and authorised, among both teachers and participants.'[58] Yet another priest says that after the pastoral training term, she was so worn out by the pressure from those of her fellow students who opposed the reform that she was on the verge of fainting throughout her ordination ceremony.[59] A fourth says that after her training period, she felt 'so lost that I did not dare to ask for ordination in any diocese at all'.[60]

This experience of the pastoral training term as being the focal point for unpleasant expressions of opposition to the reform

---

56 No. 19.
57 No. 29.
58 No. 42.
59 No. 5.
60 No. 29.

occurred at both Lund and Uppsala. There were differences, though. In the Lund case, the picture is complex. Several of the narratives mention opposition, but others paint a bright and positive picture. One priest who attended the training term at Lund in the autumn of 1958 writes: 'There was good camaraderie between the students on the training term, even during the turbulent days when the law on authorising women priests was hotly debated.'[61] However, another priest who took the training at around the same time has radically different memories:

> During that course I really felt the resistance to women priests. Not on the part of the tutors, but on that of my male fellow students. They said (one of them eventually became an archbishop) that they couldn't reconcile themselves to the idea of a woman priest [...] They wanted nothing to do with me performing services at the altar. My male fellow students got together and agreed to ignore my altar service. Since they were obliged to be present, they could not protest with their absence. They decided to behave as usual while I performed the service, but they promised one another not to take any notice of my doing so. The 'protesters' even complained to one of the teachers, as they considered their plight too difficult.[62]

The male students also felt that female students should become teachers or deaconesses instead of aspiring to the priesthood. This priest was not alone in her experience. A priest who did her training period at Lund a few years later, in the spring of 1964, has much to say about it:

> When one of us women had given a sermon in the group, we were always told: 'That's fine for a parish evening meeting, but not for the pulpit.' [...] Sometimes I was told that the ordination of a woman was ineffective in all circumstances. It could be equated with the baptism of a pig. Sometimes I was so discouraged that I could scarcely bear to go to lectures and practice sessions. Eventually, though, the end of the training period came. It was customary for the groups in the training term to end with 'quiet days'. This gave the candidates for ordination the opportunity to rally prior to their upcoming task, pray together and receive the Lord's Holy Communion. Unfortunately, our group missed out on this. Without my knowledge, the 'true believers' had decided that they could not receive Holy Communion together with a female priest-to-be. The course administrators then decided that in such circumstances they

61 No. 21.
62 No. 18.

could not arrange any 'quiet days' for us, and so we were deprived of this mustering of our strength. Naturally, this was not the fault of the administrators; rather, the reason was, of course, the prevailing atmosphere in our group.[63]

This quotation recalls a type of jargon that was employed by certain groups who opposed the reform. As we will demonstrate, this practice was common and should be viewed in the context of how influential anti-reform figures expressed themselves in public. Also noteworthy is the apparent deference by the course administrators, which seems to have been motivated by a presumption that the reform opponents were to be given precedence. The above passage also provides a striking example of the consequences of being denied recognition in a social context.

Ingrid Persson also attended the practical training at Lund at this time, in the autumn of 1959. She describes it as 'a fine term'. According to Persson, she chose Lund instead of Uppsala partly because the term leader at Uppsala was known to oppose the reform. The clear difference between the two places of study became even more obvious to her when the group from Lund visited the group at Uppsala. One of the Uppsala candidates asked to speak to her because he wanted to ensure that they would not be ordained for the same diocese and that he would be at no risk of serving alongside her. This was particularly problematic with regard to the Eucharist, he said, because the Eucharistic gifts are not transformed into the body and blood of Christ if a woman distributes them.[64]

Another priest tells of a similar experience on a visit to Uppsala after describing her happy experience of the training term at Lund. According to her, the students at Uppsala greeted her 'only after they had made the sign of the Cross'. She goes on to write: 'Making the sign of the Cross was not common at that time, but it was done to deter the powers of evil; they considered that I was not following the word of God.' In the words of this writer, this was 'the first time, but not the last, that I experienced revulsion, contempt and humiliation in a Church context'. It is interesting to note, however, that she had the support of her fellow students from Lund, 'even those who were not in favour of women priests'.[65]

---

63 No. 29.
64 Persson, 'Min väg till prästämbetet', p. 46.
65 No. 21.

The same wide range of experience is found in narratives by priests who undertook the pastoral training term towards the end of the 1960s. One difference, though, is that one priest, Margareta Brandby-Cöster, says that resistance to the reform was expressed by teachers as well. There was, she writes, one teacher who would ask things like, '[w]hat about the ladies, do the ladies know of the Confessions?' She adds that there were major disputes, but that the dissension was not so much due to the reform of the priesthood as to the fact that this was a period of theological upheaval. She also mentions that fellow students who opposed the reform might stop greeting her and would cross themselves when she walked by.[66]

However, another priest who attended the training course at Lund at the same time says that she never encountered any expression of opposition to the reform from her teachers. On the other hand, the students on the course knew who held what opinion on the matter.[67] Birgitta Fogelklou, who took the course at Lund in 1970, also seems to have had a very positive experience. 'The group is enjoyably mixed, everyone is a bit special in some way in terms of their interests and church background. But the tone is friendly and the whole atmosphere is surprisingly warm.'[68]

Priests who did their practical training at Uppsala also describe experiencing what we interpret as a denial of recognition and the consequences of that denial. One of the priests speaks about being the sole woman in her group together with 18 male candidates. She delineates the sceptical attitudes of many of her fellow students when she was to lead a practice service. On this occasion, when she sang the Salutation, only the teacher responded. The priest writes:

> Afterwards, when we were asked to comment on the service, someone said: 'You heard yourself that we didn't respond in the Salutation.' 'Yes, I heard it.' Then one of the High Church students said: 'When I think about it, I could have responded, because when [the woman's name] conducts the service, it's only playing a game.' – Talk about high-level bullying! That was the attitude I often encountered, of not being taken seriously. It's hard not to shrink up then.[69]

---

66 Brandby-Cöster, *Hur gick det till?*, pp. 40–41.
67 No. 45.
68 Letter from Birgitta Fogelklou to Stig Hellsten, dated 1 February 1970, Stig Hellsten Archive, Umeå University Library.
69 No. 18.

Other priests studied here were more favourably disposed, though, especially towards the teachers.[70] One priest who took the course in the spring of 1965 says: 'Our male colleagues were not always fun to deal with, but our teachers were interested and knowledgeable.'[71] A priest who had attended the pastoral training term the year before agrees that the teachers in the training term were not against women priests, but that a number of the other students were. In particular, to use her own words, there had been one 'High Church prime mover' who had urged the other students on.[72]

Towards the end of the 1960s there were also episodes involving explicit expressions of opposition by fellow students. The priests add that it was stressful to be unsure about who opposed the reform and how they should relate to those people. One priest talks about her training term in the late 1960s and suggests that it might actually have been a relief to have had a confrontation: 'I can't remember any heated arguments or any unpleasantness, it might have been good if there had been.'[73] Another priest who attended the practice term in the autumn of 1967 in a group of six women and 28 men writes:

> It was a good time, with no bitter divisions. Of course there were opponents in the group, both those who declared it openly and those who were opposed in their heart of hearts. Throughout all these years, the greatest difficulty has been with those of our brothers in priestly office about whom weren't sure: is he for or against?[74]

In the late 1960s there appear to have been a number of opponents to the reform among the teaching staff as well. One of the priests, who was in a group with 28 participants of whom three were women, says she was anxious before each new course because of the attitude of the teachers. One teacher who was an outspoken opponent of the reform, and later became the chairman of the Church Coalition for the Bible and Confession, took steps to ascertain which of the students were fellow opponents and did so in front of the whole group:

---

70 No. 25; No. 42.
71 No. 7.
72 No. 5.
73 No. 33.
74 No. 28.

He began the lesson by asking who was going to Gothenburg, Visby and Strängnäs. 'Just so I know where I have my people', as he put it. It was like that constantly […] It was so bad that even the opponents reacted. When the grades were presented and the teachers lined up to have their hands shaken, [the teacher's name] refused.[75]

The same priest also recounts how one homiletics teacher had refused to have the three women in his group, but because he was the only teacher of liturgy he was obliged to teach them that subject. He had then ignored the women. 'It felt very uncomfortable. I often felt like skipping his classes.'[76]

Notwithstanding the various ways in which opposition to the reform was expressed, the training term could still feel meaningful. One priest who spent the term at Uppsala in 1968 says that 'while I was taking part in it I grew into my decision to become a priest. Suddenly it became self-evident for me to be a priest. I simply could not understand why I hadn't realised long ago that my path led to the priesthood! It was incomprehensible!'[77]

Regardless of whether the vocation narratives describe the practical training term as difficult or pleasant, they share a common element: the priest's experience is connected with the behaviour of her fellow students. As some of the narratives suggest, the presence of one or more opponents to the reform did not necessarily mean that the female candidates were denied social recognition and had their identity as future priests called into question. On the contrary, a spirit of good fellowship could still exist. What, then, lay behind these expressions of opposition to the reform, expressions which come across as calculated affronts to a present-day reader?

Once again, one possible contributing cause is the Church context. When describing such expressions of opposition, both during their practical training and later when they were serving as priests, some of the first ordained women mention that the opponents belonged to the Church Coalition for the Bible and Confession.[78] Many of the modes of behaviour described by the priests were in fact recommended by the Church Coalition in what were known as 'the Seventeen Points' [de sjutton punkterna], which were an interpretation of the conscience clause [samvetsklausulen]

75 No. 42.
76 Ibid.
77 No. 8.
78 No. 29.

(see Chapter 3). Representatives of the Church Coalition expressed themselves in much the same way as the women candidates' male fellow students. What would according to Honneth's theory be understood as various expressions of denied social recognition were thus established usage within a larger context, and they were modelled on that usage.

The Church Coalition for the Bible and Confession, the conscience clause and the Seventeen Points

The Church Coalition for the Bible and Confession was formed in 1958. Most of its members were drawn from three movements within Swedish Lutheranism: Pietism (Old Church) with its roots in the nineteenth-century revivalist movements, Low Church and High Church. The leading organisers were the Bishop of Gothenburg, Bo Giertz, and the Cathedral Dean of Växjö, G. A. Danell.[79] In his book *En annan Kyrka* ['Another Church'] (2018), the practical theologian Dag Sandahl presents a detailed account of the Church Coalition and its origins. According to Sandahl, an important reason why the Church Coalition functioned as a unifying force was the personal dynamics between Giertz and Danell. Where Giertz was the diplomatic figure, appealing to those who shied away from too much confrontation, Danell rallied those who viewed the reform as a form of decay and wanted to protest. In this respect, Danell was something of a front figure for the Church Coalition.[80]

In his depiction of Danell, Sandahl emphasises his positive qualities. According to Sandahl, who was personally acquainted with Danell, he was '[p]ersonally pleasant and almost shy'. Sandahl also maintains that in all situations, Danell wanted to 'uncompromisingly state what was true and right. He could do nothing else.'[81] Even though he and Margit Sahlin prayed daily offices together, where he prayed his so-called 'litany in times of apostasy', Danell was able to be 'personally amiable' towards her.[82] This litany is an excellent example of the language that was used, even in the liturgical context. Here are some excerpts:

79 Brohed, *Sveriges kyrkohistoria*, p. 148; Sandahl, *En annan Kyrka*, pp. 197–198, 212.
80 Sandahl, *En annan Kyrka*, p. 212.
81 Ibid., pp. 197–198.
82 Ibid., p. 222.

Have mercy on your Church in our land, which has grievously offended
against you by changing your holy apostolic orders in accordance
with the ideas of this world.
    Hear us, O Lord God.
Turn away from us the just punishment of our sins, and preserve us
from being made participants in the apostasy of our people and of
our Church by false compliance and cowardly silence.
    Hear us, O Lord God.
Awaken through your Holy Ghost a right contrition and penitence
in those who by their decision have brought upon us the present
division and dishonour.[83]

Sandahl's account does not mention how Sahlin might have viewed
the situation, and she does not mention it in her diary. Instead,
Danell's name occurs in connection with the disputes that arose in
the early 1960s regarding church collections for the St Catherine
Foundation [S:ta Katharinastiftelsen], of which Sahlin was director.
The Foundation received funding via nationally collected offerings.
After Sahlin had been ordained, however, some opponents refused
to collect for this purpose. In Växjö Cathedral Danell deliberately
took up the offerings at the exit and not, as was customary, during
the service itself. In addition, Sahlin mentions Danell in connection
with her account of 'shocks that caused me [...] to weep uncontrol-
lably'. In this case, Danell had schemed to prevent a lecture that
Sahlin was to give to the Växjö diocesan women's council.[84] The
contrast between how Danell is portrayed in Sandahl's book and
how he appears in the accounts of Margit Sahlin, Inger Svensson
(Chapter 3) and Marianne Westrin (Chapter 8) is striking.

    Danell was also chairman of the Church Renewal Movement
(AKF), which was formed in 1959 with the aim of providing High
Church orientated people with a representative and coopera-
tive body at national level. The Swedish name of the association
[Arbetsgemenskapen Kyrklig Förnyelse – literally 'The working
group for Church renewal'] was taken directly from the priest
Gunnar Rosendal's (1897–1988) books *Kyrklig förnyelse* ['Church
renewal'] (1935) and *Kyrklig förnyelse i församlingskyrkan*
['Church renewal in the parish church'] (1937).[85]

---

83 Ibid., p. 222.
84 Nordlander, *Margit Sahlin*, pp. 255–266 (p. 265).
85 Mikael Löwegren, 'Leve den kyrkliga förnyelsen! Till 100-årsjubileet
   i arbetsgemenskapen Kyrklig förnyelses årsbok', in Markus Hagberg
   (ed.), *Ecclesia semper reformanda: Texter om kyrkan, kyrkans liv och*

Together with Danell, Gunnar Rosendal represented the more confrontational approach that is reflected in the episodes from the practical training term. One example can be found in the interviews Rosendal gave in connection with the General Synod's decision in 1958 and in a well-publicised lecture that he delivered. Rosendal explained to *Svenska Dagbladet* that if 'one Miss Andersson' is ordained, she is still not a priest. 'If a bishop ordains a woman and a man to the priesthood at the same time, the man becomes a priest but not the woman. The consecration does not "take" on her, profanely speaking.'[86] As we can see, there are unmistakable parallels between the ways in which Rosendal and young male theology students in the training programme expressed themselves.

The only one of the priests in this study to mention Rosendal is Margit Sahlin. An extract from her diary notes may serve as an example: 'It was harder to stomach a word uttered at a priests' meeting in Gunnar Rosendal's Osby [a locality in southern Sweden], that "a woman who speaks in public prostitutes herself." None of the priests present was seen to raise an eyebrow.'[87] Rosendal's assertion is striking to a present-day reader. The fact that he was allowed to make it unchallenged says something about the vulnerability of a woman who found herself in a one-sided male arena.

Instead of mentioning people like Rosendal by name, it is more common for the vocation narratives to use terms such as 'High Church thinking' or 'the High Church men' as a label for opponents of the reform who expressed themselves in this way. This is an indication that the priests studied here perceived that the language and behavioural patterns sometimes used by their male fellow students were influenced by theologians such as Danell and Rosendal and were found in groups such as the Church Coalition and the Church Renewal Movement.

On January 1960, when it became public that the Church of Sweden's in-principle decision to open up the priesthood to women would be put into practice, and that at least two women were to be ordained, a number of newspapers reported on this announcement. They also stated that the Church Coalition had

kyrkokritik (Skellefteå: Artos, 2017), pp. 155–159; Sandahl, *En annan Kyrka*, p. 128.

86 'Kyrkoherde Rosendal: Prästvigd fröken Andersson blir ändå inte någon präst', *Svenska Dagbladet*, 28 October 1958.

87 Nordlander, *Margit Sahlin*, p. 81.

prepared what the newspapers designated as a 'counterattack', an 'action programme' with 'guidelines for the opposing side's priests for their actions in practical situations in parish work'.[88] These guidelines, which were summarised in and later referred to as the Seventeen Points, were intended to lend concrete expression to the conscience clause, that is, the additional provision which allowed priests who opposed the reform on the grounds of conscience to avoid being ordained alongside women and serving with ordained women. The guidelines had been drawn up by two groups, one focusing on laypeople and the other on priests. The introduction reads as follows:

> The General Synod's decision to open up the priesthood to women has introduced an order into the Church of Sweden that is contrary to God's will and Christ's instructions as given to us in Holy Writ. It concerns such an important matter as the mandate to speak on behalf of Christ and to administer the sacraments in his name. If the Church gives this mandate contrary to the commandment of her Lord, such an ordination cannot be valid. It does not convey any mandate from Christ. It is an abuse of the Lord's name. Anyone who is thus ordained is not *rite vocatus*, is not rightly called to the priesthood, and is not authorised to exercise the office on behalf of Christ. The same applies, with the necessary modifications, if *venia* is conferred on a woman.[89]

The guidelines stated, among other things, that laypeople should not attend services and ordinances led by women, and should avoid engaging women for individual spiritual counselling, Communion for the sick or baptism.[90] Priests were urged, among other things, to avoid all church work in which a woman was involved as a priest.[91] The press and the general public did not react favourably to this move by the Church Coalition. They questioned whether it was possible (and Christian) to engage in 'affectionate shunning'[92] and argued that 'the now published recommendations of the Church Coalition with their elements of aggressiveness' were to be regarded as 'appeals for a blockade'.[93]

---

88 'Kyrklig samling förbereder motattack mot Sahlin-Djurle', *Dagens Nyheter*, 15 January 1960.
89 Quoted in Brohed, *Sveriges kyrkohistoria*, p. 215.
90 'Tre kvinnliga präster', *Sydsvenska Dagbladet*, 22 January 1960.
91 'Kvinnliga präster', *Upsala Nya Tidning*, 22 January 1960.
92 'Prästvigningarna', *Svenska Dagbladet*, 12 April 1960.
93 'Kvinnoprästerna', *Svenska Dagbladet*, 22 January 1960.

In his historical account of this event, Sandahl regrets that these guidelines from the opposing side were portrayed as a secret plan for battle. According to him, it was a misconception that the Seventeen Points were aimed against the ordained women. They were intended to constitute advice for those who wanted to comply with the conscience clause and who would otherwise 'give up, leave or capitulate'. They were not intended as an action plan.[94] However, the first women priests' accounts of their student days reveal that the Seventeen Points did not work like that in practice. Instead, they did indeed function as an action plan – one with grievous consequences for the female theology students. In light of this, it is not surprising that the Seventeen Points came to be perceived as 'aimed against' them, and there are good reasons to describe them as a programme which reform opponents were expected to follow.

Towards the end of 1960, the Church of Sweden was reported to the Justice Ombudsman, and Archbishop Gunnar Hultgren was called to a meeting in order to answer questions about how the Church of Sweden related to priests and laypeople who actually adhered to the Seventeen Points. The archbishop maintained that there was no way around the current provisions. It was up to each bishop to decide on the use of church premises, but if parishioners wanted a woman to officiate at a wedding or funeral, they 'could not reasonably [...] be refused', and accordingly the church premises would be used. The archbishop considered the parish registers to be so important to the Church that they could not be ignored or deviations authorised. Thus, even if an ordained woman had performed the ceremony, it had to be recorded in the parish registers.

In other words, the archbishop stressed that the Synod's decision to open up the priesthood to women should be respected. At the same time, an ambiguity existed in how he spoke about priests who opposed the reform and invoked the conscience clause.

> The archbishop emphasises that it is extremely important from the Church's point of view that respect for a priest's position based on religious convictions should be expressed by making every effort to avoid his being subjected to legal proceedings because of his actions in accordance with those convictions. Many conflicts would undoubtedly never arise if the priest who has serious misgivings were not subjected to attempts to force him to act in a manner contrary to

94 Sandahl, *En annan Kyrka*, pp. 20–21, 184–185.

his convictions by means of persuasion, and if he himself reflected on his duty to accept only the consequences of his standpoint that are necessarily linked to it.[95]

According to the archbishop, then, conflict could be avoided if only the opponents of the reform were never exposed to situations in which their convictions were questioned. Their behaviour is depicted as amounting to their accepting the necessary consequences of their point of view. While it might not have been the archbishop's intention, his words were certainly interpreted to mean that the male candidates for the priesthood who opposed the reform were subjected to coercion, and that their treatment of their female fellow students was merely a consequence of this provocation. Ultimately, it was therefore the female priests' responsibility to ensure that conflict did not arise; and if it did and led to a boycott, it was their own fault.

The fact that the archbishop's words were indeed interpreted in this way by his contemporaries is shown by some examples. The commentator Torsten Nilsson (1925–2009), who was head of the college run by the Swedish Evangelical Mission [Evangeliska Fosterlands-Stiftelsen], argued that the boycott initiated by the Church Coalition was misdirected and that criticism should instead be levelled at those who were really responsible, namely the bishops who had ordained the first women to be priests in the Church of Sweden on Palm Sunday 1960.[96]

The Church Coalition had hence presented pastoral advice that was, in practice, perceived as an action plan for reform opponents to apply. Excluding and refusing to recognise women as priests was regarded as being part of an active struggle against the reform. The more radical representatives of the Church Coalition set the tone for the use of harsh language.

Archbishop Hultgren's statement also points to a presumption which was expressed in the Church leadership's expectation that it was the women who should step aside and assume responsibility for preventing conflict situations from arising. Similarly, it was possible to regard it as justifiable to shun female candidates for the priesthood as detailed by the Seventeen Points and to speak to them

---

95 'Ärkebiskopen: Hon har full rätt till ämbetsutövning', *Aftonbladet*, 5 December 1960.

96 Torsten Nilsson, 'Kyrklig samlings handlingsprogram', *Budbäraren*, 6 (1960), 3.

in a hostile fashion. Opponents simply considered themselves to be provoked or compelled to do so.

This is what the first women priests' fellow students who opposed the reform had to relate to. It is likely that quite a few of them were influenced by the language and views expressed by the people behind the Seventeen Points. The Seventeen Points and the presumptions of the Church leadership legitimised this approach and bestowed precedence on reform opponents when it came to interpretation. There thus existed an ambivalence, a contradiction, in the General Synod's decision in principle to open up the priesthood to women and its simultaneous decision to introduce the conscience clause. That ambivalence affected what happened in practice.

As this examination of the core episodes of the student years has shown, for the women candidates this period could be a challenge in various ways – a 'Way of the Cross' of denied recognition, but also a place for growth and a deeper understanding of their vocation. After completion of their studies, the end goal finally ensued: the longed-for ordination as a priest.

Ordination

It is not surprising that ordination is a core episode. It forms the culmination and climax of many years of training and a powerful public recognition of one's vocation. That ordination is described in terms of a 'radiant celebration of joy' is only to be expected. However, the vocation narratives contain a number of testimonies to the effect that the joy of ordination was not undiluted. The media attention that women's ordinations attracted throughout the 1960s is frequently the chief concern in this context. Several of the women also raise the issue of so-called 'separate ordinations' [*särvigningar*] and other kinds of expressions of opposition that they encountered.

Joy

The joy of ordination is a recurring theme in almost all the vocation narratives. The importance of ordination as an affirmation of vocation is given particular emphasis. Using Honneth's terms, we can discuss this as recognition of the vocation on different levels – partly legal and partly social. One priest summarises this recognition: 'It is great, powerful and holy to be ordained as a priest. I'm sure everyone shares that experience. For me, it was overwhelming as an affirmation of God's call after all the years of hesitation and obstacles [...] I was so thankful.'[97] Another priest describes her feelings just before her ordination: 'Finally I was prepared to say "yes" to the Lord's Call to go out into the service of his kingdom.'[98]

The joy of having one's vocation recognised through ordination is also related to the role of ordination assistants. An assistant is an ordained individual, normally chosen by the candidate, who stands at the candidate's side during the ceremony. This is often someone who has acted as a support, role model and mentor. One priest, though, says she was given two extra assistants whom she did not know, because two 'ancient priests' had contacted her ordination bishop and had separately said they did not know any female ordinands but would like to attend the ordination of a woman.[99] Another theme that is raised in relation to the joy of ordination is parental support and involvement.[100]

The fly in the celebratory ointment

As was pointed out above, ordination was not all delight. The depictions of ordination in the vocation narratives often include a fly in the ointment, even though the joy of the ordination overshadowed it. One priest ordained in the early 1960s describes such a situation:

> The fact that TV and journalists were present during the ordination, and that there was a group of demonstrating priests and theologians – opponents of the ordination – outside the church, completely faded into the background. For me, everything became a gift and a mission to serve in Christ's footsteps.[101]

Demonstrations by opponents could thus occur, as could much media attention. The latter appears in many accounts. Priestly ordinations of women in the 1960s were widely publicised in the media, and almost every ordination was evidently considered newsworthy.

The priests could experience the media attention and protests as difficult and problematic. One priest writes: 'Journalists and

---

97 No. 28.
98 No. 24.
99 No. 34.
100 No. 44; No. 24.
101 No. 20.

photographers from various newspapers chased me. At times it was stressful. What was said in a small aside was magnified beyond recognition a number of times.'[102] Another describes a situation where newspaper reports of her upcoming ordination led to such protests in the diocese that the date had to be changed. She writes:

> But that didn't mean that there was less in the way of 'writing' in the newspapers. People were going crazy! Fake interviews abounded, and statements I had never made became like words of God. The whole thing was terrible! The only thing I could do was to keep away and be as silent as possible.[103]

The newspaper attention paid to an ordination was not always viewed in unfavourable terms, though. A third priest says that she regarded the articles written about her ordination more as an expression of caring, and that she and the other woman who was to be ordained with her felt 'supported'.[104]

One reason why the newspaper attention is portrayed as positive might be that the articles were often well disposed towards the ordinations. A telling example among many is the extensive coverage by the magazine *Vi* of the priestly ordinations in 1960. The magazine sent a reporter to each of the three ordinations. Elisabeth Djurle Olander's ordination at the cathedral in Stockholm is described as follows:

> In the oldest part of the nation's capital, the congregation at the Palm Sunday Mass experienced for the first time the controversial innovation of our Swedish Church. It was new and brave at the same time: a slender woman in simple white entered in front of six men in splendid priestly vestments, pale, the focus of attention, her own gaze on the altar, step by step closer to the prize affirming her victory in the brave struggle.
>
> And there, at the altar, an end was put to the talk about the woman being silent in the congregation. Now it was the men who suddenly kept silent and let the woman speak: Elisabeth Djurle, a young woman from Jönköping in Småland, a theology graduate from Lund, a student counsellor in Uppsala and until this moment a parish secretary in Stockholm, raised a historic voice when she took her priestly vows. A voice which did not falter and which sounded completely self-evident in this house of God. She professed her faith, and she gave answers to the five questions of the vows. The ceremony had attained its

---

102 No. 35.
103 No. 24.
104 No. 45.

most serious high point. And then something occurred that the overcrowded cathedral had until then been unable to find room for: with the woman, devotion came into the temple.[105]

Another stumbling block in connection with the ordination ceremony that took away some of the joy could also be that the choice of assistant was rejected. One priest describes how she was denied her choice of assistant because she had chosen one of the women who had been ordained a few years earlier. It was simply not considered appropriate to have an ordained woman as an assistant. Instead, the vicar of the parish she was called to serve in took over the task. The woman ordinand notes that both she and the other woman were 'saddened and offended', and she asks rhetorically in her vocation narrative whether it 'would have been too massive if the female presence at the altar had increased by one hundred per cent?'[106]

A third reason why ordinations were not always occasions of undiluted joy had to do with separate ordinations. Separate ordination was practised in all dioceses in the first decade after the first women were ordained as priests.[107] It meant that a male candidate who opposed the reform was not ordained at the same time as the women. In the early 1960s separate ordinations meant that female candidates for the priesthood had to accept being ordained on another occasion. Later on in the 1960s, it was usually the male candidates who were ordained at a different time.

Separate ordination occurs in a number of the vocation narratives. One of the priests we interviewed began her account of her ordination by showing the silver cross she had made for her ordination and pointing out that it had the wrong ordination date engraved on it. According to her, this was because 'the boys didn't want me there'. At a late stage in the planning for the ordination, just a week before, the bishop decided to let her wait until a later date because the male candidates did not want to be ordained together with her.[108]

Describing her own ordination, another priest recounts how one of her colleagues 'who could not be ordained together with women, was ordained the following Sunday during the evening service', but

---

105 Lars Öhngren, 'Mod att förkunna ordet', *Vi*, 22 April 1960.
106 No. 28.
107 For an introduction to the phenomenon of separate ordinations, see Andersson, *Den nödvändiga manligheten*, pp. 16–17, especially footnote 17.
108 No. 26.

that the ordaining bishop tried to downplay this by emphasising that it was self-evident that all the candidates for the priesthood had lunch together in connection with the regular ordination ceremony.[109] This bishop thus had no desire to organise an extra lunch for the man who wanted a separate ordination.

The final example of this use of separate ordinations again features the theme of mass-media interest. There was a clear link between the media's interest in priestly ordinations and their interest in separate ordinations, particularly as an expression of the divisions within the Church that the media thought existed. The priest in question describes how the debate in the media escalated as the time drew near when she and another woman would be ordained. The priest explains:

> [T]here was one who was ordained by himself. He was our friend anyway, so it was never a problem. Then we just accepted that things were like that. Actually, we were very accepting of the fact that there was opposition. It was only later that [...] it somehow got to me. At that point it became difficult, and I felt I had to stand up for who I am and be who I am.[110]

Several interesting themes emerge from this quotation in addition to the issue of separate ordination. Even though the priest says that she accepted that she had colleagues who questioned her vocation, she nevertheless appears to have felt upset by having her priestly identity and the validity of her ordination questioned. Despite the fact that the 1958 decision to open up the priesthood in the Church of Sweden to women has given her legal recognition, she was affected and offended by having her identity as a priest questioned. In some circles she was simply denied social recognition, to use Honneth's terminology. This denial is particularly serious when it occurs in connection with ordination, whose function is to confirm the candidate's vocation. Another theme that emerges from between the lines here is meta-reflection by the priest herself. She comments retrospectively on the difference between what she did then and how she thinks now. Back then she was silent – later she defended her identity.[111]

A fourth reason why the ordinations were not all joy and gratitude involved letters from opponents of the reform. These were

---

109 No. 44.
110 No. 45.
111 Ibid.

not infrequently worded in a way that would be considered offensive today. One of the priests, for example, describes how an obituary was sent to her home.[112] Being sent an obituary is one of the extremes, even though similar cases do exist in the material studied here. In an interview in *Svenska Dagbladet* in 1967, Elisabeth Djurle Olander, Ingrid Persson, Margit Sahlin and Ylwa Gustafsson all say that they received letters in connection with their ordination. Regarding the three who were ordained on Palm Sunday 1960, it is stated that they 'received many letters, anonymous and signed, friendly, pleading, angry and threatening'.[113]

Almost no details exist on what these letters actually contained, either in public accounts or in the vocation narratives in the LUKA archive. However, examples of what they might have sounded like emerge from letters sent to Britta Olén-van Zijl in connection with the debate about her possible ordination. Various newspaper stories published at the time of the General Synods of 1957 and 1958 made it clear that Olén-van Zijl hoped to become the first woman to be ordained in the Church of Sweden.[114] As was mentioned in Chapter 3, these hopes were dashed, partly because of her marriage to a minister in the Dutch Reformed Church and partly because she was mainly resident in South Africa.[115] The whole 'affair' gave rise to a media debate, in connection with which she received a number of letters.

In a letter dated March 1960, the sender writes that Olén-van Zijl should consider carefully so that she does not contribute to the division of the Church by persisting in her desire for ordination as a priest. The writer argues that Olén-van Zijl is in breach of Scripture and that the consequences are 'suffering or loss of the Kingdom of Heaven'. If the Church has women priests, many people will not attend services because members of the congregation will stay at home owing to conscientious objections.[116]

---

112 No. 21.
113 Wik-Thorsell, 'Kvinnlig präst söker aldrig konflikterna'.
114 'Malmölärarinna första kvinnoprästen', *Morgonbladet*, 2 September 1957. The introduction states that Olén-van Zijl 'has completed the theological background and can be ordained on the same day that the Riksdag formally confirms that the Church shall have female priests'. That Olén-van Zijl was expected to be the first woman to be ordained is also evident from a story in the news magazine *Se*, 43 (1958).
115 Olén-van Zijl, 'Att få vara präst', pp. 106–107.
116 Letter from 'Mille' to Britta Olén-van Zijl, 25 March 1960, Gunnar Olén Collection, LUL.

Citing his own interpretation of the original Greek text of 1 Corinthians 14:33–37, another writer emphasises in a letter dated about a month later that the prohibition stipulated in the Bible refers to a married woman, and that these women should therefore not speak in the church.[117] In another typewritten letter, the anonymous sender refers to Olén-van Zijl's duties as a clergyman's wife and adds that she should follow the vocation she has in that context. The writer further states that Olén-van Zijl and the three women who were ordained as priests are 'foolish' and that they risk dividing the Church through their conduct. The writer thanks God 'that there are still men like Bishop Giertz and others who fight for God's Word'.[118]

In another anonymous letter to Olén-van Zijl, the sender states that 'Jesus was a man, his disciples were men, they sacrificed themselves, they taught!' A few lines further down, the sender writes: 'The woman who allows herself to be ordained in these times only wants to get her hands on money in the laziest way.' Later in the two-page handwritten letter, the writer again emphasises that a priest 'must be a man' and 'a man with a strong faith in what the Bible proclaims'. The reason is that this strong faith has an effect on how the audience will receive the preaching:

Away with females in the pulpit. A woman's place is in the home, where she can achieve greater charity and more blessings than standing in a pulpit and making an exhibition of herself in order to make an easy living. The churches will be empty in future if things happen the way you want.[119]

These four examples have several common denominators. One is the presumption described earlier in this chapter that the split in the Church is the fault of the women priests. It is their mere presence that causes the division, and if they would only surrender their ambitions to enter the priesthood, dissension could be avoided. Another theme that we described earlier can also be discerned here: the influence of the Church Coalition, for example when the writers mention conscientious objections or refer to

---

117 Letter from [first name illegible] Karlson to Britta Olén-van Zijl, 29 April 1960, Gunnar Olén Collection, LUL.
118 Letter from anonymous sender to Britta Olén-van Zijl, undated, Gunnar Olén Collection, LUL.
119 Letter without sender to Britta Olén-van Zijl, undated, Gunnar Olén Collection, LUL.

leading representatives of the Coalition. Yet another common denominator is the view of gender roles and the different expectations and duties incumbent on women and men respectively, which we described in Chapter 3. Finally, we see here a specific type of biblical interpretation that emphasises a literal reading of the Bible.

∞∞∞∞

In conclusion, we can observe that the women priests focus attention on their student years in their vocation narratives. It is a prominent core episode in the collective narrative formed by the individual stories, and the quantity and length of these accounts testify to the fact that this was an important and, for many, also a formative period. The vocation narratives provide good insights into what it was like to study theology at this time.

When the women priests describe their student years, it is again striking to note the individual features of their narratives. The nature of their training – their course of study and choice of subjects – and the experiences they had vary greatly. It is, however, possible to make a number of general observations. During the 1960s, Lund appears to have been a more welcoming place than Uppsala for women who were studying theology with the aim of working as priests in the Church of Sweden. This may have been due to the so-called Lundensian theology [*Lundateologin*], whose adherents included teachers who took a stand in favour of the reform. The harsher climate at Uppsala was probably due to the fact that representatives of the New Ecclesiology were active as teachers there. The Stockholm Theological Institute was geographically close to Uppsala. Although its students encountered some of the teachers who also taught at Uppsala, this educational institute with its Low Church character seems to have offered an educational and social environment in which women candidates for the priesthood felt welcomed both by the teachers in charge and by their fellow students.

The vocation narratives also indicate that for many of these priests, their student years were a time of vulnerability when their vocation was often questioned. The mere fact that women as a group constituted a minority must have contributed to reinforcing this impression. There was also uncertainty about the attitude of teachers and how this might affect their conduct, and there are accounts of teachers behaving badly when the women's future career choice became known.

For many of the women candidates for ordination, their student years were also their first encounter with an explicit and personally targeted opposition to the reform. At university and during the pastoral training term, they encountered language inspired by movements that opposed the reform and also an action plan that was made explicit in the so-called Seventeen Points. At the core of the language used and the action plan lay the presumption that any conflicts, as well as the dissension that followed the 1958 decision, were the women's fault. People with this presumption held that if women would just lie low and refrain from asserting their rights, conflicts could be avoided.

In view of the 1958 decision, this behaviour on the part of fellow students and teachers might be regarded from a Honnethian viewpoint as comprising a challenge to the existing legal recognition. It might also be perceived as a manifestation of denied social recognition – a social disrespect – which sometimes turned into outright ethical violations. From this perspective, the Seventeen Points can be understood as a way of systematically and deliberately denying recognition, not only on a legal but also on a social level. In other words, these were not just random and isolated events but rather an established use of language and a systematically implemented action plan. Even in that era, this action plan was perceived as having the aim of exclusion, a shunning that some people argued was misdirected, because it affected the women who were studying to become priests and not the Church leaders who had taken the decision.

Since – according to Axel Honneth – recognition is fundamental to a human being's development, healthy self-image and identity, the contempt and denial of recognition that the ordained women faced during their study years is a serious matter. In describing such denial of social recognition, Honneth points out that acts of this kind damage the sense of being socially significant within a concrete community, and that this contempt ranges from harmless instances of not greeting someone to cases of gross stigmatisation.[120] This very much corresponds to the behaviour that the first women priests had to endure during their studies. These violations are particularly serious given that the women emphasise how intimately their vocation is linked to their identity. For some of the priests,

120 Axel Honneth, *Disrespect: The Normative Foundations of Critical Theory* (Cambridge: Polity, 2007), pp. 129–143.

the expression of opposition and the questioning of their vocation became so tangible that they could scarcely bear to complete their training.

The tone of the vocation narratives is different when ordination is described. Here, the emphasis is on joy. In a number of cases, however, the bright memories of ordination include shadowy elements. These might encompass protests, demonstrations, mass-media attention, separate ordinations, not being allowed to choose one's preferred assistant for the ceremony, and unpleasant letters.

In the vocation narratives ordination is a core episode: a natural climax to the narrative. With ordination, the women were granted a legal recognition whose foundation had been laid with the decision made in 1958 to reform the priesthood. The narratives express the joy of having received the legitimacy and affirmation of their vocation that ordination represents. In addition, the memories of the ordination ceremony are often strongly tied to the people who were present (parents, friends and colleagues). In this respect, the ordination of a priest encompasses both a legal recognition and an ample measure of social recognition.

Various forms of boycotts and protests linked to the ordination ceremony recur in the vocation narratives, indicating that this disrespect was observed by the women and that many of them were offended. Like the expressions of opposition during their training period, these manifestations constituted a questioning of their vocation. In our opinion, this disrespect may be regarded as an expression of a denial of social recognition – a denial that called their very identity into question.

As we will show in the next chapter, this mixed message also occurred with regard to recognition of the women's vocation. On the one hand, recognition was wholeheartedly dispensed by the Church of Sweden; but on the other hand the conscience clause made it perfectly possible for people who were active in the Church to deny women this recognition. This ambivalence persisted after their ordination.

Britta Olén-van Zijl together with her ordination bishop, Martin Lindström, Cathedral Dean Yngve Ahlberg, Professor Gustaf Wingren and Professor Hugo Odeberg. The image archive states that the photo was taken in connection with the ordination in 1963, but in view of the clothes worn and the composition of the group, it is more likely to have been taken at the 'priestly examination' (*prästexamen*), the occasion a couple of days before ordination when the cathedral chapter tests the knowledge of the candidates. The Lund Cathedral Chapter included, among others, the bishop, the cathedral dean and professors from the Faculty of Theology. (Image: copyright Bilder i Syd. Reproduced by permission.)

Chapter 6
Recognition of the vocation

An abundance of great kindness and lavish warmth, strong support and generous encouragement has been showered upon me from the most varied quarters of the parish, from laypeople and priests, both supervisors and colleagues, from parish councillors and church officials in general.[1]

'Get thee behind me, Satan', he said and changed seats in the bus.[2]

The warm reception given to the first Swedish women priests is depicted in almost every vocation narrative. Siv Bejerfors' words in the first quotation above aptly summarise the experience described by most of the priests. If their student years and ordination were something of a time of trial, then life in service in the parishes was often described as the exact opposite.

However, the vocation narratives also contain accounts of a very different experience, as the second quotation above bears witness to. In this case it is Ulla Nisser who describes how, during a bus journey in Israel, she ended up next to a male priest. When she told him she was also a priest, this was the reaction she received. A number of the priests in this study describe similar experiences of opposition and challenge, not so much from parishioners – such examples are very few – but from fellow clergy. We also touch on those experiences in this chapter. In addition, we examine the reception given to the first women priests by some of the bishops of the Church of Sweden. The focus here is on those bishops who favoured the reform, at least in theory.

Thanks to the vocation narratives, we are able to gain a clearer picture of a contentious issue in the historical narrative of the Church of Sweden, namely how the first women priests prepared

---

1 Bejerfors, 'Lärare och präst', pp. 115–116.
2 Nisser, *Hopp från trampolin*, p. 98.

for and began their ministry in practice. It has been claimed – especially by opponents of the reform – that active members of the Church at the parish level did not want women priests. Such claims were made, for example, in the consultation responses to the commission report of 1923, which was rejected on the grounds that these active church-goers did not want women priests.[3] As we have shown in Chapter 4, it was also Archbishop Yngve Brilioth's view that '[a] Swedish church parish envisions their priest as the head of the household in the parsonage'.[4]

This issue has been discussed by scholars such as the theologian Johanna Andersson, who has shown that the General Synod debates of 1957 to 1958 revealed a number of perceptions on how the laity viewed the reform.[5] Two narratives in particular opposed each other: on the one hand, the narrative of the parish as comprising the small majority of active parishioners [kyrkfolket] who were assumed to be negatively disposed to the reform, and on the other hand, the narrative of the parish as comprising the laity in general, of whom the large, silent majority was assumed to be favourably disposed. In the media, the latter narrative tended to dominate. Opponents of the reform were strongly critical of media claims that widespread public opinion favoured the reform.[6]

The vocation narratives contribute important elements to the academic debate on how these two overarching narratives relate to each other and the extent to which they reflect reality. These elements complement the current state of research while further emphasising the complexity of the issue by questioning the dividing lines. At the same time, our material cannot definitively settle this question. The specific nature of narrative sources means that it is not possible to generalise widely from them and claim that such circumstances existed throughout the Church of Sweden. What we can do is say something about how the first women priests

3 Betänkande och förslag i fråga om kvinnors tillträde till statstjänster: Kvinnas behörighet att inneha prästerlig och annan kyrklig tjänst, SOU [Swedish Government Official Reports], 1923:22.

4 Brilioth, Herdabrev till Uppsala ärkestift, pp. 159–173 (p. 171).

5 Andersson, Den nödvändiga manligheten, pp. 155–159; Tord Simonsson, Kyrkomötet argumenterar: Kritisk analys av argumenttyper i diskussionerna vid 1957 och 1958 års kyrkomöten om "kvinnas behörighet till prästerlig tjänst" [Studia Theologica Lundensia 23] (Lund: Gleerup, 1963).

6 More evidence of what the debate sounded like can be found in Mannerfelt and Maurits, Kallelse och erkännande, pp. 302–303.

experienced the situation in the parishes where they served and in the contexts of which they were a part.

Another peculiarity of narratives as source material is that the narrator sometimes has an unconscious or conscious agenda with his or her story, which then presents a picture that does not correspond to what actually happened. For example, in this case one might ask whether the unambiguous depiction of the parishes' warm welcome of their women priests is actually an idealised picture. Still, we believe that there are good reasons to regard the vocation narratives as reliable sources on this point. The narratives are otherwise frank in describing expressions of opposition to the reform, so it is reasonable to assume that examples of such opposition from the parishes would have been reported, too. This conclusion is further strengthened by the approach we have adopted, which entails placing many narratives side by side: the theme of welcoming parishes appears in no fewer than 23 of the vocation narratives. It is also consistent over time, in that it recurs both in the narratives that are close to the actual events in time and in the narratives that came into being at a later date.

The vocation narratives also reveal that positions were not fixed. A simplistic view according to which the laity was in favour while the clergy were against is not correct, as other source material confirms. The newspaper material shows that the clergy were also divided, and there is much to suggest that if we can speak of a dividing line among the priesthood at all, it was between different generations, older priests generally having a more favourable attitude than younger ones.[7] It is reasonable to assume that this difference of opinion between different generations of priests can be partly explained by the strong position held by the New Ecclesiology in the theological discussion at that time. In relation to the vocation narratives of the first ordained women, various theories about dividing lines are further deepened and nuanced.

7 'Kvinnliga präster behövs särskilt för männens skull', Dagens Nyheter, 11 February 1955; 'Historisk debatt om kvinnopräster: "Vi behöver dem!"', Stockholms-Tidningen, 11 February 1955; 'Kvinnlig präst ett behov: Kyrkfolket är positivt för frågan', Svenska Dagbladet, 11 February 1955; 'Ung präst vill ej ha kvinnlig kollega', Sydsvenska Dagbladet, 2 December 1948.

Recognition from fellow priests

It is striking how common it is in the vocation narratives that the external call, the call from the Church and the parish, comes through another priest. Using Axel Honneth's terminology, we can describe this as being a form of social recognition. We have previously stressed the importance of recognition by other priests in Chapters 3 and 5, which dealt with the ordained women's childhood, youth and student years.[8] But these women did not only receive their colleagues' support on their path to vocation and recognition. The encouragement given to them when they began ministering in their parish is even more evident in the vocation narratives.[9] Marianne Westrin, who emphasises that the most surprising aspect of becoming a priest was the excellent contact with her colleagues, is exuberant to say the least: 'The way in which I have been received by my brothers and sisters in the priesthood cannot be matched by anything other than the love of the first Christian congregation for their fellow Christians.'[10]

A number of the women priests also describe how encouraging the vicars [kyrkoherde] were in the parishes where they would have their first assignment. In many cases, these vicars had contacted their bishop and asked that the women be ordained for service in their parishes. This might be because the vicars wanted to call a specific woman,[11] but also because they had reported that they were in a position to accept one of the newly ordained priests, preferably a woman.[12] For example, an obituary for Kerstin Lindqvist-Bolling describes how she came to her first position as a priest:

> Sundbyberg parish received her after issuing a call. The vicar, Tore Norrby, acted according to what is good Lutheran practice when a bishop is hesitant to ordain. He had the parish call her as a priest; and according to the Lutheran order of things, the bishop must in such a case listen to the parish and perform the ordination.[13]

---

8 For example, No. 7; No. 33; No. 34; Ingrid Persson in Persson, 'Min väg till prästämbetet', pp. 49–51; Britta Olén-van Zijl in Olén-van Zijl, 'Att få vara präst', p. 107.

9 See Ingrid Persson in Persson, 'Min väg till prästämbetet', pp. 49–51.

10 Marianne Westrin, 'I elfte timmen', in Kvinnlig präst idag, p. 87.

11 No. 19; No. 26; No. 42.

12 No. 42.

13 Obituary for Kerstin Lindqvist-Bolling in Dagens Nyheter, 3 March 2015. The obituary is signed by Eva Brunne, Margarethe Isberg, Ann-Cathrin

The vocation narratives also include accounts of recognition dispensed by individual leaders of the Church of Sweden during the mid-twentieth century. Those mentioned include the Bishop of Stockholm, Manfred Björkquist (1884–1985), the Cathedral Dean of Stockholm, Olle Nystedt (1888–1974),[14] the director of the Sigtuna Foundation, Olov Hartman (1905–1982),[15] the psychotherapist and priest Göran Bergstrand (1930–2017),[16] and the aforementioned professor and priest Gösta Hök at the Stockholm Theological Institute. One priest writes of Hök: 'He took my vocation very seriously.' She also describes how, the day before her ordination, she received a telegram from 'an old professor in Uppsala' advising against her ordination. In the face of this challenge to her vocation, Hök came to 'the rescue':

> In the midst of all this thinking came Dr Hök, whom I had asked to be my ordination assistant. He was neither a man of great gestures nor of big words, but he broke my paralysing sense of chaos when he bent forward, put his head against mine and whispered: 'Do not be afraid. Go with God into what we have waited for for so long.'[17]

With regard to the difference in attitude to the reform of the priesthood between different generations of priests, as mentioned in the introduction, some of the women priests make special mention of older colleagues who treated them with great respect and expressed their personal recognition.[18] For example, one narrator recounts how a vicar in her home town who supported the reform had introduced her as a future priest to his father, also a clergyman and 83 years old: 'And then this old man [...] stood up and bowed and said: "Then I ask permission to welcome the young lady to the team." In the circumstances, that was a major gesture.'[19]

Jarl, Caroline Krook, Cecilia Wadstein and Ulla Örtberg. Tore Norrby (1909–1987) is also singled out in vocation narrative No. 30, which presents him in the role of the narrator's confirmation priest: 'He was a brilliant teacher with a tremendous sense of humour and warmth. He made us children curious about what the Church and the Bible could say to us in our lives and, at least for me, [stimulated] an interest in thinking further.'

14 Nordlander, *Margit Sahlin*, pp. 87–88.
15 No. 37.
16 Ibid.
17 No. 42.
18 No. 17; No. 34; Birgitta Nyman in Sjöberg, 'Kyrkan måste vara ömsint', p. 61.
19 No. 34.

Another example is found in the speech that Lena Malmgren gave in connection with the funeral of Stina Grönros (1942–2014, ordained 1966). Malmgren recounts how Grönros's predecessor in her new position as vicar did not want to attend her installation owing to his High Church standpoint. According to Malmgren, Grönros then received a phone call from the priest who had held the position before the unwilling colleague. Malmgren writes: 'Then Stina's phone rang: "I wonder if I might attend instead? I'm your grandfather in the job." And of course he was allowed to.'[20]

Recognition from the parishes

One of the most common themes we encountered in the vocation narratives is the recognition that the priests experienced receiving from their parishes. This theme appears in more than half – 23, to be precise – of the narratives we analyse in this study.

A number of the narrators were ordained for the diocese of Stockholm, and their vocation narratives describe a warm reception from the parishes there. To the extent that they encountered opposition to the reform, it came from individual fellow priests.[21] One priest writes in this regard: 'As a female priest, I have been met with warmth and joy from priests and parishioners throughout all my years in the diocese of Stockholm.'[22] A similar story comes from Sara Björkman (1909–2004, ordained 1967), whose obituary describes how she was given the opportunity to serve as a pastoral assistant in a Stockholm parish, a post which soon resulted in the parish requesting her ordination. 'The parish did not want to delay Sara's ordination by a single unnecessary day. At the request of the parish, Sara Björkman was ordained on 17 December 1967 in Stockholm Cathedral by Bishop Helge Ljungberg.'[23]

The circumstance whereby a parish seeks out, calls and recognises a priest is also depicted in another vocation narrative. The priest describes how she was set on becoming a teacher, but was

---

20 Speech by Lena Malmgren at Stina Grönros's funeral on 14 February 2014.
21 For example, No. 5; No. 37; No. 42; Elisabeth Djurle Olander in Sjöberg, 'Närhet och glädje', pp. 23–24; Barbro Nordholm Ståhl in Birgitta Johansson, 'Hon är en kyrklig pionjär', *Helsingborgs Dagblad*, 17 November 2013; Barbro Nordholm-Ståhl, 'Nära livet', in *Kvinnlig präst idag*, p. 25; and Barbro Nordholm-Ståhl's vocation narrative.
22 No. 37.
23 Obituary of Sara Björkman written by Barbro Ulfvarson, LUKA.

asked to serve as a pastoral assistant in her home parish during the summer. She observes that the parish council of her home parish had by then 'begun to be insistent in its desire to have a woman priest', and had therefore asked the vicar to arrange this. After her ordination she was assigned there.[24]

The great warmth of the parish welcome is also apparent in the narratives of women priests who served in the diocese of Lund.[25] When Britta Olén-van Zijl talks about the early days of her priesthood and her first parish as a priest, she emphasises the following:

> As an assistant priest I was assigned to Trelleborg. What I experienced there is something that maybe only happens once in a priest's life. Figuratively speaking, I was 'carried' by the congregation. I will always be grateful for the support of the parishioners and the boundless generosity with which they met me, something absolutely invaluable in the situation I found myself in.[26]

The picture painted by Olén-van Zijl is a powerful one. On the basis of Honneth's theories about the importance of recognition and the consequences of being denied it, it could be argued that such recognition will have been of vital importance, not least because her vocation was highly contested and involved complications owing to her marriage to a missionary and minister of a Reformed Church. She also notes: 'Of course one encounters opposition as a woman who holds the office of priest, but never from the parishioners.'[27]

It was not only in the dioceses of Stockholm and Lund that the ordained women were well received by their parishes. Margareta Brandby-Cöster observes that – despite the fact that the diocese of Gothenburg was known for its opposition to the reform – even the parishes in the city of Gothenburg generally 'gave a very good reception to the women who became priests there'.[28] In the diocese of Gothenburg, it may well have been the clergy rather than the laity who were unfavourably disposed towards the reform of the priesthood and the ordination of women. Confirmation of that assumption is provided by one of the vocation narratives in which

---

24 No. 8.
25 For example, No. 17; No. 26; No. 33; No. 34.
26 Olén-van Zijl, 'Att få vara präst', p. 107. A similar mode of expression is found in her vocation narrative, which she wrote almost thirty years later.
27 Ibid., p. 109.
28 Margareta Brandby-Cöster, 'Kvinnor som präster – också i Göteborgs stift. Reflektioner 11/11, 24 eft Trefaldighet', public lecture, 11 November 2018. See also Birgitta Nyman in Sjöberg, 'Kyrkan måste vara ömsint', p. 59.

the priest describes how she was invited by a layman to preach at a summer church in the famous beach resort of Tylösand, outside Halmstad. The person who invited her was very keen to have her as a preacher 'because he wanted to demonstrate that a woman priest was allowed to exist in the diocese of Gothenburg'. According to her, '[i]t was particularly cheering to meet grateful people on the West Coast'.[29]

The warm reception from parishes was not limited to the urban setting. One priest points out that she was 'well received in the [...] small rural parishes'. In light of the study by Benjamin Knoll and Cammie Jo Bolin of the reasons why there are fewer women than men in religious leadership positions in the United States, and what the long-term consequences of that imbalance might be, it is interesting to see that this priest also states that her presence and that of other women priests was 'a little strange', because women had previously been invisible as a group but were now accorded a different status. She concludes that for women who might have felt sidelined, 'it probably meant quite a lot that we came when we did'.[30] As we mentioned in the opening chapter of this book, Knoll and Bolin found that girls and younger women are positively influenced by having a woman as the leader of their congregation.[31] In Honnethian terms, we could thus say that the recognition given to this priest also contributed to extending recognition for other women.

Barbro Westlund reports that she was 'received with open arms and great warmth in Risinge parish' in the diocese of Linköping.[32] Her vocation narrative confirms this picture, and she writes that she had three very good years in her first parish, 'accepted both by the parishioners and by my fellow priests'.[33] Ulla Nisser also writes warmly about her first position as a parish priest, assigned to two parishes in Uppsala diocese:

> In my two parishes [...] I was received with open arms by the parishioners. As the first woman priest in Rosersberg I was cherished and accepted, and in the loneliness I experienced, their affection was helpful. I could not detect any opposition to me as a woman and a priest. No one talked behind my back, and no one took me aside to

---

29 No. 19.
30 No. 45.
31 Knoll and Bolin, *She Preached the Word*, pp. 63–146.
32 Sjöberg, 'Jag är så tacksam över att leva i en tid då det är möjligt', p. 52.
33 Barbro Westlund's vocation narrative.

discuss Bible interpretation and issues to do with my priestly office. Feeling secure, I was able to focus on my work.[34]

Although Nisser writes about the feeling of loneliness she experienced as a newly qualified priest on her first assignment, she stresses that the loyalty of her parishioners made up for it. A number of the women say that some parishes were initially careful to tell parishioners that they could choose a man to officiate at baptisms, weddings and funerals if they wished. This attitude emerges, for example, in an article in *Svenska Dagbladet* in September 1967. However, the article reports that the parishioners who were informed of this were rather surprised and that very few chose a man as officiant.[35] Marianne Westrin confirms this picture in her vocation narrative.[36] Judging from the narratives in the source material, the situation was rather the reverse: women priests were in demand as officiants at such ceremonies. Inger Svensson is one example of a priest who was appreciated in these contexts. As we describe elsewhere in this study, Svensson met with considerable resistance when the plans for her to be ordained as the first woman to serve in the diocese of Växjö became known. Nonetheless, it appears that at least initially she was welcomed by the parishioners and was often called upon to conduct funerals.[37]

Non-recognition from colleagues

When the first women priests mention the expressions of opposition to the reform that they encountered, it is almost always in relation to fellow priests.[38] These expressions of opposition could either be overtly stated or covert and implied. In both cases, it was often asserted that this was not aimed against the women priests themselves, but rather against the representatives of Church and state who had pushed through the reform. Given the existence of the conscience clause [*samvetsklausulen*], a belief also existed to the effect that these expressions of opposition were legitimate ('he could not do otherwise'). That this opposition was not theoretically directed against the first women priests may be true. Even so,

---

34 Nisser, *Hopp från trampolin*, p. 95.
35 Wik-Thorsell, 'Kvinnlig präst söker aldrig konflikterna'.
36 Westrin, 'I elfte timmen', pp. 77–78.
37 Transcript of Tom Alandh's documentary *Förlåt oss våra skulder*.
38 Brandby-Cöster, 'Kvinnor som präster – också i Göteborgs stift'.

the vocation narratives reveal that, in practice, they were the ones to suffer the consequences. To use Honneth's terminology, these expressions of opposition may be understood as a denial of social recognition that had profound consequences for the identity of the victim. Both the vocation narratives and the newspaper material contain many examples of how opposition from fellow priests might be expressed in words and actions in the late 1950s and the early 1960s. One example of such denied recognition is found in the case of Ingrid Persson, where the types of language use and actions presented in Chapter 5 recur. The newspaper material contains an article from the autumn of 1958 about how a parish priest, Assistant Vicar Folke Dahlbäck (1908–1981), had used an opportunity to make a statement from the pulpit in conjunction with a Sunday sermon in Örnsköldsvik church. In that supplementary statement he distanced himself from the General Synod's decision, which he described as the darkest defeat in the history of the Church of Sweden. Dahlbäck said that he was 'ashamed to belong to a Church that has fallen so far', that worldly leaders were blind and the Church of Sweden's bishops 'are no longer guardians on the walls of Zion'.[39] He further informed the congregation that the choice of hymns for the service reflected 'the seriousness of what has happened', and that the previous evening he had decided to fly the parish flag at half-mast. However, he had later changed his mind with regard to the flag. It appears from the article that this 'add-on sermon' came as a complete surprise to the churchgoers and that a number of them were upset about it.[40]

It was to Örnsköldsvik that Ingrid Persson came as a curate [pastorsadjunkt] after her ordination in 1960. An obituary of her states: '[i]t is very strange that the first woman priest should replace two priests in our diocese who held carefully reasoned High Church views'. They were the above-mentioned Folke Dahlbäck and Göran Granberg (1922–2000); among the places where Granberg had worked was Svartvik near Sundsvall.[41] Persson herself refers to

39 'Präst vållar Ö-viksstorm', Dagens Nyheter, 30 September 1958.
40 Ibid. Speaking of the choice of hymns, mention was made of Psalm 175:4, 'Ack, bliv hos oss, o Jesu Krist' in the 1937 hymnal, 'Abide with us, O Savior dear' [verse 5]: 'And, gracious Lord, consider too / How many teachers are untrue; / By wisdom they would know the Lord, / And set at naught His holy Word.'
41 Nils Parkman's obituary of Ingrid Persson, LUKA.

these two priests in her narrative, although she does not mention them by name. Speaking of her ordination, she says that there was 'a rather horrible letter waiting for her' at the bishop's residence in Härnösand. Although she does not say so explicitly, it is clear that this was a letter from Dahlbäck. She writes:

> He all but called down God's curse on me if I did not abstain from the ordination. The bishop and the cathedral dean had agreed to withhold the letter from me, because they guessed at its contents and felt that my joy on the day should not be ruined [...] By the time I received the letter, I had already been welcomed with great warmth in my parish. I had also experienced the great joy that actually existed in the diocese that Torsten Bohlin's idea had finally become reality. Therefore the letter did not hurt me so much.[42]

In connection with this passage, Persson reports that 'a mourning service was held in Svartvik's small church in Medelpad, with the church swathed in black fabric and with mourning and funeral hymns'. This was the parish in which the above-mentioned Göran Granberg served. Persson did not hear about this event until years later when she herself served in the parish. She says it did not offend her that much, 'because I was now well anchored in the love of my parishioners'.[43]

The vocation narratives of other women priests also describe how parish support enabled them to cope with denied recognition from their fellow priests. As we saw in Chapter 2, Kerstin Lindqvist-Bolling uses the term 'raison d'être' to suggest that the role of priest is fundamentally linked to her identity. She relates this to the recognition she received from her parishioners, which helped her to cope with the fact that '[m]any of my fellow priests have God's word that I should not be standing here'.[44]

Parish support was not the only factor that enabled the ordained women to endure expressions of opposition to the reform in the form of denied social recognition. One priest mentions a course during which a number of other priests came up to her:

> [They] declared that they were against women priests [...] Because there were so many of them, I felt my courage beginning to falter. Then another participant intervened. 'I love women priests, they're

---

42 Persson, 'Min väg till prästämbetet', pp. 49–50.
43 Ibid., pp. 49–50.
44 Lindqvist-Bolling, 'Förstadspräst', p. 41. So also, for example, No. 28.

my absolute favourite', he said and everyone laughed. The dismal atmosphere instantly disappeared.[45]

Other expressions of resistance to the principles of the reform that had practical consequences for the first women priests were job appointments. Owing to the existence of the conscience clause, this might involve not being given a job in a certain parish because another priest there opposed the reform. One example occurred in June 1968, when Vivan Krauklis (1923–2006, ordained 1967) did not obtain the position she had applied for because there were priests in the parish who refused to work with ordained women.[46] In the daily newspaper *Aftonbladet*, Krauklis underlined that she was not the only woman priest to be affected by such resistance:

> They are not fighting us openly. They are freezing us out. We are not free to apply for a job in Stockholm […] It is the insane principle of this issue that must be seen for what it is. That a single priest in a parish can refuse employment for a female colleague. If a woman has felt a calling to become a priest, she must become one out of inner compulsion. She should not then be prevented from serving.[47]

In the article the vicar, Sten Kahnlund (1903–1983), pointed out that both the parochial church council [*kyrkoråd*] and the parish assembly [*kyrkofullmäktige*] had taken unanimous decisions on the matter and that they were keen to have a female priest in the parish. Four of the five priests working in the parish were in favour, but one of them 'cannot work with a female colleague for reasons of conscience', Kahnlund said. This meant that Krauklis could not be hired 'even though the entire parish wants a female priest'.[48]

The article also interviewed the priest who refused to allow the appointment. He said that the church council was by no means unanimous, and that a number of laypeople shared his standpoint. The article stated that he was a member of the Church Coalition for the Bible and Confession. The Bishop of Stockholm, Helge Ljungberg, was also cited. He defended the procedure he had introduced, according to which male priests who had a negative view of women priests had the right of veto. Ljungberg added that there

---

45 No. 29.
46 Ann Lindgren, 'Söder får ingen kvinnlig präst', *Aftonbladet*, 12 June 1968; Magnus Briggert, 'Kvinnliga prästen drar sig självmant ur Katarina-bråket', *Expressen*, 13 June 1968.
47 Lindgren, 'Söder får ingen kvinnlig präst'.
48 Ibid.

was still 'a very critical attitude towards women priests, which the public is not aware of'.[49]

In the case of job openings, opposition might also manifest itself as a blocking tactic during the hiring procedure. During the decades in question, the procedure for appointing a priest was that applications were sent to the diocesan cathedral chapter. The chapter selected the three most suitable and best-qualified candidates for a position, and then the parish would choose between them. Because the women priests usually did not have many years of service, this meant that if a sufficiently large number of other priests with more years of service and better qualifications applied for a job, women were never even considered. For that reason, one of the women in the source material states that she slipped out the night before the deadline and posted her application.[50] That way, opponents of the reform would not have time to submit applications that might block her own.

This type of expression of opposition to the reform and denied recognition became more common in the 1970s, perhaps as a result of the ever-increasing number of women priests. One example appears in an article about a position as a priest in Vallda in the diocese of Gothenburg, which had been vacant for six months owing to a shortage of priests. When it became known that a woman had applied for the position, however, six other applications – from men – quickly ensued.[51] Newspaper reports suggest that such blocking tactics could also affect male priests who openly supported the reform.[52]

The cases described above involved opposition that was expressed openly in word and deed. It was claimed that this opposition was targeted at the principles behind the prevailing situation and at the people and institutions that had decided to implement the reform. In practice, however, it affected the women priests in the form of denied social recognition. The vocation narratives also portray expressions of opposition which were not as obvious, but which had the same consequences for the women priests' identity and self-image as more explicit forms of denied recognition. Judging from the vocation narratives, even subtle expressions of opposition from

49 Briggert, 'Kvinnliga prästen drar sig självmant ur Katarina-bråket'.
50 No. 19.
51 'Prästbrist – utom i Vallda', *Göteborgs-Posten*, 2 September 1978.
52 'Kvinnoprästernas motståndare välorganiserade', *Sydsvenska Dagbladet*, 22 August 1978.

their fellow priests took their toll on a number of the first ordained women. One of them writes as follows about the consequences of a subtle denial of recognition:

> I have been helped from within to endure the resistance from colleagues – dogged, silent, sometimes outwardly smiling. I have pushed the pain away, often with a: 'Lord, forgive them, they know no better.' But I have certainly felt disappointment at the absence of fellowship, in everyday life, and at not being able to share the deep joy before the face of God […] I have felt particular disappointment at frozen fellowship with former fellow students. Suddenly there was nothing but silence, possibly a pleasant facade. And I have backed away. I expect nothing from them, because they expect nothing from me[.]⁵³

One subtle form of opposition that might occur was to be frozen out. A number of the priests recount incidents in connection with continuing education courses for priests. One episode involved Carl Strandberg (1926–2013), who was not only co-author of the Church Coalition's Seventeen Points and a teacher of ecclesiastical law at Uppsala University's practical training term for priests, but also Cathedral Dean of Strängnäs. On the day of the course, the priest discovered that she was alone with 35 men, a situation she was quite used to. At lunch, however, it became clear precisely how alone she was:

> I did what everyone else did. I took the tray, I took food. Went and sat down at a table where four other priests were sitting. I didn't see that one of them was the dean. But all four of them picked up their trays and went and sat at another table.⁵⁴

In a similar vein, Ulla Nisser describes that the custom at longer continuing education courses in the diocese was to celebrate Holy Communion every morning. On the first morning a man always led the Communion service, and on the second morning it was always a woman. When women led the service, a quarter of the group would sleep in, citing reasons of conscience.⁵⁵ Nisser observes that '[t]he visible opposition was easier to handle than the hidden kind'.⁵⁶

The difference between open or visible opposition and concealed or unspecified resistance is also something that Caroline Krook has

---

53 No. 17.
54 No. 34.
55 Nisser, *Hopp från trampolin*, pp. 101–103.
56 Ibid., p. 100.

recognised. In her book *Prästens identitet och kyrkans trovärdighet* ['The priest's identity and the church's credibility'], she writes:

> The most painful thing I have encountered as a woman priest is not open opposition. That, I can even have some respect for, as long as it does not turn into personal attacks. The most difficult thing has been – and is – the situations where one is both accepted and not accepted. Where in certain situations one must stay away, so as not to openly reveal the division that is still a fact.[57]

However, it should also be said that those individuals who at one time opposed the 1958 decision did not necessarily remain opponents as time went by. One of the narrators writes: 'A few times, usually from colleagues, I have felt a rejection, a sense that I, as a woman, am not a real priest. Some have "reconsidered", though, and apologised to me later.'[58]

Non-recognition from other quarters

To complement other sections of this chapter, this is where there should be an account of 'non-recognition from the parishes'; but on the basis of the source material, this is not possible. Very few of the priests mention any expression of opposition from parishioners in the strict sense; there are only three examples.[59] This is not to say that there was no opposition to the reform of the priesthood among the laity in the Church of Sweden. There certainly was, but the first women priests' accounts of expressions of opposition basically refer to fellow clergy only. The explanation for this situation is probably that the first women priests were called by, assigned to and sought out parishes that had a view of the priesthood which included women.

There does, however, appear to have been some resistance from parishes to calling an ordained woman to be the vicar [*kyrkoherde*]. Welcoming a woman as an assistant priest [*komminister*] was one thing; but there appears to have been greater hesitation when it came to leadership positions such as that of a vicar. The article about Birgitta Nyman in *Du ska bli präst* ['You shall become

---

57 Krook, *Prästens identitet*, pp. 35–36.
58 No. 25.
59 No. 45; Bodil Fredfeldt in Bodil Fredfeldt, 'Vid Öresund', in *Kvinnlig präst idag*, p. 59; Elisabeth Djurle Olander in Wik-Thorsell, 'Kvinnlig präst söker aldrig konflikterna'.

a priest'] states that '[s]he applied for several jobs as a vicar and initially received none, because those parishes did not want a female vicar'.[60] Margit Sahlin and Margareta Brandby-Cöster describe similar experiences – that is, expressions of opposition to the reform had changed tack, coming to focus on preventing the advancement of women within the church hierarchy.[61]

The above-mentioned examples are the only ones we have found in the vocation narratives where the ordained women describe expressions of opposition from laypeople in the parishes. Two other examples exist where the source material discusses expressions of opposition from people other than fellow priests, but not strictly speaking from parishioners. One of these involves an undertaker's business that did not want to cooperate.[62] Another of the priests says that in her work as a hospital chaplain, she was denied recognition by some of the hospital staff. On one occasion, a chief physician encountered in one of the hospital's underground passages 'pushed me up against the wall and said: "Are you doing any good here or are you just walking around?"'[63] We heard this particular story through one of the interviews we conducted in order to supplement the source material. From our perspective, the incident – a young woman being shoved against a wall by a man in a secluded corridor – appeared striking. However, follow-up questions to the priest revealed that she did not interpret this as a form of harassment, but rather as something that was accepted in those days. The incident was not primarily related to her being a priest but to her being a woman. This demonstrates the lack of recognition that women in general in Swedish society often encountered at that time.

Recognition from bishops

The reception and recognition that the first women priests received from their parishioners and the fellow priests they encountered once they had joined the priesthood was, of course, of great importance. At least as important was the recognition – and sometimes denied recognition – that the women met with in their contacts

---

60 Sjöberg, 'Kyrkan måste vara ömsint', p. 63.
61 Nordlander, *Margit Sahlin*, pp. 272–274; Brandby-Cöster, 'Kvinnor som präster – också i Göteborgs stift'.
62 No. 25.
63 No. 26.

with the various bishops of the Church of Sweden. Since it was the bishop who decided on priestly ordination, his standpoint on the reform of the priesthood and his attitude towards implementing the 1958 General Synod decision were of the utmost importance to the individual priests.

The division within the Bishops' Conference on the issue of opening up the priesthood to women is well known, and the positions of the various bishops on grounds of principle have been discussed in detail in previous research on the reform of the priesthood.[64] In practice, however, the situation was not as simple as some bishops being in favour and others against. For example, one of the women priests tells us:

> During the spring I had enquired with the bishops who had ordained women. I had written to Bishop Ruben Josefson in Härnösand and Bishop Martin Lindström in Lund. After all, they had allowed me to serve as a pastoral assistant in their dioceses. However, I suppose they felt they had enough on their plates already and did not want to accept all female candidates. I had also visited Bishop Sven Silén in Västerås and Bishop Helge Ljungberg in Stockholm diocese, but without results.[65]

Here, then, we encounter a candidate priest who had been in contact with bishops in four different dioceses, men who had clearly stated that they would ordain women; but in practice, it was not so simple. The priest adds that she was denied ordination in her home diocese, not because the bishop was necessarily opposed, but on the grounds that the cathedral chapter was too divided on the issue of ordaining women.

The vocation narratives of the first women priests contain numerous and detailed depictions of the bishops. This is probably precisely because they are vocation narratives, in which the bishops may be taken to represent the Church's recognition and affirmation of the women's inner calling. A number of the vocation narratives reveal that the women candidates often received support, recognition and encouragement from their respective bishops; but the narratives also contain accounts of the women being challenged and even denied recognition of various kinds on the grounds that they were women.

---

64 See, for example, Andersson, *Den nödvändiga manligheten.*
65 No. 28.

The bishops most often mentioned are Gunnar Hultgren (1902–1991), Ruben Josefson (1907–1972) in Härnösand, Martin Lindström (1904–2000) in Lund, Helge Ljungberg in Stockholm and Bo Giertz in Gothenburg. Gunnar Hultgren succeeded Yngve Brilioth as archbishop (1958–1967).[66] The priests in our source material who came into contact with him generally say that Archbishop Hultgren was very accommodating. He could even act proactively to ensure that they took steps towards ordination. For example, Ingrid Persson describes how she received a personal question on Easter Saturday 1959:

> I was up in the archbishop's palace to wish the archbishop a happy Easter. We had coffee and chatted. As I was leaving, he said: 'There's something I want to talk to you about.' 'Yes?' 'I want to ask you if you would consider making yourself available to our Church as the first woman priest. We have a decision, but now we must act, too.'[67]

Here it becomes clear that Hultgren wanted the first ordinations of women to take place, and that he was keen to find suitable candidates. This attitude on his part is also emphasised by Elisabeth Djurle Olander, who says in an interview that Hultgren planned the whole thing very strategically and that part of that strategy was that at least three women would be ordained at the same time and in different places in the country.[68] Margit Sahlin also describes her dealings with Hultgren in favourable terms, highlighting how he worked strategically to make the ordination of women happen.[69]

The reason why Hultgren was so eager to move from decision to action is clear from a passage in Sahlin's diary and her correspondence with him in December 1959. She describes a conversation she had with Bishop Bo Giertz regarding her possible ordination. 'I asked Giertz if he believed there was a difference between merely

---

66 For a biographical presentation, see Klas Hansson, *Svenska kyrkans primas: Ärkebiskopsämbetet i förändring 1914–1990*, Acta Universitatis Upsaliensis: Studia Historico-Ecclesiastica Upsaliensia, 47 (Uppsala: Uppsala University, 2014), pp. 220–221 and the literature cited therein; Erik Bylund, 'Gunnar Hultgren 1902–1991', *Thule*, 4 (1991), 166–167; and Bertil Werkström, 'Parentation över Gunnar Hultgren vid Nathan Söderblomsällskapets årshögtid den 15 januari 1992', *Religion och bibel*, 51 (1992), 63–64.

67 Persson, 'Min väg till prästämbetet', pp. 44–45.

68 Brita Stendahl, *The Force of Tradition: A Case Study of Women Priests in Sweden* (Philadelphia: Fortress Press, 1985), p. 33.

69 Nordlander, *Margit Sahlin*, pp. 225, 238–239. See also No. 19.

making a decision and making a decision and then going on to implement it, too. He believed there was.'[70] To an opponent such as Giertz, a difference thus appears to have existed between making a principle-based decision and converting that decision into practice; and the practice was what mattered. This view might also reflect a hope that a decision which had not yet been implemented could be revoked. It is also interesting to note in Sahlin's letter to Hultgren that the presumption we have documented in previous chapters – that is, that the responsibility for avoiding conflict and division lay with the ordained women – appears to be in play here as well. According to Sahlin, Giertz wrote to her that she should 'refrain from utilising a freedom that is a matter of conscience for others' and that '[f]or love's sake, one should not put the other party in a situation that cannot but be untenable for them'.[71]

Judging from the vocation narratives, however, Hultgren was not always unreservedly positive. As Chapter 3 shows, the archbishop was involved in the long-running issue of Britta Olén-van Zijl's ordination. Even though he welcomed women's ordination, he appears to have believed in principle that marriage to a Reformed clergyman and residence abroad posed problems.[72]

As for Hultgren's theological starting points, these shine through in his ordination speech to Margit Sahlin on Palm Sunday 1960. The mandate as a priest is described in the speech as 'a service and nothing else'. The ordination address makes it clear how Hultgren anchors himself theologically in the concept of the folk church and the theology of service to the Word. The archbishop also emphasises that Sahlin's vocation is the same both before and after ordination, thereby acknowledging that it has been valid all along. The priestly office is depicted as a function that exists in order for the Gospel to be able to go out to people.[73] According to church historian Klas Hansson, this functional perspective is crucial to Hultgren's way of thinking about the priestly office. Hansson maintains that Hultgren linked this view to the Lutheran Confession and believed that in a Lutheran church, norms simply could not be imposed by tradition.[74]

70 Nordlander, *Margit Sahlin*, p. 227.
71 Letter from Margit Sahlin to Archbishop Gunnar Hultgren, 2 December 1959, Gunnar Hultgren Archive at the Central Church Office in Uppsala.
72 No. 18.
73 Gunnar Hultgren's speech at Margit Sahlin's ordination on 10 April 1960, Gunnar Hultgren Archive at the Central Church Office in Uppsala.
74 Hansson, *Svenska kyrkans primas*, pp. 226, 243, 260.

Hultgren's strategy was thus to conduct three ordinations at the same time. He himself would organise one of them and Ruben Josefson, Bishop of Härnösand, one of the other two.[75] It was not surprising that Josefson was chosen: not only had he voted in favour of the proposal in 1958, but in his role as editor of the magazine *Svensk Kyrkotidning*, which was written for and read by the clergy in the Church of Sweden as well as by theologians generally, he had positioned himself as an advocate of the reform.[76] It was also Josefson who later succeeded Hultgren as Archbishop of the Church of Sweden.

Josefson appears in the vocation narratives as a bishop who was keen for the Church of Sweden to ordain women as priests.[77] For example, Ingrid Persson writes that Josefson, when asked by the archbishop, 'immediately declared himself willing to receive me'.[78] He appears to have been proactive, too. One of the women priests describes how the senior priest in her home parish booked an appointment for her to talk to Josefson, because many people viewed her as a suitable candidate for the priesthood. At first she was sceptical and told the bishop that she did not feel she had received a call. 'Things became very quiet. For a long time. But then the bishop spoke in words that I cannot forget. He told me that his call of me to the priestly office was God's call. That I was needed in the diocese and must not refuse to serve in the Church and in a parish.'[79]

Josefson's theological points of departure in his view of vocation and the priestly office contain aspects of that folk church theology which stresses the concept of the priesthood of all believers. In addition, emphasis is placed on the functional aspect, whereby

---

75 Sten Rössborn, 'P L Ruben Josefson', *Svenskt biografiskt lexikon*, 20 (1973–1975), p. 414. See also Sten Rössborn, *En bok om Ruben Josefson* (Täby: Larson, 1970).

76 Boel Hössjer Sundman, 'Möta nutidsmänniskan och ge ett svar på hennes livs frågor: Om Ruben Josefsons teologi', in Hössjer Sundman (ed.), *Äntligen stod hon i predikstolen!*, pp. 150–151. According to the practical theologian Dag Sandahl, Josefson's comments on the Bishops' Conference's statement in connection with the General Synod's 'no' vote in 1957 were so critical that when he later issued a policy statement for *Svensk Kyrkotidning* that emphasised 'the Evangelical-Lutheran line', it prompted members of the Church Coalition to launch the publication *Svensk Pastoraltidskrift* in protest. Sandahl, *En annan Kyrka*, pp. 93–95.

77 For example, No. 19; Marianne Westrin in Westrin, 'I elfte timmen', p. 82.

78 Persson, 'Min väg till prästämbetet', p. 47.

79 No. 7.

the priest is regarded as an instrument for the dissemination of the Gospel. In other words, his theology is clearly that of a servant of the Word.[80]

In addition to theological reasons, there may have been practical reasons why Josefson welcomed the ordination of women. In the 1960s there was a shortage of priests in a number of dioceses, and a couple of the women priests mention this in their vocation narratives. One priest writes about Josefson and the situation in the diocese of Härnösand. After noting the lack of priests there, she writes: 'In the summer of 1962 there were only four women priests in Sweden, two of them in Härnösand diocese. Malicious tongues in Uppsala said of Ruben Josefson that "soon he will only have women and people with dispensations up there".'[81]

Martin Lindström was elected Bishop of Lund in 1960. During his ten years in the diocese, he took a clear stand in favour of ordaining women. The vocation narratives depict him as a welcoming and valued ally.[82] One priest describes how she asked the bishop if she could work as a pastoral assistant [tjänstebiträde] because her own diocese was 'closed' to women who wished to be ordained. She writes of her joy and relief after meeting with Lindström:

> When I spoke to Bishop Martin Lindström the other day, I met with the first positive response in a long time. Why didn't I apply for ordination, he wondered. He was keen to get priests into the diocese and would be happy to organise an extra ordination for me. What a blessing to finally feel like an asset after having felt like a liability for so long.[83]

The priest's words bear witness both to Lindström's attitude and to the importance for her of having her vocation recognised. In connection with her ordination, Lindström once again proved to be a support when her intended ordination assistants turned her down one by one. One of those she had asked 'had misgivings about

---

80 Ruben Josefson, *Herdabrev till Härnösands Stift* (Stockholm: Diakonistyrelsen, 1959), pp. 87–88. These features of Josefson's theology are also discussed by Boel Hössjer Sundman, who identifies 'the Bible, the Confessional writings, and the Evangelical-Lutheran tradition' as central starting points; see Hössjer Sundman, 'Möta nutidsmänniskan', pp. 150, 155–157.
81 No. 25.
82 For example, No. 34; No. 35; No. 45.
83 No. 29.

women priests', another was unable to attend and a third did not dare to take on the role. In this difficult situation Lindström personally arranged for priests to assist her.[84]

Lindström was also the bishop who ordained Britta Olén-van Zijl on 17 March 1963. As noted in Chapter 3, a number of bishops had previously refused her request for ordination on the grounds that she was married to a Dutch Reform minister. That was Lindström's initial response, too.[85] In her vocation narrative, Olén-van Zijl writes that Lindström only gave in when her husband promised him that they would stay in Sweden for a few years. '"In the name of God, then", the bishop said.'[86] It is worth observing that this was the first ordination of a woman in the diocese of Lund. After Helge Ljungberg, Lindström was the bishop who ordained the greatest number of women priests: 13 during his time in office.

Like his fellow bishops, Lindström anchored his theological position on women's ordination in the understanding of the priestly office as being 'in service to the Word'. The main objective is that the Word is proclaimed and the sacraments administered. How this is done can and should vary depending on the time and context in which the Church has to operate.[87] He also rejected the concept of representation, arguing that 'such a view of the office is completely foreign both to the New Testament and to our [Lutheran] Confession'. He points out that 'the Church's priestly office is instituted as a function, the proclamation of the Gospel and the administration of the sacraments, and as such is assigned its role'.[88] It is also worth mentioning that after retiring as a bishop, Lindström participated vigorously in the intense debate on the desirability or otherwise of the conscience clause in the late 1970s and early 1980s. One manifestation of this engagement was the book *Bibeln och bekännelsen om kvinnliga präster* ['The Bible and the Confession on women priests'], published in 1978.[89]

84 Ibid.
85 Maria van Zijl, 'Minnesord om Britta van Zijl', *Sydsvenskan*, 24 March 2017. Her path to ordination is similarly described in Olén-van Zijl, 'Att få vara präst', pp. 106–107.
86 Britta Olén-van Zijl's vocation narrative.
87 Martin Lindström, *Herdabrev till Lunds Stift* (Lund: Diakonistyrelsen, 1960), pp. 12–13 (p. 12).
88 Ibid., p. 17.
89 Martin Lindström, *Bibeln och bekännelsen om kvinnliga präster* (Stockholm: Verbum, 1978).

Ambivalent recognition from bishops

The other bishop asked by Hultgren to participate in the ordinations on Palm Sunday 1960 was Helge Ljungberg, Bishop of Stockholm from 1954 to 1971. Ljungberg had also voted in favour of opening up the priesthood to women at the 1958 General Synod.[90]

Ljungberg is mentioned in at least seven of the narratives. The picture that emerges is not as unreservedly positive as that encountered in the stories about Hultgren, Josefson and Lindström. Although some of the recollections are favourable, Ljungberg appears to have had some doubts about the reform of the priesthood and the ensuing situation. Margit Sahlin's diary entries supply examples; she describes several meetings with him. In one conversation they discussed whether she should be given a *venia*, but he did not want to issue one, stating that she was allowed to preach whenever she wanted even without a *venia*. When her application to be ordained as a priest for the diocese of Stockholm came up in the conversation, Sahlin asked Ljungberg if he wanted her to withdraw her application. He suggested that they should postpone her ordination and that Sahlin could perhaps be ordained for the diocese of Härnösand instead. Sahlin found it contradictory that he seemed unwilling to ordain her while holding the view that she could preach as much as she wanted without a *venia*.

Sahlin tried to press Ljungberg for an answer about the *venia* but received no clear response. The issue attracted the attention of the media, which also demanded a reply from him. Sahlin describes the incident in her diary:

> It was then that the bishop made his classic remark that the matter was too complicated for the public to understand. He could spend a couple of hours explaining it to the journalist, who still wouldn't get it. This failed episcopal statement set all the fuel on fire [...] Helge Ljungberg became a personification of the failed and cowardly episcopate.[91]

---

90 An account of Helge Ljungberg's time as Bishop of Stockholm can be found in Caroline Krook, *Från stor stad till storstad: Stockholms stift igår och idag* (Stockholm: Verbum, 2020), pp. 72–84.

91 Nordlander, *Margit Sahlin*, pp. 222, 238–239. The Sigtuna Foundation's archive of press cuttings contains some cuttings about Ljungberg's actions. The situation appears to have been somewhat more complex than that depicted in Sahlin's diary. For example, *Svenska Dagbladet* (30 September 1959) writes that there are some 'obscure points in the course of events' and

The question of whether or not Sahlin should receive a *venia* thus attracted media interest, and from her diary it appears that Ljungberg did not really know how he should handle the matter. He would also seem to have given Sahlin a good deal of scolding over the way the issue developed. However, Archbishop Hultgren made him realise that Sahlin had 'in reality defended him against all the virulent attacks'.[92]

In the light of this conflict, it is understandable that Sahlin wrote in her correspondence with Hultgren that she wanted the archbishop himself to ordain her and not Ljungberg, who had referred her to the diocese of Härnösand. In her letter to Hultgren, Sahlin writes the following about the Bishop of Stockholm:

> He had nothing against women priests in principle, but would find it too difficult to perform an ordination himself. It should be fairly easy to force him to take such a step with the help of the whipped-up press, but it would be a nightmare to receive ordination under such circumstances.[93]

This passage clearly shows that Sahlin did not want to be ordained by a bishop who was ambivalent and could only half-heartedly consider recognising her vocation. She also describes a meeting with Ljungberg before her ordination, when she was summoned to him together with Barbro Nordholm-Ståhl and Elisabeth Djurle Olander, the two other women who were in line for ordination in the diocese of Stockholm. Sahlin writes:

> Ljungberg received us in an unfriendly manner and immediately said that it had happened before that ministers had been made to sign death warrants against their will. He was very much against this ordination but nor could he say no. He mentioned something about yielding to state authorities, women's issues, etc. To this I replied by

---

that Ljungberg said that he had already replied to Sahlin on this issue. *SvD* argues that this was a reason why a bishop should in future not grant *venia* orally but in writing, so that there need not be any uncertainty about what has happened and that people can thereby avoid commotion and misunderstanding. The assertion that Ljungberg had claimed that the issue was too complicated for the public to understand comes from the column 'Bock i kanten', *Stockholms-Tidningen*, 21 September 1959 (written by the Court of Appeal judge Viktor Petrén), and from an item with the heading 'Bibeln' in *Expressen*, 12 September 1959.

92 Nordlander, *Margit Sahlin*, pp. 238–239.

93 Letter from Margit Sahlin to Archbishop Gunnar Hultgren, 22 September 1959, Gunnar Hultgren Archive, Central Church Office Archive in Uppsala.

presenting some observations from my standpoint. This he called women's thinking.[94]

Whereas Sahlin depicts Ljungberg as dismissive, another priest's vocation narrative says that she was supported by Ljungberg in her vocation, that it was on his advice that she remained as a pastoral assistant in one of the diocese's parishes, and that he subsequently ordained her.[95] A third priest also paints a favourable picture of Ljungberg in her vocation narrative.[96]

What is clear is that Ljungberg had difficulty navigating this sensitive issue. Yet another priest describes the contortions that occurred. She states that a phone call with the bishop revealed that he was not in favour of ordaining her and that 'he basically wanted to say no to me'. However, she plucked up her courage and requested a personal meeting. According to her, he had been 'annoyed' by the fact that two parishes in the diocese had asked for her to be ordained and assigned to their respective parishes. Ljungberg was upset by this behaviour on the part of the two vicars and stated that it was a breach of tradition to make this kind of request. According to this priest, she sensed trouble at this point, and after this meeting with the bishop she contacted a theology professor who had taught her.[97] The professor offered to talk to Bishop Ljungberg, and when she arrived at the agreed meeting, the bishop had changed his mind and booked a date for the ordination.[98] However, it turned out that the male ordinands did not want to be ordained at the same time as she. Consequently, she had to be ordained separately – a decision that came just a few days before the ordination was to take place.[99] Drawing on Honneth's concept, we could categorise this situation as being one of contradictory and ambivalent recognition.

---

94 Nordlander, *Margit Sahlin*, pp. 240–241.
95 No. 2.
96 No. 20.
97 Cf. Klas Hansson, who notes that Archbishop Josefson was convinced that it 'was the parish that controlled the office and had the task of calling office holders'. Hansson, *Svenska kyrkans primas*, p. 271.
98 No. 26. A similar arrangement, that is, that the candidate for ordination makes contact with a parish in the diocese of Stockholm, is found in No. 37: 'I became increasingly certain about becoming ordained and contacted a parish in Stockholm, which would gladly receive me as a priest.'
99 No. 26. Another case of separate ordination with Helge Ljungberg as the ordaining bishop is found in No. 33.

The picture becomes even more complex if we consult newspaper articles of that time. As we saw in previous chapters, the ordination of women often attracted much media interest, and the newspapers had caught wind of the male ordinands' refusal and demanded an answer from Ljungberg as to how the situation would be resolved. One of the articles states that the bishop felt that women should also be ordained in other dioceses than that of Stockholm, and that he wished to postpone the woman's ordination. The article suggests that priests belonging to the Church Coalition not infrequently 'try to influence bishops not to ordain women theologians'. There are many indications that Ljungberg was also subjected to such pressure.[100]

Another article states that some priests threatened the bishop with leaving the diocese if 'women priests become too prominent a feature of the Stockholm diocese'. The writer is of the opinion that Ljungberg's actions are in conflict with the legal framework that he as a bishop had chosen to adhere to, that is, the decisions of the General Synod and Riksdag. In addition, the writer states: 'The variant of ordination refusal that Bishop Ljungberg launches when he introduces a rationing of women priests is, however, not one bit more excusable than if a bishop totally refuses to deal with ordination applications from women.'[101]

Ljungberg appears to have been irresolute when faced with the women who contacted him with a desire to be ordained in order to serve in the diocese of Stockholm. It is reasonable to assume that his hesitation was not due to any conscientious objections to ordaining women, but probably stemmed from a fear of being buffeted about in yet another media frenzy, plus a desire to stay on good terms with those elements of the priesthood who rejected the 1958 reform. An episode recounted in one of the vocation narratives indicates that Ljungberg attempted to keep the diocese he headed together. It concerns a candidate for the priesthood who was

---

100 Eric Sjöquist, 'Sex dagar kvar till prästvigning. Men kvinnlig kandidat vet ännu ej om hon blir präst!' ['Six days left before ordination. But the female candidate still doesn't know if she will become a priest!'], *Expressen*, 14 December 1965. That the bishop had been on a two-month trip to South Africa is evident from *Svenska Dagbladet*, 13 December 1965, which contains an article with the headline 'Biskop Ljungberg hem från Afrika' ['Bishop Ljungberg home from Africa']. See also 'Biskop Ljungberg tvekar prästviga ännu en kvinna' ['Bishop Ljungberg hesitates to ordain yet another woman'], *Svenska Dagbladet*, 16 December 1965.
101 'För stor makt', *Expressen*, 18 December 1965.

looking for a diocese to be ordained for. She contacted Ljungberg because she had had a *venia* in his diocese. The priest writes: 'To this he gave the following peculiar answer: "Out on the islands it might be possible. With regard to the rest, my diocese is falling apart over the issue of women priests."'[102] Nevertheless, whatever the motive, the bishop's conduct viewed from the women's perspective comes across as unsympathetic and hard to interpret. Again, to use Axel Honneth's terms, we can speak of an ambivalent recognition on his part.

Ljungberg seems to have been in favour of the reform in principle. In practice, his position was less clear. As we have shown, there was considerable ambivalence about both the legal and the social recognition of the women's vocations. This ambivalence was, of course, a reflection of the ambiguity expressed by the conscience clause.

While we might be surprised at the bishop's behaviour in relation to some of the female priestly candidates and their possible ordination, it should be pointed out that the majority of the women ordained during the period 1960 to 1970 were ordained for the diocese of Stockholm. Of the 54 women ordained during this period, no less than 20 were ordained there, most of them by Ljungberg.

Among the bishops who opposed ordaining women, the Bishop of Gothenburg, Bo Giertz, is the one most frequently mentioned. This is hardly surprising, given that, as mentioned earlier, he was a rallying force for the Church Coalition and the opposition to the reform of the priesthood.[103] What might be unexpected, however, is that Giertz is portrayed in favourable terms in a couple of the vocation narratives. He is described as an important spiritual leader for some of the first women priests, both through his writings in the late 1930s and early 1940s and as a Christian. In the context of KGF, he was also a very popular lecturer.

One priest in particular, who grew up in Gothenburg and knew Giertz personally, observes that he was always pleasant, even though he knew she intended to be ordained. She goes on to say that because she intended to become a priest, she was not invited to the diocesan group's gatherings like the other women theology students who came from the diocese of Gothenburg and

---

102 No. 28.
103 For a brief biography of Bo Giertz, see Alexander Gustavsson, 'Manlig bekännelsetrohet', pp. 9–67, 173–178.

who had their sights set on becoming priests' wives or teachers. But when the bishop visited the diocesan group she was always invited to attend by a male acquaintance, and on these occasions Giertz would 'stride up' to her and greet her in a friendly manner. She says that this contrast between the bishop's goodwill and his rejection on principle of women's ordination created mixed feelings in her.[104] Yet again, an element of ambivalence is revealed in the contrast between social recognition and a denial of legal recognition.

∞∞∞∞

This chapter has shed light on historical narratives about the Church of Sweden regarding the laity's attitude to the reform: on the one hand, the narrative according to which 'active parishioners' were negative towards the reform, and on the other hand the narrative concerning the positive opinion held by members of the Church of Sweden in general. In the latter narrative, there was a strong tendency to draw a contrast between the liberal-minded laity and conservative priests who opposed the reform.

The vocation narratives complement and complicate both these narratives. They show that the first women priests received great and warm support from both fellow priests and parishes, from 'active Church people' as well as from other members of the Church of Sweden. It was far from being the case that a supposedly theologically ignorant public and secularised state authority were the only ones to welcome ordained women into service as priests. The legal recognition they received through the 1958 General Synod decision and their ordination was hence confirmed and reinforced by social recognition when they entered the ministry as parish priests.

At the same time, the vocation narratives testify to the existence of fellow priests who opposed the reform and expressed this resistance in both word and deed, sometimes explicitly, sometimes subtly. We have demonstrated that the perception that these expressions of opposition were limited to the level of principle, and were aimed against the people who decided in favour of the legal recognition of women priests, is false. In practice, these expressions of opposition primarily affected the first women to be ordained as priests. The language used and the action plan established by certain groups of opponents, for instance as expressed in the Seventeen Points, resulted in a denial of social recognition that

---

104 No. 34.

rejected the vocation which was profoundly bound up with the ordained women's identity.

This chapter has also highlighted how recognition from colleagues and parishes partly blunted the opposition, expressed as denied recognition, that the first women priests had to face. Their external call from parishes and fellow priests played an important part in the affirmation of their internal call.

In this chapter, we have also touched on recognition by bishops. These church leaders emerge as key figures in the vocation narratives of the first ordained women. With regard to the bishops who are most prominent in the material, there are a number of recurring themes. In the narratives of the first women priests, some of these bishops appear to be not only willing but sometimes even keen to ordain them. To some extent, this can probably be attributed to the genre of the vocation narrative itself. Recognition of the vocation is an essential component of the plotline, and of course it adds weight when bishops appear to be eager. At the same time, the keen bishops cannot be dismissed as a mere narrative device. The bishops' own statements in other contexts support the idea that they acted on the basis of (theological) convictions, as does the fact that the vocation narratives contain plenty of descriptions that are not so unequivocally positive.

As we have shown, the bishops could also be ambivalent about recognising the women's vocation. In principle, they favoured the reform; but in practice they were shaking in their shoes. One example of this nervousness is Bishop Ljungberg of Stockholm, who comes across as somewhat indecisive and irritable. Yet it was he who accepted and ordained by far the largest number of women.

The theological reasoning regarding vocation expressed by the first ordained women recurs among the bishops in different variants. Among the bishops, the priestly office is emphasised above all as being a function rather than a representation. The reasoning is explicitly linked to the Lutheran Confession, the priesthood of all believers, the folk church theology and the theology of the priest as a servant of the Word.

Although those bishops who favoured the reform end up in the spotlight in our discussion, the vocation narratives also contain accounts of bishops who were more hostile. It is interesting to note that the image of the bishop who was a leading figure in the opposition to the reform, Bo Giertz, is ambivalent. When he appears in the material, he is depicted as he usually appears in historical accounts: as a hardline opponent of the reform. At the same time, there are examples of his being an important influence on the spiritual development and biblical views of some of the first women priests. In other words, this is another example of how practices may shed light on principles, and how this kind of source material can complement and complicate historical narratives.

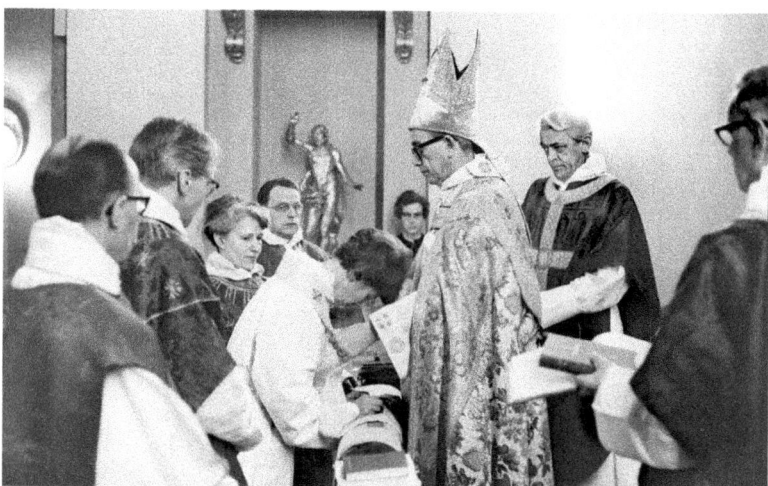

This photograph was taken at the ordination of Marianne Westrin in 1965. In the book *Kvinnlig präst idag: Tio kvinnliga präster berättar* (1967, p. 82), Westrin wrote: 'Ordination, that luminous, joyous celebration. Sole candidate for the priesthood facing the altar in the Cathedral of Härnösand. Beside me the first woman to have been ordained at that altar, Ingrid Persson, assistant priest in Njurunda. On my other side a piece of my childhood, represented by the son of the priest of Offerdal, Gunnar Åkerstedt. In the veterans' space by the altar rails the vicar of my home parish, Olof Sivertsson, the first mediator of my vocation to become a priest [...] My brother Bertil Edström, assistant priest of Björnlunda, delivered the scriptural address and administered the bread and wine to his sister. In front of me, Bishop Ruben Josefson. My future diocesan head received the small priest as if it were a great day of joy for his church. On that day, a cup full of grace was handed to me.' (Image: reproduced by courtesy of Profilbild i Härnösand AB/Kjell Jonsson.)

Chapter 7
The struggle for recognition

To me he represented the typical rigid High Church mentality, although as a human being he was endearing, humble, sweet. Now he gave an insight into his personal pain that I was grateful to share. His big question was: Are we still members of the body of Christ? Are we part of the Church? Or is all that forfeited? Is it because we no longer belong to the body of Christ that everything is out of order and not working? Or should one participate in all this suffering? From the intensity of this pain, a whole new light falls on all the anxiety about women priests. Certainly in many it is a fear of women. But it is also a despairing love for the Church of Christ. And I myself am suffering from the division of the Church and from the relationship between men and women. The children of God are suffering. Is this unnecessary suffering, which God laughs at? Or is it Christ who suffers in his broken and sickly limbs?[1]

Margit Sahlin's diary entry about a conversation with a friend who opposed the reform on the basis of his High Church view of the priesthood illustrates the narrative of division that we have repeatedly discussed in this book. According to this narrative, the ordination of women as priests led to division and conflict. Consequently, Sahlin's friend believed that the division in the Church of Sweden and the pain he felt about it was caused by her and her desire to be a priest. As we have previously shown, the narrative of division was widespread and something that everyone concerned had to deal with.

As we saw in the preceding chapter, Bishop Helge Ljungberg was affiliated with this narrative through his ambivalent attitude. Bishop Ruben Josefson referred to the narrative; however, he emphasises that the reform was not the cause of the division but had merely exposed it and thereby risked deepening pre-existing

---

1 Nordlander, *Margit Sahlin*, p. 206.

conflicts within the Church of Sweden.[2] The narrative of division is a recurring theme in the vocation narratives as well. The first women priests have had to deal with this narrative throughout their professional lives, and as a result it has been incorporated into the vocation narratives.

It is not surprising that this association between reform and division arose. As we highlighted in Chapter 3, the memory of the division that arose in relation to the revivalist movements and the Free Churches was still very much alive. In the debate that preceded the General Synod's decision in 1958, division within the Church was repeatedly mentioned as a possible consequence of the reform, and the last-minute introduction of the so-called conscience clause was a result of that concern. The striking element here is that the responsibility for avoiding this division was placed on the first women to be ordained as priests. As we will show in this chapter, the outcome was something resembling a code of conduct.

Previous chapters have shown how the narrative of division could be expressed by opponents of the reform. The narrative legitimised a use of language and a plan of action whose consequences were the denial of social recognition to the women priests. The expressions of opposition were often claimed to be targeted against the principle – that is, the legal recognition of the women's vocation. In practice, though, the vocation narratives bear witness to the fact that it was the women priests who bore the brunt through denied social recognition.

The opponents of the reform were not entirely unaware that the expressions of their opposition actually constituted blows directed against the women priests. A 1959 article by G. A. Danell may serve as an example of this awareness. Danell stresses that he wants to express his approval of the women who had abstained from being ordained as priests, and that he 'regarded the position taken by these women as a sacrifice for the unity which the Church is increasingly in need of'.[3] Drawing on Honneth's theory, we might describe his standpoint as a case of 'unjust ideological recognition'. This occurs when an institution or a group affirms oppressive social structures by extending recognition to something that will not lead to full recognition for the individual in the long run.[4]

---

2 Josefson, *Herdabrev till Härnösands Stift*, pp. 37–38.
3 'Erkännande åt de kvinnor som avstår prästämbetet', *Dagens Nyheter*, 27 January 1959.
4 Zurn, *Axel Honneth*, pp. 96–98, 113–126.

This chapter examines how the first women priests addressed and dealt with the narrative of division, with its consequences in the form of denied recognition. In this context, the value of the differences in timing among the vocation narratives becomes apparent. The early source material from the 1960s gives access to descriptions of this response, while the later source material from the 2000s gives access to the first women priests' meta-reflections on it. Meta-reflections are comments that the narrator of a narrative makes on its content. The more time that has passed since the actual event, the more common such reflections are. They can be expressed in various ways, such as 'today I realise that what happened then was really about this', 'that's not how it is today', 'one explanation for why it happened is...' or 'I would probably have done it differently now'. In connection with the content of this chapter, we want to reiterate that the first women priests are not the only ones who might have reassessed their positions over time: the same might well apply to opponents of the reform who are mentioned in the present study.

In addition, this chapter discusses the brief comments made in the meta-reflections contained in the vocation narratives about the consequences of the code of conduct in the light of Honneth's theory. Honneth argues that repeated moral violations in the form of denied recognition tend to lead to a struggle for recognition. As the preceding chapter pointed out, not many of the vocation narratives say anything about the course of events after the 1960s. This is not surprising, since they are primarily concerned with the path to ordination. An in-depth study of this topic would have required a book of its own, and that is not the purpose here.[5] However, with the help of newspaper material, we do want to paint a picture of the course of events during the 1970s and 1980s in order to contextualise and create an understanding of the meta-reflections of the narratives.

The code of conduct

We believe that the narrative of division may be said to have led to the establishment of what Margareta Brandby-Cöster calls

---

5 For a review of the tensions that arose in the Church of Sweden and the tendencies towards division from the 1970s onwards, see the works cited in Chapter 1.

a code of conduct for women in the priesthood.[6] In connection with the General Synod's decision in 1958 to open up the priesthood to women, representatives of both the state and the Church stated that they expected the first women priests not to create divisions, to refrain from all situations that might lead to division becoming visible, and to give way in favour of opponents of the reform. Speaking to the media, Archbishop Hultgren emphasised that there would be no persecution of opponents and that bishops would not be required to ordain women. He stated the following:

> The women who wish to become priests certainly will not want conflict. On the contrary, their endeavour will naturally be to support the Church, which is under attack from many quarters, and the essential thing for them will be that the Gospel be propagated and proclaimed. Through the Synod's decision, the Church will probably be spared such fruitless acts of scholastic disputation as have preceded the decision.[7]

The archbishop also pointed out that not many women even wanted to become priests because it risked increasing the division in the Church, and that he himself had received a 'strong impression of the sense of solidarity and the moderation behind their decision in what is a difficult decision for them'.[8] Considering how strategically and far in advance Hultgren had planned the first ordinations of women on Palm Sunday 1960, this statement is noteworthy. Once again an ambivalence is revealed: on the one hand, the archbishop extends his support in principle by ordaining women as priests; and on the other hand he introduces a code of conduct which, together with the conscience clause, sanctions expressions of opposition to the reform.

Minister of Education and Ecclesiastical Affairs Ragnar Edenman (1914–1998) expressed similar expectations of future women priests:

> I am particularly keen to stress that there is every reason to believe that the women who wish to become priests will avoid anything that might lead to conflict, precisely out of concern for the good of the Church, and that they will voluntarily seek out those areas of the Church's activity where they are most needed.[9]

---

6 Brandby-Cöster, 'Dubbla budskap', p. 168.
7 'Kvinnliga präster', *Sydsvenska Dagbladet*, 29 September 1958.
8 'Svar om kvinnopräst till engelsk ärkebiskop', *Svenska Dagbladet*, 22 January 1959.
9 Brandby-Cöster, 'Dubbla budskap', p. 168.

At the beginning of the 1960s and when women were first ordained as priests, there thus existed a clearly stated expectation of them. When the first women priests meta-reflect in their vocation narratives, comments about this situation are frequent.[10] In her vocation narrative, Birgitta Nyman comments as follows:

> We felt very strongly that the Church was not fully behind us. There was a decision, but no active support. The Church did not pursue a theological policy that it was desirable and good to have women in the priesthood. Rather, it felt as if the Church regarded the decision as a concession and us as a problem. It was the women priests who were supposed to get out of the way all the time, so as not to offend anyone's theological views.[11]

The theme recurs in the vocation narratives: the women tried to avoid creating conflict.[12] For example, one narrator reflecting on her situation as a newly ordained priest comments: 'I don't believe I was alone in trying to keep a low profile, not to seek conflict, to conform, to be obliging [...] We should not be too visible and above all not function or appear in a diocesan context.'[13]

The first women priests thus understood that there was such a thing as a code of conduct, and a number of them maintain that they acted in accordance with it. This compliance might mean that they repeatedly had to relate to the ruling narrative of division, particularly in relation to the media. One example occurred when Margit Sahlin, Elisabeth Djurle Olander and Ingrid Persson were interviewed in January 1960 about their upcoming ordinations. They do not describe unalloyed joy; instead they stress that they feel pain over the division. Sahlin says that she suffers as a result of causing people she is close to 'outrage and anguish'; Djurle Olander says that she is happy to be ordained, while stressing that she finds 'the division that exists within our church' painful; and Persson says that 'the division that already exists' is difficult, and that 'the first ordination of women will not help to bridge it'.[14] In this context,

---

10 For example, Margareta Brandby-Cöster in Brandby-Cöster, 'Dubbla budskap', pp. 165–166; Caroline Krook in Krook, *Prästens identitet*, pp. 35–36; Ingrid Persson in Landström, 'En stilla stund 40 år efter prästvigningen'; Barbro Westlund in Sjöberg, 'Jag är så tacksam över att leva', p. 52.

11 Sjöberg, 'Kyrkan måste vara ömsint', p. 59.

12 No. 18; No. 19.

13 No. 28.

14 'Kvinnliga prästkandidater känner glädje över beslutet', *Svenska Dagbladet*, 22 January 1960.

it should be noted that Persson, like Bishop Josefson, questions the idea that the narrative of division was caused by the reform.

Another manifestation of the code of conduct can be glimpsed in the way some of the first women priests describe their experiences of opposition to the reform. In the early source material, they emerge as highly conciliatory, respectful and placatory in the way they talk about their opponents, and they make an effort to depict good examples of well-functioning collaboration. The vocation narratives from 1967 contain a number of such examples.[15]

Siv Bejerfors devotes particular attention to this matter. She emphasises that the notion that the proponents are always good and the opponents evil is an oversimplification. Rather, the decisive factor is whether or not the standpoint in question is dictated by love of God and of humanity. The issue is hence much more complex than many people claim. She writes: 'Encountering someone with an opposing view can mean meeting a great deal of personal kindness and an honest attempt at understanding, something I have experienced many times.' Bejerfors then supplies examples of a number of such good encounters, including one with a friend who is disappointed in her because of her ordination but who nevertheless blesses her. 'My reaction can only be this: how I admire such honesty combined with love!' There is also the former fellow student who is an opponent, but who calls her in order to declare, 'I want you to know that we are just as good friends as before.'[16] In contrast to these examples, though, Bejerfors also mentions an occasion when she was not treated with the same respect: when she received a letter from an opponent writing in 'deepest distress'. Her comment on this is: 'How it saddens me that I have caused you distress, you who are a good and faithful servant of the Lord.'[17]

This conciliatory attitude is also apparent when the women who were ordained as priests in the 1960s were interviewed in the media. The title of a 1967 article 'Kvinnlig präst söker aldrig konflikterna' ['A woman priest never seeks conflicts'] says it all. The three women priests interviewed in the article stress that the situation is becoming easier all the time, that the conflicts

---

15 Lindqvist-Bolling, 'Förstadspräst', pp. 56–57.
16 Bejerfors, 'Lärare och präst', pp. 117–118, 120.
17 Ibid., p. 119.

are less noticeable, and that it is even possible to avoid many of them.[18] In another article from 1965, in which four women priests were interviewed separately about their experiences, the overall theme is that in practice, out in the parishes, the situation is peaceful. All but one of the women emphasise that they are not significantly disturbed by the opposition. Karin Svensson (1918–2009, ordained 1961) observes that she has never experienced any trouble, and that women priests are accepted by High Church male colleagues on the practical level. Barbro Nordholm-Ståhl argues that the beliefs behind the attacks by High Church priests must be respected and that it is necessary to accept differing viewpoints.[19]

Further examples of how the first women priests responded to the narrative of division by demonstrating how well they collaborated with opponents of reform exist in the many accounts of friendships with these opponents. Such friendships could date back to the time before ordination. Margit Sahlin, for example, speaks in her diary about her love for her High Church friends and role models.[20] Another example is given by Lena Malmgren, who supplied the following account in a public lecture:

And I came to Lund and the St Lawrence Foundation and made a bunch of High Church friends in addition to those who came from Gothenburg, to argue with and party with. The fact that we did both was important; we knew one another's opinions and we liked one another. 'Do you know what it costs to love?' my grandchild asked the last time we met. To yearn. Yes, I would say I know, and the pain of being separated by a chasm like the one in the Church, I always carry that with me.[21]

In an interview shortly before her death, she commented on this issue, pointing out that these friendships had built bridges and that

18 Wik-Thorsell, 'Kvinnlig präst söker aldrig konflikterna'. A similar idea – that is, that the conflicts have gradually decreased – is emphasised in Karin Algrim, 'Eve and Martha – But What about Mary? An Interview with a Woman Priest', *Hertha*, 5 (1969), 64–66.

19 'Edra söner och döttrar skola predika', *Hudiksvalls Tidning*, 28 February 1965.

20 Nordlander, *Margit Sahlin*, p. 205.

21 Lena Malmgren, '50 år med kvinnliga präster – ur mitt perspektiv, men bara med typiska händelser', lecture in Lund's All Saints Church, September 2008, LUKA. Malmgren was originally from the diocese of Gothenburg, where traditional Lutheran Church Pietism was strong.

one of her friends, a fairly high-profile opponent of the reform, had said that she had 'been a bridge' in and through her person.[22]

The bridge-builder concept recurs in other narratives, too. Another woman priest describes herself as a bridge-builder and describes in an interview how she was praised during her training for 'having such a good hand with the people of Gothenburg'[23]– that is, men from a diocese well known to be opposed to the reform. The same priest says that she experienced good collaboration with opponents of reform, collaboration that developed after her ordination through her service as a priest.[24]

Another priest tells the story of when she arrived as the new vicar of a parish where a group of High Church opponents of the reform used to be allowed to use the church to pray the Liturgy of the Hours. Over time they became friends, and the priest even says that she sometimes served as organist at their services. She acknowledges that she has sometimes been criticised for this openness towards and closeness to those who hold a different view of the priestly office:

> As human beings we are different, and I have always tried to build good relations also with those who have a different view of the office. Sometimes I have been criticised by certain female colleagues, and by others as well, for being too compliant and not having struggled more. But you cannot do violence to yourself, and I have had to act as I saw fit.[25]

A number of the other priests also describe friendship and good cooperation in their vocation narratives.[26] This conciliatory and respectful approach was noticed by their contemporaries, something that emerges, for example, in two reviews of the anthology *Kvinnlig präst idag* ('Woman priest today'). The priest and author Inge Löfström (1914–2011) writes:

> Anyone expecting to find sensational revelations and dramatic episodes from the battle over women priests will be disappointed. We read about the work of a priest throughout the week, sometimes in the form of a diary, about the changing tasks, about joys and

---

22 Lena Malmgren's vocation narrative.
23 No. 26.
24 Ibid.
25 No. 19.
26 No. 37; No. 44; No. 45.

difficulties, much as things are for male priests. The work seems to be little affected by the Church disputes.[27]

The author Rune Pär Olofsson (1926–2018) even hints at some disappointment in his review, opining that '[o]ne of these women should surely have been able to possess the moral courage to provide a frank account'.[28] He goes on to write:

[T]he positive accounts of the solidarity of the 'brothers in office' are also surprisingly numerous. Yet one cannot escape the feeling that much in this book is presented so as to be palatable to the audience: Look how well things have gone for us, we are not causing any trouble![29]

The reviewers' reactions might be regarded as a result of their expectation that the polemics existing in the Church of Sweden at the national level would be reflected in the practical work at the parish level. In view of the code of conduct, though, it is understandable that few of the first women priests wanted to talk about conflict, division and expressions of opposition.

The efforts of the first women priests to speak well of reform opponents and to highlight examples of good collaboration and friendship need not merely be an expression of the code of conduct. Many of these accounts of bridge-building, happy cooperation and close friendship also exist in the previously unpublished vocation narratives, written many years after the events described. Even four or five decades after the events, the women priests – who do not otherwise mince their words nor restrain their opinions – still have a respectful and conciliatory attitude towards the opponents of the reform. It is important to remember that this respect is often described as mutual. We could say that the above examples contain what Honneth labels 'mutual recognition'. The fact that the first women priests say that they did not notice any division at the local level, that things worked well in practice and that no conflicts arose, may therefore also be due to that actually being the case.

27 Inge Löfström, 'Att vara kvinna och präst', *Sydsvenska Dagbladet*, 8 September 1967. The name 'Inge' is a man's first name in Sweden.
28 Rune Pär Olofsson, 'tio kvinnor', *Expressen*, 7 July 1967.
29 Ibid.

Breaches of the code of conduct

The source material also contains examples of what could happen if a woman priest breached the code of conduct. If she did not choose to give way herself, others might, as it were, give way on her behalf. One example of this mode of action is the letter attached to her narrative by a priest, a letter which, according to her, 'says something about the atmosphere in 1966'.

With a background as a missionary, the woman priest had been asked to give a talk at a 'mission weekend' organised by Lunds kristliga studentförbund [the Lund Christian Students' Association]. In the letter, the organisers thank her for having accepted the invitation and having given such an 'energetic and positive response, where one immediately senses that the sender has understood what this is all about and is in agreement with the line of thinking'. The organisers continue:

> This makes it all the more painful for us that (as is clear from the letter, and we thank you for it) you are in active ministry at the relevant point in time and are accordingly preparing yourself for ordination. For many years the student movement in general, and thus also the Lund Association, have endeavoured to stay away from the political positioning within the Church. The situation is extremely exposed for us, and in order for the Association to be able to avoid boycotts from one or the other faction, thus developing an infected 'lopsidedness', we must maintain as neutral a line as possible. That we can continue to be the facilitator of matter-of-fact debates and conversations between different camps, thereby salvaging fruitful dialogue.[30]

The Lund Christian Students' Association then cancels its request and asks the priest not to take this personally: 'We both still believe that you are the most suitable person for this special task, but owing to your declared position we feel compelled to withdraw.'[31] The letter contains a concept that recurs in the source material and in the media debate: 'the neutral line'. 'Neutral' is understood to mean women priests stepping aside for the sake of domestic peace. This concept recurs in a number of cases.

The events surrounding Marianne Westrin's sermon in Skara Cathedral in the spring of 1967 are another typical example of

---

30 No. 17.
31 Ibid.

what might happen when women did not act in accordance with the code of conduct. At least some of the events were documented in the media and supply a flavour of what the situation was like. On 14 March *Svenska Dagbladet* reported that Marianne Westrin would be the first woman ever to preach in Skara Cathedral in conjunction with the annual conference of the Centre Party. Bishop Sven Danell (1903–1981) was interviewed and underlined that this did not signify any departure from his principle-based negative stance on women priests. It was a political party conference, after all, and they could invite any preachers they wanted.[32]

Two weeks later, the newspaper reported that a delegation from the Church Coalition had gone to the bishop and expressed its concern that the diocese's 'neutral' line had been violated.[33] The cathedral dean commented that he saw no biblical-theological reasons for not granting use of the cathedral, and that the faction that had accepted women priests had 'the same right to use the cathedral as the Church Coalition'.[34] The cathedral dean also pointed out to the newspapers that he objected to G. A. Danell's statement. The brother of the Bishop of Skara had spoken on the radio during the week and commented on Westrin's upcoming sermon by comparing her to Jezebel in the Book of Revelation, who claims to be a prophetess, acts as a teacher and 'leads my servants to commit fornication and to eat meat from idol sacrifices'. The cathedral dean of Skara found his fellow cathedral dean's statement alarming and emphasised the danger of people feeling uneasy about such polemics against women priests.[35]

The coverage led to a series of opinion pieces. Centerns kvin-noförbund [the women's association of the Centre Party, now Centerkvinnorna, 'Centre Women in Sweden'] registered a protest against the attempts by G. A. Danell and the Church Coalition to prevent Westrin from preaching.[36] A representative of Högerns kvinnoförbund [the women's association of the Right Party, now

---

32 'Kvinnlig cp-präst blir domkyrkopredikant', *Svenska Dagbladet*, 14 March 1967.

33 Signed 'Tenax', 'Skaradelegation angriper predikan av kvinnlig präst', *Svenska Dagbladet*, 1 April 1967.

34 Signed 'Tenax', 'Prästvigd kvinna har "lika rätt" till predikstol', *Svenska Dagbladet*, 2 April 1967.

35 Ibid.

36 'Kvinnoförbund: Domprost Danell har kränkt Bibeln', *Svenska Dagbladet*, 6 April 1967.

the Moderate Women and the Moderate Party] then submitted 'a protest against the protest' and distanced herself from the association board's demands for the introduction of women priests in 1957 and 1958.[37] John Nilsson (1898–1974), a vicar in Stockholm, also wanted to have a say. He took a firm stand against Danell's threat of God's judgement upon Westrin, declaring that he was ashamed of belonging to a Church where such oppression of women was possible.[38]

The example of Westrin shows what happened when the code of conduct was breached. Here what 'the neutral line' means becomes clear: that it is the women priests who should give way and avoid encroaching on the common territory – a territory that belongs to (ordained) men. The responsibility for keeping the division in the Church from coming to light hence rests with the women. Moreover, this case constitutes an example of what crossing this invisible boundary might cost: demonstrations, newspaper headlines, hatred and threats. The debacle in Skara is also another example of something we have discussed before, namely that the question of where the opposition's dividing lines went is complex. One cannot simply argue that it was a case of the priests versus the laity, faithful 'church people' versus secularised Swedes. Instead, we see how the bishop has a different standpoint from that of his colleague the cathedral dean, that cathedral deans might hold diverging opinions, and that 'ordinary' priests and laypeople sometimes shared the same opinion and sometimes stood on different sides of the debate.

It is also significant that Westrin herself did not speak out. In this respect she adhered to the code of conduct. However, she did comment on the Skara issue many years later. Talking about her life, she mentions this event, saying that there was a lot of upset but that 1,300 people came to the service itself, 500 of whom had to be turned away at the door. She emphasises that she respects reform opponents and is good friends with a well-known opponent of women priests despite their differences.[39] However, she adds in her vocation narrative that in connection with this affair, she received

37 Märta Håfvenström, 'Protest mot protest', *Svenska Dagbladet*, 12 April 1967.
38 John Nilsson, 'Kvinnan Jesebel i Skara', *Svenska Dagbladet*, 8 April 1967.
39 'Kvinnlig pionjär inom prästyrket', *Sundsvalls Tidning*, 29 September 2008.

a whole wad of unpleasant letters, including threats to her life, 'the ugliest of which were written on toilet paper'.[40]

Given what the women priests who broke the code of conduct had to endure in the form of media attacks, hatred and threats, it is not surprising that many of them did step aside. As gender researcher Charlotte Holgersson has pointed out in an article marking the sixtieth anniversary of Margit Sahlin's ordination, this attitude may be understood in the light of theories about 'the deviant position'. People who are very much in a minority and are perceived as deviants are often kept under observation, which leads to huge pressure to perform well. Deviants are also often consciously or unconsciously subjected to loyalty tests, in consequence of which they strive to reduce everything that might be perceived as deviant. As a result, a deviant individual becomes fairly compliant with stated and unstated expectations.[41]

However, the first women priests' meta-reflections reveal additional and stronger motives than fear. A vital driving force mentioned by some of them was gratitude.[42] One of the interviewed priests dwells on this factor: because of gratitude for being permitted to live in her vocation, a woman priest would endure having to stand aside and hence only receive partial recognition:

> It feels foolish, but there was a gratitude that we were allowed to participate, that I was allowed to become a priest, that I was allowed to conduct services [...] There were so few of us, so I suppose that made us hold back a bit [...] There were others who were more assertive and stood on the barricades and stuff like that, but as an ordinary parish priest one would perhaps not do that. At least, I didn't. But the fact that we were held back and still remained grateful, I can feel today that there we were a little too humble. Because I am still convinced that God has called me, so why shouldn't I be allowed to take part?[43]

Another reason why the code of behaviour was upheld was that the ordained women were sometimes not only expected but even urged to remain silent. There is an example in Margareta

---

40 Marianne Westrin's vocation narrative. In an international issue of *Hertha*, Westrin also comments on the events; see Algrim, 'Eve and Martha', pp. 64–66.
41 Rakel Lennartsson, 'En banbrytare med dialogen som livsluft', *Kyrkans Tidning*, 42 (2020), 18–19.
42 See Barbro Westlund in Sjöberg, 'Jag är så tacksam', p. 52; No. 28.
43 No. 45.

Brandby-Cöster's account of an incident in the diocese of Gothenburg in the late 1970s. When Bo Giertz's successor, the high-profile reform opponent Bishop Bertil Gärtner (1924–2009), was to perform the installation of a vicar, problems arose. On such occasions, all the priests in the parish are expected to take part; but one of them was a woman, Anne Strid. The solution was that Strid was given the title of 'notary', with the task of reading out the cathedral chapter's authorisation instead of participating in the installation as a priest.[44] In 1978 Brandby-Cöster wrote an opinion piece about this event. She argued that while it might seem as if a satisfactory solution to the problem had been reached, this was not the whole truth:

> The reality, of course, is that the bishop threatened not to install and the parish council was forced to refrain from allowing the parish's legally called priest to function normally [...] The bishop said: 'She herself agreed to be notary.' [...] It is very common in the Church – and probably elsewhere – for those higher-up to blame oppression on the oppressed and to put the blame on individuals who have no power. 'It was you who agreed to it...' [...] That the parish council was not strong enough to resist the bishop's pressure and defend the right of the parish to use its priests as real priests at its services is understandable but painful.[45]

Gratitude and compulsion are thus two reasons given by some of the first women priests themselves. A third, mentioned in the debate in the 1970s, was that it is a Christian ideal to be silent and forgive. In this situation it is possible to speak of ideological factors. Gustaf Wingren was one of those who shed light on this circumstance, and he did so in a series of opinion pieces in the broadsheet *Sydsvenska Dagbladet* in the autumn of 1977. In these articles, Wingren

---

44 Brandby-Cöster, 'Kvinnor som präster – också i Göteborgs stift'. One of the priests who tried to persuade Anne Strid not to serve in Guldhed church was Ebbe Hagard (1917–2008). The church historian Anders Jarlert, an expert on the history of the diocese of Gothenburg, writes: 'He never really took a principled stand on the issue of the priesthood [...] His line was that of freedom of conscience – and this was to apply both to female priests and to those male priests who could not, for reasons of conscience, serve alongside female priests'; Anders Jarlert, *Göteborgs stifts herdaminne 1620–1999: I. Domprosteriets kontrakt* (Gothenburg: Tre böcker, 2009), p. 321 (referencing Brandby-Cöster, 'Dubbla budskap').

45 Margareta Brandby-Cöster, 'Biskopsmakt eller strutspolitik?', *Göteborgs-Posten*, 22 September 1978.

criticises 'the effect that might be called "voluntary retreat". In order to avoid fierce arguments, the woman priest excludes herself from a rite in which she would normally have participated.' Why do women priests stay silent, even though, according to Wingren, they are intelligent, well-read, competent and in all other situations 'quick and incisive in their replies, bold and clear in their speech?' Wingren's answer is that they are Christians.[46]

> And this created ideal, of being 'Christian', instils in the depths of the soul a readiness to suffer, a form of inner compulsion to make concessions, which paralyses the individual in conflict situations. Biblical words such as love, peace, patience and other similar terms have been interpreted over the centuries in a way that makes it almost impossible to associate public quarrelling with Christianity.[47]

Instead Wingren calls for what he describes as a healthy conflict. Even so, he sees that few people dare to participate in such a dispute because they are 'afraid of splitting the Church, they remember the revivalist movement and how the Free Churches broke away, and they do not believe that the Church can survive another bloodletting. But perhaps the danger is not so great – the revival was a movement of the people, after all.'[48]

The narrative of division and the presumption that it was the fault of the first women priests that the division existed led to the emergence of a code of conduct. The first women priests were expected to give way, and the responsibility for preventing situations that would bring the division to light was to a very great extent placed on them. They also behaved largely in accordance with this expectation, out of fear, gratitude and coercion, and because this response was perceived as a Christian ideal.

As the above quotations imply, however, there are meta-reflections in which the priests criticise their own behaviour in relation to the code of conduct. Looking back, some of them comment that they wish they had questioned it and had demanded recognition of their vocation. One of the interviewed priests mentions the conscience clause, and when asked what she thought of it, she replies that at first she thought it was a good thing.

---

46 Gustaf Wingren, 'Kvinnliga präster och manliga samveten I: Undantaget som regel', *Sydsvenska Dagbladet*, 28 August 1977.
47 Ibid.
48 Ibid.

I thought so then, but I didn't think so later on [...] I could accept it at the time – there were many of us who were stuck in this stage of gratitude that we were allowed to participate [...] – but the more time went by, the more important it became to me to allow no retreat. That someone could not [...] say no [to collaborating with women]. And today I believe it's important that a person cannot become a priest in the Church of Sweden unless they fully accept the situation in the Church [...] In this respect, I have become more militant or left the gratitude stage. [laughs] No, but I do feel that it is important. The fact that we accepted not being accepted [...] I can feel that we were a bit too humble, those of us who didn't stand on the barricades. There were those who did.[49]

Several other priests also regard the conscience clause as being the root of the problem of the one-sided bridge-building. Ulla Nisser writes in her autobiography:

Perhaps the most insidious thing was the so-called 'conscience clause', which for years allowed bishops to avoid ordaining women. At the same time it gave the opponents of women priests the right – for the sake of their consciences – to refuse to cooperate with women. This meant that we could not feel fully accepted.[50]

The conscience clause is what makes Margareta Brandby-Cöster critical of celebrations of the 1958 decision. Because of the conscience clause, the 1958 decision was, in practice, not the signal to launch a reform but rather one that launched a wearisome struggle, because the opponents were able to behave as if the decision had never been made. The conscience clause also meant that the purpose of ordaining a priest – to confer legitimacy in the name of the Church – was overridden. Moreover, as it was formulated, it placed the responsibility for defending the decision and the women's rightful vocation not on the bishops but on each individual woman priest. The bishops could hence continue to participate in the worshipping community side by side with opponents of the reform. In this way, Brandby-Cöster says, the clause protected 'the power and the friendly relations to which we women priests were delivered up'.[51]

In view of this situation, it is no surprise that a turning point arrived at last, a reaction whereby loyalty to the code of conduct

---

49 No. 45.
50 Nisser, *Hopp från trampolin*, p. 101.
51 Brandby-Cöster, 'Dubbla budskap', pp. 163–164, 179.

was no longer perceived as a possible way forward. As Lena Malmgren puts it: 'We had backed down for quite a long time in too many ways. And had come to realise that, yes, you should respect your fellow human being, but you do not have to respect bad behaviour or bad theology.'[52] In terms of Honneth's theory of recognition, this situation is an example of how a lack of recognition combined with recurring violations will lead to a struggle for social and legal recognition.[53]

Struggle for recognition

In the following section, in which we discuss the events of the 1970s in terms of a struggle for recognition, denied recognition is not of course the sole cause of what took place. Other contributing factors existed within the overall context. Nonetheless, as this study demonstrates, for the first women who were ordained to the priesthood, denied recognition appears to have been the crucial factor.

Their struggle also fitted in with the times. The late 1960s and early 1970s was a time when many groups in Swedish society were struggling for recognition in various forms. The wave of leftism that characterised this period also contributed to strengthening conflicts between various groups and to radicalising the debate.

Denied recognition becomes visible

As time went by, there were an increasing number of media reports about the unacceptable situation of women priests and women candidates for the priesthood: their denied recognition was made visible. One of these numerous articles had the dramatic headline 'Women priests took their own lives'. In this piece, an assistant parish priest called Elly Eriksson (1934–2024) claims that at least two women priests in the diocese of Strängnäs 'took their own lives after prolonged persecution by male colleagues'. The article interviews a number of women priests who describe untenable situations. These might include 'acts of harassment, excessive workloads [and] administrative manoeuvring in relation to job vacancies'. Parishes that employed women as priests could be penalised for doing so,

---

52 Malmgren, '50 år med kvinnliga präster'.
53 Carl-Göran Heidegren, 'Inledning', in Axel Honneth, *Erkännande: Praktisk-filosofiska studier*, trans. Carl-Göran Heidegren (Gothenburg: Daidalos, 2000), pp. 11–12; Honneth, *Disrespect*, pp. 106–107.

for example by the rural dean refusing to attend the consecration of a church because a woman worked there. The harassment might assume the form of verbal abuse, too, such as being told that 'the devil is making use of us women priests'.[54]

Two of the interviewed priests, who belonged to the group ordained in 1960 to 1970, spoke in particular of shunning, 'freezing out' – a denial of social recognition: 'There is a psychological oppression that many feel very deeply. It often happens in a silent and subtle way. It is difficult to get at. Often a woman cannot bear this for long.'[55]

In addition, there were increasingly frequent reports of the hiring problems discussed in the previous chapter, as well as the plight of female theology students. Lund is singled out as being especially problematic. One such instance occurred in the spring of 1977, when some male theology students objected to Caroline Krook's being given a temporary position as a teacher in the Department of Theology at Lund to teach confirmation pedagogy and other subjects.[56] In connection with this dispute, the rector's office at the university received a report of harassment of female theology students.[57] This fuelled the fire, and in the press the conflict became known as 'the battle of the theologians'. Subsequent articles portray the deep divisions among the students in the Department of Theology, especially within the departmental student union. Some students who opposed the reform argued that any investigation into harassment should be broadened to include all forms of intimidation, including those directed against 'opponents of women priests' and/or those who had suffered persecution for their view of the Bible.[58]

The issue was also mentioned in the wake of a divine service, broadcast on the radio, on the theme 'Is the Church standing in the

---

54 Bengt Michanek, 'Kvinnopräster tog sina liv', Aftonbladet, 30 December 1983.

55 Ibid.

56 Martia Sander-Schale, 'Ny strid på Teologen – Kvinnopräst obibliskt', Sydsvenska Dagbladet, 13 April 1977.

57 The harassment report was mentioned in, for example, 'Anmälan i Lund: Kvinnor förföljs bland teologer', Dagens Nyheter, 2 April 1977. The article cites professors Gustaf Wingren (1910–2000) and Hampus Lyttkens (1916–2011), and also Bishop Olle Nivenius (1914–2002). All three appear to take the accusations seriously and welcome an investigation.

58 Jan Mårtensson, 'Teologstriden går vidare: Kvinnoprästmotståndare avgår', Sydsvenska Dagbladet, 23 April 1977.

way of Christ?', which was led by Caroline Krook. In interviews about this service, Krook said it could be regarded as a 'contribution to the debate in the Faculty of Theology at Lund'. The reporter let her address an appeal 'To her sisters, who are now being persecuted and subjected to psychological terror and bullying by a group of fanatical opponents of women priests':

> Stand firm and persevere with your ordinations! Once you are away from Theology in Lund and well settled in ordinary parish life, your work will be appreciated on merit and you will experience your professional freedom as meaningful and positive.[59]

Interestingly, Krook's words here suggest that she experienced the same contrast as discussed in the previous chapters between, on the one hand, (some) male fellow students' expression of opposition to the reform through denied recognition and the narrative of division, and on the other hand, recognition by parishes.

The disputes continued in the autumn of 1977. An article entitled 'Mobbning med Bibeln i "Förargelsens hus" där hälften av våra präster utbildas' ['Bullying with the Bible in the "House of Indignation" where half of our priests are trained'] described how female students had formed a union 'to resist the oppression from teachers and students hostile to women priests'.[60] Another big media story covered the occasion when Krook's parish in Lund hosted practice divine services for priestly candidates doing their practical training term. In connection with this arrangement, she had offered to help distribute the Eucharist, but some priestly candidates who were against the reform had reacted negatively, and the offer had not been accepted by the practice term instructors.[61]

---

59 'Är kyrkan trovärdig? Radiogudstjänst om kvinnopräster', *Dagens Nyheter*, 24 April 1977.

60 Calle Hård, 'Mobbning med Bibeln i "Förargelsens hus" där hälften av våra präster utbildas', *Expressen*, 31 July 1977.

61 For the discussions that arose in connection with Krook's appointment as a teacher on the practical training term, see, for example, 'Bara några rader om...', *Aftonbladet*, 13 April 1977; 'Mullig mansgris: – Jag är lynchad av massmedia', *Expressen*, 13 May 1977; Thomas Waldén, 'Anonyma brev mot kvinnliga präster', *Aftonbladet*, 24 September 1977; Thomas Waldén, 'Jag får ofta anonyma hatbrev', *Aftonbladet*, 25 September 1977; Elisabeth Frankl, 'Caroline Krook: "Djävulens redskap" blir vår första kvinnliga biskop' (under the heading 'Strängt personligt' ['Strictly confidential']), *Expressen*, 12 November 1977. Waldén, 'Jag får ofta anonyma hatbrev', includes a note with the text: 'The number of women theology students

The above articles are just a few of the many that serve to make this denied recognition and its consequences visible. The code of conduct discussed earlier in the chapter, based on the narrative of division and the presumption that it was the women priests' responsibility to give way, was no longer being adhered to.

Demands for recognition and the repeal of the conscience clause

Honneth's theory proposes that when denied recognition becomes visible, it can lead to demands for recognition. We believe that what happened in the Church of Sweden can be understood in these terms. As we showed earlier in this chapter, some of the first women priests regarded the conscience clause as being the root of the evil, and they were not alone. In 1975 a motion was submitted to the General Synod to remove the conscience clause. The motion was, however, rejected.

In early 1977, at the same time as the Lund debacle was unfolding, the government appointed a commission of inquiry to draft a law against sex discrimination. The chair of the commission, the Riksdag member Karin Andersson (1918–2012), demanded, among other things, that the conscience clause should cease to apply on the grounds that the discrimination against women that the 1958 reform was intended to abolish had in fact continued. The ensuing debate was heated. One example of this was mentioned in the previous chapter: the Bishop of Lund Martin Lindström's book *Bibeln och bekännelsen om kvinnliga präster* ['The Bible and the Confession on women priests'] from 1978. Another example is Bishop Ingmar Ström's sermon on New Year's Day that same year. Ström (1912–2003, Bishop of Stockholm 1971–1979) spoke of the parable of the fig tree that bore no fruit in Luke 13:6–9 and related it to opposition to the reform. He argued that remaining silent in order to keep the peace was poisoning the climate in the Church and that a decision must now be made as to whether it might be time to chop off the opposition. Newspaper reports on the sermon triggered debate and a powerful surge of

---

who drop out during their studies is alarmingly large. In recent years, an average of 170 women students started theological studies. In the final term – the "practical training" – 120 of them ended their studies without a degree.'

opinion against the opponents of reform.[62] It is notable that both Lindström and Ström questioned the presumption that it was the women priests who should give way, thus inverting the narrative of division. The view of the bishops of Lund and Stockholm was that the division was not caused by the women priests but by those who opposed the reform.

By contrast, the Bishop of Gothenburg, Bertil Gärtner, objected to the idea that it was the anti-reform priests who were the problem. In reality, he maintained, he and people who held similar views were the ones who had been 'subjected to the media's biased attacks'. In addition to distancing himself from Ström's position that the Church should adapt to the spirit of the times, Gärtner announced, 'I have never been subjected to such an attack from another bishop before, it certainly does not pave the way for trusting conversations and an open dialogue.' Archbishop Olof Sundby (1917–1996) responded that a discussion was needed, but that it should not be conducted from the pulpits.[63]

However, Ström's sermon did add fuel to the debate as well as to the initiatives. Less than a week later, under the heading 'Kvinnoprästerna som vågade höja rösterna' ['The women priests who dared to raise their voices'], it was reported that a group of priests in the diocese of Stockholm had formed what the article described as a battle group. Its leader, the priest Brita Salomon (1915–1994), said in the article: 'It feels so good to be able to say what we think! We have stayed silent for so long. It is always the men who have spoken over our heads.'[64]

It is reasonable to regard Ström's New Year's Day sermon as an overture to the Bishops' Conference a few weeks later, where the standing of the conscience clause was on the agenda. The Conference's handling of the issue was closely monitored by the media, which reported on the various positions assumed by the bishops. Of the nine bishops questioned, six said that the conscience clause should be removed; two said that it should stay; and

62 Vilhelm Bexell, 'Biskopen sa rent ut till kvinno-motståndarna: Bort med intrigerna', *Expressen*, 2 January 1978; Hans Gréen, 'Attack i nyårspredikan: Kvinnostriden förgiftar kyrkan', *Dagens Nyheter*, 2 January 1978.

63 Omar Magnergård, 'Gärtner om Ström: Otroligt påhopp', *Svenska Dagbladet*, 3 January 1978.

64 Margit Sahlin, 'Kritisk till kollegors krav', *Dagens Nyheter*, 10 January 1978.

Archbishop Sundby declined to comment until he had explained his standpoint at the Conference.[65]

Another example of how the struggle for recognition might be expressed in the public debate comes from Gustaf Wingren, the theologian mentioned by several of the first women priests as being significant for their own theological thinking about their vocation. Wingren attacked the conscience clause in a series of articles in the autumn of 1977, arguing that its application caused problems. On the one hand, the clause made it possible for priests who did not want to comply with the law on the equal right to ordination of men and women to undermine it by carefully deploying themselves in various associations of parishes. On the other hand, it led to the aforementioned 'voluntary retreat' whereby the women priests stood back in order not to create acrimonious disputes. As an example, he cited the situation when Caroline Krook was not allowed to help distribute the Eucharist during the practical training term.[66] In Wingren's view, the idea that the conscience clause would stop the Church from splitting was nonsense. The division was already a fact, and in his opinion it was not only caused by the opponents of reform – it was also 'deliberate and planned' by them.[67]

Wingren received a reply to his opinion piece from his colleague at Lund, Professor Bengt Hägglund (1920–2015), who had been the teacher in charge at the time when Krook was barred from helping to distribute the Eucharist. Hägglund presented himself as an 'ordinary, simple professor' who was unfairly accused. He said that Wingren's description of the incident was both misleading and offensive in its claim that Krook had been prevented from serving as a priest in her own church. Hägglund felt that Wingren made far too much of the incident and referred to the fact that Krook, when she herself had been allowed to speak, had not accused the leaders of the practical training term of anything.[68] According to Hägglund, the teaching staff had been in favour at first, but had changed their

65 Sören Björklund, 'Prästerna och deras samveten', *Aftonbladet*, 23 January 1978.
66 Gustaf Wingren, 'Kvinnliga präster och manliga samveten I: Undantaget som regel', *Sydsvenska Dagbladet*, 28 August 1977.
67 Gustaf Wingren, 'Kvinnliga präster och manliga samveten II: Kyrko-splittringen ett faktum', *Sydsvenska Dagbladet*, 30 August 1977.
68 Bengt Hägglund, 'Vilseledande och kränkande', *Sydsvenska Dagbladet*, 31 August 1977.

minds when they realised that the whole thing was intended as a provocation and that many participants would perceive it that way. Consequently, they had declined the offer. 'Caroline Krook was of course fully in agreement with this.'

One of several problems Wingren perceived in Hägglund's reasoning had to do with how the conscience clause was applied. Wingren replied that in Hägglund's version, it was Krook who had made a mistake and tried to provoke. 'He thereby states that the normal [situation] is provocative, and that the exception [opposition to women priests] is the only one that has an undisputed right to assert itself inside every church.' Wingren also questioned whom Hägglund was targeting via the conscience clause. Why was it not aimed at everyone who was in favour of the reform, including the bishops, but only against the women?[69] Wingren thus questioned the narrative of division, the women priests' culpability for this division, and the belief that opposing the reform by means of denied recognition was therefore legitimate.

In this series of articles Wingren also criticised Bishop Bo Giertz, maintaining that the only reason the opponents remained in the Church was because they gained financially from it. The conscience clause had to be removed and, according to Wingren, the opponents had two options: stop rejecting other ordained priests from priestly office and stay in the Church, or form their own denomination.

Giertz defended himself, arguing that opponents should have the right to continue serving the Church; neither they nor Giertz wanted to start a new Church. For this reason the conscience clause should remain in place, because through it the Church 'has shown a path that it has found more Christian and reasonable than the old, evil way of causing constant new church splits'. According to Giertz, there was no need to split the Church, as it was possible to receive the Eucharist together as long as a female priest was not leading the congregation in celebration.[70] In his response, Giertz thus upheld the narrative of division and the presumption that the split was the fault of the women priests. Bishop Giertz also brought up the situation involving the education of priests at Lund. He wrote that he did not

---

69 Gustaf Wingren, 'Tre tvivelaktigheter', *Sydsvenska Dagbladet*, 14 September 1977.
70 Bo Giertz, 'Lärostrider och samvetsfrid', *Sydsvenska Dagbladet*, 1 November 1977.

for a moment [intend] to defend clumsy actions against women theology students and priests – supposing that any such had occurred. It seems difficult to find any evidence of this. It is an unproven accusation that has made big headlines in the press. A lot of innocent people have suffered for it.[71]

Several interesting things are worth observing from this example of the public debate. One is the strident tone, which is strongly reminiscent of what the debate had sounded like back in the late 1950s. Another is the shift that occurred in the line of reasoning. In fact, when analysing the debate at the end of the 1970s in comparison with the arguments made at the time of the General Synod's decision in 1958, there is reason to speak of an inversion. This applies to both Wingren and Giertz. The conscience clause was thus no longer the solution to the split in the Church but rather the cause of it. It was not the women's vocation that was causing division but rather the ways in which the reform opponents were choosing to express their opinion. It was no longer the women who were being accused of pursuing priestly office for the sake of filthy lucre but rather the opponents of reform.

The response to the inversion of the narrative of division is interesting in more ways than one. As well as upholding the old narrative of division, Giertz and Hägglund respond by comparing degrees of suffering. The view according to which the women priests were subjected to suffering is relativised or challenged. As we saw above, this response to the inversion of the narrative also featured in the debate that followed Ingmar Ström's New Year's sermon as well as in the debate on the report about harassment in the Department of Theology at Lund. True, the women priests had suffered; but now it was the opponents of the reform who were suffering, at least as much if not more.

The consultation document

It was in this volatile situation that the government issued a clear directive at the beginning of 1978: the Church of Sweden had to find ways of ensuring that the 1958 reform worked as intended, that is, that both men and women could serve as priests in the Church of Sweden. Against this background, the Bishops'

---

71 Bo Giertz, 'Maktanspråk contra tro?', *Sydsvenska Dagbladet*, 1 December 1977.

Conference set up a broad-based consultation committee consisting of representatives of various Church contexts and positions in relation to the reform. The committee's task was to produce a document indicating how the Church of Sweden should resolve these issues in the future. The group delivered its proposal on 1 December 1978 in a document that quickly became known as the consultation document [*samrådsdokumentet*]. The press reported the main points of the document: no one might be prevented from becoming a priest on the basis of sex; and in the event of conflicts, the official view of the Church must prevail. This meant that male priests might not prevent women from serving, but they themselves might refrain from attending or participating. Both groups had to recognise that the other group's beliefs were based on the Bible and the Confessions; no one could have a monopoly on faith. However, the bishops of the dioceses of Gothenburg and Visby would be given priority as long as they remained bishops. Among other things, this meant that women theologians from those dioceses might be ordained elsewhere, by another bishop; but they were exempted from the requirement to serve at least five years in the diocese where they were ordained, so that that they could apply immediately for a position in their home diocese.[72]

The debate involved many of the first women priests, a number of whom criticised the contents of the consultation document.[73] In a letter to the editor of *Dagens Nyheter*, Lena Malmgren expresses her sadness at the outcome: 'above all because almost all those who believe it is right to have women priests are keeping silent or agreeing to "diplomatic solutions"'. She adds that laypeople are not being taken into account either:

> If this document is used as a basis, of course the parishes will continue to fear problems of cooperation. And then they will not call a woman priest if there is another priest who does not want her in the parish. Because that could easily create trouble – and so many of us have been blamed by colleagues and bosses for causing a conflict when we appeared in some context where someone else did not want to see us.[74]

---

72 'Bra "dokument" för kyrkan', *Göteborgs-Posten*, 2 December 1978.
73 For example, Caroline Krook in 'Kvinnopräst om biskopar som får egen samvetsklausul: De bör avgå', *Arbetet*, 29 December 1978; Margit Sahlin in 'Sluta hymla om kvinnopräster', *Svenska Dagbladet*, 24 December 1978.
74 Lena Malmgren, 'Kvinnoförakt?', *Dagens Nyheter*, 21 December 1978.

Malmgren is also critical of the bishops of Visby and Gothenburg being allowed to continue to go on refusing to ordain women as long as they remained in office, as this would lead to even more reform opponents being ordained during that time, while 'women have to go around begging for ordination'.[75]

In the criticism of the consultation document, the narrative of division was challenged again. Interestingly, the inversion of this narrative – which portrays the reform opponents as the ones who are actually causing the split and creating conflict – does not feature in the critical response of the first women priests. Instead, these women maintain that the problem lies in the fact that the 1958 legal recognition had been overridden by the conscience clause. As we have shown earlier in this study, this process might be described as the application of the conscience clause leading to denied social recognition and thereby to contradictory and ambivalent recognition.

When Kerstin Berglund (1930–2022, ordained 1969), the woman priest who had been a member of the consultation committee, spoke out about the consultation document, she was thus very much responding to this criticism. According to her, it was perhaps not ideal that individual bishops could continue to refuse to ordain women. However, she had managed to include a note in the minutes to the effect that anyone who accepted a bishopric in future must agree to ordain women. She was also satisfied with the group's agreement to recognise that the official position of the Church had priority while both sides wished to adhere to the Bible and the Confessions, although they interpreted the Bible differently. She added that she did not want to prevent reform opponents from studying for the priesthood, because they might change their minds during their studies. Finally, she commented on the task itself: 'The group's work has been to establish what is already clear, that is, our right to be priests. So actually it is embarrassing that a group like this one has been set up.'[76]

Berglund's reasoning again hints at the relationship between principles and practice discussed earlier in this book. Principled standpoints are formulated in a context where practical work influences how those principles can be formulated. The consultation

---

75 Ibid.
76 P. D. Lindeberg, 'Kyrkomötets kvinnoprästkompromiss: Snabbtransport till icke-motståndarstift', *Sydsvenska Dagbladet*, 2 December 1978. See also Kerstin Berglund, 'Kvinnans rätt att vara präst', *Upsala Nya Tidning*, 8 December 1978.

document embodied a proposal as to how both sides could coexist in practice. Now the only question was how the General Synod would receive this document and the government's proposed new competence law [*behörighetslag*]. Expectations were high in the lead-up to the 1979 General Synod, and the press covered the election of members. They were particularly interested in the first woman priest to be elected as a member of the General Synod, Christina Odenberg. A number of newspapers interviewed Odenberg in this connection. She stressed that she did not wish reform opponents to be expelled, '[b]ut we can no longer maintain a dual priesthood. We women priests must be given the opportunity to work undisturbed.'[77]

The 1979 General Synod led to an adjustment to the government's bill that harked back to the old system, and a decision according to which the consultation document's proposed rules would guide how cooperation would work in the future.[78] Regarding this outcome, Margit Sahlin commented in her book *Dags för omprövning? Kring bibel, kyrka och kvinnliga präster* ['Time for a rethink? On the Bible, Church and women priests'] (1980) that

> instead of resolving the tragic conflict in the Church, [the outcome] prolonged it and paved the way for divisive conflicts into an indefinite future. How could a Church with two incompatible kinds of priestly office, where one excludes the other, be able to function and gain trust? The Church's life force is leaking through the crack, and the feeling of frustration is spreading ever wider.[79]

The Riksdag did not accept the adjustments, however, and instead set up a new commission of inquiry. The bill was adopted in 1982 and came into force in 1983. It repealed the 1958 Act and with it the conscience clause.

The 'who is suffering more?' narrative

In the context of making denied recognition visible, and the demand for recognition by way of abolition of the conscience clause, what

---

77 P. D. Lindeberg, 'För första gången – kvinna på kyrkomöte – men värsta motståndarna är också valda', *Sydsvenska Dagbladet*, 16 November 1978; 'Första kvinnliga ombudet: Samvetsklausulen bör sättas ur spel', *Dagens Nyheter*, 15 November 1978.
78 *Betänkande om kvinnoprästutredningen: Omprövning av samvetsklausulen. Män och kvinnor som präster i Svenska kyrkan*, SOU [Swedish Government Official Reports], 1981:20, pp. 17–20.
79 Sahlin, *Dags för omprövning?*, p. 37.

we have chosen to call the '"who is suffering more?" narrative' became increasingly apparent. This narrative emerged in relation to the inverted narrative of division. As we saw, for example in the introductory quotation in which Margit Sahlin's High Church friend says that she has caused him pain through her desire to be ordained, an association already existed between the narrative of division and the experience of pain. This link also partly underpinned the belief that it was legitimate to express resistance to the reform by denying recognition.

When the consequences of this denied recognition began to be visible, and it became obvious what the first women priests had been subjected to, the opponents of reform increasingly began to highlight their pain, which became an important argument for retaining the conscience clause. The debate then became something akin to an arms race over who was suffering the most from the conflicts and the division in the Church, combined with the tendencies contained in the conscience clause debate between Wingren and Giertz to relativise, or even challenge, the suffering experienced by their opponents.

One example of this development arose in relation to the above-mentioned reports on the fraught situation in the Faculty of Theology at Lund University in 1977. The newspaper *Sydsvenska Dagbladet* interviewed two candidates for the priesthood who opposed the reform. Careful not to repudiate the anonymous letters and harassment, they simultaneously asserted that '[i]t is more difficult to be against women priests than to be a female theologian [...] We are constantly put under the spotlight to explain our position. We are not accepted by society.' For these candidates, however, their suffering was linked to their vocation. '"Being a priest is a kind of suffering with the responsibility you have before God", says one candidate. "It is not a profession but a vocation, and only the man is called."'[80]

Another example of the 'who is suffering more?' narrative is found in one of the debates arising in relation to the consultation

80 Ulla Nyman, 'Kvinnoprästmotståndare: Vi tar avstånd från de anonyma breven', *Sydsvenska Dagbladet*, 28 September 1977. See also the liberal opinion-maker Sven Rydenfelt's opinion piece: Sven Rydenfelt, 'Apropå kvinnliga präster: Vem bryter kyrkans traditioner?', *Göteborgs-Posten*, 29 May 1977. In it he sympathises with the young men who do not want to compromise their conscience, and asks: 'Who is being bullied the most among the young theologians? The male opponents of women priests? Or the prospective female priests?'

document. In a letter to the editor of *Dagens Nyheter*, three priests, Åke Æstius (1940–2015), Anne-Louise Eriksson (1952–) and Britt Wettle (1951–), said that they were thoroughly disappointed in the Church leadership, which twenty years earlier had taken a decision to open up the priesthood to women that did not work in practice. The leadership had then wrapped itself in 'a cloud of diplomatic phrases and a backdrop of beautiful words that committed it to nothing, when these women demand their right (twenty years later!) – well, what can we say about that Church? The worst form of cowardice, we think!'[81]

Archbishop Olof Sundby's response to this criticism of denied or ambivalent recognition is noteworthy in several respects, not least in the way he spoke about the reform opponents. He wondered if the three women critics had read the consultation document at all, which he personally believed established the right of women priests to take up space and do their job. In addition, the archbishop utilised the opportunity to make the following point:

Among our people today there exists an overwhelming majority in favour of women priests [...] The naysayers are a tiny minority. Becoming tougher with this minority only results in applause and cheers. What is needed today is courage to stand up for the right of a small minority to exist. Not an ounce of moral courage is needed to just go with the flow and conform to public opinion.[82]

Æstius, Eriksson and Wettle had an answer to that argument. They questioned the archbishop's stance, observing, '[i]t is never difficult to be tolerant if others pay the price'. They went on to give examples of how badly women priests were affected and argued that the opponents were not a small, vulnerable minority at all, but rather a group that was growing in size.[83]

In this exchange of views we see another example of how suffering is set against suffering, here confirmed by the archbishop. In his statement, he appears to be particularly concerned about the suffering of the reform opponents. This concern provokes a

81 Åke Æstius, Anne-Louise Eriksson and Britt Wettle, 'Tre präster om ärkebiskopens hållning i kvinnoprästfrågan: "Fegheters feghet"', *Dagens Nyheter*, 15 December 1978.
82 Hans Gréen, 'Ärkebiskop Sundby: – Jag är inte alls feg i kvinnoprästfrågan', *Dagens Nyheter*, 19 December 1978.
83 Åke Æstius, Anne-Louise Eriksson and Britt Wettle, 'Sundby förtiger fakta!', *Dagens Nyheter*, 24 December 1978.

response that highlights the women priests' suffering and instead questions and relativises their opponents' suffering.

The same phenomenon occurred when Martin Lönnebo (1930–2023, Bishop of Linköping 1980–1995) entered the debate and tried to pour oil on troubled waters. Arguing that everyone was suffering equally, he urged both sides not to be so implacable against each other. However, he too wanted to strike a blow for the reform-opponents minority: 'If we could ask Jesus, he would not answer: "Cast them out" but "Love your enemies and pray for those who persecute you, so that you may be children of your Father in heaven" (Matthew 5:44, 45).'[84] Together with Bertil Werkström (1928–2010, Bishop of Härnösand 1975–1983, Archbishop 1983–1993), Lönnebo also wrote a longer opinion piece entitled 'Don't inflict arson on the Church'. In it the two men likened the situation to two fires, arguing that if people blew on the fires, the entire consultation document might turn to ashes. The solution was for both parties to enter into 'the Christ pattern, which is reconciliation and forgiveness'.[85] Here, too, the writers pointed out that both parties were suffering:

> It is not easy to be a woman priest, but nor is it easy to be accused of sex discrimination [...] Unfortunately, the past has seen plenty of acts of harassment of women priests and a greatly lacking desire to cooperate. But let us not therefore try to swing the pendulum the other way, leading to acts of harassment directed against the 'orthodox' opponents of women priests.[86]

Although Lönnebo and Werkström speak in more guarded terms, between the lines there is a tendency to relativise suffering. This tendency is apparent first when the two bishops proclaim that whereas women priests did suffer in the past, now the opponents of reform were suffering (at least) as much; and, second, when they refer to a Christian approach in the view one ought to adopt towards one's opponents.

Æstius and Wettle apparently read this message between the lines as well, replying that Lönnebo's statement was characterised by the approach, 'Woman priest, be quiet and suffer in silence,

---

84 Martin Lönnebo, 'Mod att visa hänsyn', *Dagens Nyheter*, 21 December 1978.

85 Bertil Werkström and Martin Lönnebo, 'Ställ inte till mordbrand på kyrkan', *Svenska Dagbladet*, 30 December 1978.

86 Ibid.

carry your cross and you will gain respect in the long run!' They regarded it as a distortion of the Gospel when this exhortation was directed at those who 'are weak and chronically disadvantaged'. Surely it could never hurt the Church to publicly acknowledge the conflicts? 'It is a matter of making the disorder which causes people to suffer visible.'[87]

In this debate, as well as in the other examples, what we call the 'who is suffering more?' narrative can be seen in play. In the light of Honneth's theory of recognition, this situation can be understood as an expression of two opposing struggles for recognition. In practice, as Sinikka Neuhaus has noted, one group's struggle for recognition often leads to denied recognition for another group.[88] Both the events of the 1970s which led up to the abolition of the conscience clause and the ensuing debate might be regarded as expressions of the constant negotiation of the boundaries of recognition.

Interestingly, we have found no evidence that the first women priests contributed to the 'who is suffering more?' narrative. They appear to have focused on the issue of their own denied recognition and their demand for recognition. If the issue of suffering was raised, it was as the consequence of denied recognition, and no comparisons were made with the suffering of others. If the 'who is suffering more?' narrative was mentioned at all, it was in critical terms, as with Lena Malmgren, who pointedly said that '[m]artyrs stood up and complained – on both sides of the boundary'.[89]

Here Honneth's theory can help us to evaluate the various struggles for recognition, or, as he would say, to diagnose social pathologies. As discussed earlier, Honneth argues that a desirable development is increased freedom through mutual recognition. He further believes that it is essential to challenge groups who demand recognition and then use the recognition and freedom they have gained to curtail the right of others to recognition and democratic processes. This is especially true because the path to full recognition for everyone is itself a democratic process.[90]

---

87 Britt Wettle and Åke Æstius, 'Fall inte undan för hotelser', *Dagens Nyheter*, 19 January 1979.
88 Sinikka Neuhaus, *Reformation och erkännande: Skilsmässoärenden under den tidiga reformationsprocessen i Malmö 1527–1542* (Lund: Lund University, 2009), pp. 54, 83–84 (p. 83).
89 Malmgren, '50 år med kvinnliga präster'.
90 Zurn, *Axel Honneth*, pp. 155–165, 182–189.

We believe this study has demonstrated that change cannot be achieved by denying recognition to others, as the reform opponents did. Moral offence does not bring about principle-based change, only human suffering in everyday life. However, it is possible – as in the case of the 1958 reform and the abolition of the conscience clause in 1983 – to bring about change through dialogue, negotiation and democratic processes. In the meantime, judging from the vocation narratives of some of the first women priests, working side by side on the basis of mutual recognition does appear to be perfectly feasible.

∞∞∞∞

This chapter has shown how the narrative of division and the presumption that this division was the fault of the first women priests resulted in a code of conduct. The first women priests were expected to give way, and the responsibility for ensuring that situations which would expose this division did not arise was very much placed on them.

The narrative of the Anglican Church's decision to open up its priesthood to women offers an intriguing parallel. As Clare Walsh has demonstrated, the media narrative in that case also focused primarily on division. There was a 'general acceptance of opponents' construction of women priests as even more of a problem as insiders than they had been as campaigning outsiders, clamouring to be let in'.[91] The focus was on the opponents and their pain rather than on the reform being a hard-won victory. Walsh also argues that there was an expectation that whenever situations of conflict and provocation arose, women priests would form a role model of patience and understanding of their opponents' pain.[92]

The first women ordained as priests in the Church of Sweden acted largely in accordance with the code of conduct, out of fear, gratitude and compulsion, and because this was perceived as a Christian ideal. Even so, some of the later vocation narratives contain meta-reflections in which the priests are critical of their own behaviour in relation to the code of conduct. Looking back, some of them comment that they wish they had challenged it earlier and had demanded recognition of their vocation back then. In addition, this chapter has related these meta-reflections on the code

---

91 Walsh, *Gender and Discourse*, p. 183.
92 Ibid., pp. 181–189.

of conduct to Honneth's theories regarding how a repeated denial of recognition tends to lead to a struggle for recognition.

Once the first women priests had had enough and no longer upheld the code of conduct, the denied recognition became visible. The narrative of division and the presumption that it was the first women priests who were causing it were challenged. As we have shown, this narrative could also be inverted in the debate, so that the reform opponents were portrayed as the cause of the division. The struggle for recognition eventually led to the repeal of the conscience clause in 1983, whereby the ambivalence of having legal recognition alongside legitimised denied social recognition finally disappeared. In practice, however, the denial of social recognition appears to have persisted.

The chapter has also discussed how the inverted narrative of division gave rise to what we have labelled the 'who is suffering more?' narrative. The discussion of demands for recognition shifted to a comparison of who had suffered and was suffering the most, the women priests or the reform opponents. In the light of Honneth's theory, this comparison may be understood as an expression of what happens when two struggles for recognition are in opposition to each other.

On the basis of Honneth's theory and what we have seen in the vocation narratives, this is what we offer as a constructive contribution: to implement desired changes that have been decided in principle, democratic decision-making processes and respect for their outcomes are a better strategy than denying recognition. Throughout this process, mutual social recognition is a fundamental prerequisite for coexistence.

At the inauguration of a new vicar in the parish of Annedal in the diocese of Gothenburg in 1978, the then bishop, an opponent of the reform, did not wish to serve at the same altar as one of the priests in the parish, Anne Strid. The outcome was that Strid participated in the service as a notary (in general), but not as a priest (*in sacris*). The photo in the daily newspaper *Göteborgs-Posten* of the woman dressed in priest's garb left sitting on her own in the chancel, while the ordained men stood around the altar rails together with the laypeople, became iconic. The incident aroused strong feelings and created debate, in which several of the first ordained women took part. For instance, Lena Malmgren wrote as follows in the article 'Omöjligt att skilja på sak och person i prästämbetet' ['Impossible to separate the person from the issue with regard to the priestly office'] in *Göteborgs-Posten* on 31 October 1978: 'Anyone who does not respect my faith in God and in his vocation of me as a priest respects nothing of what matters to me, not the inmost core of my being, thereby inflicting an outrage on me as a person.' (Image: reproduced by courtesy of *Göteborgsposten/* Bengt Kjellin 1978.)

Chapter 8
Ecumenical entanglements

The issue of women priests is a topical one in several other countries. In England, the idea is met with fierce opposition from the Church leadership; that opposition has led to serious complications, especially in the mission fields during wartime. In Denmark, women priests appear to be able to work without interference, once the initial concerns subsided. In France, the first Protestant woman priest has just been ordained. In Norway, women have the right to hold priestly office, but the ecclesiastical authorities refuse women access to the last crucial stage of their training and can thereby exclude them from the priesthood. In Germany, the difficult situation has led to a number of women holding priestly office. In Finland, the women become youth and Sunday-school secretaries and the like.[1]

The Church of Sweden's decision in 1958 to open up the priesthood to women was not made in a vacuum. The article by 'Botilda' in *Svenska Morgonbladet* that appeared one November day in 1950 is an example of how, in the debate leading up to the decision, parallels were repeatedly drawn with the position and role of women in other churches and denominations, both in Sweden and abroad. There were plenty of contacts with and influences from other denominations that already had women as pastors or priests. The present chapter focuses on these connections, parallels and influences.

It may seem self-evident that the process in the Church of Sweden was not an isolated phenomenon, but the fact is that these connections and parallels have not come in for much attention before. There are probably many reasons for this neglect, but, as we mentioned in the introduction to this book, we believe that one contributing factor is the nature of the historical narratives. Opening up the priesthood to women has been viewed in light of

---

1 Article signed 'Botilda', *Svenska Morgonbladet*, 18 November 1950.

the so-called Church–State question – that is, as part of the con-
current discussions on the role of the Church of Sweden as the
state church in the country. From the perspective of this particular
historical narrative, the two central actors have been the Church
of Sweden and the Swedish government, and the reform has been
regarded exclusively as a political issue. Alternatively, by emphasising the importance of Lutheran theology and the concept of the
folk church as a significant driving force, the historical narrative
has focused on the Church of Sweden as the sole actor, and
the reform has been regarded exclusively as a theological issue. As
we have shown, these historical narratives – labelled the 'thesis' and
'antithesis' narratives in Chapter 1 – certainly contribute important
aspects to the understanding of the opening up of the priesthood to
women in the Church of Sweden. At the same time, their respective
focuses have contributed to a perception of the reform as a process
involving one church only: the Church of Sweden. In this respect,
research on the Church of Sweden is not an outlier either nationally
or internationally. As we pointed out in our review of the literature,
it is common for research on the reform of church offices to focus
on the process as it takes place in a specific church. At the same
time, as we have shown, the few studies that do adopt a broader
perspective emphasise that there seem to be 'intriguing parallels'
whereby experiences '"translate" from one culture to another'.[2]

However, as we mentioned in the introductory chapter, the
importance of parallels and connections has not gone unnoticed in
the Swedish context. In the 1950s debate, it was relatively common
to give 'the ecumenical argument' a brief mention – meaning a
concern that the ecumenical endeavours of the Church of Sweden,
especially its relationship with the Church of England, might be
adversely affected if the former began ordaining women as priests.
Nonetheless, how these ecumenical influences manifested themselves in practice, in concrete contexts and parallels, is very rarely
discussed.

One exception to this is church historian Gunilla Gunner. In her
article 'Om predikstolar ur ett ekumeniskt perspektiv' ['On pulpits
from an ecumenical perspective'], she places the debate about
reforming the priesthood in the Church of Sweden and the 1958
decision on this matter in the context of the nineteenth-century
Christian revival movements, and discusses the role of leadership

---

2 Jones, Thorpe and Wootton, 'Introduction', p. 7.

in various Christian denominations in Sweden. Gunner concludes: 'there is a connection between the development of the revival movement and what happened in the Church of Sweden'.[3] In this chapter and the next, we explore these under-studied connections and parallels with regard to the Church of Sweden in greater detail. How they manifested themselves, and how significant they were, becomes clear when we look more closely at the connections and parallels with other denominations – both inside and outside Sweden – that implemented similar reforms at about the same time. Above all, it becomes apparent how these influences often relate to vocation and recognition.

Background in and ties to other denominations

When we examine the core episodes in the vocation narratives that describe childhood and adolescence, connections and parallels emerge as an oft-recurring theme in addition to the themes discussed in Chapter 3. Almost half of the first women priests mention that they had a background in, or other close ties to, other religious denominations or movements in Sweden. One example is Birgitta Fogelklou (1923–1989, ordained 1970), who grew up in the Roman Catholic Church and later converted to the Church of Sweden.[4] Ties to various intra-Church revivalist movements or Free Church denominations are most common, though. Fourteen of the priests mention such a link in their vocation narratives.

A number of the first women priests, including Ingrid Persson and Stina Grönros, were greatly influenced by the Low Church movement, especially the intra-Church revivalist movement called the Swedish Evangelical Mission [Evangeliska Fosterlands-Stiftelsen, EFS].[5] Another example is Britta Olén-van Zijl. Not only was her father a Low Church priest, but her mother, Nelly Olén, née Holmström (1898–1963), was also frequently employed as

3 Gunilla Gunner, 'Om predikstolar ur ett ekumeniskt perspektiv', in Hössjer Sundman (ed.), Äntligen stod hon i predikstolen!, pp. 140–149 (p. 141). To some extent these perspectives are also discussed in Simon Sorgenfrei and David Thurfjell (eds), Kvinnligt religiöst ledarskap: En vänbok till Gunilla Gunner (Huddinge: Södertörn University, 2020).

4 Letters from Birgitta Fogelklou to Stig Hellsten, 15 June 1953 and 13 February 1968, Stig Hellsten Archive, Umeå University Library.

5 Obituary of Ingrid Persson written by Nils Parkman, LUKA; No. 24; speech given by Lena Malmgren at the funeral of Stina Grönros (1942–2014, ordained 1966) on 12 March 2014.

a preacher by both the EFS and various Free Church denominations, including the Salvation Army, the Swedish Alliance Mission [Svenska Alliansmissionen, SAM] and the Mission Covenant Church of Sweden [Svenska Missionsförbundet, SMF, now part of the Uniting Church in Sweden].[6] It was also from the EFS chapel in Karlskrona that Olén-van Zijl preached on the occasion in 1957 when she was the first woman ever to preach in a service broadcast on the radio, because the Bishop of Lund, Anders Nygren, refused to let her preach in a church.[7]

There were also a number of ties with various Swedish Free Church denominations, including congregations of the Baptist Union of Sweden [Svenska Baptistsamfundet, SBS]. For example, one of the priests says that her mother came from a Baptist congregation and that she herself attended a Salvation Army Sunday school. She adds that she spent a lot of time in the Baptist congregation and thereby gained good knowledge of the Bible. It was also there that she experienced a moment of conversion as a young woman: 'In the spring of 1954 I was converted or "saved", as they said.'[8]

While links with other denominations could be favourable, they are also described as complicated in some cases, in particular because of the mutual distrust of the various denominations, a distrust engendered by their history of conflict.[9] The priest who had roots in the Baptist Church left it when she went on to study at university: 'At Easter 1960 I left the congregation. It is easy to write but was very painful. I had a bad conscience and felt guilty

---

6 Gunnar Olén, *Kavajprästens hustru* (Jönköping: Hall, 1965), p. 75: 'She had absolutely no inhibitions regarding denominations or premises. Whenever she received a call to come and preach the gospel and she had the opportunity to get away from her many other duties, she went with joy. She gave wholeheartedly the best she could in her preaching, and as a result saw remarkable results from her labours. God commended this work. And therefore she felt safe, even though conservative priests and church people of the same calibre highly disapproved of her boldness in preaching God's word and were horrified by it.' Göte Petersson, '"En moder i Israel": Minnesruna över fru Nelly Olén', *Blekinge kyrkliga hembygdskalender* (1964), pp. 6–10.

7 Olén-van Zijl, 'Att få vara präst', p. 105.

8 No. 25.

9 The emergence of Swedish Free Churches in a society where the state church had been the sole actor for centuries was anything but plain sailing, and it was not until 1951 that Sweden gained full religious freedom.

for what I had done, as if I had let them down. Yet I knew I could not stay.'[10] Ulla Nisser sketches a Free Church background as well, with her grandmother Anna reading aloud from John Bunyan's *Pilgrim's Progress*, her confirmation in the SMF, and a revivalist meeting under SMF auspices. Nisser also describes how the Free Church 'coin' could have two sides. At the revival meeting, which took place one summer in the 1950s, Nisser says she experienced demands to be 'saved' and a form of self-righteousness among the pastors present. This experience gave her the impression that the pastors considered her to be eternally damned, even though she had a Christian faith and came from a Christian home. In contrast to the faith she encountered from the pastors at the revival meeting, she describes her parents' faith as natural and heartfelt.[11]

Other accounts of Free Church and Low Church influences are less detailed, but they do exist. In one vocation narrative, for instance, the writer states that her maternal grandparents were members of the Salvation Army and that this influenced her, but that she did not 'understand it back then'.[12] Yet another priest emphasises her ties with the SMF training school when introducing her own vocation narrative.[13] Another narrator singles out Paul Wern (1925–2007), a theologian in SAM, as an important spiritual director. She also says that the Quaker Thomas R. Kelly, through his book *A Testament of Devotion*, was an important inspiration for her.[14] One vocation narrative mentions that the Baptist Oswald Chambers (1874–1917) influenced the writer's spirituality.[15] The material also shows that one of the 54 women who were ordained during the period studied in this book was the editor of the newspaper *Dagen*, an important Free Church newspaper that originated in the Swedish Pentecostal movement.[16]

---

10 No. 25. So also No. 26, who left the Pentecostal movement, and No. 44, who left the Methodist Church.
11 Nisser, *Hopp från trampolin*, pp. 17–38 and chapter 12.
12 No. 33. Here the priest may also be referring to her grandmother, who was labelled a 'freethinker': 'I don't believe he [the narrator's father] meant that she was an atheist, but that she thought freely and about the Confession of the Church ...'
13 No. 37.
14 No. 42.
15 No. 2.
16 No. 44.

Of course, there are also priests who had no contact with intra-Church or Free Church revivalist movements at all[17] – and those who did not want this either. An example of the latter in the source material is the priest who points out that when she married a member of the EFS, she was expected to join the organisation. She says that she replied, 'It is unthinkable [...] If I were to join the EFS, it would be on theological grounds, and I couldn't see any. On the contrary.'[18]

On an individual level, almost half of the first women priests thus had a background in and ties to intra-Church revivalist movements and various Free Church denominations. This connection finds expression in their theology of vocation.

The theology of necessary preaching

Connections and parallels are also evident in relation to theological narratives about vocation. When the first women to be ordained as priests in the Church of Sweden discuss and use the concept of vocation, yet another theme emerges alongside those mentioned in Chapter 4 (that is, Lutheran folk church theology that emphasises the priestly office as a function and the servant of the divine Word, and the theological counter-narrative that questions the concept of a woman's vocation as expressed in the Lutheran doctrine of the three estates and instead highlights Galatians 3:28 as the key to interpretation). We have chosen to call this understanding of vocation, which has not received much attention in previous research on the opening up of the priesthood to women, 'the theology of necessary preaching'.

The vocation theology of necessary preaching is founded on the concept of an emergency situation and focuses on the urgent need to ensure that the Gospel is propagated. Society is perceived as secularised, time is short, and God's Word must hence reach people with immediate effect. All forces for good must be utilised; and if the Church's established practices and priests cannot cope, then God moves beyond the framework of the organisation and calls other people, on the basis of their personal faith and suitability. For this reason, the individual often cannot refuse the call – there is an element of compulsion, even though the person who is called also frequently expresses a sense of longing.

---

17 Leif Olsson, 'Det har varit en obehaglig upplevelse', *Dagen*, 26 June 2002.
18 No. 34.

This theological understanding is central to the view of vocation that existed in the intra-Church revivalist movements and the Free Church denominations. Considering how many of the priests in the source material explicitly state that they had a background in and/ or contacts with such movements and denominations, it is not surprising that this vocation theology appears in the narratives. How the connection between vocation and preaching might be understood in a Swedish Free Church context has been discussed in detail by the practical theologian Sune Fahlgren, who highlights a number of central concepts and phenomena. One such phenomenon is lay preachers, described by Fahlgren in relation to the preaching of P. P. Waldenström (1838–1917). Waldenström was a lay preacher, first in the EFS and later in the SMF.[19] According to Waldenström, *rite vocatus* (being 'properly called') consists of the external vocation from the true Church, that is, 'the true believers', in combination with the internal vocation. To Waldenström, the concept of the 'royal priesthood' (1 Pet. 2:9) was essential, too. This concept bears some resemblance to the Lutheran priesthood of all believers, but it is through personal experience of God, rather than through baptism, that an individual comes to belong to a kind of priesthood. Like the Old Testament Levitical priests, these 'priests' have a threefold task: to teach (preach), to pray and to sacrifice (to live a giving Christian life). The task of preaching was particularly important, since faith derives from preaching.[20]

Waldenström was first active in the EFS, the movement that five of the first women priests say they grew up in. Church historian Henry Wiklund describes how the EFS was formed in the mid-nineteenth century, with the aim of conducting mission work among nominal Christians in Sweden and 'reviving' them to faith and involvement in the congregations of the Church of Sweden. Although the early EFS statutes did recognise the official priesthood, Wiklund says that the EFS indirectly criticised the Church of Sweden when it expressed the opinion that a special foundation was needed for preaching activities. The lay preacher C. O. Rosenius (1816–1868), one of the founders of the EFS, argued that if the regular, ordained priesthood was insufficient, then

---

19 Waldenström was ordained as a priest in the Church of Sweden but resigned from the priesthood in 1882.

20 Sune Fahlgren, *Predikantskap och församling: Sex fallstudier av en ecklesial baspraktik inom svensk frikyrklighet fram till 1960-talet* (Uppsala: Uppsala universitet, 2006), pp. 138–141.

the priesthood of all believers in the form of 'revived' Christians would be obliged to intervene and preach in order to bring about a revival.[21] At the same time, the EFS felt that a person's inner vocation had to be placed within a context. A *rite vocatus* was needed for lay preachers too.[22]

The vocation theology of necessary preaching was also often linked to eschatological perspectives and to the idea that time is short. That idea was also central to the emerging missionary movement and was a major reason why missionaries went out into the field, even though doing so could be extremely dangerous.[23]

The notion that time is short is especially evident from four priests in our source material.[24] One of these was Sara Björkman (1909–2004, ordained 1967), a missionary sent out by the Mission Covenant Church of Sweden. In her 1955 poetry collection *Meditationer* ['Meditations'], she wrote a number of poems that are strongly influenced by the vocation theology of necessary preaching. In some of her poems, thoughts about the need to preach are linked to a concrete mandate to be God's 'messenger'. She writes:

A deed, unreasonably large,
you dare
call me to. You entrust
the work to my hands,
while I hesitantly ask,
why do you send me of all people?

A drop of dew can reflect
a flood;
and a tiny key can turn the lock –
and I do know, God Almighty,
with a human destiny
you can send eternal tidings.[25]

---

21 Henry Wiklund, *Predikant, pastor, präst: EFS samfundsproblematik 1940–1972* (Stockholm: EFS-förlaget, 1979), p. 23.

22 Ibid., pp. 22–24.

23 At least four out of ten Swedish missionaries died in the field. Pia Lundqvist, *Ett motsägelsefullt möte: Svenska missionärer och bakongo i Fristaten Kongo* (Lund: Nordic Academic Press, 2018), p. 75.

24 No. 35.

25 Sara Björkman, *Meditationer* (Stockholm: Kvinnliga Missionsarbetare, 1955), p. 20.

It is, of course, impossible to ascertain whether Björkman is writing about herself in her poems, or the extent to which she draws on her own experience. It is better to regard her lines as an example of a way of thinking theologically about vocation, an expression of the theological narrative – the discourse – we want to substantiate. The 'I' in the poem who is called and sent forth to bear the message of the poem's divine 'you' never has a specific sex or office. It is a vocation that cannot be refused, and a person may be 'a drop of dew' or 'a speck of dust' and still be given the mission.

This theological understanding of vocation recurs in Björkman's biography of the missionary Signe Ekblad (1894–1952), who worked for many years as headmistress of the Swedish school in Jerusalem.[26] Björkman's biography of Ekblad provides an insight into how the theology of necessary preaching was expressed in literature. A key theme in Björkman's portrayal of Ekblad is that a vocation is unavoidable and powerful, and that it comes both from within and as an external call from other people and in relation to the suffering that Ekblad saw. Björkman quotes from Ekblad's diary about what it was like to be consecrated as a missionary: 'Trembling before the act, but then constantly happy and joyful to be one of the many who have been set apart for a vocation by the laying on of hands.'[27]

As Björkman describes it, nothing is allowed to stand in the way of this vocation; the suffering is pressing, and Ekblad can do nothing but give her all. A recurring theme is that despite her health problems, Ekblad cannot bring herself to rest: 'Signe was dead

---

26 In this context, Signe Ekblad viewed her role as headmistress as a calling from God. When asked what drove her, she responded by quoting St Bridget: 'I am only a messenger from a great and powerful God. He is responsible for the tasks I receive and where he sends me. I have only to obey him.' See Sune Fahlgren, 'Signe Anna Charlotta Ekblad', *Svenskt kvinnobiografiskt lexikon*, https://skbl.se/sv/artikel/SigneEkblad [accessed 2 February 2021].

27 Sara Björkman, *Signe Ekblad* (Uppsala: J. A. Lindblads Bokförlag, 1954), pp. 21–27 (p. 27). To be 'set apart' is a term used in many Free Church denominations for the ritual act of confirming a person's calling for a particular task by a denomination or congregation. Similar to, for example, the ordination of a priest, this is done by a representative of the denomination/congregation laying hands on and praying for the individual who is called and designated. This indicates that the person is officially sent out and authorised.

tired, sleepless and worried, but she simply could not be satisfied with just looking after her health. Greater values were at stake.'[28] The theology of necessary preaching recurs with Ingrid Persson as well. As mentioned earlier, she had a background in the EFS. Her answer to the question of whether she had ever doubted her calling was that '[i]t was the women and not the fancy disciples who were allowed to go with the message on Easter Day that Jesus lived. So why shouldn't I be allowed do it?'[29] Her first sermon as a priest, at the main Easter Sunday service in Härnösand in 1960, focused on this Easter motif. Towards the end of the following section of the sermon, she describes the task of 'spreading the message' as incumbent on everybody:

> Surely the two women who came to the tomb with the slow, heavy steps of mourners had never dreamed that, when the Easter morning sun rose, they would leave it with the dancing, light steps of the joyful. But so it was. They are no longer in charge of themselves. The Easter miracle has them in its power. What has happened forces them inexorably to do one thing, the way an intense internal joy exerts force: to spread the news, to carry the message further. Our text says of them: 'with fear and great joy [they] ran to tell his disciples'. And now it is our turn. How could we do otherwise? If we have received a living, risen Saviour through the Easter miracle, it is neither a question of will nor of courage to spread the message about that. We just have to. To spread the message to all those who do not know, do not ask for the one thing needful.[30]

This quotation contains several components of the theology of necessary preaching. God's call applies to everyone, and it is compulsory in relation to all who have not yet been reached by the good news, 'the one thing needful'. In her vocation narrative Persson states that if God so wills, he may move beyond the established order of the Church of Sweden. 'God is not dependent on the Church or on human laws and opinions. He may go beyond.'[31]

The vocation theology of necessary preaching is sometimes connected to a wish to show how unnecessary the debate on

28 Björkman, *Signe Ekblad*, p. 123.
29 Yvonne Landström, 'En stilla stund 40 år efter prästvigningen', *Västernorrlands Allehanda*, 5 July 1997.
30 Ingrid Persson, 'Påskdagen: Matt 28:1–8', in *Postilla: 49 kvinnor predikar* (Stockholm: Verbum, 1990), p. 136.
31 Persson, 'Min väg till prästämbetet', p. 32.

reforming the priesthood is in relation to the present emergency.[32] One example is the case of the future priest who was a missionary in India and happened to catch a Swedish radio programme discussing the Seventeen Points (see Chapter 5). Her thoughts on that occasion were: 'Here I am in a country up to its neck in incredible misery, and some people in a small country near the Arctic Circle know exactly what God wants: that having women priests is wrong.'[33]

These individuals are not the only ones to express the theology of necessary preaching; rather, it constitutes a kind of interdenominational discourse about vocation that is also embraced by priests and theologians with no personal connection to any Free Church denomination. For example, the theology of necessary preaching is a theme that permeates the view of vocation expressed by the priest who had a Roman Catholic background. In her letters to her spiritual director Stig Hellsten, Birgitta Fogelklou repeatedly returns to this topic. In a letter from 1953, she writes as follows:

> And where is the woman in the church supposed to go? She is permitted to be a bench filler – but to be fervent in spirit? We are being drowned in all types of official reports – what fun the devil will have. Can we really afford to refuse a woman's desire to serve? Or, oh horror, will there be no one left for the priests to preach to? This is indeed serious – it runs like a tremor or madness through humanity – do we not therefore need many more people who dare to go unarmed and face all this human loneliness with faith?[34]

This passage is an example of how the theology of necessary preaching in relation to vocation did not always involve ties to Low Church thinking or to the Free Church denominations, even though that was where it was most clearly expressed as an established way of theologically understanding vocation.

While the theology of necessary preaching in relation to vocation formed a powerful legitimisation of women, enabling them to take their place as preachers, it also had an unfavourable aspect. When the emergency was no longer considered so acute, and there were men to fulfil the functions, the women often had to take a back seat again. As the theologian Andrew Mark Eason, who has studied

---

32 Lindqvist-Bolling, 'Förstadspräst', pp. 50, 56–57.
33 No. 19.
34 Letter from Birgitta Fogelklou to Stig Hellsten, Thanksgiving Day 1953, Stig Hellsten Archive, Umeå University Library.

gender and equality in the Salvation Army up to 1930, puts it: the authority that comes from being called by the Holy Spirit to speak publicly in an emergency situation got women up into the pulpit, but not much farther. Because the Salvation Army's organisation was structured in accordance with (theological) conceptions of women's distinctive nature and subordination, the women, with very few exceptions, did not move beyond the pulpit.[35]

As was pointed out in Chapter 5, the group that mustered not only High Church but also Low Church opponents of the reform – the Church Coalition for the Bible and Confession – offers a telling example that the vocation theology of necessary preaching did not always lead to the conclusion that women could indeed serve as priests and pastors.

Predecessors in other denominations and movements

Some of the first women priests in the Church of Sweden, especially those with links to intra-Church revivalist movements and Free Church denominations, thus found theological resources for discussing vocation in these movements and denominations. Some of them also mentioned that they found predecessors and role models there. As Ylwa Gustafsson, for example, observed in an interview in 1967, it was nothing new for women to 'stand in the service of the Word': 'Since the end of the nineteenth century, women have been functioning as priests around the world. After all, the important thing is that the Gospel is disseminated.'[36]

In the Swedish context, there were plenty of examples of predecessors in the revivalist movements and Free Church denominations. One of these was Nelly Hall (1848–1916), one of the first women to preach in Sweden, who preached for the Swedish Holiness Union [Helgelseförbundet]. Hall was a so-called 'travelling preacher' who came and preached when summoned by congregations.[37] According to a news item in *Svenska Dagbladet* from June 1911, Hall was apparently the first woman to stand in a Swedish pulpit. In 1885 she gave 'religious lectures that drew much attention' in Sköllersta

---

35 Andrew Mark Eason, *Women in God's Army: Gender and Equality in the Early Salvation Army* (Waterloo, Ont.: Wilfrid Laurier University Press, 2003), pp. 156–157 (p. 156).

36 Wik-Thorsell, 'Kvinnlig präst söker aldrig konflikterna'.

37 Fahlgren, *Predikantskap och församling*, pp. 156–164.

church, two miles south of Örebro. The news item also contains another interesting remark:

> Moreover, quite a good story is told about Miss Hall's appearance in Sköllersta church. Those who approached Dean Tillman in order to request the church for Miss Hall were at first refused. Although the broad-minded and friendly Tillman personally had nothing against it, he did not dare in view of the expected repercussions from the cathedral chapter and bishop. After a few heartfelt parting words, however, the dean added that he could not promise them the church, but that the keys were there and there. They winked at the dean, picked up the keys and let the people into the church. Later, when the higher authority demanded that Tillman explain what had happened, he could freely say that he had never sanctioned the use of the church.[38]

This anecdote shows not only that women preached in the churches of the Church of Sweden at an early date, but also that the Church's priests were not necessarily opposed to it.

The mention of Nelly Hall as the first woman in a Swedish pulpit was probably prompted by another example of a predecessor, the Methodist pastor and feminist Anna Howard Shaw (1847–1919), who gave a sermon on 11 June 1911 in the Gustav Vasa church in Stockholm. Shaw, who was born in the UK but moved to the US in early childhood, visited Stockholm to attend the Sixth Conference of the International Woman Suffrage Alliance and preached in conjunction with that gathering. It is claimed that some 1,100 delegates from 22 countries and four continents listened to Shaw's sermon. However, the sermon was not given in conjunction with the regular 11 a.m. service; the large audience did not gather until 2.30 in the afternoon. Perhaps this was because it would have been too controversial to have a woman preach, and in English to boot, during the congregation's main service. It was probably also out of consideration for the critics that Shaw was not permitted to preach from the pulpit but instead had to stand in the chancel of the church.

Shaw's sermon was based on Psalm 68:12, which speaks of the role of women in spreading the message of victory. The sermon centred on the suffrage movement's positive relationship with Christianity. The following day, the newspaper *Dagens Nyheter* quoted excerpts from the sermon. Shaw is reported to have said the following:

---

38 'I marginalen', *Svenska Dagbladet*, 19 June 1911.

Never has there been a time when so much great and good has been achieved as now. It is the spirit of God in the hearts of human beings that impels them to do good. In the time of Christ, women were still considered to be in the same relationship with God as men, but later on the men found that there was so much sin and so much evil in the world. It had to be somebody's fault, and so the Church began to interpret Scripture to mean that it was women who were evil and had to be suppressed. Jesus expressed the right of all people to freedom [...] Achieving political freedom is only one more step of many in our work for the Kingdom of God. What is the spirit that drives you forward, and how will you use your right to vote? On your answer depends the value of your freedom. We should use it to work to make the world better, to live a more holy life. The suffrage movement signifies religious awakening. It does not contradict Christianity, but it seeks to infuse the Gospel with a new spirit, a spirit consistent with Christ's own words.[39]

According to the writer of this article, Shaw thus perceives a reciprocal influence whereby the suffrage movement's struggle for recognition gives contemporary relevance to 'Christ's own words' about everybody's right to freedom, and to the contention that women and men stand in the same relationship to God and therefore have the same mission to work for the Kingdom of God. In other words, what emerges in Shaw's sermon is the counter-narrative of vocation based on Galatians 3:28.

Shaw's biographer, Trisha Franzen, briefly mentions Shaw's visit and sermon in Stockholm in 1911: 'She was to be the first woman to preach in the Swedish Church but the momentous became the sensational when the Church of Norway denied Shaw a similar right to preach.' According to Franzen, Shaw felt that she was under great pressure with the world's eyes upon her, and that she was required to deliver a good sermon. Even so, Shaw described the occasion in the Stockholm church as a spiritual experience.[40]

---

39 *Dagens Nyheter*, 12 June 1911. Our thanks to Bishop Emerita Eva Brunne who, through her lecture 'To love a great cause – om Anna Howard Shaw' on 7 March 2022 in the Gustav Vasa church, drew our attention to this sermon and provided us with quotations and sources.

40 Trisha Franzen, *Anna Howard Shaw: The Work of Woman Suffrage* (Urbana, IL: University of Illinois Press, 2014), p. 133. Shaw's visit to Stockholm and her sermon in the Gustav Vasa church are also described in Märta Tamm-Götlind, *Anna Howard Shaw: Den kvinnliga prästen och människovännen* (Uppsala: J. A. Lindblads Bokförlag, 1920), pp. 68–70.

Shaw is best known to posterity as a woman suffragist and president of the National American Woman Suffrage Association. However, interesting parallels exist between her life story and the experiences of the first women to become priests in the Church of Sweden. Franzen observes that the role of pastor gave Shaw a platform and room to manoeuvre, stressing that it was thanks to her vocation and her claim to have a divine mission to preach that she was able to enter arenas previously reserved for men.[41] Similarly, the nineteenth-century revivalist movements were important in Shaw's American context in that they enabled women to become ordained as pastors. There, too, women had taken on roles as evangelists and preachers. In American society, the Quakers had long given both women and men equal access to preaching, although other Dissenting denominations were more hesitant. Not least the issue of women's respectability – that is, the expectation at that time that a woman's primary role was to be a good wife and mother – meant that many denominations rejected women preachers. According to historian of religion Catherine A. Brekus, women preachers were most common in marginalised denominations whose members were poor or from a lower social class, and/or which were located in comparatively remote areas of the expanding United States. In such circumstances, it was not unusual for congregation leaders or reform-minded men to support those women who felt a call to preach. The efforts by Shaw's own Methodist Church to create a 'counter-culture' in American society might also have contributed to the welcoming of women evangelists.[42]

Like many of the first women priests in the Church of Sweden, Shaw experienced denied recognition during her student years. When she began her theological studies at Boston University School of Theology in 1875, Shaw was the only woman in her class

---

41 Franzen, *Anna Howard Shaw*, pp. 2, 7 and 38 (p. 7).
42 Ibid., pp. 36–37; Brekus, *Strangers & Pilgrims*. In the case of the major Lutheran church bodies – the Lutheran Church in America (LCA) and the American Lutheran Church (ALC), two bodies that would later become the Evangelical Lutheran Church in America (ELCA), the largest Evangelical Lutheran church in the United States – the decision to ordain women would not be made until 1970. Tradition and ecumenism – especially in relation to Roman Catholics – were viewed as obstacles to this decision. Gracia Grindal, 'Women in the Evangelical Lutheran Church in America', in Catherine Wessinger (ed.), *Religious Institutions and Women's Leadership: New Roles Inside the Mainstream* (Columbia, SC: University of South Carolina Press, 1996), p. 180. See also Makant, *Holy Mischief*.

of 40 men and appears to have had no allies. Franzen writes that 'Shaw faced what might best be described as a very hostile tolerance'. Life in this almost exclusively male environment seems to have been particularly difficult because, unlike men in the same situation, Shaw also lacked access to helpful scholarships and housing that might have facilitated her studies.[43]

There are parallels between Shaw and the first women priests in the Church of Sweden in another respect, namely with regard to the Church's recognition of their vocation. After her theological studies, Shaw continued to work as a pastor but was denied ordination. It was not until the autumn of 1880, after changing from one Methodist denomination to another, that she could be ordained as a pastor. Other pastors were among those who refused to recognise her, both before and after her ordination. Franzen writes that 'Shaw never forgot how badly the men of the cloth treated her throughout the entire episode. Apparently even after she was ordained, the young men in the Methodist Protestant Conference went out of their way to make her week there miserable.'[44]

Alongside famous examples such as Nelly Hall and Anna Howard Shaw, there were a number of other role models in the Swedish context. Women preachers appeared early on in the Salvation Army, whose view of vocation influenced the revivalist movements in Sweden. Incidentally, the Swedish branch of the Salvation Army was established in 1882 by a woman, Hanna Ouchterlony (1838–1924), a bookseller from Värnamo, who served as Commissioner (supreme leader) in Sweden.[45]

At this point, it is important to note that in the revivalist and Free Church movements, not only were there historical examples of women called to the ministry in various ways; women were also engaged in writing the life stories of such predecessors. They created narratives about their own movement, individual congregations, preachers, evangelists, missionaries and so on in order to foster identity, inspire and educate. These efforts included stories about women that were documented in book form. As we showed

---

43 Franzen, *Anna Howard Shaw*, pp. 39–43; Tamm-Götlind, *Anna Howard Shaw*, pp. 32–38.

44 Franzen, *Anna Howard Shaw*, pp. 47–48 (p. 48); Tamm-Götlind, *Anna Howard Shaw*, pp. 43–44 (describing her transition from one branch of Methodism to another).

45 Lundin, *Predikande kvinnor och gråtande män*, pp. 11–12.

above, one of the first women priests, Sara Björkman, contributed to the formulation of such a historical narrative.

One of the better-known Swedish cases of history writing by and about women was that of Signe Walder (1875–1963), a teacher and missionary in the Congo, posted there by the SMF.[46] She wrote a number of books, two of which are about women's contributions to the revivalist movement. One individual Walder names is the Baptist Ida Andersson of Skara.[47] This is the same Ida Andersson that Britta Olén-van Zijl's father, Gunnar Olén, held up as a predecessor and example of the need for women priests (see Chapter 3). As was mentioned earlier, Olén-van Zijl also regarded her own preaching mother, Nelly Olén, as a role model. Some 200 of her mother's sermon manuscripts are preserved in the archives of the University Library in Lund. Judging by the number of dates and places written on each manuscript, most of the sermons were delivered a number of times.[48] Another of the first women priests also states that she had a female family member who preached in public, an aunt who had been an evangelist.

In addition, there were more recent predecessors in the Free Church denominations. Both the Mission Covenant Church of Sweden and the Baptist Union of Sweden officially permitted women to become pastors a few years before the Church of Sweden. It was therefore natural for contemporary debaters to draw parallels between developments in these denominations and the Church of Sweden. The parallels should be viewed in relation to the changes in society in the course of the twentieth century, not least the expanded recognition of women; but they were not solely due to the fact that the three denominations operated within the same social context.[49] The ties and connections between the denominations were closer than that. This closeness becomes even more apparent when the changes in the Church of Sweden are compared with developments in the Mission Covenant Church of Sweden and the Baptist Union of Sweden, and more specifically in relation to

---

46 Signe Walder herself is portrayed in, for instance, Lundqvist, *Ett motsägelse-fullt möte*, p. 245.

47 Maria Lundahl and Signe Walder (eds), *I striden och vid trossen* (Stockholm: Svenska missionsförbundet, 1938), p. 145.

48 Gunnar Olén Collection, LUL.

49 See, for example, Hirdman, Björkman and Lundberg (eds), *Sveriges historia, 1920–1965*, pp. 581–582, which describes how the labour market was opened up to women in the 1960s and 1970s.

two of the first women pastors in these denominations: Ingegärd
Dackerud (1929–2024) and Ulla Bardh (1936–).

The Mission Covenant Church of Sweden and Ingegärd Dackerud

At its 1950 General Conference, the Mission Covenant Church of
Sweden (SMF) formally decided to allow women to be ordained
as pastors. As was pointed out above, the vocation theology
of necessary preaching did not necessarily involve a favourable
attitude towards women in church leadership. In fact, there was
such disagreement on this issue that the decision was formulated
as 'each congregation decides for itself what position to take on
the question of a woman being leader of the congregation'.[50]
The determining factor in the decision was thus the fact that the
SMF was a congregationalist denomination, which meant that it
was not necessary to reach theological consensus at the General
Conference.[51]

There is an interesting connection here between the Church of
Sweden and the Mission Covenant Church of Sweden, a connection
which Gunilla Gunner has emphasised. Greta Bredberg, who served
as an expert in the group that investigated the issue of women's
access to the priesthood in the Church of Sweden and delivered the
report in 1951 (see Chapter 4), also sat on the SMF committee that
was commissioned to investigate the issue of women's ordination as
pastors back in 1948. At the first meeting of the 1948 committee,
Bredberg was commissioned to report on the working process in
the discussions in the Church of Sweden. Gunner believes that this
shows 'that there were largely parallel processes going on within

---

50 Rune W. Dahlén, Ulf Hållmarker and Lennart Molin, *Missionsskolan
Lidingö* (Skåre: Votum, 2016), p. 165.

51 According to Rune W. Dahlén, this congregationalist stance has been
important for enabling the preservation of unity throughout a number
of different crises in the SMF's history, not only over the issue of women
pastors. On the issues of historical-critical biblical interpretation, homo-
sexual pastors and same-sex marriage, the ability of each individual
congregation to decide how to act has also prevented division. Rune W.
Dahlén, 'Pastoral Education and Controversy in the Mission Covenant
Church of Sweden', in Hanna Ondrey and Mark Safstrom (eds), *Essays in
Honor of Philip J. Anderson: Sacred Migration: Borderlands of Community
and Faith* (Chicago: The Swedish-American Historical Society, 2020),
pp. 215–231.

the SMF and the Church of Sweden'.[52] International influences also appear to have been at work. The theologian Rune W. Dahlén argues that the discussions within the SMF took off in earnest when the English Methodists and the Congregationalists in the USA opened up to women pastors in 1945.[53]

The investigation prior to the 1950 General Conference had been prompted by the fact that in the autumn of 1946, the Alster Mission Covenant congregation had called Signe Eriksson (1913–1996) as pastor and director. She had not been trained at the mission school, as was customary for pastors, but she was an evangelist, and it was possible to be 'set apart' if one had served for at least two years in an SMF congregation. Two years later, Alster, supported by the Värmland-Dalsland District Council, requested that Eriksson be declared a regular pastor.

In January 1950 the committee presented its proposal, suggesting that the SMF board accept women pastors. However, one of the members of the committee registered a dissenting opinion and instead proposed that a special position be established that made better use of the special gifts of women. Essie Eklund (1919–2013) was the first woman to be admitted to the pastor training programme on Lidingö, an island in the inner Stockholm archipelago, in 1952, and Ingegärd Dackerud was admitted in the following year. In 1957 Dackerud became the first woman in the SMF to be appointed as the pastor of a congregation after being made a pastor.

On 8 June 2020, in conjunction with the seventieth anniversary of the SMF's decision to allow women to be ordained, a filmed interview was published entitled 'Ingegärd Dackerud – pionjär som kvinna och pastor' ['Ingegärd Dackerud – a pioneer as a woman and a pastor'], in which Dackerud discusses her vocation for and service as a pastor. Among other things, Dackerud states that she felt a calling when she was young, but she believed it was to become a missionary, since the SMF did not have women pastors. Like a number of the first women to be ordained as priests in the Church of Sweden, Dackerud thus sought to be 'something like a priest/pastor'. She began training as a missionary in 1949, but injured her back as a result of the heavy practical work involved in doing medical care. While she was in hospital, her father brought her an issue of the SMF's in-house newsletter, *Svensk Veckotidning*: 'And there it said that "Now the SMF Board has decided to admit

---

52 Gunner, 'Om predikstolar ur ett ekumeniskt perspektiv', p. 145.
53 Dahlén, 'Pastoral Education', p. 231.

women pastors and has opened the seminary to them." Oh, I said in a hushed voice, was that what you were thinking, God?'[54]

Another similarity with the future women priests in the Church of Sweden is the need to have one's vocation recognised through some kind of ordination ceremony. Dackerud says that she wanted to train as a pastor and be 'set apart' as one, because she had seen what had happened to other women who had not been designated in that way. She mentions Signe Eriksson as an example of the importance of gaining the social recognition that came with a theological education, and says that Eriksson had found it difficult to be recognised as a pastor because she lacked such training.[55] Another similarity is that Dackerud emphasises that there is no difference between being a woman pastor and simply being a pastor.

> For me it was quite unnatural when they came and asked 'what is it like to be a woman pastor?' I replied: you might at least ask what it feels like to be a pastor [...] For me, this term 'woman pastor' has never applied. I am a pastor.[56]

Like some of the first women to be ordained as priests, Dackerud also says that she chose not to have a family so that she could fully embrace her vocation, and she describes the pressure to do well because failure would have given opponents of the reform the opportunity to say 'We told you so.'

There were also direct links between Dackerud and one of the first women to be ordained as a priest in the Church of Sweden. Dackerud says she had known Margit Sahlin since her student years at Uppsala. She believes that she had played the role of mentor to Sahlin until Sahlin's ordination, to which Dackerud was actually invited, 'to the great horror of the bishops'. Dackerud also believes that Sahlin had a harder time with the opposition than she did, and states that they had 'an open phone line' so that Sahlin could call from time to time and talk about how she was feeling.[57]

Serving as a pastor, Dackerud experienced both support and opposition from male priests in the Church of Sweden, who, unlike their male pastor counterparts, would sometimes show their claws.

54 'Ingegärd Dackerud – pionjär som kvinna och pastor', YouTube, 8 June 2020, https://www.youtube.com/watch?v=-ZjX3ThbMak [accessed 3 July 2020].
55 Ibid.
56 Ibid.
57 Ibid.

However, the Bishop of Visby, Algot Anderberg (1893–1963), proved to be an unexpected ally. Dackerud says that he phoned and invited her as the new SMF pastor to the Church of Sweden's gathering of the priests in his diocese in order to introduce her.

Then he said that he was very pleased to receive the first woman to be ordained as a priest – those were his words – in his diocese. I went into that [priests' meeting] He introduced me [...] we continued to chat and then he said that 'I'm so proud that we have you here', adding, 'Listen, if any one of my lads is nasty to you, just call Papa Anderberg.'

The next week I was to go in with my priestly certificate [...][58] A priest was there who didn't like the idea of this business of women pastors and women priests in general, so he refused to register me as a pastor. He would register me as a preacher. Then I said: 'my title is pastor, I am ordained as a pastor, and I have done just as much schooling as you have, and my profession is pastor.' 'Pastor is not a profession', he said, 'it is a practice. You are a woman so I cannot register you as a pastor.' [...] When I got home [...] I phoned Papa Anderberg, because he had given me his personal phone number, and I said: 'It's Pastor Dackerud.' – 'Aha, has someone been nasty?' And I told him what had happened. 'Rubbish', he said. 'Boyish nonsense.' [...] Then after a while, when I was sitting at the dinner table, the phone rings: 'Hello, it's [the priest]. I've changed my mind, so I've registered [the priestly certificate].' 'Oh, did the bishop phone you?' I said. 'Yes. I've been told off.' 'Well, you deserved it', I said.[59]

A number of interesting things emerge from this passage. First, it portrays vigorous recognition from the bishop – who belonged to a different denomination from Dackerud herself – who expresses his joy and pride in having a woman pastor in his diocese. It is also interesting to note that, according to Dackerud, the bishop referred to her as a 'priest' and not as a 'pastor'. The bishop also gives his support to Dackerud when she is denied recognition by a priest in the diocese.

Ingegärd Dackerud's narrative provides examples of parallels and connections between the SMF and the Church of Sweden. Considering the historically close ties between these two denominations, this is perhaps not very surprising. However, it is

58 At this time, the Church of Sweden was in charge of the national population register, and Dackerud had to see the local clergyman in order to be registered as residing at her new domicile.
59 Ibid.

significant that these connections and parallels also apply to the other Free Church denomination that opened up to women pastors shortly before the Church of Sweden: the Baptist Union of Sweden.

The Baptist Union of Sweden and Ulla Bardh

The Baptist Union of Sweden decided on the issue of women pastors in 1955. As in the SMF, the issue had been raised by the fact that women had already been hired as pastors by local congregations. They included Eva Hedqvist (1911–2006), who had been pastor and leader of the congregation in Solna since 1953, and Thora Thoong (1909–1999), who was called to the post of youth pastor in Västerås in 1951.[60] According to Gunilla Gunner, the debate was 'lively', but here, too, the issue was resolved thanks to the Baptist Union's congregationalist standpoint. Each congregation could decide for itself whether or not to call a woman as pastor.[61]

The same year that the decision was made, three women were admitted to the pastor training programme at the Bethel Seminary in Stockholm: Ulla-Cajsa Axelson (1932–), Ulla Bardh and Birgit Karlsson (1935–). In May 1958 they were interviewed by *Dagens Nyheter*. When the journalist raised the issue of opposition, they replied that Baptist congregations were generally favourably disposed towards women pastors. Birgit Karlsson explains this by saying that it had already been the practice for a long time: 'That it is going so well for us is probably connected to the Free Church having had female evangelists for a long time. Women in the pulpit are no novelty to us; the only difference is that we will be called pastors when we have finished training.' There is no explicit mention of the Baptist congregationalist standpoint as a reason why there was less strenuous opposition in this denomination, but it is implied when the journalist asks about the future. 'Baptist pastors don't get to choose where they go, it depends on where the calls come from. So none of the women know much about what the future will hold. Only that they don't need to be afraid of not getting a position – it is already clear that the congregations

---

60 *Vägmärken för baptister: Tro, frihet, gemenskap. Svenska baptistsamfundet 1848–2012* (Karlstad: Votum, 2016), pp. 104–105.
61 Gunner, 'Om predikstolar ur ett ekumeniskt perspektiv', pp. 145–146.

want them.'[62] However, in an interview from 2016 Birgit Karlsson makes the following point:

> It was during these years that the great debate about women priests in the Church of Sweden was going on. In the face of that debate, we realised what freedom is involved in living with the congregational view represented by the Baptist Union of Sweden. It created space. Not all congregations were prepared to accept women pastors in 1955, but none were forced to either.[63]

The three pastoral candidates lend unambiguous expression to the theology of necessary preaching in relation to vocation, stressing its compelling nature – that it cannot be refused, and that they would not have been able to carry out their mission if they had not had a vocation to do so. 'Without the inner calling, none of us would have ventured into this, and nor would we have been able to endure it, because it is not only bright and glorious but also dark and difficult at times.'

There is nothing in our source material that corresponds to the interview with Dackerud. In order to shed light on the issue of connections and parallels between the Church of Sweden and the Baptist Union of Sweden, we will instead make a few selections from Ulla Bardh's writings. Bardh was ordained as a pastor in 1958, has a doctorate in ecclesiology and has held a number of important positions. In various ecumenical contexts she has repeatedly discussed issues of vocation and the priestly/pastoral office.[64]

In an interview about her childhood, Bardh says that she was the child of a pastor and that she viewed her father as a role model. 'I wasn't going to have a girl's career – to get married and have children. I identified with my father Emil, the preacher!' Throughout the article she talks about being in service to the Word, and about how a Free Church and pietistic environment fosters the desire and inclination to preach.[65] As with some of the first women priests, having a priestly or pastoral lineage is thus important, and the theology of vocation as serving the Word is an essential

---

62 'Kvinnor i predikstolen: "Pastorn" hjälper med disken: Skriver uppsats mot Paulus', *Dagens Nyheter*, 5 January 1958.

63 *Vägmärken för baptister*, p. 98.

64 Ulla Bardh, *Församlingen som sakrament: Tro, dop, medlemskap och ekumenik bland frikyrkokristna vid 1900-talets slut* (Örebro: Libris, 2008).

65 Kerstin Vinterhed, 'När jag var barn: Kyrkan var aldrig ett tvång. Baptistpastorns dotter. Ulla Bardh växte upp med en lust att predika', *Dagens Nyheter*, 5 May 1997.

component. The theology of necessary preaching in relation to vocation is not foregrounded in this article, but it is all the more prominent in an interview on the future of the Free Churches. The newspaper headline summarises the essence of Bardh's message: 'When people are in need, we have no time for internal squabbling'. It is noteworthy that she says this in relation to the need for ecumenical cooperation.[66]

Other connections can be found upon taking a closer look at the 1974 study book written by Bardh – *Här är icke man och kvinna* ['Here is neither man nor woman'] – whose purpose is 'to stimulate dialogues about the relationship between woman and man in the home, congregation and society'. As the title suggests, Galatians 3:28 is central to Bardh's presentation of a biblical interpretation that evokes 'the spirit of Christ himself'.[67] It is interesting to observe the task assigned at the end of one chapter, a task that the study groups who are reading the book are told to discuss. They are to read a statement about the relationship between husband and wife, which describes the husband as being the head of the family and of the wife in the same way that Christ is the head of the Church – in other words, the Lutheran doctrine of the three estates. That Bardh herself does not agree with the content of this quotation is clear, not least in the statement 'he was unchallenged...'. The speaker was Bishop Bo Giertz, a high-profile opponent of women priests (see Chapter 6).[68] In other words, not only are the same biblical words used as a central key to interpretation in both of these churches, but the proponents of women's access to the office of pastor or priest opposed the same dominant theological narrative and consequently faced the same opponents.

In another text on the theology of vocation, Bardh points out that according to Baptist thinking, the vocation is sent out to all the people of God. At the same time, in the Baptist tradition the term 'vocation' engenders unmistakable associations with the individual vocation to be set apart as a pastor, a call that is confirmed by the call made by the local congregation. The Baptist vocation has a strong link to serving the Word. 'The word "vocation", understood

---

66 Daniel Wärn, 'Ulla Bardh: När människor är i nöd har vi inte tid med internt tjafs', *Dagen*, 12 June 2008.
67 Ulla Bardh, *Här är icke man och kvinna* (Stockholm: Moderna läsare, a publishing activity organised by the Free Church Adult Educational Association, 1974), p. 5.
68 Ibid., pp. 20–33.

theologically, still applies in particular to the call to preach the Word as the work of a lifetime.'[69]

For the purposes of this study, the conclusion of Bardh's text is particularly interesting. She raises the issue of women's access to the offices of pastor and priest, mentioning a number of things that also recur in the narratives of the first women priests:

> Throughout my life my vocation has been called into question, while at the same time it feels like my only wealth and identity [...] It cannot be reasonable to hold a conference on the question of the Office without touching on what still constitutes a wound in Nordic Christianity: namely, the issue of women's right to the office of pastor or priest. It is with sorrow that I realise how far we have come and yet sometimes we seem to be at the end of the road, with no way forward or through. Still I am convinced that for Christendom as a whole – no matter how strong, well-organised or respectably concealed the resistance is – there is never any way back. In the Kingdom of God, the question of male and female is primarily not about equality in a worldly or sociological sense but about the fact that Christ cannot be divided. Insofar as it is true that both men and women are created in the image of God, that all are redeemed and baptised into his death and resurrection, it follows, in my view, that the fullness of Christ and thus the mission of the Church cannot be made visible unless it is embodied in the jointly human: the female and the male.[70]

Bardh mentions the lack of recognition, establishing that vocation is an integral part of one's identity and that it is a theological issue, not one of equality between the sexes. She also emphasises that this issue is applicable to all the Nordic denominations, not just to one of them.

Obviously, then, there are a number of parallels and connections between the first women to become priests and those who became pastors, particularly in their descriptions of how they experienced recognition and their theological understanding of their vocation. There are also a number of connections and parallels between the processes in the respective churches, both with regard to what happens in practice and in respect of reflections engendered by these processes.

---

69 Ulla Bardh, 'Kallad – av vem?', in *Präst och pastor: Ämbete, kallelse, tjänst*, Nordic Ecumenical Series, 28 (Uppsala: Nordic Ecumenical Council, 1996), pp. 84–87 (p. 84).
70 Ibid., p. 87.

Naturally, there are differences as well. For example, both Ingegärd Dackerud and Ulla Bardh point out that there was less resistance to women pastors in a Free Church context. Contributing factors include the vocation theology of necessary preaching; a congregationalist view of the Church; and the fact that these denominations had a long tradition of women serving in the role of pastor. At the same time, it is clear from their statements that the process was not all plain sailing. Both Dackerud and Bardh mention the importance of recognition at various levels and their own experiences of denied recognition.

∞∞∞∞

This chapter has focused on an under-studied theme in research on the Church of Sweden's reform of the priesthood: connections and parallels, above all between the Church of Sweden and the Free Church denominations in the country. These connections and parallels are manifested in close relationships. As we have shown, almost half of the first women priests mention in their vocation narratives that they had a background in, or other close ties to, intra-Church revivalist movements or other Christian denominations in Sweden. Low Church influences are particularly evident in this context. Connections and parallels also appear in relation to how a number of the first women priests express themselves theologically with regard to vocation, the phenomenon that we have chosen to call the theology of necessary preaching. According to this understanding of vocation, all means of spreading the Word of God in secularised society must be utilised. Time is short, the matter is urgent, and the vocation is, in essence, a compelling force: 'We just have to', as Ingrid Persson puts it. This theological understanding of vocation is prominent in the intra-Church revivalist movements and the Free Church denominations, and it has influenced the ways in which many of the first women priests perceived their vocation.

The vocation narratives of some of the first women priests mention predecessors in other denominations, both in Sweden and abroad. Narratives about such predecessors were common in the daily press and in scholarly texts, and this chapter has drawn attention to Nelly Hall of the Swedish Holiness Union, the feminist and Methodist pastor Anna Howard Shaw, the Baptist Ida Andersson, Signe Walder and Signe Ekblad of the Mission Covenant Church of Sweden, and Hanna Ouchterlony of the Salvation Army.

In addition, this chapter has brought out parallels and connections with some of the Free Church denominations at the time. The first women who were ordained, or 'set apart', to serve as pastors in the Mission Covenant Church of Sweden and the Baptist Union of Sweden in the 1950s encountered – in the words of Axel Honneth – forms of recognition and denial of recognition that were similar to those that the first women priests in the Church of Sweden would experience a decade later, and the women pastors understood and justified their vocation in similar ways.

Although previous research has largely neglected the link between the Church of Sweden and developments in the intra-Church revivalist movements and the Free Church denominations in terms of the view of preaching and the priestly office, this link seems to have been self-evident for the first women priests and other actors in the Church of Sweden. Indeed, looking to and being inspired by developments in other denominations was a matter of course. While this chapter has focused on parallels, connections and influences between various denominations in Sweden, the next chapter turns towards other countries, especially neighbouring Denmark and Norway.

Chapter 9

Links and parallels in the public debate and the Scandinavian Lutheran state churches

Since the aftermath of the First World War, a growing public opinion had been lobbying the authorities to recognise the right of women to be ordained as clergy in the established national churches. In 1948 Bishop *Øllgaard* of Odense took the important step of ordaining the first three women priests in Denmark, despite the opposition of the other eight bishops and the fact that 514 of the country's 1,300 clergymen threatened to leave their posts. In Denmark's Scandinavian neighbouring countries, there were also strong feelings both for and against the event, which took place with great solemnity in Odense Cathedral on 28 April. The 514 male priests gave up, and all of them remained in the service of their Church.[1]

Links and parallels with other churches and denominations are not only depicted in the narratives of the first women to join the clergy; they were also very much part of the public debate, especially in the 1950s. As was pointed out above, this situation has not received much attention in the Swedish historical narrative. Where links and parallels have been highlighted, it has mainly been in relation to 'the ecumenical argument'. As we have seen, the Church of Sweden's ecumenical endeavours since the beginning of the twentieth century had been particularly aimed at deepening relations with the Church of England – at least at the highest level. Because that church did not ordain women as priests, the Church of Sweden believed that a decision to open up the priesthood to women in Sweden would endanger ecumenical relations. 'The ecumenical argument' was thus actually a counter-argument.

Upon closer examination, however, it becomes clear that the contemporary debate also included another, and different, ecumenical argument. This one looked at the position adopted by

---

1 Märta Tamm-Götlind, *Kvinnliga präster jorden runt* (Stockholm: Svenska kyrkans diakonistyrelses bokförlag, 1957), pp. 90–91.

other churches in respect of women's ordination, and on the basis of these experiences the opening-up of the priesthood to women was advocated. Unlike the ecumenical counter-argument, this argument never explicitly claimed that failing to open up the priesthood to women in Sweden would endanger cooperation with other churches. Nonetheless, it was an ecumenical argument in the sense that it pointed to what other churches were doing and argued that the Church of Sweden should do the same.

This chapter draws on three contemporary voices in the debate – Margit Sahlin, Yngve Brilioth, and the author, debater and folklorist Märta Tamm-Götlind (1888–1982) – supplying examples of how various ecumenical arguments could be expressed in the Swedish debate during the 1950s. We will also look at the links and parallels between the processes of opening up the clergy to women in the three state churches in neighbouring Denmark, Norway and Sweden. As the Danish church historian Lone Kølle Martinsen noted in an anthology published in 2023, in connection with the seventy-fifth anniversary of the first women ordained in the Evangelical Lutheran Church in Denmark [Folkekirken], there is a need for transnational studies that examine and compare developments in Denmark, Sweden and Norway.[2]

As was the case with the Mission Covenant Church of Sweden and the Baptist Union of Sweden, the reform of the clergy was implemented more or less concurrently in these other Scandinavian churches, and (as we will show) there were close links between the Church of Sweden and these other churches. It is fair to say that these parallels and connections influenced developments in the Church of Sweden. Further, we will show that vocation and recognition were key drivers of change.

'The ecumenical argument' – the cases of Margit Sahlin and Yngve Brilioth

'The ecumenical argument' is an expression used by Margit Sahlin in her first book on women in priestly office, *Man och kvinna i Kristi kyrka* ['Man and woman in Christ's Church'], published in 1950. As was mentioned earlier, there is a paragraph towards the end where Sahlin discusses some of the arguments against

---

2 Lone Kølle Martinsen, 'Apostelinder – Grundtvig og spørgsmålet om kvindelige praester', in Else Marie Wiberg Pedersen (ed.), *Guds Ord i kvindemund: Om køn og kirke* (Aarhus: Nord Academic, 2023).

women priests. The argument to which she pays the most attention, and which she describes as 'the most weighty', is what she calls 'the ecumenical argument'. Ecumenism must not be jeopardised. At the same time, she cautions that we still do not know what the consequences might be. The idea that the time is not ripe, that people are not ready for women priests, also weighs heavily. Therefore, 'in the existing situation, owing to the urgent need, we must look for other, more navigable ways to achieve the necessary female ministry in the church'.[3]

One reason why Sahlin discussed the ecumenical argument, as well as the claim that 'the time is not ripe', in depth is likely to have been that this view was particularly current in the debate at this time. It is relevant that this was the argument emphasised by the newly appointed Archbishop Yngve Brilioth. When he came to formulate his pastoral letter, or episcopal 'programme statement', to his diocese in 1950, the issue was so topical that he had no choice but to address it. Because Sahlin's and Brilioth's books were published at about the same time, they were often discussed in relation to each other, especially when the report of the General Synod's inquiry was published in early 1951.

Brilioth writes relatively little about his own view of the reform, and then only against the background of his own understanding of the Church of Sweden. His view of the Church is distinguished by what he discusses in the first and longest chapter of his pastoral letter: ecumenism. Under the heading 'the Church's division – the Christians' unity', he lists the achievements of the ecumenical movement and singles out 'a line that is close to my own heart: the link with the Church of England'.[4] After this chapter on ecumenism, he describes 'the Church of Sweden's internal problem', concluding that '[a]t the time of writing, it appears to be an essential task that the various groups within the Church of Sweden should seek, more than they have done so far, to understand one another without any self-aggrandisement and to share with one another the gifts that have been entrusted to each of them'.[5]

It is on the basis of ecumenism and internal division that Brilioth finally concludes that the time is not ripe for opening up the priesthood to women. While he believes it is not against the Bible to ordain women, it is against the tradition of many of the churches

---

3 Sahlin, *Man och kvinna*, pp. 200–208 (p. 208).
4 Brilioth, *Herdabrev till Uppsala ärkestift*, p. 61.
5 Ibid., p. 85.

with which he would like to have a deeper unity. It is noteworthy that he explicitly dismisses the Danish and Norwegian churches as being less important than, for example, the Anglican Church and the American Lutheran churches.[6]

At the same time, it is not only in response to the archbishop's views that Sahlin regards ecumenism as the most important argument. In her diaries, edited by Elisabeth Nordlander, ecumenism appears to be very close to her heart. Sahlin describes herself as strongly influenced by High Church thinking, from which she draws her spiritual role models and whose aesthetic expression she is drawn to with 'her whole being'.[7] She was also deeply involved in the Vadstena movement, a movement 'for personal and ecclesiastical renewal' that brought together people from various church movements, above all the Oxford Group and the High Church movement. During the 1940s and 1950s Sahlin was close to both these movements and – through her involvement in the Vadstena movement – sought to mediate between these diverging ways of thought.[8]

Sahlin came to experience the weight of the ecumenical argument in relation to her involvement in the Vadstena movement. As church historian Andreas Wejderstam has shown, 1958 to 1959 became 'a turning point in the history of the Vadstena meetings'. One expression of this development was that the invitations to the annual meetings were no longer signed by name, as the organisers held opposing views about the reform of the priesthood and presumably did not wish to be associated with their opponents. Wejderstam adds that for the same reason, including names might discourage other participants from attending the meetings. Sahlin herself took part for the last time as co-organiser of the Vadstena meetings in 1957, following a gap of a few years.[9]

Crucial to Sahlin's decision to request priestly ordination in spite of everything was her experience at an ecumenical meeting in Switzerland in the autumn of 1958, when she asked fellow participants how they would respond if the Church of Sweden began to ordain women. She breathed a sigh of relief when she learned that the English delegate felt that the Church of England was in fact unlikely to cut any ties for that reason, and when the Catholic

6 Ibid., pp. 159–173.
7 Nordlander, *Margit Sahlin*, pp. 205, 210.
8 Wejderstam, *Personlig och kyrklig förnyelse*, pp. 15–19, 201–202.
9 Ibid., pp. 198, 201–202.

Cardinal Yves Congar (1904–1995) assured her that such a move would have no impact on the Church of Sweden's relations with Rome. It was in this environment that an event occurred which – according to Nordlander – Sahlin often recounted: 'On 7 September I was sitting on a bench overlooking Lake Geneva, filled with a kind of serene peace. I had gained clarity on the issue of ordination: Yes, in the name of Jesus!'[10]

Although Sahlin and Brilioth adopted different positions on the reform of the priesthood, they both belonged to the line of High Church piety and therefore paid particular attention to, and cherished the ecumenical ties with, the Church of England (although Sahlin was, as has been said, critical of the 'High Anglican and Catholic' concept of apostolic succession). They hence both perceived the ecumenical argument as one of the weightiest reasons against opening up the priesthood to women. Upon closer inspection, however, it becomes apparent that this was not the sole ecumenical argument in this context.

Another ecumenical argument – the case of Märta Tamm-Götlind

On that June day in 1911 when Anna Howard Shaw preached in the Gustav Vasa church, her audience included Märta Tamm-Götlind, then 23 years old.[11] A biographical article about her states that she was a marshal at the Sixth Conference of the International Woman Suffrage Alliance in Stockholm in 1911, that Shaw's sermon was 'a memorable experience' for her, and that Tamm-Götlind 'would henceforth fight throughout her life for women's right to be priests in Sweden too'.[12] Shaw clearly made a very strong impression on Tamm-Götlind, whose first book, published in 1920, was about the American Methodist pastor and women's rights activist.[13]

---

10 Nordlander, *Margit Sahlin*, p. 224.
11 The importance of ecumenical perspectives and 'another ecumenical argument' are also discussed in Frida Mannerfelt, 'Ekumeniska influenser i 1958 års ämbetsreform i Svenska kyrkan', in Karin Rubenson and Karin Tillberg (eds), *Vigd till tjänst: Om ämbetet i Svenska kyrkan* (Stockholm: Verbum, 2024), pp. 361–387.
12 Gunnel Furuland, 'Märta Elisabet Katarina Tamm-Götlind', *Svenskt kvinnobiografiskt lexikon*, www.skbl.se/sv/artikel/MartaTammGotlind [accessed 24 February 2023]. See also Tamm-Götlind, *Kvinnliga präster jorden runt*, p. 10.
13 Tamm-Götlind, *Anna Howard Shaw*.

In her preface Tamm-Götlind writes that Shaw, during her visit to Stockholm, 'attracted particular attention in her capacity as a *priest* truly ordained to the office'.[14] Tamm-Götlind goes on to describe the American confessional landscape and the fact that ordained women were present in a number of denominations.[15]

Tamm-Götlind thus became deeply involved in the issue of women's right to ordination. She approached the issue by making ecumenical comparisons. For decades she encouraged people to be inspired by other churches and denominations, and especially the situation that prevailed in other countries. She returned to this topic in a number of articles and opinion pieces. For example, in an article in 1955 she stressed the importance of including a comparative element in the debate. 'In the face of Swedish dithering, studying how churches in several other countries have dared to ordain women to serve as priests supplies food for thought.'[16]

The existence of good examples in other churches, both in and outside Sweden, was a recurring argument for Tamm-Götlind. That same year, news reports quoted her as saying the following at a discussion evening held by Kvinnliga studentförbundet [the Women's Student Association]:

> 'There are actually women priests in our country, too, even if most people don't realise it', she says. 'But so far they only exist within the Free Churches. In the State Church resistance is still fairly strong, although our neighbouring countries have proved to be more liberal and are now allowing highly deserving women to be ordained – with excellent results.'[17]

This passage not only shows that comparison with other churches constitutes Tamm-Götlind's main argument; it is also a clear example of the phenomenon labelled 'the language issue' in Chapter 2. Tamm-Götlind calls the Free Church pastors 'priests', something that, for example, Brilioth and Sahlin, on the basis of their understanding of the concept 'priest' (*präst*), would probably not have done. Tamm-Götlind's broader, more *vocation*-based and functional understanding of the 'priest' concept is clearly present

---

14 Ibid., p. 7. Italics in the original.
15 Ibid., pp. 24–25.
16 Märta Tamm-Götlind, '"Jag skall bli präst som mor och far!"', *Stockholms-Tidningen*, 10 January 1955.
17 '"Kvinna i predikstolen" ämne för het diskussion i Uppsala', *Svenska Dagbladet*, 2 February 1955.

in the main expression of her comparative approach: her book *Kvinnliga präster jorden runt* ['Women priests around the world']. The book was published in 1957 as a direct contribution to the intense debate on opening up the priesthood to women. In the introduction, Tamm-Götlind points out that the Bible is often read contextually and that such a reading has led to 'a large number of Christian denominations around the world [...] taking women fully into their ministry, not only as teachers, evangelists and missionaries, but they have *been consecrated to the priestly vocation* with all that it entails, not least to the administration of the sacraments'.[18] With her compilation of various churches and denominations that ordain women, Tamm-Götlind wanted to show how women ordained to the clergy 'work where they are *allowed to* work'. She adds that she hopes the book can contribute to the ecumenical argument (more on this below).[19]

The book's six chapters are based on Tamm-Götlind's extensive correspondence with women ordained to the clergy in other countries, plus her many tours and study visits. She gives space to many leading women in various denominations. For instance, she writes about a trip to England and Scotland in 1955 and describes a visit to the suffragette and preacher Maude Royden (1876–1956) and Rosamond Fisher (1890–1986), wife of the Archbishop of Canterbury. Her overview of women clergy and women leaders in the UK also mentions Elsie Chamberlain (1910–1991), who in 1956 became the first woman to lead the Congregational Union of England and Wales. In addition to presenting the situation in the Church of England and among Congregationalists, Tamm-Götlind discusses Methodists, Baptists and Presbyterians. In the case of the Baptists, she mentions the Revd Gwenyth Hubble (1906–1972), who was ordained in 1939 and whom she also met. Interestingly, Tamm-Götlind also raises the subject of women in liberal Judaism, specifically mentioning the position of Lily Montagu (1873–1963) in progressive Judaism.[20]

In her chapter on the situation in the United States, Tamm-Götlind discusses Antoinette Brown Blackwell (1825–1921). Brown Blackwell is said to have been the first woman to be ordained as a minister of an established Protestant denomination in the USA

---

18 Tamm-Götlind, *Kvinnliga präster jorden runt*, p. 8. Italics in the original.
19 Ibid., p. 9. Italics in the original.
20 Ibid., pp. 12–27. For Maude Royden, see Sheila Fletcher, *Maude Royden: A Life* (Oxford: Basil Blackwell, 1989).

in 1853. Naturally, Tamm-Götlind returns to Anna Howard Shaw in this chapter. With regard to the situation in the USA, Tamm-Götlind presents the arguments for and against the ordination of women as clergy in various churches and denominations. As regards North and South America, Tamm-Götlind also reviews the situation in Canada, Cuba and Argentina. In the last-mentioned case, she mentions the first woman to be ordained in Latin America, Jorgelina Lozada (1906–1995).[21]

Tamm-Götlind also devotes a chapter to women working as clergy in the mission field.[22] In addition, she discusses the situation in the Netherlands and France, noting that the Lutheran Church in the Netherlands had ordained women pastors but that a woman pastor who married had to leave her post. According to Tamm-Götlind, the same attitude applied in relation to the two ordained Lutheran women in France. The Dutch Reformed Church in the Netherlands had a number of women theologians, but they had not been granted ordination. Speaking of the Reformed tradition, she also describes her contacts with the Reformed Church in Switzerland, which she visited in the summer of 1954, meeting several ordained women who preached and baptised.[23] In addition, she had been in contact with ordained women in Austria and Czechoslovakia. In the latter case, she tells the story of Darina Bancíková (1922–1999), a pioneer of the Lutheran Church in what was then Czechoslovakia. Bancíková, who had obtained a Bachelor of Theology degree, felt an inner calling to become a pastor, but initially had to work as a Christianity teacher. However, she was the first woman to be ordained in 1951.[24]

In addition, Tamm-Götlind discusses the situation in Germany, noting that the first woman was ordained in 1927 and that during the Second World War several women theologians took on priestly duties because there was a shortage of clergy. Naturally, she also describes developments in the neighbouring Nordic countries of

21 Tamm-Götlind, *Kvinnliga präster jorden runt*, pp. 28–40. For Antoinette Brown Blackwell, see Elizabeth Cazden, *Antoinette Brown Blackwell: A Biography* (New York: The Feminist Press at The City University of New York, 1983). For a brief presentation of Jorgelina Lozada, see Pablo R. Andiñach, *The Book of Gratitudes: An Encounter Between Life and Faith* (Eugene, OR: Wipf & Stock, 2016), pp. 49–50.
22 Tamm-Götlind, *Kvinnliga präster jorden runt*, pp. 41–49.
23 Ibid., p. 67.
24 Ibid., p. 77.

Denmark and Norway.[25] Some of the Swedish Free Church denominations are mentioned under the heading 'Women priests work in several Swedish Free Churches': the United Methodist Church in Sweden [Metodistkyrkan i Sverige], which ordained its first female elder in 1954, and the Mission Covenant Church of Sweden and the Baptist Union of Sweden, which opened their respective training programmes to women in 1954. Tamm-Götlind emphasises that the Baptist Union of Sweden made no distinction between male and female pastors.[26]

In a chapter near the end of the book, Tamm-Götlind compares the situation in other countries with that in Sweden. She concludes that although women in Sweden make an indispensable contribution in sewing circles and as deaconesses and youth secretaries, they have been better utilised in the Church's ministry in other countries – especially those women who have a theology degree. She notes that '[w]e know that some of them would have liked to have been ordained as priests so they could have devoted themselves entirely to the vocation of preacher and spiritual adviser'.[27] Besides, she emphasises that the main justification for opening up the priesthood to women is a religious one:

> The issue of women priests cannot be dismissed as a 'women's issue', because that term implies something inferior, which would be contrary to the sanctity of the Church.
>
> It is a catchphrase that has acquired its meaning in many contexts in human history whenever women have had to fight for their development and education, and indeed for their human rights in general. Women's demand and longing for permission to follow an inner vocation can be formally labelled a 'women's issue', but deep down it is an issue for the whole of humanity, with ideological justification in the ancient proclamation in St Paul's Letter to the Galatians: 'There is no longer slave or free, there is no longer male and female...'
>
> History has shown that even venerable traditions and customs *can* stand in the way of life's growth if they prevent people – be they men or women – from following the highest calling of their being.[28]

In other words, the significance of vocation is at issue here: Tamm-Götlind is of the opinion that traditions and customs cannot

---

25 Ibid., pp. 89–94.
26 Ibid., pp. 108–109.
27 Ibid., p. 112.
28 Ibid., p. 123.

result in individuals being denied the opportunity to follow their vocation.[29]

Tamm-Götlind was not only extremely active in the debate; she also corresponded directly with some of the first women to become priests. In a letter to Britta Olén-van Zijl, she reflects on her own role in the public debate and calls herself a 'propaganda person'.[30] The correspondence between them began earlier, however, when Olén-van Zijl applied to be ordained as a priest for the diocese of Lund in the summer of 1959. In this first letter, Tamm-Götlind wished to express her support for Olén-van Zijl by telling her about other women who had been in similar situations of strenuous and difficult resistance. Through her husband, Olén-van Zijl had connections to South Africa and the Dutch Reformed Church, which is probably why Tamm-Götlind writes about the situation of women clergy in Africa and the Netherlands. However, she also tries to express encouragement by pointing out that despite this resistance, women are in fact working as pastors in both South Africa and the Netherlands.[31] Tamm-Götlind also wrote to Olén-van Zijl on 20 March 1960, three weeks before the first three women were to be ordained as priests in the Church of Sweden. As mentioned earlier, Olén-van Zijl's request for ordination had been refused. With her letter, Tamm-Götlind wanted to put Olén-van Zijl in contact with a woman pastor, Darina Bancíková, in the Lutheran Church in what was then Czechoslovakia. Tamm-Götlind also mentions that there are a number of women pastors in various Lutheran denominations in Czechoslovakia.[32] Tamm-Götlind thus points to parallels between the Church of Sweden and other churches, but also wants to help create ties by connecting women who are struggling for recognition and for permission to be ordained as priests.

Tamm-Götlind, Sahlin and Brilioth are important examples of how people who participated in the debate about opening up the priesthood to women in the Church of Sweden very much recognised the existence of parallels and connections between their own

---

29 Ibid., p. 123.
30 Märta Tamm-Götlind to Britta Olén-van Zijl, 20 March 1960, Gunnar Olén Collection, LUL.
31 Märta Tamm-Götlind to Britta Olén-van Zijl, 24 June 1959, Gunnar Olén Collection, LUL.
32 Märta Tamm-Götlind to Britta Olén-van Zijl, 20 March 1960, Gunnar Olén Collection, LUL.

church and other churches. Clearly, these 'ecumenical arguments' did influence how the debaters viewed the reform.

Sometimes ecumenical arguments could be pitted against each other, as occurred in an exchange of views between Tamm-Götlind and the lecturer, debater and textbook author Bengt Åke Häger (1927–2019) in *Aftonbladet* in the summer of 1955. Under the heading 'Kvinnan och prästämbetet' ['Women and the priestly office'], Häger argued that the shared communion with the Anglican Church would be endangered if the General Synod decided to open up the priesthood to women. He also addressed the situation in the neighbouring countries of Norway and Denmark, noting that although the ordination of women to priestly office was permitted in Norway, no woman had yet been ordained there; and of the three women ordained as priests in Denmark, none had been given a post as a parish priest.[33] In a rejoinder a week later, Tamm-Götlind rejected Häger's claims about the ordained Danish women. She added that any fears that joint communion with the Anglican Church was under threat were probably unfounded, and that opinion favouring women's ordination as priests in the Church of Sweden was strong even among 'those heavily involved in Church matters'.[34]

The Swedish debate hence frequently looked towards the two Nordic neighbours, Denmark and Norway. Closer inspection reveals that this was also done in practice.

Links and parallels with the Church of Norway

In terms of the actual course of events, there were many parallels between Norway and Sweden.[35] The issue of women's access to priestly office was raised and discussed in the two neighbouring countries at about the same time. In both Norway and Sweden, demands for women's emancipation increased in the latter part of the nineteenth century. Over time, these emancipation endeavours led to a change in who was considered a full member of society. The milestone in this process of broader recognition was universal and equal suffrage – introduced in Norway in 1913 and in Sweden in 1921.

---

33 Bengt Åke Häger, 'Kvinnan och prästämbetet', *Aftonbladet*, 26 July 1955.
34 Märta Tamm-Götlind, 'Kvinnan och prästämbetet: Ett genmäle', *Aftonbladet*, 4 August 1955.
35 This section is based on Mannerfelt and Maurits, 'Kallelse och erkännande'.

In both countries the issue of women's rights and position in society also encompassed women's right to hold public office, which in both Norway and Sweden's state churches included the clergy. This right became a subject of intense debate in both countries, in Norway as early as the 1910s. However, according to Synnøve Hinnaland Stendal, a researcher in practical theology, the issue of women's ordination as clergy was to be considered as a matter of principle only, as the time was not yet ripe for this to be done in practice. But as a matter of principle, it was given a prominent position – both in Norway and Sweden – in the women's movement's programme and the struggle for recognition.[36]

The parallels and connections between the two processes can be linked not only to the concept of recognition but also to the concept of vocation. Both opponents and proponents turned to their neighbouring country. The church historian Aud Tønnessen notes that Norwegian opponents of the reform were influenced by how resistance was expressed in the Swedish context.[37] Similarly, the theologian Mari Saltkjel argues that '[t]he processes in the neighbouring countries infused strength and were messages of hope that change was possible', which empowered the women who aspired to ordination.[38]

The various ways of theologically understanding vocation and the priestly office that existed in the Swedish context thus had parallels in the Norwegian situation. Hinnaland Stendal's analysis of the debate in the Norwegian Parliament, the Storting, in the 1930s outlines four categories: the view of women, the view of the church, contemporary understanding, and the view of the politician's task. As was discussed above, the last of these categories relates to the fact that reforming the clergy was regarded as a political issue, that of equality between the sexes. It is noteworthy that the proponents invoked national pride: it was a favourable development that Norway had been an early adopter of equal rights for women, and having women clergy could be regarded as a step in this process.[39]

---

36 Synnøve Hinnaland Stendal, 'Kvinnelige prester i Den norske kirke – kirke og stat på kollisjonskurs?: om behandlingen av spørsmålet om kvinners adgang til de geistlige embetene', *Kyrkohistorisk årsskrift*, 108 (2008), 120.

37 Aud Valborg Tønnessen, *Ingrid Bjerkås: Motstandskvinnen som ble vår første kvinnelige prest* (Oslo: Pax, 2014), p. 74.

38 Mari Saltkjel, *Som en krone på hodet: Fortellinger om kvinners prestekall* (Oslo: Verbum, 2011), p. 10.

39 Hinnaland Stendal, 'Kvinnelige prester i Den norske kirke', p. 284.

With regard to the view of women, Hinnaland Stendal identifies two theological understandings of womankind. On the one hand, women possessed religious equality with men on the basis of Galatians 3:28 and how Jesus interacted with women. The reform proponents asserted that Jesus gave women vindication, recognition, and human and religious value on a par with that of men. On the other hand, women were subordinate to men on the basis of the order of creation and the Lutheran doctrine of the three estates. The reform opponents argued that the woman's vocation is not to lead but to be a suitable helper for the man.[40]

In discussing the 'view of the church' category, Hinnaland Stendal presents a number of arguments. Both proponents and opponents referred to models in the early Christian church, in the New Testament but also among the Church Fathers. Notably, she cites the ecumenical counter-argument, that is, that women priests constitute a violation of the tradition of a shared universal church. However, Hinnaland Stendal points out that this counter-argument was not accorded much prominence, believing its comparative obscurity to be due to the Church of Norway having relatively little in the way of High Church thinking while possessing a vigorous lay movement. This argument was linked to the church–state issue, too, and to the question of how much influence the state should actually have in internal church matters.[41]

The category of 'contemporary understanding' brings up viewpoints that were related to contemporary trends of thought, such as emancipation movements of various kinds. It is noteworthy in this context that Hinnaland Stendal dwells briefly on how the position of women in the Free Church denominations was used as an argument in favour of female clergy. The Salvation Army and the Methodist Church were singled out and, just as in the Swedish context, Anna Howard Shaw was held up as a role model.[42]

Not only did the arguments find parallels in the two debates; so did the ways in which people responded to the arguments. With regard to the situation in Norway, Hinnaland Stendal argues that two traditions of canon law came to oppose each other: 'Those who wanted to open up for women priests put more emphasis on the state side of the issue, whereas those on the opposite side believed that more weight should

---

40 Ibid., pp. 343–377.
41 Ibid., pp. 284–342.
42 Ibid., pp. 233–262.

be given to internal Church conditions.'[43] A lively debate ensued about who had the right to rule over the Church, and the reform opponents – who were in the majority in parish councils – argued that the women's movement was 'not sufficiently Christian/Church-orientated'.[44] As we discussed in Chapter 4, this tendency among the opponents of reform to view themselves as being more faithful to the Bible and the Confessions had its counterpart in the Church of Sweden. In other words, reform opponents in both countries displayed an unmistakable tendency to emphasise that the push for change was underpinned by reasons of equality between the sexes, not by theological arguments.

Proponents of the reform reacted in similar ways. As Chapter 4 showed, in almost every context in which they spoke about the reform, the first women priests in the Church of Sweden stressed that it was introduced not for reasons of sex equality but on theological grounds.[45] This line of argument was much to the fore in Norway. Tønnessen points out that women theologians did not wish to be associated with or assisted by the feminist movement.[46]

The way women theologians dealt with the failure of their churches to recognise their vocation to priestly office was similar, too. They pursued alternative ways of living their vocation and having it recognised. As we have seen, a number of the first women to become priests in the Church of Sweden looked for ways of at least acting as 'something like a priest'.[47] This also seems to have been the case in Norway. Tønnessen notes that in 1960 there were 40 women who had received a Bachelor of Theology degree. Some of them had also completed the practical part of the training that was a prerequisite for ordination. Among them, some women had tasks in the parish that were reminiscent of the position of women in the church which had been outlined in Norway as early as the 1930s, and which developed into what was called 'parish secretaries' in Sweden. One example frequently cited in the Norwegian debate was that of Agnes Vold (1912–1994), who was ordained to work as something akin to a hospital chaplain.[48]

Although the formal decision to open up the clergy to women was made on 24 June 1938, it was not until 1961 that the first woman

---

43 Ibid., p. 120.
44 Ibid., p. 121.
45 Mannerfelt and Maurits, *Kallelse och erkännande*, pp. 267–270.
46 Tønnessen, *Ingrid Bjerkås*, p. 73.
47 Mannerfelt and Maurits, *Kallelse och erkännande*, pp. 184–200.
48 Tønnessen, *Ingrid Bjerkås*, p. 72.

was ordained as a priest in the Church of Norway. On 19 March 1961, Ingrid Bjerkås (1901–1980) was ordained by Bishop Kristian Schjelderup (1894–1980) in Vang church. The reason why the ordination took place there was that the cathedral dean had refused to allow the cathedral in Hamar to be used for this service. Just as for her Swedish colleagues, there was a fly in the ointment for Bjerkås in the form of protests. Likewise, her ordination also attracted much media interest. It is interesting to note that the bishop actually wanted to do what had previously been done in Denmark and Sweden, that is, ordain three women at the same time. However, the two other women he asked declined citing the following reasons, among others: they did not wish to be associated with Bjerkås because they did not share her views, including her view of Christianity; and they did not want to cause the unrest and division in the Church against which several bishops had uttered warnings.[49]

In her biography of Bjerkås, Tønnessen describes how she justified her desire to be ordained by referring both to current legislation and to the issue of women's rights, but also to her feeling a call from God. This mingling of theological and legal arguments was not common practice and was considered by many to be inappropriate; but Tønnessen argues that this approach was perhaps necessary for someone like Bjerkås, 'who had her religious vocation so thoroughly rejected'.[50] Bjerkås had been in contact with various bishops for a long time to find out if anyone was prepared to ordain her, and for a while she was sent back and forth between different bishops. As she had a theological degree, she also applied for various posts in the Church, but opponents of women's ordination encouraged male candidates to apply for the posts in question. This strategy is also recognisable from Sweden (cf. Chapter 6).[51]

In her autobiography, *Mitt kall* ['My vocation'], Bjerkås describes her path to ordination. She outlines her experiences of opposition, singling out the statement made by six of nine bishops in connection with her ordination. This episcopal statement is referred to as 'a dark cloud in the sky':

> Six of the nine bishops in the country had published a statement via the radio, the Norwegian news agency Norsk Telegrambyrå

---

49 Ibid., pp. 86, 90–101.
50 Ibid., p. 85.
51 Ibid., pp. 86, 90–101.

and all the newspapers in which they claimed their right to distance themselves from me, and also the right of all pastors and parishioners throughout the country to freely oppose me without being reproached for it.[52]

Tønnessen observes that the bishops' statement was, in essence, a call for a boycott of women clergy.[53] The statement is thus a kind of equivalent to the Swedish Seventeen Points, which provided guidelines for how opponents of the reform might act and thereby legitimised the denial of recognition. Interestingly, Tønnessen shows how the call for a boycott was linked to the risk of Church division if women were to be ordained.[54] The narrative of division is thus repeated here.

So is the presumption which we have referred to in this book as the 'code of conduct', which was a consequence of the narrative of division. Tønnessen shows that just as in Sweden, the responsibility for a possible Church split was placed on the women theologians and prospective clergy: 'The women theologians tried as best they could to create as little noise as possible to minimise the impression that they wanted to destroy the Church. For this reason, they did not want to apply for a position and become a cause of division.'[55] This attempt to keep a low profile was discussed in the Swedish press, too, for example in *Göteborgs Handels- och Sjöfartstidning* in December 1958:

So what is the situation in Norway now – more than two years later? In Oslo there is one female priest and two female parish workers. But so far no woman has been fully ordained. Despite changes in the law, there is obviously still discrimination, and no one wants to try to force themselves on a congregation against its will. One of the female theologians said that she would never seek a position without being asked, and this is probably a common standpoint among those concerned.[56]

In this article, the denied social and legal recognition is described as discrimination. This is unusually strong language for the time and the debate.

---

52 Ingrid Bjerkås, *Mitt kall* (Oslo: J.W. Cappelen, 1966), p. 54.
53 Tønnessen, *Ingrid Bjerkås*, p. 92.
54 Ibid., p. 92.
55 Ibid., p. 73.
56 Anne-Mari Arnesen, 'Om kvinnliga präster i Norge', *Göteborgs Handels-och Sjöfartstidning*, 8 December 1958.

As in the Swedish context, the refused recognition was made possible and legitimised by a proviso added to the decision to open up the clergy to women. When the Storting decided to take this step in 1938, it ended in a compromise. The so-called 'Lex Mowinckel' established that women had the same right as men to hold public office in Norway, but that they would not be employed as priests 'where the parishes object to it for reasons of principle'.[57] The principle on which the Lex Mowinckel is based exhibits great similarities to the Swedish conscience clause. We believe there are good reasons to assume that the Swedish Riksdag used Norway as a model when formulating its conscience clause. Although the right of refusal in the Church of Norway was granted to the parish and in the Church of Sweden to the individual male priest, the intentions behind the provisos were very similar. In other words, the ambivalent recognition of women's vocation to priestly office took similar forms in the two countries.

It is quite clear that Sweden took the Norwegian context into account. According to the theologian Johanna Andersson, there were three reasons why the topic of opening up the priesthood to women came to be discussed at the Church of Sweden's General Synod in the autumn of 1938: because a number of Swedish women's organisations had demanded that the priesthood be opened up to women; because the school headmaster Manfred Björkquist (1884–1985, Bishop of Stockholm 1942–1954) had argued that a special post should be created for women in the Church; and because 'the Church of Norway legally opened up the clergy to women on 24 June 1938'.[58] Andersson does not discuss this further, but it is worth observing that the contents of Björkquist's proposal to the Swedish General Synod for a special post for women in the Church is very similar to the contents of the report prepared by the Norwegian Bishops' Conference in 1937. However, neither proposal was realised.[59]

To summarise, there are a number of parallels and links between the Church of Norway and the Church of Sweden. People in Sweden looked at the developments in Norway, referred to them in the debate and appear to have been inspired in terms of proposals and decisions. This connection forms an important complement to our understanding of the historical course of events in the Church of Sweden.

---

57 Hinnaland Stendal, 'Kvinnelige prester i Den norske kirke', p. 122.
58 Andersson, *Den nödvändiga manligheten*, p. 31.
59 Hinnaland Stendal, 'Kvinnelige prester i Den norske kirke', p. 122.

Links and parallels with the Evangelical Lutheran Church in Denmark

The Evangelical Lutheran Church in Denmark formally decided to ordain women as priests on 4 June 1947, and the first ordination was held on 28 April 1948. As the theologian Else Marie Wiberg Pedersen observes, Denmark thus became the first mover in this respect.[60] It was hence not surprising that both Norway and Sweden turned their attention to the Evangelical Lutheran Church in Denmark. Like its Norwegian counterpart, the Evangelical Lutheran Church in Denmark differs from the Church of Sweden in a number of respects. Despite these differences, interesting parallels regarding the processes of opening up the clergy to women appear in respect of the Evangelical Lutheran Church in Denmark as well.

Just as in Norway and Sweden, the reform of the clergy in Denmark was related to the struggle for women's equality and wider recognition in Danish society as a whole. In Denmark, too, this reform occurred in parallel with, and was very similar to, the processes in the neighbouring Scandinavian countries. The right to hold public office at the state and municipal levels and the possibility for women to pursue academic studies were introduced at about the same time. In Sweden women gained access to university studies in 1873, in Denmark in 1875 and in Norway in 1884. Danish women were admitted to the Faculty of Theology at the University of Copenhagen in 1904; and a year later, in 1905, the King of Sweden issued the first dispensation for a woman to study theology in Sweden. Women were also granted the right to vote at about the same time: in Denmark in 1915 and, as mentioned above, in 1913 in Norway and 1921 in Sweden. Permission to hold public office was introduced in Denmark in 1921, with the exception of military service and the clergy. In Sweden, the same right – and with the same exceptions – was introduced in 1925.[61]

---

60 Else Marie Wiberg Pedersen, 'Kirke mellem kønsballade och kønsbalance', in Wiberg Pedersen (ed.), *Guds Ord i kvindemund*, p. 14. Wiberg Pedersen also notes that the Evangelical Lutheran Church in Denmark is nevertheless not recognised internationally as the first mover. That role has been credited to the Church of Sweden (p. 36).

61 Marianne Rasmussen, 'Da *Mænd* blev til *Personer*', in Else Marie Wiberg Pedersen (ed.), *Se min kjole: De første kvindelige præsters historie* (Copenhagen: Samlerens Forlag AS, 1998), pp. 108–112; Pia Fris Laneth, 'En kjole, to køn: En fortælling om et samfund i forandring', in Eva

However, the Danish context differs in that the women's movement there was even more involved in the struggle to open up the clergy to women. Ever since the issue of women's access to the clergy had been put on the political agenda in earnest at the end of the 1910s, organisations such as the Danish Women's Society [Dansk Kvindesamfund] and the Women's Council in Denmark [Danske Kvinders Nationalraad] had been engaged in extensive advocacy work to promote equality of the sexes in the Evangelical Lutheran Church in Denmark. For the Danish Women's Society, this became one of the most important issues in the struggle. In this respect the Danish debate differed from that in Sweden, where the issue was not discussed as thoroughly from an equality perspective.[62]

The more prominent role of the women's movement is reflected in Danish research on women's right to be ordained, research that emphasises the emancipatory side of the issue and thus the importance of the women's movement. It should be underlined, however, that the involvement of the women's movement in this cause did not mean that the debate was devoid of theological arguments; quite the contrary: the proponents of women's rights were able to advocate women's right to be ordained on the basis of their interpretation of the Bible and their theology.[63]

With regard to the various theological understandings of vocation put forward in the debate, the arguments for and against reform were also similar.[64] The opponents emphasised an order

Holmegaard Larsen (ed.), *Kvinde – Mand – Kirke: Folkekirken og den lille forskel* (Copenhagen: Forlaget Anis, 2012).

62 'Kampen om de kvindelige præster', Det Kgl. Bibliotek, https://www. kb.dk/inspiration/kvinders-kamp-medborgerskab/kampen-om-de-kvindel ige-praester [accessed 24 April 2023]; Lis Bisgaard, 'Johanne Andersen – præst', *Dansk Kvindebiografisk Leksikon*, https://kvindebiografiskleksikon. lex.dk/Johanne_Andersen_–_pr%C3%A6st [accessed 23 April 2023]; Rasmussen, 'Da *Mænd* blev til *Personer*', p. 120. That women's access to the clergy in Denmark was largely a feminist issue is also evident from Birte Andersen and Lene Sjørup (eds), *Bid i æblet: Feministiske præster 1968+50* (Frederiksberg: Eksistensen, 2020), and Christina Fiig and Bettina Lemann Kristiansen, 'Køn, magt og rettighedskonflikt i folkekirken', in Wiberg Pedersen (ed.), *Guds Ord i kvindemund*, pp. 189–223.

63 Bisgaard, 'Johanne Andersen – præst'.

64 For a thorough review of the debate on women in the clergy over time, see Else Marie Wiberg Pedersen, 'Kirkens kønsskifte? Nedslag i medieomtalen af kvindelige præster', in Wiberg Pedersen (ed.), *Guds Ord i kvindemund*, pp. 281–315.

of creation in which the sexes complement each other, citing the Lutheran doctrine of the three estates. A woman's vocation is to be a wife and mother, and it is not compatible with the vocation to be a priest.[65] By contrast, proponents turned the argument of the complementary nature of the sexes around, claiming that the ranks of the clergy should be opened up to women precisely because of their unique qualities. Johanne Andersen (1913–1999), who became Denmark's first woman priest when she was ordained in 1948, was one of those who made this argument. On the one hand, she said that women should be ordained because a new age – which had broken with Christian tradition in many ways – required that women, too, should serve as clergy. On the other hand, she thought it obvious that not all tasks were congenial to a woman priest. Instead, like other women, an ordained woman usually had an aptitude for various forms of children's and youth activities (such as teaching Sunday school and confirmation classes) and caring for the sick and infirm.[66]

In her overview of arguments in the Danish debate on ordaining women from 1919 to 1947, church historian Liselotte Malmgart identifies four types of argument. All of these are recognisable from their Swedish counterparts. Alongside equality between the sexes, the proponents emphasised the functional aspect of the office of priest, arguing that the key issue was that the Word was proclaimed and the sacraments administered, and that the Bible could not be used as an argument against ordaining women. Representatives of intra-Church revivalist movements cited the Bible as the reason why women could not become priests, while opponents of a more High Church persuasion stressed that the ordination of women would constitute a breach of tradition.[67]

'The ecumenical (counter-)argument' made itself felt in the Danish debate as well. In a petition entitled 'Adressen til Regering og Rigsdag imod kvindelige præster' ['Address to the Government and Parliament against women priests'], published in *Præsteforeningens Blad* on 28 February 1947, 514 male priests warned that ecumenical

65 Lis Bisgaard, 'Debatten om kvindelige præster', in Wiberg Pedersen (ed.), *Se min kjole*, p. 167; Wiberg Pedersen (ed.), *Guds Ord i kvindemund*, pp. 290–294.

66 Bisgaard, 'Debatten om kvindelige præster', pp. 171–172.

67 Liselotte Malmgart, 'Går livet forud for loven? Den danske frihedslovgivning og de kvindelige præster', *Kyrkohistorisk Årsskrift*, 108 (2008), 99–107.

relations would be jeopardised 'with all other major denominations in the world, but also with a two-thousand-year-old interdenominational tradition based on the vision of Holy Scripture'.[68] For many of those who opposed the ordination of women, ecumenism was thus a key argument.

That the reform would constitute a break with Church tradition and make ecumenical relations more difficult was also cited as an objection by the Danish bishops in 1944, when a group of women theologians petitioned the College of Bishops to have Ruth Vermehren (1894–1983) ordained. Vermehren had been a substitute prison chaplain in two women's prisons in Copenhagen since 1929, and in the late 1930s and early 1940s there were discussions about whether she should be allowed to work as an ordained priest. The bishops rejected this request. At the same time, it can be noted that one bishop regarded the lack of apostolic succession in the Evangelical Lutheran Church in Denmark as a bigger problem for ecumenical relations, and he felt that the Church would therefore not be harmed by ordaining women as priests.[69]

The ecumenical argument was considered to be important in Denmark as well as in Norway and Sweden, not least for government minister Carl Martin Hermansen (1897–1976, Minister for Ecclesiastical Affairs 1945–1947), who proposed an amendment to the law that would allow women to join the clergy. In doing so, he relied on two Nordic bishops who were then considered to possess authority in the ecumenical field, the Norwegian Eivind Berggrav (1884–1959) and the Dane Valdemar Ammundsen (1875–1936). As neither of them had any reservations about women being priests, Hermansen hoped that others would not either. Hermansen also anchored his reasoning in the theological counter-narrative of the

---

68 Rasmussen, 'Da *Mænd* blev til *Personer*', pp. 139–140. It can be noted that when the Council on Interchurch Relations of the Evangelical Lutheran Church in Denmark, in connection with the celebration in 2023 of the 75th anniversary of the ordination of the first women priests, asked whether the reform was (and is) 'a challenge for ecumenical co-operation', the two theologians who spoke stated that this was not the case, and that in terms of practical work, the differing views of the priestly office had not affected ecumenical relations. Article entitled 'Kvindelige præster – en udfordring for det økumeniske samarbejde?', https://www.interchurch.dk/aktuelt/nyheder/kvindelige-praester-en-udfordring-for-det-oekumeniske-samarbejde [accessed 24 April 2023].

69 Rasmussen, 'Da *Mænd* blev til *Personer*'.

sexes and argued – alluding to Galatians 3:28 – that 'although women priests are a new phenomenon, it has grown out of the equality between slave and free, between male and female, which is fundamental to Christianity'.[70]

The Danish approach might be said to form a parallel to the Swedish and Norwegian contexts. Just as in their neighbouring Scandinavian countries, opponents of the reform maintained that the issue was driven primarily by secular considerations of equality between the sexes, and they maintained that the demands for reform were very much a women's issue – not a theological one.[71] Like their Swedish and Norwegian colleagues, however, the Danish women who became priests also resisted viewing women's access to the clergy as a women's issue. This was the case for Johanne Andersen, for example, who believed that the ordination of women was in itself a central issue for the Church. Talking about the whole thing as a women's issue risked obscuring this fact.[72] Ruth Vermehren and Edith Brenneche Petersen (1896–1973) emphasised that they did not view ordination as the result of a women's struggle, but rather as 'a natural historical development within the Evangelical Lutheran Church in Denmark'.[73] Leading advocates of the reform, such as Lis Blauenfeldt (1905–2004), even argued that help from the organisations working for women's emancipation should be rejected in order to highlight the theological arguments more clearly.[74]

Furthermore, as in the Swedish and Norwegian contexts, there were a number of women who worked as 'something like a priest', with or without a theological degree. Just like their Swedish counterparts, they were employed as teachers, parish secretaries, YWCA secretaries, missionaries and deaconesses.[75] As the practical

---

70 Ibid., pp. 135–136; see also Fris Laneth, 'En kjole, to køn', pp. 29–30.
71 Bisgaard, 'Debatten om kvindelige præster', p. 167.
72 Bisgaard, 'Johanne Andersen – præst'.
73 Ole Hyldegaard Hansen, *Helga Jensen – Jyllands første kvindelige præst* (Hammel: Forlaget AKKA, 2012), p. 28.
74 Bisgaard, 'Debatten om kvindelige præster', p. 177.
75 See, for example, Hans Raun Iversen, 'Tolv danske kvindelige apostle – I det 20. Århundrede', in Holmegaard Larsen (ed.), *Kvinde – Mand – Kirke*, pp. 188, 193; Hyldegaard Hansen, *Helga Jensen*, p. 28; Fris Laneth, 'En kjole, to køn', pp. 27–28; Tine Elisabeth Larsen, *Anne Marie Petersen, a Danish Woman in South India: A Missionary Story 1909–1951*, Lutheran Heritage Archives, 3 (Chennai: Lutheran Heritage Archives, 2000); Hans Raun Iversen and Harald Nielsen, 'Fra fruentimmere til diakonisser og

theologian Hans Raun Iversen has repeatedly pointed out, the fact that women were seen to be working in such roles broke down preconceptions about women's limitations and helped pave the way for women to be ordained in Denmark.[76]

On 28 April 1948 Johanne Andersen, Ruth Vermehren and Edith Brenneche Petersen were ordained by Bishop Hans Øllgaard (1888–1979) in Odense. Bishop Øllgaard, who favoured the ordination of women, stressed that this action was not a women's issue but rather a matter of the true nature of Christianity. At the ordination he cited Galatians 3:28.

The ordination was condemned by a church group calling itself 'Kirkeligt konvent af 1946' ['the Church convention of 1946'], which claimed that the bishop and the three ordained women had placed themselves outside the Church community; they did not recognise the three women as priests; and they could not regard the bishop as a legitimate supervisor in the Evangelical Lutheran Church in Denmark.[77] In other words, in the Danish context recognition was denied not only to the ordained women but also to the bishop who ordained them. It is reasonable to assume that this situation was a contributory factor in Swedish Archbishop Gunnar Hultgren's strategy of not only ordaining three women as priests, but also having the ordinations performed by three different bishops.

The open denial of recognition was made possible by the inclusion of reservations in the Danish context, too, reservations which make it possible to speak of ambivalent recognition. In the debate leading up to the decision, opponents of the reform repeatedly expressed concern about having a system imposed on them that would violate their conscience. Minister Hermansen's 1947 bill therefore contained two additions geared to meeting the opponents' needs. The law would have a time limit, and a woman could not be appointed as a priest unless the parish council as a whole explicitly

kvindelige missionærer', in Wiberg Pedersen (ed.), *Guds Ord i kvindemund*; Kølle Martinsen, 'Apostelinder – Grundtvig og spørgsmålet om kvindelige præster'.

76 Raun Iversen, 'Tolv danske kvindelige apostle', pp. 188, 193; Raun Iversen and Nielsen, 'Fra fruentimmere til diakonisser og kvindelige missionaerer', p. 155.

77 Johnny Wøllekær, 'For 70 år siden: For biskoppen var kvindelige præster ikke kvindesag – det var teologi', *Århus Stiftstidende*, 25 April 2018, https://stiften.dk/debat/for-70-aar-siden-for-biskoppen-var-kvindelige-praester-ikke-kvindesag-det-var-teologi-2022-12-4 [accessed 8 May 2023].

recognised the right of women to be ordained.[78] Given the similarity
to the Norwegian Lex Mowinckel discussed above, it is reasonable
to assume that the Evangelical Lutheran Church in Denmark was
influenced by the Church of Norway in this respect.

Nevertheless, these restrictions were not enough in the Danish
context. When the amendment was finally passed, it led to conflicts
within the Evangelical Lutheran Church in Denmark; for example,
a number of bishops refused to ordain women or to cooperate with
women priests.[79] To achieve the ordination of women, another
proviso was therefore needed: a law that permitted bishops not to
ordain women and, in some cases, also not to have to supervise a
parish and its clergy. In 1978, when Denmark gained its current
law on 'equal treatment' of men and women in the labour market,
a clause was added preserving this right.[80]

The narrative of division was present in the Danish context as
well as in Sweden and Norway. For example, the aforementioned
petition from 1947 in which 514 clergymen opposed reform argued
that not only ecumenism was endangered, but also the unity of
the Evangelical Lutheran Church in Denmark.[81] We have not been
able to establish whether there was also a 'code of conduct' within
the Evangelical Lutheran Church in Denmark in relation to the
narrative of division.

As for direct links between the two state churches of Sweden
and Denmark, it is clear that these did exist among both proponents and opponents. One example is the Danish priest Helga
Jensen (1923–2009), the fourth woman to be ordained in the
Evangelical Lutheran Church in Denmark in February 1956. She
visited Sweden and preached to a packed church and a large media
audience.[82] She was also invited to preach in a couple of churches
in Norway in the spring of 1957. The Norwegian news agency
Norsk Telegrambyrå described this as 'a historical event in church

78 Fiig and Kristiansen, 'Køn, magt og rettighedskonflikt i folkekirken',
    pp. 200–212.
79 Fris Laneth, 'En kjole, to køn', pp. 32–33.
80 Fiig and Kristiansen, 'Køn, magt og rettighedskonflikt i folkekirken',
    pp. 200–212.
81 Rasmussen, 'Da Mænd blev til Personer', pp. 139–140.
82 The event was reported in a number of Swedish newspapers on 11 March
    1957: 'Kyrkohistoria i Arvika', *Dagens Nyheter*; 'Fullsatt tempel såg
    kvinnlig präst döpa', *Göteborgs Handels- och Sjöfartstidning*; 'Kvinnlig
    präst', *Svenska Dagbladet*.

history'.[83] Jensen was ordained in Aalborg in 1956 by Bishop Erik Jensen (1906–1975) after a long controversy with the Bishop of Viborg, Christian Baun (1898–1972). Baun belonged to the Church Association for the Inner Mission in Denmark [Kirkelig Forening for den Indre Mission i Danmark], a pietistic revivalist movement within the Evangelical Lutheran Church in Denmark which, like Swedish traditional Lutheranism, emphasised personal piety, as well as the authority of the Bible and the Lutheran Confessional texts.[84] In connection with the amendment to the law in 1947, the Church Association for the Inner Mission had also strongly rejected the new law and 'renounced all forms of cooperation with female priests'.[85]

1959 saw another instance of close links between Denmark and Sweden. Bishop Baun wrote to his Swedish episcopal colleague, Bo Giertz, about the latter's involvement in the Church Coalition for the Bible and Confession. Baun wanted to subscribe to the organisation's publications and receive information about its operations: 'Here in Denmark we are rather passive and very much desire the encouragement we can get from your energetic work.'[86] Giertz responded a few days later by sending over that year's edition of the magazine *Kyrka och Folk* ['Church and people'] and the new magazine *Svensk Pastoraltidskrift* ['Swedish pastoral magazine']. He described the situation in Sweden and added that he was looking forward to reading a forthcoming Danish publication containing an exchange of views between a reform opponent, Professor Regin Prenter (1907–1990), and a reform proponent, the Bishop of Lolland-Falster, Halfdan Høgsbro (1894–1876).[87]

---

83 Bisgaard, 'Debatten om kvindelige præster', pp. 185–187. The quotation is from Hyldegaard Hansen, *Helga Jensen*, p. 76.

84 Fris Laneth, 'En kjole, to køn', p. 16.

85 Ibid., p. 31.

86 Letter from Bishop Christian Baun to Bishop Bo Giertz, 12 May 1959, Bo Giertz Archive, LUL.

87 Letter from Bishop Bo Giertz to Bishop Christian Baun, 20 May 1959, Bo Giertz Archive, LUL. Giertz is probably referring to the book published in connection with the tenth anniversary of the first ordination of women clergy in Denmark: Johannes. I. Hansen, Dag Monrad Møller and Verner Schroll, *Kvinden og kirkens embede: En meningsudveksling mellem pastor Dag Monrad Møller, pastor Johs. I. Hansen, pastor Verner Schroll, professor Regin Prenter og biskop Halfdan Høgsbro* (Copenhagen: Nyt Nordisk/Arnold Busck, 1959). For an analysis of the book, see Else Marie Wiberg Pedersen, 'Reformationen og køn: Kvinder og kirkens embede', *Dansk Teologisk Tidsskrift*, 80 (2017), 146–165.

In October that same year, Giertz wrote to Baun asking him to come to Uppsala for a 'gathering of Scandinavian, English and German churchmen and theologians to exchange thoughts and experiences on the issue of women priests'. The initiator was the Professor of Dogmatics Hjalmar Lindroth.[88] Baun replied that he was unable to attend but 'would *very much* have liked to be there' [emphasis in original]. He recommended inviting Regin Prenter as a speaker instead. Baun added that he and Prenter had been inspired by the work of the Church Coalition in Sweden and that they had discussed the possibility of inviting 20 to 30 people to a meeting to discuss the situation and what they should do.

> The main topics would be the new High Church movement, which is stirring things up a great deal here, and a clarification of our relationship with women priests, an issue about which we have once again had a heated dispute. Prof. Prenter and I would be delighted if you could and would come down here and inform us about the situation in Sweden and your work plans in the Church Coalition.[89]

Giertz expressed his willingness to come in January, but Baun wrote back to say that they had had to postpone the meeting because of three events: first, the conflict in Skive (where the bishop had refused to attend a foundation-stone-laying ceremony for a church building if Helga Jensen was allowed to participate) which, according to the bishop, had created a terrible mess and great anger towards him personally; second, the eighth ordination of a woman which was soon to take place and had reopened the debate; and third, the new High Church movement, which was causing problems. He therefore wondered whether Bishop Giertz could come at a later date.[90] Replying that he was happy to do so, Giertz wrote, with reference to the dismaying situation with the Danish High Church movement, that his experience from the Church Coalition's work suggested that it was not necessary to sort out mutual conflicts. Instead, it was 'sufficient to note that our belief in Scripture as the Word of God means that we must oppose women priests [...] It has been one of the sources of satisfaction to find that

88 Bishop Bo Giertz to Bishop Christian Baun, 26 October 1959, Bo Giertz Archive, LUL.
89 Letter from Bishop Christian Baun to Bishop Bo Giertz, 2 November 1959, Bo Giertz Archive, LUL.
90 Letter from Bishop Christian Baun to Bishop Bo Giertz, 11 December 1959, Bo Giertz Archive, LUL.

the High Church men are far more traditionally Lutheran than the slander had claimed.' He stated that it was possible to unite in fully recognising the divinity of Christ and 'when it comes to counting on the authority of his word, his ability to lead his church to the whole truth and to speak through his apostles'. Giertz also returned a newspaper clipping sent by Baun. The text contained an interview with a woman priest. Giertz stated that he had copied the most important points to use as examples in the Swedish debate.[91]

This correspondence from 1959 illustrates the links and connections between the Danish and Swedish contexts. The letters demonstrate that the reform proponents were not the only ones to support and influence one another; the opponents did so too, and to an equally high degree.

∞∞∞∞

This chapter has deepened the discussion about connections and parallels that began in the previous chapter. We have mapped a number of connections and parallels between the Church of Sweden and the two Scandinavian sister churches in Denmark and Norway. Further, the present chapter has shown how these connections and parallels often relate to the concepts of vocation and recognition. There was an active exchange of views on theological concepts and arguments. In all three countries, the processes of opening up the clergy to women were related to an expanded recognition of women's rights and the emancipation movement. All decisions to open up the clergy to women came with reservations – an ambivalent recognition that made it possible to deny the first women clergy recognition at various levels. When decisions were to be made, implemented and managed, those in charge looked to their neighbouring countries.

It is likewise obvious that parallels and connections were extensively discussed in the Swedish debate. We have looked at the discussion about the so-called 'ecumenical argument' – the idea that a reform might threaten the Church of Sweden's ecumenical cooperation with, for example, the Church of England – in some depth. We have also noted that the reform debate involved additional ecumenical arguments – ones that urged the Church of Sweden to derive inspiration from churches that had already implemented reform.

---

91 Letter from Bishop Bo Giertz to Bishop Christian Baun, 17 December 1959, Bo Giertz Archive, LUL.

This ninth chapter has explored how the 'intriguing parallels' observed by the editors of the anthology *Women and Ordination in the Christian Churches: International Perspectives* could be expressed in a church, finding that these were not only parallels but also direct connections.[92] Including such perspectives in historical narratives about reforming the clergy would appear to be both fruitful and crucial.

---

[92] Jones, Thorpe and Wootton, 'Introduction', p. 7.

Chapter 10
Conclusion

Our time together is drawing short, my reader. Possibly you will view these pages of mine as a fragile treasure box, to be opened with the utmost care. Possibly you will tear them apart, or burn them: that often happens to words.

Perhaps you'll be a student of history, in which case I hope you'll make something useful of me: a warts-and-all portrait, a definitive account of my life and times, suitably footnoted; though if you don't accuse me of bad faith I will be astonished. Or, in fact, not astonished: I will be dead, and the dead are hard to astonish.

I picture you as a young woman, bright, ambitious. You'll be looking to make a niche for yourself in whatever dim, echoing caverns of academia may still exist by your time. I situate you at your desk, your hair tucked back behind your ears, your nail polish chipped – for nail polish will have returned, it always does. You're frowning slightly, a habit that will increase as you age. I hover behind you, peering over your shoulder: your muse, your unseen inspiration, urging you on.

You'll labour over this manuscript of mine, reading and rereading, picking nits as you go, developing the fascinated but also bored hatred biographers so often come to feel for their subjects. How can I have behaved so badly, so cruelly, so stupidly? you will ask. You yourself would never have done such things! But you yourself will never have had to.[1]

When Margaret Atwood's novel *The Handmaid's Tale* (1985) was adapted as a television series in 2017, it was hotly debated. What did not emerge in the series was the framing supplied in the book. The final section, 'Historical Notes', is set more than 200 years after the events in the narrative at a research symposium about

---

1 Margaret Atwood, *The Testaments* (New York: Nan A. Talese/Doubleday, 2019), p. 403.

the regime of Gilead. Historians have gathered to hear Professor Pieixoto present his work on publishing a new collection of sources to advance historical research about the regime. In contrast to the protagonist Offred's deeply moving story of abuse and oppression, friendship and love, hope and despair, the professor's dry, academic description of the potential credibility of the historical source appears distant and belittling. He concludes his talk by stating:

> As all historians know, the past is a great darkness, and filled with echoes. Voices may reach us from it; but what they say to us is imbued with the obscurity of the matrix out of which they come; and, try as we may, we cannot always decipher them precisely in the clearer light of our own day.
> *Applause.*
> Are there any questions?[2]

The sequel to the book, *The Testaments*, was not published until 2019. It is set within the same framework narrative. Historians have accessed new sources, which now include the story of Aunt Lydia. In the light of her unreserved support for the Gilead regime, the first book portrayed her as the embodiment of incomprehensible evil; now she suddenly gains added dimensions and it becomes possible to understand her. These new perspectives supplement the historical narrative, making it more complex.

Aunt Lydia's last words in the novel are those quoted in the introduction to this chapter. Her fears about what will happen to her story beautifully encapsulate all that is difficult about writing history on the basis of narratives. Can a history writer, sitting at a distance in time and space and applying theoretical perspectives, really understand? What are his or her aims in writing? Does he or she have the experience and perspective needed to make a fair interpretation? The risk of appearing like a Professor Pieixoto hovers in the shadows.

Even though we cannot fully understand and decipher everything in the narratives that form the core of our source material from our position in time and space, we hope that we have still been able to extract enough to ensure that the historical narrative about the opening up of the Church of Sweden's priesthood to women can be complemented and given more profound dimensions in all its complexity. We also hope that the quotations we

---

2 Margaret Atwood, *The Handmaid's Tale* (London: Vintage, 1985), p. 324.

have supplied from the source material have contributed to the reader's own sense of the voices represented by the vocation narratives.

A fundamental perspective in both of Atwood's novels is that people create meaning and understanding through storytelling. Both Offred and Aunt Lydia come into being through their stories. In Atwood's novels, stories are also always linked to power. For both of her protagonists, writing down their stories is an act of resistance, a way of challenging the common narrative of the Gilead regime's seizure of power as a form of liberation. This book has also centred on this theme: about narratives as meaning- and identity-makers and about their connection to power; about the importance of recognising the vocation to the priesthood; about the consequences for a person's identity when this recognition is denied and how such a moral violation can lead to reactions and struggle; and about the writing of history and what happens to it when practice sheds light on principle, when people's personal narratives complicate and complement the prevailing ways of describing the past.

A number of conceptual pairs – vocation and recognition, complicating and complementing, principles and practices, links and parallels – have run through this book like a common thread. The present chapter reviews and then sums up our conclusions on the basis of these concepts.

The first two chapters discussed the narratives in our source material and their relation to the common historical narrative of the Church of Sweden. The primary source material comprises 34 narratives about what the path to priestly ordination and the initial time in office were like for the first women to be ordained as priests in the Church of Sweden between 1960 and 1970. This source material has been supplemented by narratives derived from other contexts. The women have been interviewed and portrayed in documentaries and memoirs; they have written their own books, diaries, opinion articles, theological works, novels and poems; they have delivered lectures, and so on. As far as possible, all these voices have been included. The first purpose of this book was linked to this function: making these narratives known and heard. In so doing, this book becomes part of the research on women in church leadership roles that starts out from their own narratives.

These chapters have also presented various ways of understanding and shaping the historical narrative about the 1958 reform of the priesthood in the Church of Sweden. We noted that this historical narrative could be summed up through a particular model.

Many scholars have promoted the thesis that the reform resulted from political pressure, that is, that the Church was steered by the secular state, which was primarily motivated not by theological considerations but by emerging ideals of equality between the sexes plus a secularised theology of the folk church. In contrast to this thesis, other scholars have created what might be described as an antithesis: that is, that the reform of the priesthood was primarily motivated by theological considerations, and that it came about after comprehensive theological preparation. The latest trend appears to be a synthesised historical narrative that takes both of these perspectives into account and recognises the complex connections that actually lay behind the reform and its effects.

The second purpose of this book has therefore been to complement and add complexity to Swedish historical narratives about the twentieth century and the opening up of the priesthood in the Church of Sweden. This discussion also ties in with an international scholarly discussion about the writing and use of history in relation to women's leadership in the Christian church. A central theme has been how other types of sources than the accepted official, normative, theological and canonical documents have contributed to deepening and questioning the prevailing historical narrative. The Swedish historical narratives constitute a similar case. They are usually based on material at the level of principle, such as General Synod and church council minutes, commissions of inquiry, and writings and statements by bishops or other church leaders. Hardly any historical narratives have been based on materials that focus on practice, such as narratives about what happened when these decisions of principle 'hit' individuals and parish communities.

In analysing the vocation narratives, our methodological starting point has been the connection between writing a narrative and writing history. Both of these practices involve parallel and partly intertwined processes that create meaning and are closely tied to issues of identity and power. This is why we have worked with narrative analysis. When analysing narratives, two steps are crucial: to identify the plot of the narrative, and to anchor one's analysis in theories and secondary sources.

We have argued that the 34 narratives can be understood and analysed as vocation narratives. In other words, we maintain that the narrative thread – the plot – on which the narrative 'beads' – the episodes, ideological circumstances and meta-reflections – are strung is the theological concept of *vocation*. Further, we have chosen to anchor our analysis of the narratives in the historical and theological context, in the debate in the media and in Axel Honneth's theory of *recognition*. We thus look at the source material from two perspectives: vocation and recognition. As we showed in the research overview, the most common approach to analysing this type of narrative is to emphasise *either* a theological *or* a theoretical – often sociological or power-critical – perspective. In this book we use both.

In addition, we believe that the two concepts of vocation and recognition are connected, because the Reformation's emphasis on the priesthood and vocation of all believers can be viewed, in the light of Honneth's theories, as a struggle for recognition. Furthermore, the opening up of the priesthood to women can be viewed as part of a longer struggle for the recognition of women's rights.

The following five chapters (Chapters 3 to 7) described crucial core episodes and ideological circumstances in the ordained women's chronological narratives that relate to vocation and recognition. The analysis consistently shows that the first women to become priests are definitely not a homogeneous group and should not be treated as such. There is nothing typical about women who are priests, which by extension means that generalising statements along the lines of 'all women priests …' should be used with great caution and preferably not at all.

A recurring theme in these women's descriptions of how they experienced their vocation is that it was deeply connected to their identity. As several of them point out, this is why they experienced having their vocation questioned as a violation. In the light of Honneth's theory of the importance of recognition for a person's identity and self-esteem, the serious consequences of denied recognition become obvious.

In Chapter 3 we highlighted a number of frequently recurring core episodes. We first discussed childhood, the confirmation period and church involvement during adolescence, all of which were regarded in relation to the historical social context. We described a time of great social change, urbanisation, modernisation, secularisation and, not least, a time of struggle for the recognition of women's rights. We also singled out core episodes on the theme of 'something like a priest' – that the first women ordained as priests had previously sought out professions where they could perform tasks similar to those of a priest. A number of these women had worked as missionaries, deaconesses, parish secretaries or teachers before becoming priests. This may be seen as an in-practice strategy of manifesting their vocation in their lives and work. However, the material also shows that for these women this was not enough. A number of them make it clear in their narratives that they wanted their vocation to be confirmed by ordination. This appears to have been an important goal, and, to use Honneth's words, the 1958 reform provided the opportunity to obtain this key legal recognition.

Chapter 3 also discussed the core episode of being from a clerical family. We showed how two of the first women priests' fathers, who were also priests, acted to have their daughters' vocation recognised by the Church. The result was a picture of how difficult it could be to put a decision of principle into practice, and how the efforts of men could be necessary for the women to obtain recognition. This portrayal also problematises historical narratives according to which the reform of the priesthood was something that was forced on a reluctant Church by the state.

Chapter 4 analysed how the first women priests thought theologically about vocation in the context of contemporary theologians and theological currents. Simply put, we can say that the contemporary debate revolved around function versus essence. Alongside a number of influential theologians, the first women to become priests emphasised that being a priest is something you do and not something you are. From this viewpoint, a priest's key task – or function – is to point to Christ, but not to represent him. Advocates of this view based their theological reasoning on the Lutheran concept of the priesthood of all believers and the ordained priesthood. In doing so, they rejected the alternative 'representation' concept which, invoking apostolic succession, had become increasingly influential among theologians who opposed the reform of the priesthood. Further, we found that in the case of the first women priests, the theology of the folk church played a major role, as is often described in the prevailing historical narrative. Being a servant of the Word was a central theological concept in their description of what they were called to do and who they were called to be.

In Chapter 4 we showed how the dominant narrative of vocation and biological sex – the Lutheran doctrine of the three estates, in which woman is subordinate to man – was challenged by a counter-narrative. This counter-narrative viewed the relationship between the sexes in terms of Paul's Epistle to the Galatians, which states that in Christ we are no longer male and female. At the same time, there was a tension between, on the one hand, this neutral view of the relationship between the sexes and, on the other, a complementary view that employed the idea that men and women have different characteristics to justify the need for women in the priesthood.

Chapter 5 and Chapter 6 focused on the core episodes of formation, ordination, and early years as a priest. In both chapters we applied Honneth's theories of different levels of recognition to identify and discuss recurring themes in the vocation narratives. We observed that the first women to become priests received a great deal of recognition at both a fundamental and a social level from parents, fellow students, worshippers, bishops and future fellow priests. That recognition brought great joy to these women. This was particularly true of their ordination, which is often described as a combination of recognition of vocation on all three of Honneth's levels, and features as the crowning point of the vocation narratives.

However, we also showed that the opposite was true: that the first women to become priests were denied recognition in various contexts. It was primarily the opponents of reform who expressed their resistance through a denial of social recognition, and the women encountered this from fellow students, university teachers, fellow priests and anonymous letter writers. We further noted that a discrepancy existed between the intention behind the actions and their actual consequences. The years of study, especially the concluding practical training term, appear to have been a trial by fire.

Opponents to the reform claimed that they were being true to their conscience by opposing a decision that was based on a principle. Still, this supposed opposition to a principle ended up involving real harm to the first women priests. Opposition to the reform was not expressed in a random and spontaneous way, as we showed by focusing on one of the groups that mustered many opponents: the Church Coalition for the Bible and Confession and its 'Seventeen Points'. Previous historical narratives have argued that the Seventeen Points were intended to constitute pastoral advice to opponents on how they should proceed in order not to have to betray their principles. On the basis of our source material, though, we have been able to show that, in practice, this advice functioned as an action plan that reform opponents were expected to follow. Furthermore, harsh and offensive language was accepted practice in certain circles. In the light of Honneth's theory of recognition, this situation may be viewed as a systematic and deliberate denial of recognition at the social level. This denied recognition was made possible by the 'conscience clause' [*samvetsklausulen*], a reservation in the law that allowed male priests to refrain from cooperating with female priests on grounds of conscience.

The tension between principle and practice is also expressed in how the bishops of the Church of Sweden related to the reform. We have shown that although one bishop claimed to support the reform and the principle-based decision to open up the Church of Sweden's priesthood to women, he might in reality demonstrate an ambivalent attitude. Even a bishop who supported the reform in principle could, in practice, display a hesitant – or even evasive – attitude towards the women who came to him requesting priestly ordination. Judging from the vocation narratives, it was precisely because they were women that the bishops did not want to ordain them, not because they lacked personal suitability.

In addition to the conscience clause, another factor contributing to this ambivalence was the fairly widespread narrative of division resulting from the reform. Church leaders not infrequently expressed a desire for coexistence. This desire derived from the idea that the division that had emerged as a result of the reform would subside again, if only the women priests would maintain a low profile. This narrative of division helped to justify expressing opposition by denying recognition to women priests, as well as viewing such actions as a legitimate response to a provocation: quite simply, a reform opponent could not do otherwise.

Our source material was also able to help complement the historical picture in terms of how the laity responded to the reform. One narrative has claimed that people with active functions in the Church, laity and priests alike [kyrkfolket], opposed the reform; another has claimed that the members of the Church of Sweden as a whole were generally in favour of it. The latter narrative is strongly inclined to contrast a liberal-minded laity with a conservative clergy who opposed the reform. The vocation narratives complement and add nuance to both these narratives. They reveal that the first women priests received great and warm support both from fellow priests and parishes, and from active Church people as well as from other members of the Church of Sweden. A supposedly theologically ignorant public and a secularised state were far from being the only ones to welcome women priests.

In Chapter 7, we returned to the issue of the 'code of conduct' to which the first women priests were expected to adhere. In the context of the narrative of division, an expectation prevailed according to which it was the responsibility of the first women priests to give way, in order to avoid situations that might expose this division.

The example that we used to illustrate how this principle of a code of conduct could be expressed in practice – the invitation to Marianne Westrin to preach in Skara Cathedral – brought out the complexity of the ways in which various people related to the reform. The dividing lines over the reform rarely ran where previous historical narratives had indicated: both proponents and opponents existed among laypeople as well as among priests and bishops.

In addition, we demonstrated that the first women priests largely behaved in accordance with the code of conduct, out of fear, gratitude and compulsion, and because such behaviour was regarded as a Christian ideal. However, some of the later recorded vocation narratives contain meta-reflections in which the priests are critical of their own conduct. Looking back, some of them wish that they had questioned the code of conduct and demanded that their vocation be recognised. Chapter 7 contextualised these meta-reflections on the code of conduct and discussed the women priests in the light of Honneth's assumption that repeated denial of recognition leads to a struggle for recognition. Drawing on the media debate in the 1970s, the chapter depicted something of what happened after the period covered by the vocation narratives. The narrative of division was questioned; it was also at times inverted, so that it was the reform opponents who were accused of causing division. This struggle for recognition eventually led to the repeal of the conscience clause in 1983, whereby the possibility of legally legitimising ambivalent or denied recognition finally disappeared.

We also showed how this inverted narrative of division gave rise to a new narrative, which we have chosen to call the 'who is suffering more?' narrative. The debate over demands for recognition shifted to a comparison of who had suffered and was suffering more: the women priests or the opponents of reform. We also discussed the 'who is suffering more?' narrative in the light of Honneth's theories. It is not unusual for a recognition that is expanded to include a new group to lead to a questioning of the recognition extended to other groups. This problem is discussed by Honneth in his later writings, in which he clarifies how struggles for recognition can be evaluated. Increased freedom through mutual recognition is the benchmark for good development. Because development occurs through democratic processes, groups that demand recognition with the intention of using it to limit other groups' right to recognition should be challenged.

The last two chapters of the book discussed connections and parallels between what was happening in the Church of Sweden and what went on in other denominations and churches at the time. By using narratives as source material and taking a close look at what was actually happening in practice, the chapter shed light on connections and parallels that had been obscured by the sources and approaches used for previous historical narratives. Both the 'thesis' and the 'antithesis' historical narratives about the reform of the Church of Sweden's priesthood have portrayed it as a process involving two actors only: the state and the Church. As we showed in our overview of the relevant research, this pattern is not unusual in historical accounts of the opening up of the priesthood to women. Indeed, it is rather the rule, and studies that apply a comparative perspective are the exception. The few discussions about connections and parallels between churches and denominations that do exist usually appear in introductions or postscripts to anthologies and argue that the debate about such perspectives needs to go deeper. We also observed that such comparative approaches tend to lead to reflection on the relationship between two key drivers of reforms of the priesthood: on the one hand, theological motives, and on the other, social changes in the form of emancipation and women's movements. In other words, themes to which this book has referred as vocation and recognition.

This insight is germane to the third and final aim of this book: to show how the processes of opening up the priesthood to women in one church influence and are influenced by the processes in other churches. We have sought to achieve this by examining connections and parallels between the process of change in the Church of Sweden and that which took place in other denominations at the time. The narratives uncovered a number of connections and parallels with other churches and denominations. These existed in the background of the first women priests, with almost half of the vocation narratives describing close ties to Free Church denominations and intra-Church revivalist movements. This background was also strongly manifested in the first women priests' theological understanding of vocation, which we have chosen to call 'the vocation theology of necessary preaching'.

The vocation theology of necessary preaching involves a conviction that time is short and secularisation is looming, and that all forces for good must therefore be utilised to preach the Gospel. Personal faith and the gift of preaching are the key factors, not biological sex. This way of thinking about vocation was prominent in, for example, the Mission Covenant Church of Sweden and the Baptist Union of Sweden, but it could also be articulated in the context of the Church of Sweden.

Besides, the first women priests perceived connections and parallels themselves, and a number of them commented that they had been inspired and influenced by female predecessors in other denominations and revivalist movements. Discussions about possible ecumenical influences, connections and parallels also featured prominently in the public debate in the decades leading up to the General Synod's decision to open up the priesthood to women in 1958, both among supporters and opponents of the reform.

We have also demonstrated a number of connections and parallels between the process of opening up the priesthood to women in the Church of Sweden and in other denominations and churches at the time. The Mission Covenant Church of Sweden and the Baptist Union of Sweden, as well as the Church of Norway and the Evangelical Lutheran Church in Denmark, influenced and were influenced by developments in the Church of Sweden.

Our exploration of these connections and parallels makes it clear that a double common thread runs through the narratives – both those of the individual women and those written by historians – which relates to vocation and recognition. This realisation brings us back to the first aim of this study and the discussion about how narratives about women's access to church leadership positions might be analysed. In this context, the value of having *both* a theological *and* a theoretical (for example, sociological) eye open when analysing this type of narrative becomes apparent.

One final point: in Margaret Atwood's novels the historians' discussions about the narratives contained in their sources are merely a framework. The core is formed by the women's own voices, their own stories. It is our hope that in this book, the voices of the first women priests have been heard at least as much as the analyses of church historians and theologians. It is therefore right and proper that one of these women should have the final word.

Although a mere sixty-five years have passed since the reform was implemented, from a historical perspective things have changed quickly. One indication of this rapid development is that in the summer of 2020 as many women as men were serving as priests in the Church of Sweden. On that Palm Sunday in 1960, when Elisabeth Djurle Olander, Ingrid Persson and Margit Sahlin became the first three women to be ordained as priests in the Church of Sweden, such a situation would have been impossible to imagine. The contrast between the decades that we have studied for this book and the situation in the Church of Sweden today is overwhelming.

With time comes inevitable change, even if it is not always obvious when you are right in the middle of it. Some of the first women to become priests have reflected on this process.[3] They include Caroline Krook (ordained in 1969), who has the final word:

I sometimes put it this way: My grandmother died young, and when she died women did not have the right to vote in Sweden. But her granddaughter became a bishop. It gives you a perspective on women's issues and equality between the sexes. We may think that things are moving slowly, but from a historical perspective the change has been extremely swift.[4]

3 'I have always believed that it is time that works for us. From a historical perspective, forty years is not that much, and we are already many in number.' No. 19. See also Christina Odenberg in Lina Sjöberg, 'Kristus som livshypotes: Christina Odenberg, prästvigd 1967', in Hössjer Sundman and Sjöberg, *Du ska bli präst*, p. 46.
4 Anna Lena Persson, 'Caroline Krook växte upp med Strindbergs teater', *Kyrkans Tidning*, 4 August 2011.

Image credits

1 Lena Malmgren, ordained for the diocese of Karlstad in 1967. Copyright Bilder i Syd. Reproduced by permission.
2 Ingrid Persson, ordained in 1960. Reproduced by courtesy of Profilbild i Härnösand AB/Kjell Jonsson.
3 Britta Olén-van Zijl, ordained in 1963. Copyright Bilder i Syd. Reproduced by permission.
4 Margit Sahlin, one of the first three women to be ordained in the Church of Sweden in 1960. Copyright TT Nyhetsbyrån. Reproduced by permission.
5 Britta Olén-van Zijl in 1963 with her ordination bishop Martin Lindström, Cathedral Dean Yngve Ahlberg, Professor Gustaf Wingren and Professor Hugo Odeberg. Copyright Bilder i Syd. Reproduced by permission.
6 The ordination of Marianne Westrin in 1965. Reproduced by courtesy of Profilbild i Härnösand AB/Kjell Jonsson.
7 Anne Strid. Reproduced by courtesy of *Göteborgsposten*/ Bengt Kjellin 1978.

Bibliography

Unpublished sources

Lund University Archives
Lund University Library (LUL)
    The Bo Giertz Collection
    The Gunnar Olén Collection
Lund University Church History Archive (LUKA)
    The vocation narratives of the first women ordained as priests in Sweden
Umeå University Library
    The Stig Hellsten Archive
Uppsala, The Church Chancellery
    The Gunnar Hultgren Archive
Uppsala, National Archives
    The Gunnar Hultgren Archive

Newspapers

Aftonbladet
Arbetet
Dagen
Dagens Nyheter
Expressen
Göteborgs Handels- och Sjöfarts-Tidning
Göteborgs-Posten
Helsingborgs Dagblad
Hudiksvalls Nyheter
Hudiksvalls Tidning
Kyrkans Tidning
Norrköpings Tidningar
Nya Dagligt Allehanda
Stockholms-Tidningen
Sundsvalls Tidning
Svensk Kyrkotidning

Svenska Dagbladet
Svenska Morgonbladet
Sydsvenska Dagbladet
Upsala Nya Tidning
Västernorrlands Allehanda

Published sources

Algrim, Karin, 'Eve and Martha – But What about Mary? An Interview with a Woman Priest', *Hertha*, 5 (1969), 64–68.

Andersen, Birte, and Lene Sjørup (eds), *Bid i æblet: Feministiske præster 1968+50* (Frederiksberg: Eksistensen, 2020).

Andersson, Johanna, *Den nödvändiga manligheten: Om maskulinitet som soteriologisk signifikant i den svenska debatten om prästämbete och kön* (Gothenburg: Institutionen för litteratur, idéhistoria och religion, Gothenburg University, 2019).

Andiñach, Pablo R., *The Book of Gratitudes: An Encounter Between Life and Faith* (Eugene, OR: Wipf & Stock, 2016).

Andrews, Molly, Corinne Squire and Maria Tamboukou, *Doing Narrative Research* (London: Sage, 2008).

Antikainen, Ari, 'Introduction: In Search of Life History', in Ivor Goodson (ed.), *The Routledge International Handbook on Narrative and Life History* (Abingdon: Routledge, 2017), pp. 131–143.

Appold, Kenneth G., 'Frauen im frühneuzeitlichen Luthertum: Kirchliche Ämter und die Frage der Ordination', *Zeitschrift für Theologie und Kirche*, 103 (2006), 253–279.

Aronsson, Peter, *Historiebruk: Att använda det förflutna* (Lund: Studentlitteratur, 2004).

Asol Kapinde, Stephen, and Eleanor Tiplady Higgs, 'Global Anglican Discourse and Women's Ordination in Kenya: The Controversy in Kirinyaga, 1979–1992, and its Legacy', *Journal of Anglican Studies*, 20 (2022), 22–29.

Atwood, Margaret, *Alias Grace* (London: Bloomsbury, 1996).

Atwood, Margaret, *The Handmaid's Tale* (London: Vintage, 1985).

Atwood, Margaret, *The Testaments* (New York: Nan A. Talese/Doubleday, 2019).

Augsburgska bekännelsen [Svenska kyrkans bekännelseskrifter] (Stockholm: Verbum, 2000).

Austen, Jane, *Pride and Prejudice* (New York: W.W. Norton, 2001 [1813]).

Bajramovic Jusufbegovic, Sanela, 'Muntliga berättelser om kvinnoaktivism i Bosnien-Hercegovina – med källkritik och analys i fokus', in Greger Andersson, Christina Carlsson Wetterberg, Carina Lidström and Sten Wistrand (eds), *Berättande, liv, mening* (Örebro: Örebro University, 2014), pp. 107–115.

Bardh, Ulla, *Församlingen som sakrament: Tro, dop, medlemskap och ekumenik bland frikyrkokristna vid 1900-talets slut* (Uppsala: Teologiska institutionen, Uppsala University, 2008).

Bardh, Ulla, *Här är icke man och kvinna* (Stockholm: Moderna läsare, a publishing activity organised by the Free Church Adult Educational Association, 1974).

Bardh, Ulla, 'Kallad – av vem?', in *Präst och pastor: Ämbete, kallelse, tjänst*, Nordic Ecumenical Series, 28 (Uppsala: Nordic Ecumenical Council, 1996), pp. 84–87.

Bejerfors, Siv, 'Lärare och präst', in *Kvinnlig präst idag: Tio kvinnliga präster berättar* (Stockholm: Natur och Kultur, 1967), pp. 114–139.

Berglund, Sven-Oscar, *Laurentiistiftelsen i brytningstid: Minnen från ett studenthems tillkomst och uppbyggnad* (Lund: Lunds universitets kyrkohistoriska arkiv, 2000).

Berntson, Martin, Bertil Nilsson and Cecilia Wejryd, *Kyrka i Sverige: Introduktion till svensk kyrkohistoria* (Skellefteå: Artos, 2012).

Betänkande och förslag i fråga om kvinnors tillträde till statstjänster: Kvinnas behörighet att inneha prästerlig och annan kyrklig tjänst, SOU [Swedish Government Official Reports], 1923:22.

Betänkande om kvinnoprästutredningen: Omprövning av samvetsklausulen, Män och kvinnor som präster i Svenska kyrkan, SOU [Swedish Government Official Reports], 1981:20.

Bexell, Oloph, 'Kyrkligheter i Svenska kyrkan', in Stephan Borgehammar (ed.), *Kyrkans liv: Introduktion till kyrkovetenskapen* (Stockholm: Verbum, 1993), pp. 123–138.

Bexell, Oloph, *Präster i S:t Sigfrids stift: Minnesteckningar till prästmötet i Växjö 1990* (Gothenburg: Pro caritate, 1990).

Bexell, Oloph, *Sveriges kyrkohistoria, 7: Folkväckelsens och kyrkoförnyelsens tid* (Stockholm: Verbum, 2003).

Bexell, Oloph, Kjell Hagberg and Viveka Posse, *Kvinnliga präster i Växjö stift?! Handlingarna i en kyrklig stridsfråga* (Uppsala: Pro Veritate, 1969).

Bible, The, translated into Swedish in 1917. The English edition used for this translation is the New Revised Standard Version.

Bischoff-Mikkelsen, Lene, 'Alt fra den levende Gud til den svedende krop', in Else Marie Wiberg Pedersen (ed.), *Se min kjole: De første kvindelige præsters historie* (Copenhagen: Samlerens Forlag AS, 1998), pp. 70–107.

Bisgaard, Lis, 'Debatten om kvindelige præster', in Else Marie Wiberg Pedersen (ed.), *Se min kjole: De første kvindelige præsters historie* (Copenhagen: Samlerens Forlag AS, 1998), pp. 144–188.

Bjerkås, Ingrid, *Mitt kall* (Oslo: J. W. Cappelen, 1966).

Björkman, Sara, *Meditationer* (Stockholm: Kvinnliga Missionsarbetare, 1955).

Björkman, Sara, *Signe Ekblad* (Uppsala: J. A. Lindblads Bokförlag, 1954).

Brandby-Cöster, Margareta, 'Dubbla budskap – vilket ska firas?', in Boel Hössjer Sundman (ed.), *Äntligen stod hon i predikstolen! Historiskt vägval 1958* (Stockholm: Verbum, 2008), pp. 162–180.

Brandby-Cöster, Margareta, *Hur gick det till? Hur blev jag präst? Erinringar 50 år efteråt* (Stockholm: BoD – Books on Demand, 2020).

Brandby-Cöster, Margareta, 'Vad skall kyrkan förkunna i klimat-orons tid?', in *Sagt och gjort: Texter och tal från mitt prästliv* (Stockholm: BoD – Books on Demand, 2015), pp. 232–257.

Brandby-Cöster, Margareta, 'Wingrensk homiletik', *Svensk Teologisk Kvartalsskrift*, 2 (2011), 87–90.

Brandby-Cöster, Margareta, Birgitta Nyman and Anne Strid, *Kvinna – kyrka* (Stockholm: Verbum, 1977).

Brekus, Catherine A., *Strangers & Pilgrims: Female Preaching in America, 1740–1845* (Chapel Hill, NC: University of North Carolina Press, 1998).

Brilioth, Yngve, *Herdabrev till Uppsala ärkestift* (Stockholm: Diakonistyrelsen, 1950).

Brohed, Ingmar, 'Review of *Äntligen stod hon i predikstolen! Historiskt vägval 1958*', *Kyrkohistorisk årsskrift*, 109 (2009), 267–273.

Brohed, Ingmar, *Sveriges kyrkohistoria, 8: Religionsfrihetens och ekumenikens tid* (Stockholm: Verbum, 2005).

Brunne, Eva, et al., *Myten om madonnan: En bok om kvinna och man under förtryck och befrielse* (Stockholm: Verbum, 1978).

Bylund, Erik, 'Gunnar Hultgren 1902–1991', *Thule*, 4 (1991), 166–167.

Carlquist, Gunnar (ed.), *Lunds stifts herdaminne: Från reformationen till nyaste tid: Ser. II Biografier 13A Östra och Medelstads kontrakt* (Lund: Bokhandeln Arken, 2006).

Cazden, Elizabeth, *Antoinette Brown Blackwell: A Biography* (New York: The Feminist Press at The City University of New York, 1983).

Christiansson, Elisabeth, *Kyrklig och social reform: Motiveringar till diakoni 1845–1965* (Skellefteå: Artos & Norma, 2006).

Claesson, Urban, 'Introduktion', in Urban Claesson and Sinikka Neuhaus (eds), *Minne och möjlighet: Kyrka och historiebruk från nationsbygge till pluralism*, Forskning för kyrkan, 22 (Stockholm: Makadam, 2014), pp. 7–11.

Claesson, Urban, 'Lutherska begrepp och nordisk samhällsteologi', in Jenny Ehnberg and Cecilia Nahnfeldt (eds), *Samhällsteologi: Forskning i skärningspunkten mellan akademi, samhälle och kyrkan*, Forskning för kyrkan, 41 (Stockholm: Verbum, 2019).

Coelho da Silva, Eliana, 'Chamadas por Deus: características do pastorado feminino na cidade de Fortaleza', PhD dissertation, Universidade Federal do Ceará (UFC), 2014.

Dahlbacka, Jakob, *Framåt med stöd av det förflutna: Religiöst historiebruk hos Anders Svedberg* (Åbo: Åbo Akademi, 2015).

Dahlén, Rune W., 'Pastoral Education and Controversy in the Mission Covenant Church of Sweden', in Hanna Ondrey and Mark Safstrom (eds), *Essays in Honor of Philip J. Anderson: Sacred Migration: Borderlands of Community and Faith* (Chicago: The Swedish-American Historical Society, 2020), pp. 215–234.

Dahlén, Rune W., Ulf Hållmarker and Lennart Molin, *Missionsskolan Lidingö* (Skåre: Votum, 2016).

Den svenska psalmboken (Stockholm: Verbum, 1986).

Eason, Andrew Mark, *Women in God's Army: Gender and Equality in the Early Salvation Army* (Waterloo, Ont.: Wilfrid Laurier University Press, 2003).

Edgardh, Ninna, *Diakonins kyrka: Teologi, kön och omsorgens utmattning* (Stockholm: Verbum, 2019).

'Eko efter kyrkomötet: KVINNO-präster NEJ/JO', *Kyrka och hem: Kyrkligt månadsblad för Växjö stift*, 11 (1957), 230–233.

Fahlgren, Sune, *Predikantskap och församling: Sex fallstudier av en ecklesial baspraktik inom svensk frikyrklighet fram till 1960-talet* (Uppsala: Uppsala University, 2006).

Fahlgren, Sune, 'Ämbete, kallelse och tjänst', in *Präst och pastor: Ämbete, kallelse, tjänst*, Nordic Ecumenical Series, 28 (Uppsala: Nordic Ecumenical Council, 1996), pp. 15–40.

Fletcher, Sheila, *Maude Royden: A Life* (Oxford: Basil Blackwell, 1989).

Fransson, Tomas, *'Kristi ämbete': Gunnar Rosendal och diskussionen om biskopsämbetet i Svenska kyrkan* (Skellefteå: Artos 2006).

Franzén, Georg, *In memoriam: Minnesteckningar av präster i Lunds stift 1987–93* (Lund: Arcus, 1994).

Franzen, Trisha, *Anna Howard Shaw: The Work of Woman Suffrage* (Urbana, IL: University of Illinois Press, 2014).

Fraser, Nancy, and Axel Honneth, *Redistribution or Recognition? A Political-Philosophical Exchange* (London: Verso, 2003).

Fredfeldt, Bodil, 'Vid Öresund', in *Kvinnlig präst idag: Tio kvinnliga präster berättar* (Stockholm: Natur och Kultur, 1967), pp. 58–76.

Fridrichsen, Anton, *Fyrahanda sädesåker: En kommentar till Evangeliebokens högmässotexter* (Stockholm: Svenska kyrkans diakonistyrelses bokförlag, 1958).

Fris Laneth, Pia, 'En kjole, to køn: En fortælling om et samfund i forandring', in Eva Holmegaard Larsen (ed.), *Kvinde – Mand – Kirke: Folkekirken og den lille forskel* (Copenhagen: Forlaget Anis, 2012), pp. 15–38.

Fry, Alex David James, 'Gender Attitudes amongst Anglo-Catholic and Evangelical Clergy in the Church of England: An Examination of How Male Priests Respond to Women's Ordination as Priests and their Consecration as Bishops', PhD dissertation, Durham University, 2019.

Goodson, Ivor, 'Introduction: Life Histories and Narratives', in Ivor Goodson (ed.), *The Routledge International Handbook on Narrative and Life History* (Abingdon: Routledge, 2017), pp. 3–10.

Goodson, Ivor, 'The Rise of the Life Narrative', in Ivor Goodson (ed.), *The Routledge International Handbook on Narrative and Life History* (Abingdon: Routledge, 2017), pp. 11–22.

Goodson, Ivor, 'The Story of Life History', in Ivor Goodson (ed.), *The Routledge International Handbook on Narrative and Life History* (Abingdon: Routledge, 2017), pp. 23–33.

Goodson, Ivor (ed.), *The Routledge International Handbook on Narrative and Life History* (Abingdon: Routledge, 2017).

Grindal, Gracia, 'Women in the Evangelical Lutheran Church in America', in Catherine Wessinger (ed.), *Religious Institutions and Women's Leadership: New Roles Inside the Mainstream* (Columbia, SC: University of South Carolina Press, 1996), pp. 180–210.

Gubrium, Jaber F., and James A. Holstein, 'Analyzing Novelty and Pattern in Institutional Life Narratives', in Ivor Goodson (ed.), *The Routledge International Handbook on Narrative and Life History* (Abingdon: Routledge, 2017), pp. 156–166.

Gunner, Gunilla, 'Om predikstolar ur ett ekumeniskt perspektiv', in Boel Hössjer Sundman (ed.), *Äntligen stod hon i predikstolen! Historiskt vägval 1958* (Stockholm: Verbum, 2008), pp. 140–149.

Gustafsson, Johanna, *Kyrka och kön: Om könskonstruktioner i Svenska kyrkan 1945–1985* (Eslöv: B. Östlings bokförlag Symposion, 2001).

Gustafsson Lundberg, Johanna, *Medlem 2010: En teologisk kommentar* (Uppsala: Church of Sweden Research Unit, 2010).

Gustavsson, Alexander, 'Manlig bekännelsetrohet i motvind: En mikrohistorisk studie av prästen Bo Giertz', in Anders Jarlert (ed.), *Bo Giertz – präst, biskop, författare* (Gothenburg: Församlingsförlaget, 2005), pp. 9–67.

Hammar, Inger, *Emancipation och religion: Den svenska kvinnorörelsens pionjärer i debatt om kvinnans kallelse ca 1860–1900* (Stockholm: Carlsson, 1999).

Hansen, Johannes I., Dag Monrad Møller and Verner Schroll, *Kvinden og kirkens embede: En meningsudveksling mellem pastor Dag Monrad Møller, pastor Johs. I. Hansen, pastor Verner Schroll, professor Regin Prenter og biskop Halfdan Høgsbro* (Copenhagen: Nyt Nordisk/Arnold Busck, 1959).

Hansson, Klas, *Svenska kyrkans primas: Ärkebiskopsämbetet i förändring 1914–1990*, Acta Universitatis Upsaliensis. Studia Historico-Ecclesiastica Upsaliensia, 47 (Uppsala: Uppsala University, 2014).

Heidegren, Carl-Göran, 'Inledning', in Axel Honneth, *Erkännande: Praktisk-filosofiska studier*, trans. Carl-Göran Heidegren (Gothenburg: Daidalos, 2000), pp. 7–19.

Hermansson, Mikael, *'En allians av något slag': Förändrade relationer mellan Svenska kyrkan och Church of England, 1909–1954* (Malmö: Universus Academic Press, 2018).

Hessler, Carl Arvid, *Statskyrkodebatten* (Stockholm: Almqvist & Wiksell, 1964).

Hinnaland Stendal, Synnøve, 'Kvinnelige prester i Den norske kirke – kirke og stat på kollisjonskurs? om behandlingen av spørsmålet om kvinners adgang til de geistlige embetene', *Kyrkohistorisk årsskrift*, 108 (2008), 119–125.

Hirdman, Yvonne, Jenny Björkman and Urban Lundberg (eds), *Sveriges historia, 1920–1965* (Stockholm: Norstedts, 2012).

Holm, Ulla Carin, *Hennes verk skall prisa henne: Studier av personlighet och attityder hos kvinnliga präster i Svenska kyrkan* (Båstad: Plus Ultra, 1982).

Honneth, Axel, *Disrespect: The Normative Foundations of Critical Theory* (Cambridge: Polity, 2007).

Honneth, Axel, *Erkännande: Praktisk-filosofiska studier*, trans. Carl-Göran Heidegren (Gothenburg: Daidalos, 2000).

Honneth, Axel, *The Fragmented World of the Social: Essays in Social and Political Philosophy* (Albany, NY: State University of New York Press, 1995).

Honneth, Axel, *The Struggle for Recognition: The Moral Grammar of Social Conflicts* (Cambridge: Polity, 1995).

Horsdal, Marianne, 'The Narrative Interview – Method, Theory and Ethics: Unfolding a Life', in Ivor Goodson (ed.), *The Routledge International Handbook on Narrative and Life History* (Abingdon: Routledge, 2017), pp. 260–269.

Horsefield, Peter, *From Jesus to the Internet: A History of Christianity and Media* (Chichester: Wiley Blackwell, 2015).

Hyldegaard Hansen, Ole, *Helga Jensen – Jyllands første kvindelige præst* (Hammel: Forlaget AKKA, 2012).

Hössjer Sundman, Boel, 'Möta nutidsmänniskan och ge ett svar på hennes livs frågor: Om Ruben Josefsons teologi', in Boel Hössjer Sundman (ed.), *Äntligen stod hon i predikstolen! Historiskt vägval 1958* (Stockholm: Verbum, 2008), pp. 150–161.

Ideström, Jonas, *Folkkyrkotanken – innehåll och utmaningar: En översikt av studier under 2000-talet* (Uppsala: Svenska kyrkans forskningsenhet, 2012).

Janzon, Göran, 'Driftig församlings- och kapellbyggare', in Göran Janzon and Berit Åqvist (eds), *I kallelsens grepp: Om sex baptistkvinnors liv och tjänst* (Karlstad: Votum & Guller, 2016), pp. 43–61.

Jarlert, Anders, *Göteborgs stifts herdaminne 1620–1999: I. Domprosteriets kontrakt* (Gothenburg: Tre böcker, 2009).

Jarlert, Anders, 'Reform in Sweden: From Confessional Provincialism towards World Ecumenism', in Anders Jarlert (ed.), *Piety and Modernity: The Dynamics of Religious Reform in Northern Europe 1780–1920*, III (Leuven: Leuven University Press, 2012), pp. 286–306.

Johansson, Anna, *Narrativ teori och metod: Med livsberättelsen i fokus* (Lund: Studentlitteratur, 2004).

Jones, Ian, Kirsty Thorpe and Janet Wootton, 'Introduction', in Ian Jones, Kirsty Thorpe and Janet Wootton (eds), *Women and Ordination in the*

Christian Churches: International Perspectives (London: T&T Clark, 2008), pp. 1–18.

Jones, Ian, Kirsty Thorpe and Janet Wootton (eds), *Women and Ordination in the Christian Churches: International Perspectives* (London: T&T Clark, 2008).

Jonson, Jonas, *Missionärerna: En biografisk berättelse om Svenska kyrkans mission 1874–1974* (Stockholm: Verbum, 2019).

Josefson, Ruben, *Herdabrev till Härnösands stift* (Stockholm: Diakonistyrelsen, 1959).

Kerby-Fulton, Kathryn, 'Introduction: Taking Early Women Intellectuals and Leaders Seriously', in Kathryn Kerby-Fulton and J. Van Engen (eds), *Women Intellectuals and Leaders in the Middle Ages* (Martlesham, Suffolk: Boydell & Brewer, 2020), pp. 1–18.

Kjöllerström, Sven, *Sätt till att ordinera en vald biskop 1561–1942* (Lund: Gleerup, 1974).

Kling, David W., *The Bible in History: How the Texts Have Shaped the Times* (Oxford: Oxford University Press, 2023).

Knoll, Benjamin, and Cammie Jo Bolin, *She Preached the Word: Women's Ordination in Modern America* (Oxford: Oxford University Press, 2018).

Koivonen Bylund, Tuulikki, '"Ett ytterligare #metoo?" Berättelsernas egenvärde', *Svensk Kyrkotidning*, 11 (2018), 328–330.

Kolfeldt, Margit, 'Långt mellan byarna', in *Kvinnlig präst idag: Tio kvinnliga präster berättar* (Stockholm: Natur och Kultur, 1967), pp. 97–102.

Kristensson Uggla, Bengt, *Becoming Human Again: The Theological Life of Gustaf Wingren* (Eugene, OR: Cascade Books, 2016).

Kristensson Uggla, Bengt, *Gustaf Wingren: Människan och teologin* (Stockholm: B. Östlings bokförlag Symposion, 2010).

Krook, Caroline, *Från stor stad till storstad: Stockholms stift igår och idag* (Stockholm: Verbum, 2020).

Krook, Caroline, *Prästens identitet och kyrkans trovärdighet* (Stockholm: Verbum, 1996).

Kvinnas behörighet till kyrkliga ämbeten och tjänster. Betänkande av inom ecklesiastikdepartementet tillkallade sakkunniga, SOU [Swedish Government Official Reports], 1950:48.

Kvinnlig präst idag: Tio kvinnliga präster berättar (Stockholm: Natur och Kultur, 1967).

Kølle Martinsen, Lone, 'Apostelinder – Grundtvig og spørgsmålet om kvindelige praester', in Else Marie Wiberg Pedersen (ed.), *Guds Ord i kvindemund: Om køn og kirke* (Aarhus: Nord Academic, 2023), pp. 157–188.

Lagerlöf Nilsson, Ulrika, and Birgitta Meurling, 'Vid hans sida – en introduktion', in Ulrika Lagerlöf Nilsson and Birgitta Meurling (eds), *Vid hans sida: Svenska prästfruar under 250 år – ideal och verklighet* (Skellefteå: Artos & Norma, 2015), pp. 7–12.

Larsen, Tine Elisabeth, *Anne Marie Petersen, a Danish Woman in South India: A Missionary Story 1909–1951*, Lutheran Heritage Archives, 3 (Chennai: Lutheran Heritage Archives, 2000).

Larsson, Göran, *Geo Widengren: Stridbar professor i en föränderlig tid* (Stockholm: Bokförlaget Langenskiöld, 2023).

Lindqvist-Bolling, Kerstin, 'Förstadspräst', in *Kvinnlig präst idag: Tio kvinnliga präster berättar* (Stockholm: Natur och Kultur, 1967), pp. 41–57.

Lindström, Martin, *Bibeln och bekännelsen om kvinnliga präster* (Stockholm: Verbum, 1978).

Lindström, Martin, *Herdabrev till Lunds stift* (Lund: Diakonistyrelsen, 1960).

Lundahl, Maria, and Signe Walder (eds), *I striden och vid trossen* (Stockholm: Svenska missionsförbundet, 1938).

Lundin, Johan A., *Predikande kvinnor och gråtande män: Frälsningsarmén i Sverige 1882–1921* (Malmö: Kira, 2014).

Lundqvist, Pia, *Ett motsägelsefullt möte: Svenska missionärer och bakongo i Fristaten Kongo* (Lund: Nordic Academic Press, 2018).

Lyttkens, Carl Henrik, *The Growth of Swedish–Anglican Intercommunion between 1833 and 1922* (Lund: Gleerup, 1970).

Lövheim, Mia, and Stig Hjarvard, 'The Mediatized Conditions of Contemporary Religion: Critical Status and Future Directions', *Journal of Religion, Media & Digital Culture*, 8 (2019), 206–225.

Löwegren, Mikael, 'Leve den kyrkliga förnyelsen! Till 100-årsjubileet i arbetsgemenskapen Kyrklig förnyelses årsbok', in Markus Hagberg (ed.), *Ecclesia semper reformanda: Texter om kyrkan, kyrkans liv och kyrkokritik* (Skellefteå: Artos, 2017), pp. 153–200.

Macy, Gary, *The Hidden History of Women's Ordination: Female Clergy in the Medieval West* (Oxford: Oxford University Press, 2008).

Makant, Mindy, *Holy Mischief: In Honor and Celebration of Women in Ministry* (Eugene, OR: Cascade Books, 2019).

Malmgart, Liselotte, 'Går livet forud for loven? Den danske frihedslovgivning og de kvindelige præster', *Kyrkohistorisk årsskrift*, 108 (2008), 99–107.

Mannerfelt, Frida, 'Ekumeniska influenser i 1958 års ämbetsreform i Svenska kyrkan', in Karin Rubenson and Karin Tillberg (eds), *Vigd till tjänst: Om ämbetet i Svenska kyrkan* (Stockholm: Verbum, 2024), pp. 361–387.

Mannerfelt, Frida, 'Kontrast och kontinuitet: Predikoideal i Svenska kyrkans prästutbildning 1903–2017', in Stephan Borgehammar (ed.), *Predikan – i tid och otid*, Svenskt Gudstjänstliv (Skellefteå: Artos, 2018), pp. 123–158.

Mannerfelt, Frida, and Alexander Maurits, *Kallelse och erkännande: Berättelser från de första prästvigda kvinnorna i Svenska kyrkan* (Stockholm: Makadam, 2021).

Mannerfelt, Frida, and Alexander Maurits, 'Kallelse och erkännande: Perspektiv på de första prästvigda kvinnorna i Svenska kyrkan', *St Sunniva*, 2 (2021), 6–24.

Manning, Philip, *Erving Goffman and Modern Sociology* (Cambridge: Polity, 1992).

Mathiasen Stopa, Sasja Emelie, 'Women as Wives and Rulers in Martin Luther's Theology', *Dialog* (April 2023), 1–14.

Maurits, Alexander, *Den vackra och erkända patriarchalismen: Prästmannaideal och manlighet i den tidiga lundensiska högkyrkligheten, ca 1850–1900* (Malmö: Universus Academic Press, 2013).

Maurits, Alexander, 'Prästfrurollen under förändring: Prästfruar verksamma i Växjö stift omkring 1920–1987 berättar', in Ulrika Lagerlöf Nilsson and Birgitta Meurling (eds), *Vid hans sida: Svenska prästfruar under 250 år – ideal och verklighet* (Skellefteå: Artos, 2015), pp. 75–100.

McAdams, Dan P., 'How Stories Found a Home in Human Personality', in Ivor Goodson (ed.), *The Routledge International Handbook on Narrative and Life History* (Abingdon: Routledge, 2017), pp. 34–48.

McLeod, Hugh, *The Religious Crisis of the 1960s* (Oxford: Oxford University Press, 2007).

Mei, Miki, 'A Church with Newly-opened Doors: The Ordination of Women Priests in the Anglican-Episcopal Church of Japan', *Japanese Journal of Religious Studies*, 44 (2017), 37–54.

Moyaert, Marianne, *Christian Imaginations of the Religious Other: A History of Religionization* (Chichester: Wiley Blackwell, 2024).

Nesbitt, Paula D., *Feminization of the Clergy in America: Occupational and Organizational Perspectives* (Oxford: Oxford University Press, 1997).

Neuhaus, Sinikka, *Reformation och erkännande: Skilsmässoärenden under den tidiga reformationsprocessen i Malmö 1527–1542* (Lund: Centre for Theology and Religious Studies, Lund University, 2009).

Neuhaus, Sinikka, 'Vad är det vi gör när vi berättar historia?', in Urban Claesson and Sinikka Neuhaus (eds), *Minne och möjlighet: Kyrka och historiebruk från nationsbygge till pluralism*, Forskning för kyrkan, 22 (Stockholm: Makadam, 2014), pp. 44–52.

Nilsson, Torsten, 'Kyrklig samlings handlingsprogram', *Budbäraren*, 6 (1960), 3.

Nisser, Ulla, *Hopp från trampolin: Mitt liv som flicka, kvinna och präst* (Mjölby: Atremi, 2016).

Nordbäck, Carola, '"Att återvända till början". Historia och identitet inom Missionsprovinsen', in Urban Claesson and Sinikka Neuhaus (eds), *Minne och möjlighet: Kyrka och historiebruk från nationsbygge till pluralism*, Forskning för kyrkan, 22 (Stockholm: Makadam, 2014), pp. 132–162.

Nordbäck, Carola, 'Kyrkohistorisk historiebruksforskning', in Urban Claesson and Sinikka Neuhaus (eds), *Minne och möjlighet: Kyrka och historiebruk från nationsbygge till pluralism*, Forskning för kyrkan, 22 (Stockholm: Makadam, 2014), pp. 14–43.

Nordholm-Ståhl, Barbro, 'Nära livet', in *Kvinnlig präst idag: Tio kvinnliga präster berättar* (Stockholm: Natur och Kultur, 1967), pp. 24–31.

Nordlander, Elisabeth, *Margit Sahlin: På väg mot verklighet* (Skellefteå: Artos 2010).

Nykvist, Martin, *Alla mäns prästadöme: Homosocialitet, maskulinitet och religion hos Kyrkobröderna, Svenska kyrkans lekmannaförbund 1918–1978* (Lund: Nordic Academic Press, 2019).

Nykvist, Martin, 'A Superfluous Legislation? Historical and Contemporary Perspectives on Religious Freedom in Sweden', *Religion – Staat – Gesellschaft: Zeitschrift für Glaubensformen und Weltanschauungen*, 18.1–2 (2017), 95–108.

Odenberg, Christina, 'The Ordination and Consecration of Women in the Church of Sweden', in Ian Jones, Kirsty Thorpe and Janet Wootton (eds), *Women and Ordination in the Christian Churches: International Perspectives* (London: T&T Clark, 2008), pp. 113–122.

Olén, Gunnar, *Kavajprästen berättar: Del II. Mannaåldern och livsinsatsen* (Stockholm: Gummesson, 1962).

Olén, Gunnar, *Kavajprästens hustru* (Jönköping: Hall, 1965).

Olén, Gunnar, *Möte på vägen* (Jönköping: SAM-förlaget, 1967).

Olén-van Zijl, Britta, 'Att få vara präst', in *Kvinnlig präst i dag: Tio kvinnliga präster berättar* (Stockholm: Natur och Kultur, 1967), pp. 103–113.

'Om bogen', in Else Marie Wiberg Pedersen (ed.), *Guds Ord i kvindemund: Om køn og kirke* (Aarhus: Nord Academic, 2023), pp. 8–12.

Orr, Lesley, 'To Build the New Jerusalem: The Ministry and Citizenship of Protestant Women in Twentieth Century Scotland', *Religions*, 13 (2022), 1–17.

Persson, Ingrid, 'Min väg till prästämbetet', in Urban Råghall (ed.), *Härnösands stiftshistoriska sällskap: Studier och uppsatser IV* (Härnösand: Härnösands stiftshistoriska sällskap, 1994), pp. 29–51.

Persson, Ingrid, 'Påskdagen: Matt 28:1–8', in *Postilla: 49 kvinnor predikar* (Stockholm: Verbum, 1990), pp. 133–137.

Persson, Per Erik, 'Glädjebudet – det allt avgörande', in Boel Hössjer Sundman (ed.), *Äntligen stod hon i predikstolen! Historiskt vägval 1958* (Stockholm: Verbum, 2008), pp. 43–60.

Persson, Per Erik, *Kyrkans ämbete som Kristus-representation: En kritisk analys av nyare ämbetsteologi* (Lund: Gleerup, 1961).

Petersson, Göte, '"En moder i Israel". Minnesruna över fru Nelly Olén', *Blekinge kyrkliga hembygdskalender* (1964), pp. 6–10.

Petrén, Erik, *Kyrkan och synoden* (Lund: Signum, 1984).

Plummer, Ken, 'Narrative Power, Sexual Stories and the Politics of Storytelling', in Ivor Goodson (ed.), *The Routledge International*

Handbook on Narrative and Life History (Abingdon: Routledge, 2017), pp. 280–292.

Rasmussen, Marianne, 'Da *Mænd* blev til *Personer*', in Else Marie Wiberg Pedersen (ed.), *Se min kjole: De første kvindelige præsters historie* (Copenhagen: Samlerens Forlag AS, 1998), pp. 108–143.

Raun Iversen, Hans, 'Tolv danske kvindelige apostle – i det 20. århundrede', in Eva Holmegaard Larsen (ed.), *Kvinde – Mand – Kirke: Folkekirken og den lille forskel* (Copenhagen: Forlaget Anis, 2012), pp. 183–206.

Raun Iversen, Hans, and Harald Nielsen, 'Fra fruentimmere til diakonisser og kvindelige missionaerer', in Else Marie Wiberg Pedersen (ed.), *Guds Ord i kvindemund – Om køn og kirke* (Aarhus: Nord Academic, 2023), pp. 117–156.

Ricoeur, Paul, *Time and Narrative*, I (Chicago: University of Chicago Press, 1984).

Rüsen, Jörn, *History: Narration – Interpretation – Orientation* (Oxford: Berghahn Books, 2005).

Rüsen, Jörn, *Zeit und Sinn: Strategien des historischen Denkens* [Neuausgabe] (Frankfurt am Main: Humanities Online, 2012).

Rössborn, Sten, *En bok om Ruben Josefson* (Täby: Larsson, 1970).

Rössborn, Sten, 'P L Ruben Josefson', *Svenskt biografiskt lexikon*, 20 (1973–1975), 414.

Sahlin, Margit, *Dags för omprövning? Kring bibel, kyrka och kvinnliga präster* (Stockholm: Proprius, 1980).

Sahlin, Margit, *Man och kvinna i Kristi kyrka* (Stockholm: Diakonistyrelsen, 1950).

Sahlin, Margit, *Ordets tjänst i en förändrad värld: Några linjer till ett kyrkligt program* (Stockholm: Diakonistyrelsen, 1959).

Salmon, Christian, *Storytelling: Bewitching the Modern Mind* (London: Verso, 2010).

Saltkjel, Mari, *Som en krone på hodet: Fortellinger om kvinners prestekall* (Oslo: Verbum, 2011).

Sammet, Kornelia, *Frauen in Pfarramt: Berufliche Praxis und Geschlechterkonstruktion* (Würzburg: ERGON, 2005).

Sandahl, Dag, *En annan Kyrka: Svenska kyrkan speglad genom Kyrklig samling och Kyrklig samling speglad genom Svenska kyrkan* (Helsingborg: Gaudete, 2018).

Sandahl, Dag, *Förnyarna: Mer än en historia om arbetsgemenskapen Kyrklig förnyelse* (Skellefteå: Artos, 2010).

Sandahl, Dag, *Kyrklig splittring: Studier kring debatten om kvinnliga präster i Svenska kyrkan samt bibliografi 1905–juli 1990* (Stockholm: Verbum, 1993).

Sarja, Karin, *'Ännu en syster till Afrika': Trettiosex kvinnliga missionärer i Natal och Zululand 1876–1902* (Uppsala: Svenska institutet för missionsforskning, 2002).

Schmidt, Frederick W., '"How Long, O Lord?"': Women, Ordination and the American Baptist Churches, USA', *American Baptist Quarterly*, XXXVIII (2019), 369–386.

Sidenvall, Erik, 'Frikyrkligheten i Sverige 1920–1965', in Yvonne Hirdman, Urban Lundberg and Jenny Björkman (eds), *Sveriges historia 1920–1965* (Stockholm: Norstedts, 2012), pp. 83–88.

Simonsson, Tord, *Kyrkomötet argumenterar: Kritisk analys av argumenttyper i diskussionerna vid 1957 och 1958 års kyrkomöten om"kvinnas behörighet till prästerlig tjänst"* [Studia Theologica Lundensia 23] (Lund: Gleerup, 1963).

Sjöberg, Lina, 'Jag har aldrig blivit bibringad föreställningen att livet skulle vara enkelt: Astrid Andersson Wretmark, prästvigd 1966', in Boel Hössjer Sundman and Lina Sjöberg, *Du ska bli präst: Livsberättelser 50 år efter kyrkomötets beslut* (Stockholm: Verbum, 2008), pp. 29–38.

Sjöberg, Lina, 'Jag är så tacksam över att leva i en tid då det är möjligt: Barbro Westlund, prästvigd 1967', in Boel Hössjer Sundman and Lina Sjöberg, *Du ska bli präst: Livsberättelser 50 år efter kyrkomötets beslut* (Stockholm: Verbum, 2008), pp. 47–56.

Sjöberg, Lina, 'Kristus som livshypotes: Christina Odenberg, prästvigd 1967', in Boel Hössjer Sundman and Lina Sjöberg, *Du ska bli präst: Livsberättelser 50 år efter kyrkomötets beslut* (Stockholm: Verbum, 2008), pp. 39–46.

Sjöberg, Lina, 'Kyrkan måste vara ömsint och stå på människors sida: Birgitta Nyman, prästvigd 1970', in Boel Hössjer Sundman and Lina Sjöberg, *Du ska bli präst: Livsberättelser 50 år efter kyrkomötets beslut* (Stockholm: Verbum, 2008), pp. 57–64.

Sjöberg, Lina, 'Närhet och glädje: Elisabeth Djurle Olander, prästvigd 1960', in Boel Hössjer Sundman and Lina Sjöberg, *Du ska bli präst: Livsberättelser 50 år efter kyrkomötets beslut* (Stockholm: Verbum, 2008), pp. 21–28.

Sjösvärd Birger, Carl, *'Den katolicerande riktningen i vår kyrka': högkyrklig rörelse och identitet i Svenska kyrkan 1909–1946* [Acta Universitatis Upsaliensis: Studia Historico-Ecclesiastica Upsaliensia 52] dissertation (Uppsala: Uppsala University, 2022).

Skytte, Göran, *Biskop Christina: Ett samtal med Göran Skytte* (Lund: Arcus, 1998).

Sorgenfrei, Simon, and David Thurfjell (eds), *Kvinnligt religiöst ledarskap: En vänbok till Gunilla Gunner* (Huddinge: Södertörn University, 2020).

Steen, Jane, 'Women's Ordination in the Church of England. Conscience, Change and Law', *Ecclesiastical Law Journal*, 21 (2019), 289–311.

Stendahl, Brita, *The Force of Tradition: A Case Study of Women Priests in Sweden* (Philadelphia: Fortress Press, 1985).

Södling, Maria, 'Ingen kvinna synes än: En historia om kvinnliga präster', in Boel Hössjer Sundman (ed.), *Äntligen stod hon i predikstolen! Historiskt vägval 1958* (Stockholm: Verbum, 2008).

Södling, Maria, *Oreda i skapelsen: Kvinnligt och manligt i Svenska kyrkan under 1920- och 30-talen* [Acta Universitatis Upsaliensis: Uppsala Studies in Faiths and Ideologies 26] (Uppsala: Uppsala University, 2010).

Tamboukou, Maria, 'A Foucauldian Approach to Narratives', in Molly Andrews, Corinne Squire and Maria Tamboukou (eds), *Doing Narrative Research* (London: Sage, 2008), pp. 102–120.

Tamm-Götlind, Märta, *Anna Howard Shaw: Den kvinnliga prästen och människovännen* (Uppsala: J.A. Lindblads Bokförlag, 1920).

Tamm-Götlind, Märta, *Kvinnliga präster jorden runt* (Stockholm: Svenska kyrkans diakonistyrelses bokförlag, 1957).

Taylor, Joan E., and Ilaria L. E. Ramelli, 'Introduction', in Joan E. Taylor and Ilaria L. E. Ramelli (eds), *Patterns of Women's Leadership in Early Christianity* (Oxford: Oxford University Press, 2021), pp. 1–10.

Thorne, Helen, *Journey to Priesthood: An In-depth Study of the First Women Priests in the Church of England* [CCSRG Monograph Series 5] (Bristol: Department of Theology and Religious Studies, University of Bristol, 2000).

Thurfjell, David, *Det gudlösa folket: De postkristna svenskarna och religionen* (Stockholm: Molin & Sorgenfrei, 2015).

Thurfjell, David, 'Världens mest sekulariserade land?', in Kjell Östberg and Jenny Andersson (eds), *Sveriges historia 1965–2012* (Stockholm: Norstedts, 2013), pp. 156–160.

Tønnessen, Aud Valborg, *Ingrid Bjerkås: Motstandskvinnen som ble vår første kvinnelige prest* (Oslo: Pax, 2014).

Vägmärken för baptister: Tro, frihet, gemenskap: Svenska baptistsamfundet 1848–2012 (Karlstad: Votum, 2016).

Walsh, Clare, *Gender and Discourse: Language and Power in Politics, the Church and Organizations* (Harlow: Longman, 2001).

Wejderstam, Andreas, *Personlig och kyrklig förnyelse: Svenska kyrkan och Vadstenamötena 1943–1985* [Acta Universitatis Upsaliensis: Studia Historico-Ecclesiastica Upsaliensia 51] (Uppsala: Uppsala University, 2020).

Wejderstam, Andreas, 'Recension av *Kallelse och erkännande*', *Svensk pastoraltidskrift*, 11 (2023), 27–28.

Wejryd, Cecilia, 'Kallelse och erkännande', *Kyrkohistorisk årsskrift*, 122 (2022), 196–198.

Wejryd, Cecilia, *Svenska kyrkans syföreningar 1844–2003* (Stockholm: Verbum, 2005).

Werkström, Bertil, 'Parentation över Gunnar Hultgren vid Nathan Söderblom-sällskapets årshögtid den 15 januari 1992', *Religion och bibel*, 51 (1992), 63–64.

Wessinger, Catherine, 'Women's Religious Leadership in the United States', in Catherine Wessinger (ed), *Religious Institutions and Women's Leadership: New Roles Inside the Mainstream* (Columbia, SC: University of South Carolina Press, 1996), pp. 3–36.

Westrin, Marianne, 'I elfte timmen', in *Kvinnlig präst idag: Tio kvinnliga präster berättar* (Stockholm: Natur och Kultur, 1967), pp. 77–88.

Wiberg Pedersen, Else Marie, 'Kirke mellem kønsballade och kønsbalance', in Else Marie Wiberg Pedersen (ed.), *Guds Ord i kvindemund: Om køn og kirke* (Aarhus: Nord Academic, 2023), pp. 13–40.

Wiberg Pedersen, Else Marie, 'Kirkens kønsskifte? Nedslag i medieomtalen af kvindelige praester', in Else Marie Wiberg Pedersen (ed.), *Guds Ord i kvindemund: Om køn og kirke* (Aarhus: Nord Academic, 2023), pp. 281–315.

Wiberg Pedersen, Else Marie, 'Reformationen og køn: Kvinder og kirkens embede', *Dansk Teologisk Tidsskrift*, 80 (2017), 146–165.

Wiberg Pedersen, Else Marie (ed.), *Guds Ord i kvindemund: Om køn og kirke* (Aarhus: Nord Academic, 2023), pp. 6–7.

Wifstrand, Mailice, 'Dröm, plan och verklighet', *Svensk Kyrkotidning*, 10 (2004), 138–139.

Wiklund, Henry, *Predikant, pastor, präst: EFS samfundsproblematik 1940–1972* (Stockholm: EFS-förlaget, 1979).

Wiklund, Martin, 'Inledning', in Jörn Rüsen, *Berättande och förnuft: Historieteoretiska texter*, trans. Joachim Retzlaff (Gothenburg: Daidalos, 2004), pp. 13–25.

Williams, Rowan, *Why Study the Past: The Quest for the Historical Church* (London: Darton, Longman & Todd, 2005).

Wingren, Gustaf, 'Bekännelseskrifterna och högkyrkligheten', *Svensk Kyrkotidning*, 10 (1954), 149, 155.

Wingren, Gustaf, *Kyrkans ämbete* (Lund: Gleerup, 1958).

Wingren, Gustaf, *Luther on Vocation* (Eugene, OR: Wipf & Stock, 2004).

Witte, Jr., John, *Law and Protestantism: The Legal Teachings of the Lutheran Reformation* (Cambridge: Cambridge University Press, 2002).

Young, Frances, 'Hermeneutical Questions: The Ordination of Women in the Light of Biblical and Patristic Typology', in Ian Jones, Kirsty Thorpe and Janet Wootton (eds), *Women and Ordination in the Christian Churches: International Perspectives* (London: T&T Clark, 2008), pp. 21–39.

Zurn, Christopher F., *Axel Honneth* (Cambridge: Polity, 2015).

Östberg, Kjell, and Jenny Andersson (eds), *Sveriges historia 1965–2012* (Stockholm: Norstedts, 2013).

Österlin, Lars, *Churches of Northern Europe in Profile: A Thousand Years of Anglo-Nordic Relations* (Norwich: Canterbury Press, 1995).

Österlin, Lars, *Svenska kyrkan i profil: Ur engelskt och nordiskt perspektiv* (Stockholm: Verbum, 2004).

Östling, Johan, Anton Jansson and Ragni Svensson Stringberg, *Humanister i offentligheten. Kunskapens aktörer och arenor under efterkrigstiden* (Stockholm: Makadam, 2022).

Other

Bisgaard, Lis, 'Johanne Andersen – præst', *Dansk Kvindebiografisk Leksikon*, https://kvindebiografiskleksikon.lex.dk/Johanne_Andersen_-_pr%C3%A6st [accessed 23 April 2023].

Brandby-Cöster, Margareta, 'Kvinnor som präster – också i Göteborgs stift. Reflektioner 11/11, 24 eft Trefaldighet', public lecture, 11 November 2018.

'Changing Laws and Patriarchal Attitudes Go Hand in Hand', online article, The Lutheran World Federation, 23 May 2016, https://www.lutheranworld.org/news/changing-laws-and-patriarchal-attitudes-go-hand-hand [accessed 20 September 2023].

Christoffersen, Lisbeth, 'Professor i religionsret om muligt nej til kvindelige præster: Det værste vil være ikke at gøre noget', *Kristeligt Dagblad*, 30 May 2023.

Fahlgren, Sune, 'Signe Anna Charlotta Ekblad', *Svenskt kvinnobiografiskt lexikon*, https://skbl.se/sv/artikel/SigneEkblad [accessed 2 February 2021].

Förlåt oss våra skulder, documentary by Tom Alandh, broadcast on Swedish Television on 13 February 2014, transcription.

Furuland, Gunnel, 'Märta Elisabet Katarina Tamm-Götlind', *Svenskt kvinnobiografiskt lexikon*, www.skbl.se/sv/artikel/MartaTammGotlind [accessed 24 February 2023].

'General Synod to Discuss Ordination for Fifth Time', *Lutheran Church of Australia*, 17 June 2022, https://www.lca.org.au/general-synod-to-discuss-ordination-for-fifth-time/ [accessed 9 February 2023].

'Ingegärd Dackerud – pionjär som kvinna och pastor', YouTube, 8 June 2020, https://www.youtube.com/watch?v=-ZjX3ThbMak [accessed 3 July 2020].

Interview with Isaac Munther, 27 February 2023.

Irving, Mattias, 'Caroline och kärleken', på Seglora Tankesmedja, https://seglorasmedja.se/post5876/caroline-och-karleken/ [accessed 7 April 2020].

'Kampen om de kvindelige præster', Det Kgl. Bibliotek, https://www.kb.dk/inspiration/kvinders-kamp-medborgerskab/kampen-om-de-kvindelige-praester [accessed 24 April 2023].

'Kvindelige præster – en udfordring for det økumeniske samarbejde?', https://www.interchurch.dk/aktuelt/nyheder/kvindelige-praester-en-udfordring-for-det-oekumeniske-samarbejde [accessed 24 April 2023].

Wøllekær, Johnny, 'For 70 år siden: For biskoppen var kvindelige præster ikke kvindesag – det var teologi', *Århus Stiftstidende*, 25 April 2018, https://stiften.dk/debat/for-70-aar-siden-for-biskoppen-var-kvindelige-praester-ikke-kvindesag-det-var-teologi-2022-12-4 [accessed 8 May 2023].

Index

Whenever names occur both in the running text and in footnotes on the same page, references to the latter have been omitted. Editors of edited volumes who are quoted in that capacity are indexed with reference to the first mention of the book in question. Persons with two surnames are indexed under the first. Names of journalists in the daily press are not indexed.

EU authorised representative for GPSR:
Easy Access System Europe, Mustamäe tee 50,
10621 Tallinn, Estonia
gpsr.requests@easproject.com

www.ingramcontent.com/pod-product-compliance
Lightning Source LLC
Chambersburg PA
CBHW070341100426
42812CB00005B/1388